Frontiers of World Socialism Studies

Yellow Book of World Socialism

Frontiers of World Socialism Studies
Yellow Book of World Socialism
Year 2013

edited by Li Shenming

Volume I

CANUT INTERNATIONAL PUBLISHERS

Istanbul - Berlin - London - Santiago

This edition is an authorized translation from the Chinese language edition, published in cooperation with **Social Sciences Academic Press**, Beijing, China.

Published with financial support of the Innovation Program of the Chinese Academy of Social Sciences

Frontiers of World Socialism Studies
Yellow Book of World Socialism - Year 2013 - Volume I-II
Edited by Li Shenming
Chinese Title: 世界社会主义跟踪报告 (2012-2013), (ISBN: 978-7-5097-4482-6)
Copyright © SSAP China, 2013

Canut International Publishers
Canut Int. Turkey, Teraziler Cad. No.29. Sancaktepe, Istanbul, Turkey
Canut Int. Germany, Heerstr. 266, D-47053, Duisburg, Germany
Canut Int. United Kingdom, 12a Guernsay Road, London E11 4BJ, England
Copyright © Canut Internation Publishers, 2016
All rights reserved. No part of this book may be used or reproduced in any manner whatsoever without the written permission of the publishers.
ISBN: 978-605-9914-33-8
Printed in UK
Lightning Source Ltd. UK
Chapterhouse, Pitfield Kiln Farm
MK11 3LW
United Kingdom
www.canutbooks.com

About the Editor of the Book

Li Shenming, born in 1949, native of Wenxian city of Henan Province. For long years he served in the PLA and PLA Medical Research Institute, led major central publications and newspapers of the PLA, later worked as the secretary of Central Military Commission in 1998 he was assigned as the vice president of the Chinese Academy of Social Sciences and was elected as the director of World Socialism Research Center attached to CASS. His major research areas include world socialism, global economic and political crises, international strategies of major world powers, and Mao Zedong Thought. He has authored and co-authored and edited abundant books and articles, including *Globalization and Party Building* (1991), *Globalization and Chinese Strategy* (2007), *Trend of History, The Reasons Behind The Collapse of the CPSU and the Soviet Union, History's Reflection: Memorial for the 20th Anniversary of the Disintegration of Soviet Union* (2013), *Return to Truth* (History of Mao Zedong Thought and Truth of Facts Related To Mao Zedong, co-edited by Lie Jie, (2015) published by Social Sciences Press, Beijing. His two major articles in recent years include: "At the End of Hegemonism and Power Politics Is the Revival of Socialism" and "The New Features of the Present Capital Empire: Financial, Scientific and Technological, Cultural and Military Hegemonies."

Contents

Acknowledgements by the English Editor . . . i
Acknowledgement by the Chinese Publisher . . . iii
List of Scholars of the WSRC attached to CASS . . . v

PART ONE
General Theory

Y. 1
The Issue of Era and Historical Location:
On Marxism and the Historical Destiny of Socialism
  Wang Weiguang . . . 1

Y. 2
New Features of the Present Capital Empire:
Financial, Scientific and Technological, Cultural and Military Hegemony
  Li Shenming . . . 11

PART TWO
Analyses of the Crisis of Capitalism

Y. 3
Big Crisis, Big Differentiation and Big Transformation:
A Reanalysis of the Profound Changes in the World Pattern
  Cao Suhong and Wang Liqiang . . . 38

Y. 4
"Occupy Wall Street" Movement and the Crisis of the US Capitalism
  Wang Jing . . . 55

Y. 5
Class Analysis of Global Capitalism and Its Main Features
  Jiang Hui . . . 67

Y. 6

In the West, Capitalism is like the Sun

Zhang Wenmu   77

Y. 7

Where are the "Dangers" of Capitalism?

Jiang Hui   87

Y. 8

On the Increasing Risk of Economic Turmoil: U.S. and Europe's Transfer of Losses of Economic Crises, Domestic and External Transfer

Yang Bin   97

Y. 9

The Domination of Financial Monopoly Capital and the Formation of the Global Rentier Empire

Chen Renjiang   109

Y. 10

The Crisis of the Capitalist System and the Future of Socialism

Song Lidan   123

Y. 11

A Preliminary Exploration on the Early Warning System of the Financial Crisis

Wang Liqiang   139

Y. 12

Suggested Research and Formulating Long-term Strategy in China– Some Observations about Capitalism

Li Changjiu   151

Y. 13

Reflections on the Predicaments of Capitalism in the West Today

Zhao Minghao   163

Y. 14
Some Thoughts on the International Strategy
He Bingmeng   173

Y. 15
Social Crisis Induces the Resurgence of French Left-wing Thoughts
Shen Xiaoquan   183

Y. 16
From Iran to Xinjiang: The Swirl in the "Oval-shaped" Zone under the Shadow of the US Middle East Strategy
Ma Zhongcheng   193

Y. 17
The US-Style Oligarchy: Paul Krugman's Critique of Social Inequality in the United States
Yu Haiqing   205

Y. 18
Pursuit of "Universal Values" as Part of the US Foreign Strategy
Xie Xiaoguang   213

Y. 19
How Has "State Capitalism" Become the "New Pet" of the West?
Cheng Enfu and Hou Weimin   223

Y. 20
Neoliberalism Worsens Global Labor Relations
Cui Xuedong   233

Y. 21
The Decline of the Western Market Fundamentalism
Yu Zuyao   248

Y. 22
A Research on the Policy of Neoliberalism and
Its International Influence
   Tian Chunsheng   *261*

Y. 23
Problems of The Western Labor Movement as
Demonstrated in the "Occupy Wall Street" Movement
   Wu Jinping   *271*

Y. 24
Occupy the System: Confronting Global Capitalism–
A Commentary on International Left Forum 2012
   Lu Weizhou   *281*

Y. 25
"Occupy Wall Street Movement" on Its First Anniversary:
Gains, Losses and Prospects
   Zhang Xinning   *293*

Y. 26
Some Questions to be Heeded in the Research of
"International Secretive Groups"
   Jing Xianghui   *299*

Y. 27
An In-depth Investigation among the Working Class of Beijing:
An Experience and Reflection
   Lu Gang   *309*

PART THREE
Studies on the Theories of Socialism
Theoretical Consciousness and Having Confidence in the System

Y. 28

On Democracy and Socialist Democracy

Wang Weiguang

Y. 29

Several Issues of Deepening the Concept of Socialism with Chinese Characteristics

Zhu Jiamu

Y. 30

Following the Basic Line of the Party Unswervingly throughout One Hundred Years: A Review on Deng Xiaoping's South China Speeches

Zhu Jiamu

Y. 31

Socialist State-owned Enterprises and Capitalist State-owned Enterprises Are Essentially Distinct

Yu Bin

Y. 32

Building the Chinese Discourse System Based on the Practice of Reform and Opening Up

Cao Suhong

Y. 33

A Popular Theoretical Reader That Clarifies the Causes of the End: Be Vigilant Against Danger: World Socialism Book Series Well Received after Release

Yi Yuan

Y. 34

What Do People Live For?

Li Shenming

Y. 35

Why is there a Lack of Consensus on the Core Values of Socialism?

Hou Huiqin

PART FOUR
Communist Party and Workers' Party around the World in the Struggle

Y. 36
Grasp the Hypocritical Nature of "Universal Values" and
Refine Socialist Core Values
Li Zongfang

Y. 37
The Major Changes and Transformation of Contemporary World
Socialist Movement
Nie Yunlin

Y. 38
Communist Party of the Russian Federation and Russia: Their Future
Ouyang Xiangying

Y. 39
The Successful Practice of Chavez's Socialist Exploration
Zhu Jidong

Y. 40
The New Struggle of Communist Party of Greece
Under the European Debt Crisis
Yu Haiqing

Y. 41
The Positive Action of the Communist Party of Greece in the Debt Crisis
Tong Jin

Y. 42
The Views of Swedish Communist Parties on the Capitalist Economic Crisis
Li Kaixuan

Y. 43

Alliance of the Vulnerable Countries: Help Yourself
The Present Situation and Prospects of the Bolivarian Alliance for the Peoples of Our America (ALBA)

Chen Airu

Y. 44

Revisiting Marx: Why Marxism Is On the Rise Again?

Stuart Jeffries

Y. 45

The Communist Party of India (Maoist) as
Viewed by the Indian Communist Movement

Wang Jing

Y. 46

Review of the New Programme of the Communist Party of Belarus

Kang Yanru

Y. 47

New Exploration of the Socialist Development Path of the South African Communist Party in the New Period

Nie Yunlin and Cheng Guangde

Y. 48

Post-War History of the Japanese Communist Party as Narrated in the Autobiography by Mrs. Tetsuzo Fuwa

Zheng Ping

Y. 49

On the Nature of the Current International Meetings of Communist and Workers' Parties

Nie Yunlin

Y. 50

Remolding the World: Establishing the New Sustainable Development Pattern
  Tan Yangfang

Y. 51

An Analysis of the "International Annual Meetings of Communist and Workers' Parties" from 1999 to 2011
  Wang Ximan and Wang Zifeng

Y. 52

The Brussels Meetings:
The Analysis of the 21st International Communist Seminar
  Wang Ximan

Y. 53

For Equality, Democracy, Peace and Socialism
  Wang Ximan and Wang Zifeng

Y. 54

Imperialism in the Era of Globalization as Viewed by the 20th Congress of the Communist Party of India (Marxist)
  Yang Chengguo and Liu Chunyuan

Y. 55

The 17th and 18th Meetings of the Sao Paulo Forum and the Consolidation and Development of the Latin American Left Forces
  Xu Shicheng

Y. 56

Review of the Eleventh Congress of the Communist Party of Turkey Forging Socialist Alternative against Reactionary Power and Push Forward Socialism
  Yu Weihai

PART FIVE
Lessons Drawn from the Collapse of the Soviet Union

Y. 57

Ideological Realm and the Intelligentsia during the Evolution of the Soviet Union
  Zhou Xincheng

Y. 58

Twenty Years since the Fall of the USSR: Whose Fault? And What to Do?
  Yuri Prokofyev

Y. 59

The Disintegration of the Soviet Union and the International Financial Crisis: A Round Table Talk held by Li Shenming and Guests from the Austrian Academy of Sciences led by Helmut Denk
  Wang Xiaoju

Y. 60

Soviet Scholars' Debates on the 20th Congress of the CPSU and "the Sixties"
  Ma Xiaoming

Y. 61

The Social Situation in the Territory of the Former U.S.S.R., 20 Years after Its Disintegration
  Xu Hua

Y. 62

The Russian Scholars Beginning to Explore the Contemporary Value of the "Soviet Civilization"
  Li Ruiqin

Y. 63

A Proposal to Translate and Publish the Revised Editions of Stalin's Collected Works, Volume 14-18
  Ouyang Xiangying

Y. 64

The Analysis of Social Structure and Classes of Russia by the Russian Communists - "Theory and Practice of Foreign Communists" Research Report II

Liu Shuchun

Y. 65

The Collapse of the Soviet Union and East Europe:
Reflection and Criticism by the Communist Party of Australia

Yang Chengguo

Y. 66

Scientifically Reveal the Reasons behind the Collapse of the Soviet Union

Gao Yong

Y. 67

Unveiling the Real and Thought-provoking "19/8" Event - The Archives of the Beijing Television (BTV)

Disintegration of the Soviet Union: Inside Stories of the "19/8" Event Receives Massive Echoes

Li Yan

Y. 68

The Party Committees of Various Regions and Departments Have Organized A Campaign of Group Watching of the TV Documentary: "20 Years' Reflections on the Soviet Union's and Soviet Communist Party's Perishing: It Has Received Intensive Echoes and Responses"

A News Report by China Fangzheng Press

Y. 69

A Review of A Spectacular Event: The Educational TV Film "20 Years' Reflections on the Soviet Union's Collapse and the Soviet Communist Party's Decline"

Liu Ruisheng and Li Yan

English Editor's Acknowledgement

The Yellow Book, a yearly catalogue book of world socialism studies of 2 volumes has been a valuable book created by the World Socialism Research Center attached to China Academy of Social Sciences and published by Social Sciences Academic Press in Beijing for years, and it is one of best in China among its kind in this sphere. It is the first time such a meticulous work has been translated into English and made available for the global readers. With the publishing this catalogue, I have intended to reflect the current trend and mature level of Marxism and socialism studies in China, especially the researches on the history of the world socialism, history of the socialist camp and the Soviet Union.

Due to several other reasons and especially due to language barriers, little is known about Chinese academic studies of Marxism and socialism.

Most of the academic journals in China are published in Chinese, which means that much of the current research achievements are not readily available to non-Chinese readers. Those who are interested can only read an abstract of the work in English, from the national data base, www.cnki.net. But it is no secret that China's scholars in this sphere are very keen to communicate with their colleagues throughout the world, some have already started to write and publish in foreign languages, yet being rare.

Throughout my editing work, I have experienced that the studies on the theoretical system of Marxism, and scientific socialism in China enjoys an unprecedented vitality and academic diversity plurality in this country, especially their studies on the newly added characteristics of capitalism and the inevitable crises of capitalism, focusing on the new phasic developments of the capitalist monopoly which is the core of hegemonism and power politics or imperialism. Also in my deep conversations and interviews, I have personally experienced that Chinese socialism academy sticks to the fundemental tenets and methodology of Marxism and Leninism in revealing the essence of current realities and trends of capitalism, monopoly capitalism and imperialism, which is misinterpreted by some, outside this country. Besides this sphere of academy has nurtured an abundant number of masters which lead an army of middle age and young theoreticians, which means that China is still following the desire mentioned by Mao Zedong and Deng Xiaoping.

Marxism is gaining anew brightness and attraction, and concurrently the development of the world socialist movement shows clear signs of recovery and re-union, the current facts have proven that "barbarism" and wars can only be a temporary trend, and the prospects of socialist development trend is bright and its victory is inevitable as Wang Weiguang, Li Shenming and Nie Yunlin have firmly analyzed in this book. In this respect the readers will find valuable informative articles, related to communist, socialist and progressive movements in Russia, Japan, India, Greece, South Africa, Belarus, Turkey, USA, Australia, Sweden, Venezuela and Israel. In the book, there are 4 articles analyzing the great "Occupy Wall Street" struggle of the American people which has inspired and moved millions of people in Western Europe.

Prof. Nie Yunlin has especially focused on the International cooperation and meetings of the communist and workers' parties, their scope of cooperation, their cooperation mode and mechanisms which has blazed a trail in the studies of international cooperation and its improvement. I hope this book will increase the exchange of debates and theories among Marxism and socialism scholars of the world.

I am thankful that Canut International Publishers has assigned me this task of editing and proof reading of this valuable book with rich content and write this with acknowledgment for it. I am thankful to scholars of the World Socialism Research Center and Social Sciences Academic Press in Beijing who have very cooperatively helped me in accomplishing this task and especially the latter who enabled the co-realization of this book.

Daivya Jindal
September, 2016
Bombay, India

Chinese Publisher's Acknowledgement for the Chinese Edition

The Yellow Book of World Socialism is a collection of authoritative, cutting-edge and representative research achievements made by the World Socialism Research Center (WSRC) in 2012. During the past year, the economic crisis in the Western capitalist have continued deepening, also the sovereign debt crisis which spread especially to European countries and to others has been persistent, besides the uncertainties and risks in the world economy rose sharply. In spite of deepening crises and uncertainties throughout the world, the theory and practice of building socialism with Chinese Characteristics has made world-acclaimed achievements. With the current crisis the theories of Marxism has been popular again and revisited by people with foresight, the issue of direction and fate of human development has become a new reflection and study subject, globally.

The yellow book consists of 5 parts: Part I, on the general theories of Marxism and socialism, which may also be read as an introduction; Part II includes articles on the crisis of the capitalist system; Part III includes articles probing into the theories of socialism; Part IV includes articles debating on the struggles of world's communist and workers' parties fighting against exploitation and oppression; Part V includes articles debating on the lessons drawn from the disintegration of the Soviet Union and demise of its historical party, the CPSU.

In the Part I of the book the first article by the president of China Academy of Social Sciences, Prof. Wang Weiguang has addressed the historical destiny of Marxism and Socialism from the perspective of temporal and historical development and on the basis of capitalism analysis, which represents the major foci and views of the WSRC scholars. And the second article in the part I, written by Li Shenming, "The New Features of the Present Capital

Empire: Financial, Scientific and Technological, Cultural and Military Hegemonies" reflects the WSRC's new findings and understanding of the contemporary capitalism.

In the Part II of Yellow Book readers can find recent important research articles and critical studies written by the WSRC scholars, debating aspects of the current financial crisis issues and many other themes such as financial hegemony, neoliberalism, monopoly capitalism, cyber warfare and hegemony, the "universal values" promoted by the West, and the Western market fundamentalism. And there are also several articles analyzing the storm of "Occupy Wall Street" movement, which has spread to many Western countries. We hope that readers from all walks of life can benefit and broaden their views on the issues of socialism, the current world socialism and other crucial issues of the contemporary world. The book includes two valuable articles written by foreign scholars Stuart Jeffries and Yuri Prokofyev, to whom we owe special thanks.

We would particularly thank to the executive leaders and staff of the WSRC, who have cooperated with us during the realization process of the book, and we are grateful to Mr. Huang Changzhuo who has proofread the English parts of the book.

Social Sciences Academic Press
Beijing, 2016

List of Consultants and Scholars Contributing to World Socialism Research Center attached to Chinese Academy of Social Sciences as of 2013

Consultants

Chen Kuiyuan, Former Vice Chairman of the CPPCC and Chinese Academy of Social Sciences

Wang Jiarui, Vice Chairman of the CPPCC National Committee, the Minister of Foreign Relations attached to CPC Central Committee

Dai Bingguo, Former State Councilor

Wang Weiguang, Dean of the Chinese Academy of Social Sciences, Party Secretary

Liu Huaqiu, Former Director of the Foreign Affairs Leading Group Office of the CPC Central Committee

Li Anan, Former General Secretary of the Central Advisory Commission

Zhang Panjing, Former Minister of the Organization Department of the CPC Central Committee, the president of the National Party Building Research Association

Zheng Keyang, Former Deputy Director of the Central Policy Research Office, vice chairman of the Party Building Research Association

Yu Hongjun, Vice Minister of the International Department attached to CPC Central Committee

Wei Jianhua, Former Director of the Compilation and Translation Bureau attached to CPC Central Committee

Director of the World Socialism Research Center

Li Shenming

Executive Directors of the World Socialism Research Center

Xia Weidong, Wu Enyuan, Cheng Enfu, Hou Huiqin, Deng Chundong Wang Xuedong, Yan Shuhan, Li Hongqi, Zhang Shuhua, Jiang Hui, Fan Jianxin, Wang Liqiang, Wang Tingzhi, Wang Yicheng, Wang Lei, Wang Zhenya, Wang Xuejian, Wang Wen, Chung Yeung, Ma Yan, Feng Gang, Feng Jinhua, Tian Yongxiang, Anqi Ren, Huayu Wu, Liu Shulin, Liu Shuchun, Liu Tong, Liu Ruisheng, Lu Weizhou, Ren Zhijun, Sun Haiquan, Xu Xingya, Xu Zhengfan, Zhu Bingyuan, Zhu Jidong, Zhuang Qiansheng, Chen Xueming, Chen Zhanan, Chen Zhihua, Chen Yue, He Bingmeng, He Qianqiang, He Junchen, Li Bingyan, Li Chongfu, Li Hanlin, Li Jianping, Li Qiqing, Li Xinggeng, Li Xiangjun, Li Jun (ambassador), She Zhiyuan, Song Xiaoping, Li Xiangjun, She Zhiyuan, Song Xiaoping, Wu Bo, Wu Shangmin, Wu Xiongcheng,

Zhang Guozuo, Zhang Guanzi, Zhang Shunhong, Zhang Haibin, Zhang Zaixing, Zhang Shulin, Zhang Wenmu, Yang Haijiao, Fang Guangshun, Fang Ning, Meng Jie, Lin Gang, Luo Wendong, Luo Hong, Wu Zhaoling, Zhou Zhaoguang, Zhou Hong, Zhou Qi, Zhou Xincheng, Zhao Jianying, Hu Lemin, Hu Zhenliang, Hu Zhenliang, Jiang Shanyian, Shihe An, Rao Ninghua, Jin Baoping, Gao Yongzhong, Gao Qiufu, Gao Xiang, Guo Yuzhou (ambassador), Guo Jiezhong, Guo Jianning, Qin Xuan, Sang Yucheng, Tang Kunxiong, Xu Chongwen, Xu Shicheng, Cui Yaozhong, Huang Haotao, Huang Jinhui, Huang Xiaoyong, Huang Rongsheng, Huang Ping, Mei Rongzheng, Huang Rongsheng, Huang Hong, Mei Rongzheng, Cao Yaxiong, Cheng Wei, Dong Jingquan, Dong Xiaoyang, Dong Zhengping, Jiang Lifeng, Wen Bo, Xie Shouguang, Jinhui Ming.

Visiting Scholars of World Socialism Research Center

Ding Bing, Ding Yuanhong, Ding Xiaoqin, Ding Shujie, Yu Zuyao, Yu Haiqing, You Suzhen, Wei Jianlin, Ma Xiaoquan, Ma Zhongcheng, Ma Xiaoming, Ma Weixian, Wang Jing, Wang Shaoxian, Wang Zhongbao, Wang Wene, Wang Zhengquan, Wang Lincong, Wang Jiafei, Wang Jingli, Wang Zhenhua, Wang Xiaoquan, Wang Xiaoju, Wang Haiyun, Wang Ximan, Mao Xianglin, Kong Tianping, Lu Gang, Ye Weiping, Shen Yajie, Tian Chunsheng, Qiu Jin, Feng Yumin, Feng Shaolei, Feng Yanli, Qu Wei, Qu Yanming, Zhu Andong, Quan Lin, Yuan Liu, Liu Junmei, Liu Zhiming, Liu Guoping, Liu Chunyuan, Liu Haixia, Qi Fengtian, Jiang Shixue, Xu Hua, Xu Xin, Xu Yuanrong, Sun Li, Sun Hongbo, Ji Jun, Su Zhenxing, Du Han, Du Xiaolin, Li Qian, Li Weil, Man Liyan, Li Changjiu, Li Fenglin, Li Weiheng, Li Zhengle, Li Minqi, Li Yazhou, Li Kaixuan, Li Zongfang, Li Yanyan, Li Runhai, Li Ruiqin,

Li Fuchuan, Yang Shuang, Yang Bin, Yang Shengguo, Yang Chengguo, Yang Huichun, Yang Jianmin, Yang Chengxun, Yang Zugong, Yang Hongxi, Xiao Feng, Xiao Lian, Xiao Bin, Xiao Guozhong, Wu Qian, Wu Jian, Wu Guoping Wu Jinping, He Xin, Tong Yuhua, Yu Li, Yu Bin, Yu Wenli, Yu Jincheng, Yu Weihai, Wang Tingyou, Shen Qiang, Shen Xiaoquan, Shen Zongwu, Song Lidan, Song Mengrong, Zhang Li, Zhang Jie, Zhang Ji, Zhang Zhongyun, Zhang Wendai, Zhang Yuliang, Zhang Ximing, Zhang Xinghui, Zhang Shouhua, Zhang Xiaodong, Zhang Tiezhu, Zhang Haipeng, Zhang Xinning, Lu Shucheng, Chen Yue, Chen Renjiang, Chen Chengxin, Chen Airu, Chen Shuoying, Fan Lei, Lin Xinhai, Ouyang Xiangying, Shang Wei, Luo Yunli, Jin Ying, Jin Liqun, Zhou Miao, Zhou Zhiwei, Zhou Suiming, Pang Dapeng, Pang Zhongying, Zheng Ping, Zhao Shi, Zhao Yao, Zhao Minghao, Zhao Changqing, Hu Junqing, Zhong Yaping, Duan Lijuan, Duan Qizeng, Hou Aijun, Yu Su, Jiang Li, Jiang Lin, Jiang Weiping, He Shuangrong, Geng Lihua, Yuan Qun, Nie Yunlin, Xia Dongmin, Gu Yumin, Chai Shangjin, Xu YunFeng, Xu Zhongwei, Xu Xiaofeng, Xu Haiyan, Luan Wenlian, Gao Yong, Gao Hong, Gao Gexiu, Gao Yixin, Gao Zengjie, Guo Yuanzeng, Guo Jianping, Tang Xiuzhe, Tang Yanlin, Huang Dengxue, Cao Changsheng, Cao Suhong, Chang Weiguo, Cui Xuedong, Kang Yanru, Yan Zhimin, Yan Hongju, Liang Xiao, Ge Xinsheng, Jinghui Zhichun, Cheng Chunhua, Fu Ning, Fu Junsheng, Shu Chang, Tong Jin, Xie Xiaoguang, Pei Yuanying, Liao Jian, Tan Suo, Tan Yangfang, Xue Xinguuo, Xue Fuqi, Wei Yongwang, Wei Nanzhi.

PART ONE

General Theory

Y. 1

The Issue of Era and Historical Location: On Marxism and the Historical Destiny of Socialism

Wang Weiguang[1]

Abstract: This article uses the materialistic conception of history and makes a scientific judgment on the issue of the era we are living in and our historical location through a systematical analysis of the Marxist theory of the evolution of social formations, and scientifically addresses the major strategic issues of our development: we are precisely in a historical era when capitalism gradually moves towards doom and is gradually replaced by socialism. In this era, the working class is in the historical location of diligently carrying out socialist revolution and socialism building. This article is one of the articles discussing the historical destiny of Marxism and socialism.

Key words: Marxist theory of the evolution of social formations; era and historical location; an important period of strategic opportunities

---

[1] Prof. Wang Weiguang, President, General Secretary of the Leading Party Group of China Academy of Social Sciences.

In the great historical endless river of the history of human society, in what kind of era and historical location is China, and the Chinese nation now? Which direction will China and the Chinese nation develop? How will their historical destiny and future? Under the premise of scientifically judging the era and historical location of China and the Chinese nation, how to understand the domestic and foreign situation for developing socialism with Chinese characteristics? How to judge the period of important strategic opportunities for China's development? How to advance the scientific development of socialism with Chinese characteristics? All these are major strategic issues that call for scientific answers.

I. Marxist theory on the evolution of social formations

In the 1980s, the Chinese theorists had a debate on the Marxist theory of the evolution of social formations (morphology)—the debate between the "five formations doctrine" and the "three formations doctrine". The so-called "five formations doctrine" is, according to Marx's and Engels' writings about the elaboration and summarized argument on the evolution of the social development formations, namely that, usually said, the development of the human society inevitably and successively passes through the five stages of primitive communist society, slave society, feudal society, capitalist society and communist society (socialist society as its first stage of development)

The so-called "three formations doctrine" is according to Marx's view and summarized argument on the historical course of human society in his *Economic Manuscripts of 1857-1958* (namely "London Manuscripts") where Marx pointed out, "The relations of personal dependence are the first social forms in the midst of which the human productive activity develops (but) only in reduced proportion and in isolated places. Personal independence based on material dependence is the second great form within which is constituted a general metabolism made of universal relations faculties and needs. Free individuality based on universal development of the individuals and their domination of their common, social productivity as their (own) social power is the third stage. The second stage creates the conditions for the third." According to Marx's division of the three major stages, namely the relation of personal dependence, relation of material dependence and the all-round development of man, it is believed that human society will successively pass through three stages, namely the natural economy, the market economy and the product economy.

The debate between "five formations doctrine" and "three formations doctrine" has produced some mental confusion. Some have used the latter to negate the former, thinking that Marx had never said such a thing that the human society has five fundamental alternation of social forms, that it was

Stalin who brought forward the "five formations doctrine" and it was not what Marx truly meant and it was not the general law of historical development, while others failed to realize that human society must inevitably pass through the market economy stage in order to transit into the ultimate product economy stage. In fact, whether the "five formations doctrine" or the "three formations doctrine", both are based on Marxism's the scientific summary of the development historical development course of social formations based on the historical conditions of the development of the productive forces. The "five formations doctrine" has been quite familiar to us. If we carefully study all the classical works by Marx and Engels, we can find that they had explicitly sketched the historical course of "the five formations" of the development of human society. According to the "three formations doctrine" by Marx and Engels, the first stage—"relations of personal dependence"—is actually the natural economy society in which, due to backward productive forces, the primitive man depends on the community, the slave personally depends on the slave owner, and the peasant personally depends on the landlord, displaying man's dependence on others and man's dependence on the social organization; the second stage—"relations of material dependence"—is actually the market economy society where individuals depend on commodities and money, and as such expressed as the domination of men by things; the third stage—"the all-round development of man"—is the product economy society after the market economy society withers away, where men become their own masters.

The "three formations doctrine" actually does not contradict the "five formations doctrine". These two kinds of division on the evolution of social formations by Marx and Engels are according to the analysis the evolution of social formations of the materialistic conception of history and are correct conclusions. They are consistent, but their angles are different. The "three formations doctrine" looks from the perspective of natural historical course that human society must inevitably experience, that is, from the nature and status of matter, the productive forces and the economy. The "five formations doctrine" looks from the perspective of the nature and status of the production relations determined by the productive forces and the superstructure and form the nature and status of the social system.

The essence of the debate is whether the Marxist judgment on the development law of human society and on the evolution of social formations constitutes an objective truth, whether socialism and communism are historically necessary, whether the market economy and the public ownership can be combined, whether socialism must develop a market economy or not. The crux of the related issue lies in whether socialism and communism are inevitable trends or not, whether Marxism is the truth or not, whether it has vitality or not.

Like all things the human society has an unceasing historical development process from lower to higher stages. Historical materialism holds that human society has experienced the primitive society, the slave society, the feudal society and the capitalist society and must develop into the future communist society (socialism is the first stage of the communist society). Each social formation experiences the course from birth to death. Looking from the perspective of the natural-historical course of material conditions, of the conditions of productive forces and of economic conditions, the five social formations can separately belong to three major stages, namely the natural economy, the market economy and the product economy. In this case we can say, the primitive society, the slave society and the feudal society (three of the five formations) belong to the natural economy society, while the capitalist society (the fourth among the five formations) is the market economy society. At present, it seems that the market economy should be vigorously developed at least in the primary stage of socialism. The product economy society is the future communist society (fifth formation). Marx and Engels analyzed the development of the capitalist society and concluded that it will ultimately perish because of its insurmountable inherent contradiction and be replaced by the communist society, a more advanced social formation, while communism will first pass through the stage of socialism in its development course.

(1) So far, it has been empirically proved by archaeology, anthropology and sociology that the Marxist judgment that humanity has successively experienced the primitive society, the slave society and the feudal society is correct.

(2) The historical facts in the 150 years from the birth of the first socialist country after the death of Marx and Engels, the setbacks met by the development of socialism to today's success of socialism with Chinese characteristics and then the fact of the financial crisis and the decline of capitalism in the West, all these have proved that the Marxist judgment that socialism will inevitably supersede capitalism in conformity with the laws of historical development is correct.

(3) Marx and Engels have just revealed the general laws and overall trend of historical development, but they did not exclude exceptions and accidents among the general laws and overall trend, because the social progress of humanity is made up of numerous exceptions and accidents and the general laws and overall trend also often relies on exceptions and accidents and pave the way. That is to say, the human history as a whole has experienced "five formations", but taken specifically, each country or each nation will not necessarily experience each social form successively, because such historical course is seen from the aspect of human society as a whole. The natural economy, the market economy and the product economy which

are inevitably experienced by the human society as revealed by Marx and Engels is the insurmountable natural historical course that the human society must experience.

(4) The Marxist scientific conclusions about socialism and future communist society are based on the trend and objective laws of historical development. Marx and Engels only predicted on the newly born phenomenon in the objective trend of historical necessity which is socialism, but as for how socialism concretely is they gave nothing more than an overall description at that time. But there is at least one thing: since socialism comes out of the womb of capitalism, certain new factors of socialism are already generated in the womb of capitalism, such as the socialized mass production, the social security system and the stock-holding system. Socialism, as a newly born phenomenon will inevitably experience a long process of growth and development with twists and turns and how to build socialism in the end has to be touched on in the practice.

(5) Contemporary capitalism has still a certain space for development. Many people often ask the question: why more than 150 years after the death knell sounded for capitalism as declared by Marx and Engels capitalism has not perished yet? It is not difficult to answer the question: Marx and Engels' judgment on the overall historical trend that capitalism necessarily perishes and socialism necessarily flourishes is scientific, but what they describe was a long interval and certain process of history. For example, the eve mentioned by them was not the eve in astronomy and Earth's nature. When it came to the necessity of socialism, Marx and Engels held that the socialist revolution would occur, when the capitalist productive forces have become highly mature and mature to such a level that the capitalist production relations can no longer accommodate the development of the capitalist productive forces. For them socialism which is established after the revolution should have: firstly, the public ownership system of whole society, secondly, implementation of planned economy without commodities and currency and thirdly, distribution according to labor, and will ultimately realize man's all-round development and the association of free men. The contradiction between productive forces and production relations is the innate motive power of social change. Production relations are like the eggshell, while productive forces are like the eggyolk. When they suit each other, the eggshell will promote the eggyolk; otherwise, it will hinder the eggyolk. Therefore, when the chick is mature, it will break through the shell. Of course, for a revolution to succeed, there must be certain objective conditions as well as certain subjective conditions. Through subjective efforts, the socialist revolution of underdeveloped countries can be launched in advance, but after the success of revolution, it is necessary to develop the productive forces vigorously and the production relations can't straightly

go beyond, cannot adapt to the productive forces. Marx and Engels' judgment is based upon the following: first, the insurmountable sharpness and intensification of the contradiction between productive forces and production relations of the laissez-faire capitalism, secondly, the living reality had shown that the eve of the socialist revolution had arrived and, third, the death knell of capitalism had sounded, while the conclusion derived from such an objective state was: "This is the final struggle / Let us group together and tomorrow". The then situation was just as reflected in *The Internationale*. But afterwards the fact that the contradictions of monopoly capitalism further intensified, leading to a series of wars, crises and revolutions, urged capitalism to adjust the production relations and make reforms until contemporary capitalism and enter into today's period of a relatively moderate development, which also has an aspect of adaptation of capitalist production relations to the productive forces. Therefore, capitalism is still alive, and its time of death has not come. As to socialism, because socialist revolution and socialism building were carried out in underdeveloped countries, objectively, it does not have any "ready-made" development path to walk and faces many difficulties. Besides, subjectively, mistakes made by leaders of the socialist countries and especially the traces that the old society leaves in the new, such as bureaucratism made appear conditions that hindered the development of the productive forces and caused setbacks in the system.

II. Scientific judgment of the current era and historical location

Applying historical materialism properly and making analyses with the Marxist theory of evolution of social formations help us to judge the current era and our historical location. Generally, in the long river of human history, we are now in a historical era where capitalism is going to its doom and gradually replaced by socialism. In this era, the working class strives to wage the socialist revolution and build socialism. We are along such a historical development path, i.e. the era we are in and the historical location we are at.

1. So far, the general features of the era have not changed, but in the overall development process of the era, the first historical stage has passed, the second has passed. We are now in the third historical stage.

Each three stages display different stage characteristics. In the modern history, the first stage was the stage of capitalism of free competition and of emergence of workers' and socialist movements. Due to the sharpening of inherent contradiction of laissez-faire capitalism, which had been totally exposed, class antagonisms, and bipolar division, the working class as the representative of the new productive forces had come on the stage of politics. The class struggles between the working class and the capitalist class were unfolded, workers' movements and socialist movements had emerged. Marx and Engels made a scientific judgment of this stage. The second stage was the stage of monopoly capitalism, or the stage of imperialist wars and the proletarian revolution. Lenin revealed the features of such stage. We are now in the third historical stage whose features have been generalized by the Communist Party of China and Comrade Deng Xiaoping.

Marx and Engels made a bright scientific judgment on the features of laissez fare capitalism. After them, Marxists have made two important judgments related to the latter two historical stages. One was made by Lenin in 1916—the world was in the era of imperialist wars and proletarian revolutions, that is, the theme of the era was war and revolution. According to him, this change conformed to the features of the era back then, that the capitalism of free competition had developed into the stage of monopoly capitalism, and that capitalism was going to its doom at the turn of the 19th and 20th centuries. With the passage from free competition to monopoly, the inherent contradiction of capitalism was intensified, which led to wars and revolutions. World War I triggered the October Revolution; the World War II triggered a series of socialist revolutions (including those in China.) All these facts prove that Lenin had made a proper judgment. Thus Lenin's judgment has played a critical role in guiding the socialist revolutions in China and the world. After WWII, in a fairly long period after the founding of new China, faced by the Cold War and evaluating the confrontation between the West and the East (socialism versus capitalism), the containment and encirclement of imperialism, and intensified conflicts between China and the Soviet Union, the Communist Party of China followed the evaluation that the era of war and revolution still continued.

This evaluation was crucial for China's domestic and foreign policies, and guided the judgment on China's external environment and the development of its domestic and foreign policies. On September 29, 1965, Vice Prime Minister Chen Yi expressed at a press declaration to Chinese and foreign reporters, "Just bring it on—the Soviets from the north, the Indians from the west, the Americans and Taiwanese from the south. We have been waiting for you for so long." This was a famous speech with the aspect of war and revolution. In the 1970s, when judging the then international situation, Mao Zedong said, "The wind sweeping through the tower heralds a rising storm in the mountains. The wind is blowing harder and harder, and nothing can prevent the storm." So Mao Zedong indicated that a war was approaching. The war to resist U.S. aggression and aid to Korea shortly after the founding of new China, the bombing of Jinmen (Taiwan) in 1958, the counterattack for self-defense on China-India border in 1959, the supporting of Vietnam against the U.S. in the 1960s, the self-defense counter-attack in Zhenbao Island against the Soviet Union in 1969; the border conflict with the Soviet Union at the borders of Xinjiang on May 9, 1969, the counter-attack in self-defense in Xisha Islands in 1973, the counter-attack at the borders of China and Vietnam in 1979, etc., among these wars only the war to resist U.S. aggression and aid to Korea was massive; the others were smaller. Mao Zedong estimated the situation and warned China to "get ready for the war," "get ready to fight a world war," "smash the pots and pans first and then carry out the construction," "dig deep holes; gather grain extensively, be prepared against natural disasters for the people". He warned China to focus on constructing "the Third Front", decided to invest less or none in the eastern coastal areas, and his whole strategy was preparing for war, which demonstrated the views of the Communist Party of China on the war. Of course, we can say that this was an overestimation of the seriousness of the situation, but the grave threat of hegemony and power politics against China indeed existed then. China won the war to "resist U.S. aggression and aid Korea" and the war to resist U.S. aggression and aid Vietnam, tightened its belt and developed its nuclear and hydrogen bombs and man-made satellites before obtaining the status as a world power and before ushering in the era of peace and development.

The third judgment was made by Deng Xiaoping in 1978. With the change of the international situation, the overall historical process underwent a new change of stage and new stage characteristics emerged, according to which a new judgment should be made. If China had still maintained its former judgment, it would inevitably negatively influence the adjustment and formulation of its domestic and foreign policy. Of course, in his late years, Mao Zedong also began to make policy adjustments like building diplomatic relations with the U.S. But it was Deng Xiaoping who first proposed to change the judgment of the Communist Party of China on the stage characteristics of the era. In the 1960s and 70s, the Cold War between the West and the East was not fully over, the East-West conflict and the contest between the U.S. and the Soviet Union were still the main aspects of the international situation. However, entering the 1970s and 80s, the international situation encountered gradual changes: later in 1989, the Berlin Wall collapsed; in 1991, the Soviet Union transformed, Eastern Europe dissolved, the Cold War ended, thus the history was reversed. Deng Xiaoping was the first one to judge that "the general era did not change, but we have new changes in the characteristics of the stage" He believed that the world was faced with two major issues—peace and development instead of war and revolution; that peace and development were the world's two major themes, and both goals and demands had not yet been met. His strategic judgment led to a major change in the general policy guideline, effecting China's domestic policies and diplomatic relations which led China to adjust its strategy for dealing with domestic and international issues. Consequently China started to implement the grand policy of socialist reform and opening-up, strive to build a peaceful external environment, focus on domestic (especially economic) construction, and take the road of peaceful development of socialism with Chinese characteristics. The judgment of Deng Xiaoping was a scientific analysis on the current change of stage in the relative strength of capitalism and socialism, which did not affect the judgment on the overall characteristics of the era (passage from capitalism to socialism). The scientific judgment made by Deng Xiaoping enabled China to seize a great development opportunity.

The era being themed as peace and development does not mean that the basic contradiction of capitalism—between socialization of production and private nature of ownership—has disappeared. The current world-wide financial crisis indicates that this basic contradiction of capitalism still exists and is still insurmountable. Despite its different forms of manifestation, the overall historical trend of capitalism has not changed. For example, due to the development of capitalism in the West, the South/North gap and the gap between the rich and the poor have further expanded. Poor people who are living with less than 1 US dollar per day on average have reached 1.2 billion in the world. Of the 6.7 billion world population, or more than 6.9 billion as shown by some statistics, one out of six is utterly poverty-stricken. Two billion world people, that is, 1/3 of the total world population, live with less than 2 US dollars per day on average. People living in poverty account for a considerable proportion in world population. The world is not tranquil at all. The unrest and local wars worldwide today are fundamentally rooted in the inherent contradiction of the world capitalism.

2. We are still in the overall and big era judged by Marxism-Leninism. The overall characteristics of the era is, in essence, still the repeated contest between the new social form and the old social form, between capitalism and socialism, between the working class and the bourgeoisie, which are the two forms of society, two paths and two big strengths.

At present, in the contest over the two big themes of peace and development, China and the other developing countries want peace and development, so do the Western capitalist countries. However, the Western capitalist countries are against the development of China and that of the other developing countries. They can instigate local wars at will, thus become opposed forces to peace and development of China and the other developing countries. In the contest, these two major forces and two historical trends sometimes confront each other, sometimes strive to develop along and sometimes compromise, showing a very complicated battle situation. However, on the whole, capitalism is declining, but remains strong; socialism is newly born, but remains weak.

3. The contest between the two social forms, two paths and two classes inevitably display themselves in the field of ideology.

Such contest finds its expression in repeated confrontation and contest between the Marxist, socialist ideology and value orientation and the bourgeois, capitalist ideology and value orientation. It is closely intertwined with today's complicated national interests, people's interests and demands, with today's ethnic and religious issues, the common demand of worldwide protection of living environment of humanity, with the struggle for interests of peace and development. In order to cover its nature, the capitalist ideology is usually beautified under the guise of universality, human rights, whole humanity, neutrality and abstractness, which misleads people about its essence.

4. At present and in a period to come, the development of socialism with Chinese characteristics is still in a rare period of strategic opportunities in which it can make great achievements.

The period will witness both opportunities and challenges, achievements and problems, and peace and struggle. It is a golden period of development, but also a period of emergent contradictions. The theme of the era—peace and development—has not changed, the basic national conditions of China has not changed, the basic task taking economic construction as the core has not changed. That China is in a period of strategic opportunities for development and the basic pattern that the opportunities are bigger than challenges have not changed. As a whole, the overall trend that the international environment is conducive to the peaceful development of China has not changed. Therefore, China is at a crucial period for marching into a well-off society in an all-round manner as well as a period for deepening its reform and opening-up, can speed up transforming its mode of development and can promote a comprehensive social and economic development.

Y. 2

New Features of the Present Capital Empire: Financial, Scientific and Technological, Cultural and Military Hegemony

Li Shenming[1]

Abstract: The outbreak and deepening of the international financial crisis will inevitably further promote intense and profound changes in the world pattern. Presently, the grand era that opened with 1917 has not changed, but theme and trend of the era will develop and change and even transform along with development and change of the era. The world is on the eve of big changes and big adjustments and severe turbulence, which is the necessary outcome of long-term accumulation of conflicts arising from various major contradictions in the world. Although in decline, the US-led Western world still tries hard to lead the international political and economic order, the financial, scientific and technological, cultural and military hegemony, the so-called "four in one" hegemony, which constitutes the new features of the present world capitalist imperialist era. Although the US-led Western world still possesses an overall hegemony, particularly in the high-tech area, the new S&T revolution driven by the IT revolution and economic globalization led by the United States presents a double-edged sword for the international monopoly bourgeoisie. They further intensify the basic contradiction of capitalism between the socialization of production and the capitalist private ownership of the means of production in the global scale. The inevitable result is the global widening gap between the rich and the poor which will have far-reaching consequences. Therefore, we firmly believe that socialism will surely see a worldwide revival.

Key words: international financial crisis; world pattern; revival of socialism

---

[1] Li Shenming, Deputy President of the Chinese Academy of Social Sciences (CASS), and the Director of the World Socialism Research Center attached to CASS.

I. It is very likely that the world is on the eve of great upheavals, adjustments and reforms

On July 23, 2012, Hu Jintao clearly pointed out in his speech at the opening ceremony of the working seminar attended by leading cadres at provincial and ministerial levels: "Based on a comprehensive analysis of the domestic and foreign situation, China is faced with unprecedented opportunities and challenges. It is a period of important strategic opportunities for the development of China". When expounding on the issue of Party building, he especially pointed out: "External risks are unprecedented". The above judgment is of great significance.

The drastic changes in Eastern Europe and the disintegration of the Soviet Union in 1991 marked an intense change in the world pattern, which promoted the further development of a new round of economic globalization dominated by the US-led Western world, further aggravated the contradiction between the socialization of production and even globalization of production and the private ownership of the means of production, and between unlimited expansion of production and the limited demand of society being the basic contradiction, thus further intensified the polarization between the rich and the poor in the aspects of income and wealth. In a sense, we can say the international financial crisis that erupted in 2008 was an inevitable product of the drastic change in Eastern Europe and the disintegration of the Soviet Union in 1991. The outbreak and deepening of the current international financial crisis will surely promote sharp and profound changes in the world pattern.

After the outbreak of the international financial crisis, the governments of major world countries, instead of "flying separately faced with the imminent disaster", have further intensified close cooperation, explored the expansion of original or the new establishment of different levels of big power groups so as to settle different levels of corresponding issues and collaborate in seeking an "effective prescription" for the international financial crisis. Around the outbreak of the international financial crisis, some figures related with the U.S. put forward the concept of "Chimerica" and the concept of US-China "two blocs theory", namely "G2" one after another. "Chimerica" refers to the interest community made up of the U.S, the world's biggest consuming country, and China, the world's biggest savings country. "G2" means that China is a super economic power evading its economic responsibilities, so it is necessary to regulate China's economic behaviors through a bilateral system like G2. Neither "Chimerica" nor "G2" means that U.S. and China share the authority to jointly govern the world. China is a socialist country, whose nature and essence determines that China cannot seek world hegemony. On May 3, 2012, Dai Binguo, the

State Councilor of China, declared that China and US will not engage in a G2 "as a "two-nation bloc" or in a Sino-US domination of the world or in a Sino-US confrontation, but they can engage in "bilaterally coordinated" G2. This not only expressed an opposition to the U.S attempt to intervene in China's internal affairs and demonstrated China's principled stance of not seeking hegemony, but also expressed the demand of the Chinese government to cooperate with the U.S. government. Later, some figures related with the U.S. and the U.K. put forward the idea of G3, that is, with American military strength and purchasing power, Chinese capital, namely huge foreign exchange reserves and cheap labor force and European regulations and technology, the three—the U.S., China and Europe—can cooperate to save international finance. G2 and G3 propose on the one hand to interpret the strategy of the US-led Western world, and unmistakably express what it demands from China. Although the formulation of G2 and G3 is not widely accepted, it does not affect a relevant coordination and cooperation in substance. The former G7 and G20 are both playing their established unique roles. However, G7 will continue its efforts to lead the deepening development of economic globalization, and assume some important missions in U.S's "Pivot to Asia" strategy. In G20, the US-led G7 demands the developing countries therein, especially China, from now on assumes more responsibility for G7. The five countries of BRICS will continue to cooperate, but among them especially India will be able to be strongly contained and split apart by G7. G7 has a strong demand to blur ASEAN 10+3 (China, Japan and the Republic of Korea) and the Shanghai Cooperation Organization. The US-led Trans-Pacific Strategic Economic Partnership Agreement, namely TPP, which excludes China, will possibly be given substantial content constantly. Under certain conditions, it may take on the role of "NATO" in the U.S.'s "Pivot to Asia" strategy. Now both in the international community and in China, people are worried about a G0, a "polar-less" "world broken into pieces", and think that this is "a new dark age meaning anarchism", which will be a "more dangerous and turbulent" era. I believe that a G0 world pattern will not emerge in the foreseeable 20 to 30 years. The reason for this estimation is that mainly today and possibly so in a fairly long period of time to come there will be still the basic state of "West is strong and we are weak". This is not only because the US-led West has a quite strong economy, including hard powers such as finance and military strength, but also because at the present time there did not appear any strong rival that can really compete with it in terms of the so-called soft powers like the formulation of international rules and ideological manipulation. Although the international financial crisis has still not bottomed out and is still deepening, seen from international debt, the U.S. government has already gone bankrupt, but the US-led Western world still has a lot of and big space of regulation. In the years to come, they will be able to employ political to economic counteractions right up to the highest political means—war—for its economic services. Therefore, generally speaking, the U.S. as a nation state will not decline soon. Even if it declines, it will possibly be a quite slow process. However, the U.S. as an empire may see the obvious signs of decline in the years to come, and may need the help of Europe and Japan to delay its decline process. We can also make the following judgment: Along with the accumulation and development of various basic contradictions in the world, around 2050, it is very likely that a number of socialist countries being on par with the US-led Western world as a whole will appear. If in our world a G0 can truly appear, it would be a golden opportunity for the world's left-wing and the revival of socialism. Of course, we have to be highly alert to the great might of extreme "multi-polarization" where under certain conditions several new empires simultaneously emerge and the big socialist country lacks independence, and then the new imperialist countries re-divide the world between themselves and restage the tragedies of WWI and WWII.

Today, peace, development and cooperation are undoubtedly the universal demand of various countries and the main trend which indeed exists. However, we should soberly understand: Firstly, under certain conditions, peace, development and cooperation, the three have an inherent degree of unity, but each also has different connotations, they are not of equal rank. War is different in nature, so are peace and development different in nature. The US-led Western world tries to realize peace under their rule in order to achieve their development under peaceful conditions and to ensure the eternity of the capitalist system. When G.W. Bush and President Obama held an office in the National Security Council, Paul D. Miller, who was an assistant professor of international security affairs at the U.S. National Defense University in Washington, recently wrote an article and pointed out clearly: "the United States has been pursuing at least one pillar of an implicit grand strategy since the end of the Cold War: building the democratic peace."[2] In a sense, peace under certain conditions is a state a certain subject hopes to achieve, cooperation under certain conditions is a means a certain subject adopts, while specific development is the aim a certain subject hope to achieve. Before the human society reaches the world commonwealth, peace and cooperation should have specific connotations to different subjects that will not pursue peace and cooperation for peace and cooperation, but for the fundamental aim of its own development. Secondly, along with the continuous deepening of the international financial crisis, not only among major powers in both hemispheres, but also particularly among the numerous Third World countries, enhanced cooperation should be possible or become

---

2 Paul D. Miller: American Grand Strategy and the Democratic Peace, British Bimonthly Survival, April/May 2012.

the mainstream of world development. In October 2006, the Sino-African Cooperation Forum attended by the heads of the states and government leaders or representatives of 48 African countries, the chairman of the African Union Commission, representatives of regional and international organizations was held in Beijing. It was an important result of the enhanced cooperation of developing countries. The Sino-African cooperation is deepening at all levels. In July 19 and 20, 2012, the fifth ministerial level conference of the Sino-African Cooperation Forum between China, the foreign ministers and ministers in charge of economic cooperation of 50 African countries, as well as the chairman of the African Union Commission was held in Beijing. According to the statistics, the Sino-African cooperation has achieved an unprecedented extent and depth in politics, economy, culture and other fields in the new century that the volume of trade between China and Africa leaped from 12 million US dollars in 1950 to 129.6 billion US dollars in 2010, and even exceeded 160 billion US dollars in 2011. China has become Africa's biggest trading partner. It is predictable that, as long as correctly formulation and implementation of strategy is correct, China and the numerous developing countries, namely the Third World, can certainly present a new situation of cooperation that we anticipate. This will certainly continue to provide a relatively stable external environment for China's accelerating development in the new century. Thus, it can also be achieved to gradually weaken the hegemonism and power politics acting continuously around the globe and to gradually fulfill the conception of a harmonious world constructed by China. Thirdly, behind peace, development and cooperation there is competition, gaming and even contest. Therefore, peace, development and cooperation exist if they are sought through struggle; peace, development and cooperation die, if they are sought through compromise. China should take full advantage of the current unprecedented opportunity primarily through maximum cooperation, correctly deal with the rare and serious challenge so as to achieve its strategic goal of peaceful development; but it can never rule out the adoption of other means, including anti-aggression wars, to protect its sacred sovereignty and territorial integrity and protect the aspect of peace, development and cooperation. Only with such determination and confidence, especially with sufficient ideological, material and military preparation can China truly make good use of the period of important opportunities while it can achieve domestic and international progress.

Meanwhile, we must fully understand that in the next 20-30 years it is very difficult to say the results of the mutual cooperation, competition, gaming and contest among each major power and each strategy group in the world. There are various of possibilities, while an impressive rise of socialism with Chinese characteristics and a remarkable revival of the world socialist movement is extremely probable. Of course, the possibility that China and the Third World countries encountering new greater difficulties in their development, and socialist movement falling into a new lower tide should not be excluded. No matter which above prospect emerges, one thing can be fully affirmed: the wheel of history has begun to drive into the fast lane of historical development and that highly turbulent, even leaping situation may very possibly occur in the world pattern from the outbreak of this international financial crisis and to the first 20 and 30 years of the 21st century and even till the first half of the 21st century. It is an inevitable result of the contradiction between long accumulated major conflicts in the world. Reasons can be attributed to the following:

First, the world economy has stepped into a longer period of recession. Along with the disintegration of the Soviet Union other socialist countries of the East Europe and setbacks of the communist parties in 1990s, and the global proliferation of neoliberalism, the "global privatization" wave which was started by Thatcher and Reagan has led the world economy into a dilemma. The top 1% US citizens grab nearly 1/4 of the U.S. national income. Almost all countries of different types around the globe see more and more poor people who are poorer and poorer on the one hand and fewer and fewer rich people who are getting increasingly rich on the other hand. The sharp rise in their debts and fiscal deficits serve as the fundamental sign that almost all these countries are becoming poorer and poorer. In 2011, the public debt and fiscal deficit of the U.S. accounted for nearly 100% and 11% of its GDP respectively. In the same year, the average proportion of public debt and fiscal deficit to the GDP of the 17 countries in the EU region have exceeded 87% and 6% respectively. Till the end of 2012, Japan's proportion of public debt and fiscal deficit to GDP will reach 232% and over 10% respectively, far higher than the redline of 60% and 3% set by the EU's Stability and Growth Pact. The effective demand of the general population in the world is drastically reduced. Thus the fundamental contradiction between the socialization and even globalization of production and the private ownership of the means of production and the fundamental contradiction between the unlimited expansion of production and the limited social demand further intensify, the economy of the capitalist world will certainly further decline, and the world socialist tide and world socialist movement will further revive. The competition, gaming and contest between the two fundamental systems, capitalism and socialism, system will be lasting, fierce and sometimes even take brutal and violent forms.

Second, a more serious international financial crisis may be yet to come. This is because various major countries deal with the crisis mainly from the viewpoint of fiscal and monetary policy either tightening government expenditures or implementing monetary expansion; from the viewpoint of immediately increasing temporary fiscal revenue, they sell out state-owned assets, including state-owned enterprises, to raise fund for government debts or they reduce necessary government subsidies. These measures can alleviate contradictions within the framework of capitalist production relations temporarily and partially, but in the long run, they create conditions for more serious economic and social crises. As to tightening government expenditure, it will directly lead to the reduction of the limited social consumption, then aggravate unemployment, causing more enterprises to go bankrupt, thus further push up the high unemployment rate and trigger social unrest. For example, Greece and Japan now adopt the measure to directly cut the salaries of officials. As to implementing monetary expansion, another large-scale monetary expansion after adopting several rounds of monetary expansion policies will directly trigger hyper-inflation, sharp reduction of the limited wealth and limited consumption accumulated by ordinary people, which will similarly cause more enterprises to go bankrupt, thus push up the employment rate and trigger social unrest. As to selling out state-owned assets including state-owned enterprises to raise fund for government debts or to reduce necessary government subsidies, its direct consequence is that private capital or foreign capital will even more grasp the energy, public transportation and other fundamentally strategic enterprises as well as land, mines, among other resources, which are originally controlled by the state. Greed is the nature and life of capital and leaves no hole undrilled. After controlling these enterprises and resources, capital will try to squeeze out more labor and wealth from ordinary people, which will further intensify social polarization. Such as Greece's deep-seated debt crisis, it is accelerating the privatization process, and plans to complete privatizing its state-owned gas companies and gas supply network by the end of September 2012. Over 90% of the privatization plans of the Greek government cover leasing and selling out state-owned land and infrastructure. Poland, which is in the so-called economic transformation, has carried out 159 privatization projects in the first half of 2012, of which 60 have been successfully privatized. The Polish government got 3,760 million złote (nearly 1,145 million US dollars) from privatization in the first half of 2012. This privatization will intensify the gap between the rich and the poor in Poland. As to realizing economic transformation through hi-tech innovations, under the conditions of international monopoly capital-dominated economic globalization where the means of production are privately owned, it also ultimately reduces labor income and increases capital income around the globe, then further intensifies of the most fundamental contradiction between the socialization of production and even globalization of production and the private ownership of the means of production and between the unlimited expansion of production and limited social demand. For example, the Foxconn production line had only 10,000 sets of robots in 2011, reached 300,000 units in 2012, and will be as high as 1 million units in 2014, that is, equivalent to the total number of its current workers. When all workers in major industries have been replaced by machines, the ordinary working people accounting for the overwhelming majority of the world population will lose their sources of wages and salaries, then who will buy and consume the commodities flooding the market, even the globe? The above measures, instead of solving the fundamental issue of polarization between the rich and the poor, a pressing issue for world countries now, will further push the overwhelming majority of the people in the society, even the world to impoverishment and lead a handful of people to get rich overnight. When the overwhelming majority of ordinary people is living on the verge of death and when fighting back may be a way out, then social change has to occur inevitably.

Third, the US-led Western world is declining, but its quite strong economy including the so-called hard power such as financial and military strength, the so-called soft power such as the formulation of international rules and ideological manipulation, is still occupying the domination or the monopolistic position globally. Despite the obvious signs of decay in the US-led Western world, we should fully realize that it has a variety of "regulation" methods. In the cooperation, competition and gaming with the numerous Third World countries, in order to save the economic downturn, the US-led Western world will of course first of all use its so-called soft power or hard power. However, once conventional means do not work, it will resort to nonconventional means to achieve its ultimate aim. Along with the unceasing deepening of the international financial crisis, the contest in the aspects of energy, food, finance, Internet, even territory and sea areas among major world countries behind cooperation, competition and gaming will be fierce. It may be extremely violent and the highest method is war. Of course, it is the best option for the US-led Western world to look for proper war agents. In today's Asia, the best attempt is utilizing the current conflicts between China and Vietnam, North Korea and South Korea, and those between Iraq and Iran, in future the conflicts between China and Japan and that between China and India and even repeating the old trick of selling arms to both sides and profiting from the war as in the WWI and the WWII. We must resolutely protect our sovereignty and territorial integrity, upon which we should never feel uncertain or waver, or we will become sinners of the Chinese nation. However, in the extremely complicated international situation today, we must meticulously plan and maneuver among various forces with a broader vision.

Fourth, the U.S. has bumptiously targeted its spear to two great nations, Russia and China. Paul Craig Roberts, former Assistant Secretary of the Treasury for Economic Policy, recently wrote an article and clearly pointed out, "The evidence is simply overwhelming that Washington–both parties–have Russia and China targeted. Whether the purpose is to destroy both countries or merely to render them unable to oppose Washington's world hegemony is unclear at this time."[3] It is often said that "One can never discern the true face of the mountain Lu, if one can only look out from within these hills." Yet, often there is also a case, that one can discern the true face of the mountain Lu, if one can only look out from within these hills.

I agree with Paul Craig Roberts' judgment that Washington targeted both parties, Russia and China. As to US's aim to destroy these two countries, whether it is merely to render them incapable to resist Washington's world hegemony, depends on the strengths of each party and their strategies to cope with each other. Rendering Russia and China incapable to resist the U.S. is a phased aim, destroying both is the most ideal goal of the U.S. In order to save itself, even the entire Western world, the U.S. may probably enter a long period of economic recession. Without a grand global strategy, it is almost impossible to achieve the aimed utopia. The U.S. targets Russia and China mainly because Russia has abundant resources and a very strong military industry, while China has a huge market and a rising economic strength. Moreover, in the eyes of the U.S., Russia is restoring its nationalist "autocracy" under the leadership of President Putin, while China is vigorously developing socialism with Chinese characteristics, which are fatal threats to the U.S., both in ideological and value terms. The US politicians generally follow pragmatism, and seldom practice formalism. Between July 5 and 17, 2012, US Secretary of State, Hillary Clinton, made a 13-day, 43,450 km-long continuous visit (3,220 km longer than going once around the earth) to 9 countries including France, Afghanistan, Japan, Inner Mongolia, Vietnam, Cambodia, Egypt and Israel. In a sense, her ultimate target was Russia and China. Of course, China has also to prevent the US-led Western world from succeeding in driving a wedge between Russia and China under certain conditions, in order to establish the broadest "international united front": at first, it will concentrate its main power on encircling China, and then march northward to dismember Russia, in order to achieve its aim of world domination. I firmly believe that the great Russian and Chinese people will definitely not wait for capture with tied hands. Their resistance of the two nations and people against this strategic aim of the US will be magnificent. Fundamentally speaking, nationalism and socialism are ultimately irreconcilable with hegemonism and power politics; between the two a "win-win" and harmony in terms of strategic aims can never be achieved; the biggest confluence and merger of interests between the two can be only achieved in the cooperation mode of strategic mode when our fundamental goal is a limited goal in a certain period.

---

3 Paul Craig Roberts: Can the World Survive Washington's Hubris? The World [Spanish], July 1, 2012.

Fifth, the harvest period of neoliberalism carried out by the US-led Western world is to end in 3 to 5 years, or in 10 years at the most. After the drastic changes in Eastern Europe and the disintegration of the Soviet Union, the world economy entered a period of rapid economic development, mainly due to the world-wide implementation of neoliberalism, which has a certain inherently rationality and historical necessity. Developing countries have a variety of rich and cheap material resources, very cheap labor force, abundant talented people including hi-tech personnel as well as an urge for economic development, not hesitating to attract some high-pollution foreign-investment projects at the expense of environmental degradation in order boost their total GDP, thus increase their tax revenue and solve the pressing problem of unemployment. On the one hand, the developed countries happen to make a large-scale transfer of some high-pollution, high-energy consuming and high-labor cost enterprises to developing countries. On the one hand, they can accelerate their S&T and industrial product innovations so as to achieve the transformation of their mode of economic development, in order to prepare a new strategy and concrete conditions for developing a higher-level of advanced economy around the globe. Looking from the present, this way of cooperation which is beneficial for both the investor and the investee countries may last for some years, that is to say, the harvest period of neoliberalism in the developing and especially emerging countries will possibly last 3-5 years, or even 10 years. Because of this, many experienced bourgeois politicians, thinkers and economists have a strong sense of urgency, are fiercely criticizing neoliberalism and strongly demanding resolute improvements to liberal capitalism. In a sense, such cooperation between the developed and the developing countries usually means the trading at the expense of long-term interests of developing countries for temporary interests. Once this "win-win" harvest period of temporary interests ends, conflicts between these two types of countries will be inevitable. In fact, in the so-called major emerging countries, material resources have begun to become scarce, labor costs have increased, the environmental costs of investment have been on the rise and some foreign capital has begun to withdraw the already earned huge profits from these emerging countries and moved to less developed countries with lower costs. When foreign capital is withdrawn on a large scale, the emerging countries will encounter difficulties, which will further intensify the so-called "economic imbalance" around the globe and trigger a severer global turmoil.

Sixth, along with the deepening of the international financial crisis, various conflicts and issues left over from history will be further exposed and intensified. Some inherent ethnic and religious conflicts, some territorial sovereignty disputes and disputes over economic interests will possibly intensify.

In summary, we can draw an initial conclusion: The big era has not changed, but the theme and trends of the era will change along with the development of the era, even transform along with the unceasing development and change of the era. The world is on the eve of a great turmoil, great adjustments and great change. Of course, the eve here does not mean a day of 24 hours or a period of 3 or 5 years, but a period of 10 to 20 years. If eve is narrowly understood, academic, theoretical, even strategic discussions will lose their proper premise, will impossibly be deepened and lead to correct conclusions which can stand the test of practice and history.

The world is on the eve of such a great turmoil, such great adjustments and such great change, that it will see predictable and even lots of unpredictable new situations and problems. China should be mentally fully prepared to this and ready to deal with concrete strategies. Only in this way can China seize unprecedented strategic opportunities timely and correctly and face unprecedented strategic challenges.

II. Financial, scientific and technological, cultural and military hegemony is the new feature of the present capital empire

In 2005, General Secretary Hu Jintao explicitly pointed out, "Peace, cooperation and development are the main themes of our times... At the same time, peace and development, the two overriding questions before the world, have not yet been fundamentally resolved" "All this has made our road towards universal peace and common development a bumpy and challenging one"[4] Practice has proven that the judgment made by Mr. Hu was quite right, fully consistent with the one made by Deng Xiaoping in 1992 in his famous "Southern Tour Talks" that "peace and development are the two major issues in the world, and neither one has been resolved;"[5] and with the judgment made by Jiang Zemin in 2000 that "the economic globalization in the current world is led by the Western developed countries".[6]

Demanding peace, promoting development and seeking cooperation and is without doubt the universal and strong demand of the peoples all over the world, as well as the direction of the objective efforts between the governments of major world countries today. Nobody can deny that hegemony and power politics have been enormously enhanced after the drastic changes in Eastern Europe and the collapse of the Soviet Union, while its main feature

---
4 Hu Jintao: Build Towards a Harmonious World of Lasting Peace and Common Prosperity—Statement by H.E. Hu Jintao President of the People's Republic of China At the United Nations Summit New York, People's Daily, September 16, 2005.
5 Selected Works of Deng Xiaoping, Vol. 3, p. 383,.People's Publishing House, 1993.
6 Jiang Zemin: Statement at the 2000 APEC CEO Summit Lunch Meeting, People's Daily, November 16, 2000.

is the unceasing enhancement into one of financial, scientific and technological, cultural and military hegemonies and its increasing integration. The US-led Western world attempts to lead the situation and direction of the current world peace, development and cooperation. The primary purpose why the US-led Western world maintains and strengthens its world hegemony is to firmly control and orderly plunder the limited resources on earth that are hurriedly reducing.

Financial hegemony: The era of free competition capitalism is characterized by the dominant position of industrial capital and the control of major economic resources and decisive political institutions by industrial capital. But today finance is the lifeblood of contemporary national economies and world economy. Financial capital, the highest and most abstract manifestation form of capital, is the highest form of capital which rules over the human society. Such international monopoly financial capital based on international industrial product monopoly monopolizes not only almost all the sources of raw materials of the world, but also major industries of the world, all kinds of scientific and technological talents and skilled manual labor forces, seizes major thoroughfares and various production tools and controls and holds more capital through banks, a variety of financial derivatives and shareholding systems, so as to take the global order under its control. In a sense, the current world is a huge global stock-holding company held by the US-led Western world. Taking the IMF as an example, in June 2012, 12 countries including China, Brazil, Russia, India and South Africa pledged to increase their funding to the IMF at the G20-meeting, with China injecting another 43 billion US dollars, the highest increase at that time. Brazil, India and Russia pledged each to aid another 10 billion US dollars.

China's funding increase has at least the following three advantages: China's share in the IMF will increase from 3.72% to 6.39%. China's vote will also increase from 3.65% to 6.07%, thus surpassing Germany, France and Britain and ranking after the U.S and Japan. The security level of China's investment in the IMF is high, and the proceeds are safer, which is more conducive to further promote the reform of the governance structure of the IMF and enhancement of the voice of developing countries in the IMF policies. But, it deserves our attention that the adoption of major IMF decisions requires at least an approval of 85%, while the U.S. holds 17.67% of the voting rights. The reform of the IMF has a long way to go. Today, the international financial monopoly capitalism has formed such a world economic system, making the tentacles of the financial capital stretch to every corner of the world, making both international financial monopoly capital countries and financial capital importing countries form such socioeconomic relations which are the most favorable for the international monopoly financial capital to seize maximum benefits.

Secondly, economic globalization led by the international financial monopoly capital is in fact also a process of commercializing and monetizing all material objects of the world gradually carried out by international monopoly capital. All the material objects are first monetized, and then gradually involved into the field of financial circulation. All sovereign states are forced to open their currencies, which then realizes financial globalization. Thus, international monopoly capital controls the material wealth of all countries, directly or indirectly. Please look at the following sets of data: In 1980, U.S.'s ratio of financial assets to GDP was 158%, which soared to 420% in 2010. Also in 2010, the profits of the financial sector accounted for 45% of total corporate profits. When the proportion of profits of the financial sector further climbs over 50%, the U.S. will have to witness a qualitative change and become a thorough financialized country. If the U.S. implements a new quantitative easing, its financial economy will fully overtake its real economy quantitatively. In 2009, the GDP of the United States was only 14.7 trillion US dollars, and its real economy was about 2.77 trillion US dollars, that is, one fifth of its GDP. Besides, by trade deficit or by other means, the U.S. outputs at least 50 million US dollars to overseas per hour on average. So, each year, it has shifted a material wealth worth at least 400 billion US dollars from overseas to home. In a sense, finance hegemony is the major means to satisfy the international financial monopoly groups' plunder of world countries' wealth crazily and to keep capitalism alive and ensure its development. It is the economic basis which ensures the prosperity of the US-led Western powerful nations and reconciles their domestic class contradictions. International financial hegemony is the new highest stage of the development of hegemonism and power politics.

Finance is the bewildering and dazzling kaleidoscope played by the international monopoly capital. Today, in the face of economic globalization or financial globalization, the U.S. can be compared to the heart of a body of global finance—almost all the other countries and each of their cities in the world are covered by blood veins with which the U.S. sucks their blood. Stocks, futures, exchange rates and international bulk commodity prices, all these can rise and fall, because the greater the height of a water dam is, the more will be the generated energy. And the key behind is the manipulation of big international financial monopoly capital. Now, the global GDP is 70 trillion US dollars, while the bond market reaches 95,000 trillion US dollars, being over 1,000 times more than the global GDP; the value of various financial derivatives have reached 466,000 trillion US dollars, that is, more than 6,657 times greater than the global GDP. The total capital flowing every 2.4 hours in the world is equivalent to the global GDP in a year.[7] Such vast and numerous financial derivatives have stretched their tentacles to

---

7 World economy to see another crisis in 2012, Rebellion [Spanish] October 2, 2011.

each corner, even to each family in the world to grab the money directly without passing through the production link.

Scientific and technological hegemony: Looking from the aspect of R&D investments, if we take the domestic R&D budget in 2007 as an example, the U.S. used one third of its domestic R&D budget for investment, the highest in the world, followed by EU (23.1%), Japan (12.9%) and China (8.9%). Looking from the aspect of investment in education, U.S.'s absolute amount of education expenses has been the highest in the world for many years. In 2009, the per capita public expenditures on education of the U.S. accounted for 6.1% of the per capita GDP income, and the same index was 4.28% in Japan, 3.01% in South Korea, 1.87% in Russia, 2.29% in Brazil, but only 0.82% in China. That of the U.S. was 7.44 times greater, that of Russia was 2.28 times greater, and that of Brazil was 2.79 times greater than that of China. Therefore, China lags far behind the developed countries, even ranks at the bottom of the BRICS countries in terms of its expenditures on education. The U.S.'s education implements a "youth" strategy in universities, even middle schools with a variety of favorable conditions to attract outstanding talented people from various countries of the world, so as to achieve its "scientific and technological hegemony" in a sustainable way. In 2011, the US universities have enrolled 725,000 overseas students, setting a historical record. In terms of revenues from copyright and licensing fees, the U.S. ranks first in the world. During 2000 and 2009, its revenues in this regard grew from 43.2 billion US dollars to nearly 90 billion US dollars, being far ahead of Japan and that of Germany, ranking second and the third. Seen from the number of academic papers published in scientific journals, the U.S. has been far ahead in the world for many years. Especially seen from the Internet, in the creation of the Internet, the U.S. also designed a DNS rule. In the DNS resolution process any number of bytes from big to small pages are all finally subject to the root server. Who controls the root servers controls the huge power of the Internet. Of the 13 root servers in the world which are in charge of the Internet, the only A root server and another 9 secondary root servers (B-M) are in the U.S. The other three secondary root servers are in Britain, Sweden and Japan, respectively. In their resolution process, the three secondary root servers must pass through the A root server of the U.S. to enter the net. Theoretically, each e-mail, cell phone text message sent by ordinary citizens and each phone call can be recorded by the A root server of the U.S. About 80% of the global Internet business volume is related with the U.S. Over 80% of the huge Internet database is controlled by the U.S.. and almost all the rules of Internet operation are formulated by the U.S.. China, with 500 million native netizens, accounts only for 0.1% of information inflow rate and 0.05% of information outflow rate of the Internet. The following deserves special attention:

First, in May and June, 2012, there appeared a computer virus named "the flame" in Western Asia, reaching a code volume of 650,000 lines, equivalent to 2400 meters of printed pages. Some scholars pointed out that this virus came from one ore two developed country.

Second, currently the U.S. has at least 90,000 cyber troops, that is, equivalent to eight 101 airborne divisions and possesses over 2,000 kinds of actual combat viruses.

Third, the U.S. stepped up to R&D of "off-line network" assault weapons, which can connect to the physically isolated network system in order to directly attack military, financial, electricity, traffic, medical services and other network systems.

Cultural hegemony: Cultural hegemony in the current world today is controlled by the best funded international financial monopoly capital. In 2010, the U.S. cultural industry accounted for 43% of the world cultural industry, and the figure of China was less than 4%, that is, weaker than 1/10 of the U.S. cultural industry. The cultural industry of the US accounts for 25% of the GDP, 20% of the GDP in Japan; but only 2.5% of the GDP in China. That the U.S. defines the Internet as a "domain of military activities" parallel to the army, the navy, the air force and space has further demonstrated its cultural hegemony. In fact, the U.S. acts as the police of the global internet information highway and attempts to let only those cultures conforming to the US-led Western values on the road. Not only the most popular websites, but also worldwide-known and broad TV programs, radio stations, newspapers, magazines and movies as well as the universities, research and consulting agencies that serve them indirectly are all controlled by the US-led Western world. On March 19, 2012, the National Computer Network Emergency Response Technical Team/Coordination Center of China (known as CNCERT or CNCERT/CC) released 2011 China Internet Cyber Security Report, in which it pointed out that the U.S. controls with over 9,500 IP addresses 8.85 million mainframes in China, has over 3,300 IP addresses which control more than 3,400 websites in China. With the IP addresses under its control, through stealth machine mass mailings, the U.S. can also send nearly 700,000 pieces of fake news of fabricated rumors to major Chinese websites within two hours. Besides, in 2011, the U.S. government has released the white paper Federal Cloud Computing Strategy and its cloud computing industry has started to march into a rapid development track. U.S. monopoly capital does not only control the core technologies of cloud computing, but also takes the Internet as the channel of the highest level in cloud computing. It will have a significant impact on China's information security and even national security. We should not only notice that it is an industry which is expensive to invest in, but highly profitable, but also see that today a thriving world cultural industry is actively propagandizing the values of the US-led Western world and fabricates all kinds of public opinions for its permanent domination of the world. Therefore, the US-led Western world praises the U.S. as the "empire of values". What are American values? As stated in its 2002 National Security Strategy report, "America will encourage the advancement of democracy and economic openness…because these are the best foundations for domestic stability and the international order".

Military hegemony: On September 27, 1840, A.T. Mahan was born in the professors' building of the US Military Academy in West Point. In 1890, he published his work—The Influence of Sea Power Upon History—which had a far-reaching impact on the American history. His basic concept is: a country's economy depend on its global trade volume. In order to trade as much as possible, one must prevent his competitors from intervening in his own business as much as possible. Therefore, global trade volume is inseparable from military strength. Thomas Friedman, the most influential journalist in the U.S. and author of the bestseller The World Is Flat pointed out, "The hidden hand of the market will never work without a hidden fist. McDonald's cannot flourish without McDonnell Douglas, the designer of the F-15 war planes"; "the emerging global order demands an enforcer. That's America's new burden"[8]

A Spanish journalist recently pointed out, "the US does depend on its political or diplomatic theories or democratic and military speeches to rule the world, but only carries out the indestructible logic of US dollar and military and economic strength to other countries." "To destroy the 'dollar empire', a brand-new international economic and financial order must be brought forward and designed, and the U.S. must be persuaded to forget its nuclear arsenals, aircraft carriers and (thousands of) military bases all over the world, and to 'peacefully' give up itself in the hegemonic position in the capitalist system"[9] The US strategist Thomas Barnett once said, "We trade little pieces of paper (our currency, in the form of a trade deficit) for Asia's amazing array of products and services. We are smart enough to know that this is obviously an unfair deal unless we offer something of great value along with those little pieces of paper. That product is a strong U.S. Pacific Fleet, which squares the transaction nicely" According to him, the hi-tech-military hegemony is without doubt the pillar of pillars, and the "U.S. Pacific Fleet" needs to be supported by "the little pieces of paper". Since the U.S. military expenditures amounts to nearly half of the world's total, the US dollar-financial hegemony is indeed indispensible at

---

8 U.S.-China Policy: Hiding the Military-Economic Link, available at http://history-newsnetwork.org/ on July 8, 2012.

9 Manuel Freitas: Why can't the US and US dollar fall? Spanish newspaper Rebellion, August 4, 2011.

the moment.[10] I repeatedly quote remarks of Western scholars or strategists for the main purpose of explaining that the Cold War mentality has never vanished from the brains of the Western politicians, thinkers and strategists, or from their strategic operations. Letting the Cold War mentality "steps aside, rest at ease" and even letting it die in its dead is nothing more than a wishful thinking of some good or unique thinking persons. Along with the gradual deepening of the international financial crisis, global military expenditures surge, global armament race is fierce, which fully shows that financial hegemony and military hegemony are a pair of mutually dependent, mutually conditioned conjoined twins. The previously mentioned US and British scholars put forward the idea of G3, that is, the three economic entities, the US, EU and China should rule the world together, of which the U.S.'s powerful military strength is one of its superiorities. Due to the economic crisis, the U.S. cuts its military expenses, but has a substantial increase in its arms trade, and military presence in nearly 130 countries, that is, more than 2/3 of all world countries. The U.S. military spending was 661 billion US dollars in 2009, not counting the US Department of Energy's spending on nuclear weapons. U.S. military spending accounts for 43% of the global total, and is equivalent to the sum of the military expenditures of 14 countries ranking from the 2nd to the 15th. If we look at the statistics of military industry in the broad sense, in which all the military industry-related industries and enterprises are included, over 70% of the U.S. GDP is output by its military industry and enterprises. According to the common sense, the U.S. should substantially cut its military spending after the Cold War, but the facts are reverse: its military expenses grew by 75.8% between 2000 and 2009, and its per capita military expenditures have reached 2,100 US dollars, ranking first in the world. The U.S. is also far ahead of other countries in terms of its strategic nuclear weapons, space exploration capability, stationed troops and military bases overseas. The U.S. is a country that best knows the economical input-output ratio. To maintain its military hegemony, it usually intimidates the other countries to capitulate, thus supports its finance, scientific and technological and cultural hegemony, ensures the normal operation of its economic, political and cultural systems which contributes to its domination of the world; and when necessary, wages hi-tech regional wars without hesitation.

In a sense, financial hegemony, military hegemony and cultural hegemony are respectively the concentrated expressions of the present economic, political and ideological hegemony of international monopoly capital. Scientific and technological hegemony is wisely imbued into its economic, political and cultural hegemonies. In another sense, if we say financial,

---

10 http://thomaspmbarnett.squarespace.com/globlogization//2010/8/8/blast-from-my-past-asia-the-military-market-link-2002.html.

scientific and technological and cultural hegemonies are expressions of its soft power, military hegemony is the expression of its hard power. This financial, scientific and technological, cultural and military "four in one" hegemony is the new feature of the Capital Empire in the current world.

What is the purpose of dominating the world? On May 9, 2009, Obama explicitly declared to the world through the TV, "if over a billion Chinese citizens begin to follow the same living patterns as Australians and the US people do, right now then all of us will face a very miserable time, the planet just can't sustain it…" According to Obama, it is not the U.S. that intends to restrict the development of China, but China that has to assume international responsibilities when planning its development. The Chinese can become rich, but Chinese leaders should come up with a new model and do not let the Earth what it can't afford. In a sense, Obama's words are the key to interpret the essence of the current US strategy.[11]

We all know that the U.S, has a population less than 5% of the world, but consumed 20% of the global energy, 16% of the fresh water, and 15% of the woods and produces 10% of the waste and 25% of carbon dioxide of the world. The U.S. will do everything it can and resort to various means to maintain and even expand its share. In the past we always talked about "geo"-politics. Now, it seems that we can add four more types of politics: "currency" politics, "information" politics, "military" politics and "resources" politics. It seems safe to say that "geographic", "currency", "information" and "military" politics are the methods, ultimately utilized for plundering and holding resources. Adding together "geographic", "currency", "information", "military" and "resources" politics seems to be able to explain all the major events in the current world.

III. The end of hegemonism and power politics is the revival of socialism

While hegemonism and power politics have greatly strengthened at the global level, the fundamental contradiction between the socialization production and the capitalist private ownership of the means of production and between the unlimited expansion of production and effective social demand is exacerbated, which will inevitably call for the revival of socialism in the world. The end of hegemonism and power politics is the revival of socialism, which is an irresistible law of history.

The US-led Western world has been leading the process of economic globalization since the drastic changes in Eastern Europe and the disintegration of the Soviet Union. It is pushing forward the new hi-tech revolution, constantly strengthening its financial, scientific and technological, cultural

---

11 http://apps.hi.baidu.com/share/detaiL/5816647.

and military hegemony, seemingly unexcelled in the world. Some scholars in China believe that the US-led Western world is too powerful and prospects for world socialism look bleak. Others believe that the international financial crisis is deepening and socialism will soon set off a new upsurge. These viewpoints are worth discussing. I believe that people who hold a pessimistic view about the prospects of world socialism in the near future and in the medium term are in majority. This pessimistic view is not without reason, but we should be thorough historical materialists, that is, we should not only see the objective conditions provided by history, but we should also give full play to our subjective initiative as communists. As long as we have a firm confidence, have a correct ideological and political line, as long as our strategy and tactics are correct, we can surely overcome all the difficulties and achieve various glorious history-making victories. As for the U.S., embodying all sorts of hegemony, we must certainly study all sorts of its strengths, never categorically excluding any of them, but there is no reason to fear them. Strategically, we shall despise the U.S., but tactically, we should take the U.S seriously and in science and technology, we should study the US. Only in this way, can we peacefully coexist with the US and even achieve a win-win situation. Mao Zedong said, "Imperialism and all reactionary forces are paper tigers". This is not only because Mao Zedong saw the strength of the people, but also the existence of imperialism and reactionary forces themselves and their self-destructive contradiction which is ultimately insurmountable. This contradiction determines the philosophical basis of its essence as "paper tigers". Based on this, true communists have strategically no reason to fear the U.S. Nobody has foreseen and only few people have expected that the U.S. with a so strong hegemony would be sucked into a war quagmire in the little Iraq. The Chinese nation, no matter how many disasters it has encountered, has always found a way out, even rose from its ashes, and created the Chinese nation which are world-scale victories one after the other. The classical Western philosophy has the concept of antinomy, the ancient Chinese philosophy has the concept "things turn into their opposites when reaching their extreme" and true communists are mastering historical materialism and dialectical materialism. Fully understanding this law, we will have great confidence, a grand wisdom and grand strategies. Seeking world hegemony is just like a boomerang, nothing in the world can escape this law.

Those people who lack confidence about the future prospects of the communist party are often amazed by the hi-tech penetration in economical, political, cultural and military fields that the US-led Western world possesses and will constantly possess. The domestic and international rivals of the communists are proud of this, too. Now let's make a brief analysis of the IT-driven high technology of the U.S. to see how its hi-tech hegemony can weaken, even can bring a disaster to the basic capitalist system in the future.

First, in the present world, the US-led new IT-revolution makes the number of people hired by capital fewer and fewer, but makes the product prices and product quality the more competitive so that the product markets become even more globalized. From modernized communication tools, computer software and other hi-tech products to daily necessities like toothpaste and washing powder, on the whole there are several world famous brands that have a monopolistic status around the globe. Ordinary people around the world all like and can use Colgate toothpaste on an equal footing with the former US President George W. Bush or the Russian President Vladimir Putin. The constant development of high technology, the endless stream of new products with good quality and cheap prices allow the international monopoly capital to accumulate great wealth through excessive monopoly profits or through small profit but rapid turnover.

Second, the widespread use of the Internet so that the world wide flow of international capital speeds up in a geometric progression. International financial capital can be divorced from the real economy and the production chain in the financial and massive financial derivatives domain just by just clicking a little mouse, thus achieve that its value shows growth in geometric progression. In a sense, under circumstances where the capitalist production relations are dominant, all the global stock markets, futures, exchange rates and all sorts of bulk commodities and other financial derivatives are the organic components of the unified big world casino.

It is mainly based on the above two points, globalization of the product markets and high level of financial monopoly which suck the wealth from poor countries and poor people at the same time that inevitably lead to the most basic economic phenomenon in this era of economic globalization, in the global scope: the poor are getting more and more and poorer and poorer, the rich are getting fewer and fewer and richer and richer. World's various countries' money quantity is increasing, but it finally goes into the accounts of a handful of people. In 1976, the richest US families had 8.9% of the total income of the US, but in 2007, on the eve of the outbreak of the international financial crisis, these one percent richest US families had nearly 25% of the total income of the US. In simple words, the overwhelming majority of the poor have not much money for the rich to be exploited again, which is the inevitable result of the contradiction between globalization of production, including the globalization of financial products, and the private ownership of the means of production. Comrade Hu Jintao said on many occasions that the international situation is experiencing profound changes. It is safe to say that the polarization between the rich and the poor around the globe is the most profound and fundamental aspect of the deep changes in the international situation, and the basis and root of all the other changes as well. All the other changes are its derivatives.

The nature of capital is its greediness and short-sightedness, so it does not see this point at all. In *Capital*, Marx pointed out: "The ultimate reason for all real crises always remains the poverty and restricted consumption of the masses as opposed to the drive of capitalist production to develop the productive forces as though only the absolute consuming power of society constituted their limit."[12] It is precisely for this reason that capital never understands the fundamental principle that "it is not that producing food becomes more difficult, but obtaining food by the working masses"[13], thus it unavoidably encounters crises.

It is the most fundamental knowledge of Marxism that the productive forces determine the production relations. Advanced tools of production have always been the decisive material force of the accumulation of wealth, the generation and development of advanced revolutionary ideas. The production relations change and develop with the change and development of productive forces, which are primarily initiated with the change and development of the tools of production. In a certain sense, the Stone Age determines the primitive social formation, the Bronze Age determines the slave social formation, the Iron Age determines the feudal social formation; and the steam engine and electricity era determines the capitalist social formation. The IT-led hi-tech revolution, namely the rapid development of the era of information economy is most likely the latest tool of production to push forward a new social formation on a global scale, namely the tool of production for the great development of the socialist and communist social formation. Their emergence and rapid development, on the one hand, create rich material conditions for the new social formation; on the other hand, the generation and aggravation of the fundamental economic phenomenon that the rich countries and rich persons becoming richer and richer, while poor countries and poor persons becoming poorer and poorer will necessarily make even more fully manifest the iron historical law "Where there is oppression, there is resistance" as said by Mao Zedong and will necessarily make Marxism which is the most advanced theoretical idea in the human history so far enormously innovate and develop.

Third, the Internet, as one of the signs of hi-tech revolution, will also make the spread of advanced revolutionary theories as convenient and as swift as the plunder of the wealth of other countries and people by the international financial capital, let the wings of the scattered growth of the "ghost of socialist revival" quickly spread and gather around the globe, which will undoubtedly and enormously help push forward the resistance and struggle of the world working class and other working masses become from in-themselves to for-themselves, and let them unite and join up closely.

---

12 Collected Works of Marx and Engels, Vol.25, People's Publishing House, 1972, p.548.
13 Collected Works of Lenin, Vol. 5, People's Publishing House, 1972, p.89.

The US-led Western world during the evolution of the Soviet Union has formed a whole set of mature technologies and means. Among them they employed radio stations, TV programs and newspapers which have played a unique and significant role. For example, they repeatedly instilled lots of fake information and wrong things into the Soviet people, and made many people believe them. However, the Internet is a new type of medium in human history whose biggest feature is not its high speed and big capacity, but the interaction between the promulgator and the audience. Once fake information or wrong things are issued on the Internet, insiders who know what is really going on are likely to immediately expose and rebut them. Such interaction is exactly what radio, TV, newspapers and other media lacks. Of course, regarding such exposition and rebuttal, promulgators of world culture hegemonism can carry out a control within a certain range, but it can succeed only within a certain range and period of time. It doesn't change with man's will. We can put it this way: due to the birth of the Internet, world culture hegemons' attempts to employ the Internet to culturally erode other countries' Internet, especially to Westernize the socialist countries, have great obstacles. Of course, the Internet is home to a variety of views, where so to speak "mud and sand flow together", good and bad are mingled, but in a sense, it has paved the way "to let a hundred flowers blossom and a hundred schools of thought contend". People who contend about something can compare, distinguish and improve which is enormously conducive to enhance the theoretical level of various countries in the world. Looking from the local and short run perspective, the Internet has many shortcomings, but in the long run and fundamentally, the Internet is a rare good thing. The emergence of this brand-new tool of production may push us closer to a thorough socialist social formation.

Thus it can be seen that the hi-tech revolution led by the information revolution and the US-led economic globalization are undoubtedly a double-edged sword to the international monopoly bourgeoisie. On the one hand, they have pushed forward the development of the productive forces of the capitalist society to a certain extent, in a certain period of time, made the basic contradiction within the capitalist society alleviate to a certain extent; on the other hand, while we make a full estimation of the vitality of capitalism, we have also to see: along with the further deepening and development of economic globalization and the new hi-tech revolution, the contradiction between the socialization of production and the capitalist private ownership of the means of production is impossible to extinguish, but will further intensify on a global scale. Along with the further intensification of this contradiction, the contradiction between capitalist production and capitalist consumption, that between the monopoly bourgeoisie and the proletariat and the working people, that between the developed Western countries and the vast Third World countries, that between the developed capitalist countries as well as global problems such as the further deterioration of the eco-environment on a global scale will also be intensified. These contradictions and problems are impossible to be fundamentally solved within the framework of the capitalist system.

The further strengthening of hegemonism and power politics will only further intensify these contradictions and problems. Just as Marx has pointed out 156 years ago, "This antagonism between modern industry and science on the one hand, modern misery and dissolution on the other hand; this antagonism between the productive powers and the social relations of our epoch is a fact, palpable, overwhelming, and not to be controverted." For this reason, for the capitalist society, "steam, electricity, and the self-acting mule were revolutionists of a rather more dangerous character than even its citizen...Blanqui [Blanqui was the great standard-bearer against the feudal monarchy in France in the 19th century, and was 'the leader, head and the heart' of the early proletarian party (Marx), resolutely opposing the capitalist exploitation system and private ownership system. In his 76 years of life, Blanqui led uprisings many times, failing many times and being sentenced to death twice including spending 36 years in 30 prisons. Blanqui advocated to overthrow the bourgeois rule through political revolution, but its fundamental strategy was revolt or conspiratorial means by a minority, which was fundamentally different from seizing power relying on the strength of broad masses advocated by Marxism. In 1871, the Paris Commune succeeded a revolution and he was absently elected the honorary chairman of the commune. After he passed away on January 1, 1881, 200,000 Parisians gave him a send-off spontaneously.]"[14]

In summary, we have further deepened our understanding of the law of the replacement of formations of human society revealed by the founders of Marxism. That is to say, the rapid development of economic globalization and hi-tech revolution led by the information technology will necessarily aggravate such conditions that rich countries and rich persons are becoming richer and richer, while poor countries and poor persons are becoming poorer and poorer on a global scale, will necessarily bring up thinkers, theorists, politicians and revolutionaries "of a rather more dangerous character than Blanqui" against the international monopoly capital wave after wave, and then strengthen the ranks of the proletariat and working people armed with advanced theoretical weapons. Along with continuous strengthening of the ranks of the grave-diggers of the bourgeoisie, one can imagine the prospects and destiny of capitalism. It is in this sense that, seen from the overall trend of historical development, the rapid development of economic

---

14 Selected Works of Marx and Engels, Vol. 1, People's Publishing House, 1995, pp.774-775.

globalization and hi-tech revolution led by the information technology, instead of getting farther and farther from socialism and communism will move closer and closer to socialism and communism. Of course, no one can deny that it is a fairly protracted process, possibly with big and even bigger twists and turns.

Capitalism and the bourgeoisie place their hope of social stability in the Western world in the continuous growth of the so-called middle strata, namely the strata with middle income. Regarding the necessary victory of socialism, Marxism and the proletariat are based on the fact that, along with the deepening of the financial crisis, the middle-income strata of the bourgeois states will necessarily and constantly witness increasingly greater class polarizations one by one, i.e. more people will necessarily fall into absolute poverty. According to statistics of the Fed, due to the steep fall in house prices and the stock market, the US household's median net value shrank %39 and 50% of the "middle class" saw significant decline of its economic status during economic recession during 2007 and 2010.

As the polarization between the rich and the poor becomes more aggravated and the purchasing power of the ordinary people of different countries gradually drops to a certain level, a large number of enterprises go bankrupt to some extent; a vast number of citizens from middle-income strata are forced to join the ranks of absolute poverty; when the sovereign debts of different countries brake through the unbearable limits, large-scale social unrest and turmoil will be unavoidable, and the ranks of the working class will see an unceasing vigor in the struggle. Moreover, the overwhelming majority of the middle-income strata mentioned here constitutes "white-collars" stratum as we usually call it. The struggles launched by the "blue-collar workers" stratum in the ranks of the poor unifying with the "white-collars" stratum are quite different from those in the previous economic crises in terms of form and effect.

On September 17, 2011, over a thousand people demonstrated in New York, and launched the "Occupy Wall Street" movement. Impassioned people have raised and shouted slogans like "Revolution Now", "We are the 99 percent", "A government accountable to the people, freed up from corporate influence", etc. Its root cause was the polarization in wealth and income distribution and one can also get a glimpse of some clues from the form of struggle. It is safe to say that if world's other major countries are able to deal with the deepening international financial crisis in a correct manner, the domestic and foreign debt of the U.S. will further deteriorate, its gap between the rich and the poor will further aggravate and various deep-level conflicts are bound to erupt massively in the coming years. In a sense, "Occupy Wall Street" has just begun. Since 2010 mass demonstrations and riots have occurred in economically and socially quite stable countries like Italy, Germany and Israel. These new phenomenon is worth paying close attention to and deserves our study.

It is absolutely safe to predict that the global financial crisis that has started in 2008 is far from being over, and is still evolving and may even be just at the beginning. More profound and comprehensive socioeconomic crises, which therefore will pose more serious challenges to the socialist countries may be yet to come. Without a doubt, the road will be twisted, full of hardships and dangers, but the future will be bright and glorious. The inevitable victory of socialism and the inevitable demise of capitalism, declared by Marx and Engels in *The Manifesto of the Communist Party* are inevitable.

John Feffer, the director of Foreign Policy In Focus at the Institute for Policy Studies, has recently pointed out, "We await a modern Marx who can shake up the Left just as surely as the Right with a trenchant critique of the current economic orthodoxy and a game plan for transformation." "If the next Marx is out there somewhere scribbling away, the future might bring an entirely different economic system altogether"[15] Some scholars pointed out that it is unnecessary to await a modern Marx, because Marxism has not become out of date. I deeply agree with this. In the world today, there are numerous big, middle and little Marxes just carrying on Marx's then enterprise, scribbling away in each corner of the world. As the capitalist international financial crises evolves, Marxism which represents the fundamental interests of the overwhelming majority of the mankind and eventually represents the fundamental interests of all human beings will be inevitably reborn in the world.

The revival of the world socialist theories pioneers the revival of the world socialist movements. That is the fundamental reason why Mao Zedong, Deng Xiaoping, Jiang Zemin and Hu Jintao have repeatedly stressed the necessity for the careful study of the Marxist classics by cadres at different levels, especially by senior Party cadres.

When we flip through the clouds of smoke of the history of the WWII and the rising winds of the national and democratic liberation movements in the 1950s and 60s, we can see many brilliant thinkers, politicians, revolutionaries and strategists with great achievements. It is predictable that earthshaking leaders will definitely grow waves upon waves along with the torrential arrival of the revival of the world socialist theories and movement and along with the maturity and strengthening of the working classes of various countries.

15　John Feffer: The Next Marx, available at the website of Foreign Policy in Focus at the Institute for Policy Studies on January 31, 2012.

The interests, wisdom and struggles of the overwhelming majority of the world people are calling for and creating world-class thinkers, politicians, revolutionaries and strategists who will lead the overwhelming majority of the world people to struggle together for the civilization and progress of the entire mankind. The broad masses of people are the ultimate decisive force of historical development, while the important role of leaders of different eras and different classes in the historical development process should be admitted. Such important role is often the decisive role under certain conditions and in certain periods. Lenin's theory on "the Leaders, the Party, the Class, the Masses" before realizing communism has an eternal power.

PART TWO

Analyses of the Crisis of Capitalism

Y. 3

Big Crisis, Big Differentiation and Big Transformation: A Reanalysis of the Profound Changes in the World Pattern

—An Overview of the Release of the "Yellow Book of World Socialism 2011-2012" and the Symposium "World Pattern and Social Structure - Neoliberalism and Financial Hegemony"

Cao Suhong and Wang Liqiang[1]

Abstract: This article gives an overview of the release of the Yellow Book of World Socialism 2011-2012 and an overview of the academic symposium "World Pattern and Social Structure - Neo-liberalism and Financial Hegemony", which was co-sponsored by the World Socialism Research Center and the Social Sciences Academic Press on March 2, 2012. Regarding the international financial crisis, the symposium has focused on topics such as changing class forces, the international bourgeoisie reconstructed by neo-liberalism and the continuous deepening of the changes in the world pattern. The symposium has pointed out that under the current leadership of international monopoly capitalism the aggravation of polarization, the intensification of social conflicts and the crisis of capitalism once more highlight the importance of class division. The participants believe that the international monopoly capital is innovating its methods of exploitation for the pursuit of excess profits, to create the conditions for accelerated development of state monopoly capitalism into international monopoly capitalism and that the international monopoly bourgeoisie is engaged in a restructuring: (1) Another restoration of the power of capital; (2) promotion of the fusion of commercial capital and financial capital. The international financial monopoly capital has launched a new economic colonization of the world. Emerging economies emerge as a new force to be reckoned with, while the world socialist movement is reviving and realizing a new transformation.

Key words: Yellow Book of World Socialism 2011-2012; world pattern and social structure; neoliberalism and financial hegemony

---
1 Wang Liqiang, deputy director of the CASS World Socialism Research Center, researcher of the CASS Bureau of Scientific Research Management.CaoSuhong, visiting researcher of the CASS World Socialism Research Center, director and associate senior editor of the editorial office of Trends in World Socialism Research.

The Yellow Book of World Socialism 2011-2012 and the Symposium on World Situation and Social Structure - Neoliberalism and Financial Hegemony, which was co-sponsored by the CASS World Socialism Research Center and the Social Sciences Academic Press, was held in Beijing on March 2, 2012. Li Shenming, CASS vice president and director of the CASS World Socialism Research Center, Zhang Quanjing, former minister of the Organization Department of the CPC Central Committee, Zheng Keyang, former deputy director of the Policy Research Office of the CPC Central Committee, Wang Yanzhong, director of the CASS Supervision Bureau, among others, attended the symposium and delivered a speech. More than 230 people, including the persons in charge of relevant ministries and departments such as the Organization Department of the CPC Central Committee, the Publicity Department of the CPC Central Committee, the Liaison Department of the CPC Central Committee, the Policy Research Office of the CPC Central Committee, the Central Party School, Xinhua News Agency and Chinese Academy of Social Sciences, relevant universities like Peking University, Tsinghua University, Renmin University of China, Central China Normal University, China Youth University of Political Studies, Chongqing University of Posts and Telecommunications, newspapers and magazines like Xinhua News Agency, People's Daily, Guangming Daily and "Red Flag", as well as expert scholars Zhang Quanjing, Zheng Keyang, Cheng Enfu, Wu Enyuan, HouHuiqin, Zhao Yao, Wu Xiongcheng, Wu Jian, Zhou Xincheng, Wang Zhengquan, Xu Chongwen, Xu Shicheng, Xu Zhongwei, Nie Yunlin and Li Ling attended the symposium.

At the symposium, Li Changjiu, researcher of the Centre for World Issues Studies of Xinhua News Agency, was invited to make a presentation entitled Reunderstanding Capitalism; Cheng Enfu, dean of the CASS Academy of Marxism, was invited to make a presentation entitled New Theory on Classes and Strata; Jiang Hui, Party Secretary of CASS Institute of Information Studies, was invited to make a presentation entitled Class Polarization Caused by Global Capitalism and Its Main Features; Zhao Minghao, researcher of World Today Center of the Liaison Department of the CPC Central Committee, was invited to make a presentation entitled Reflections on Capitalism by the West; Zhu Andong, deputy secretary of Party Committee of Tsinghua University, was invited to make a presentation entitled Consequences of the Unchecked Spread of Neoliberalism; Wang Wen from Global Times was invited to make a presentation entitled 2012, the Prelude to Great Global Changes; Zhang Wenmu from Beijing University of Aeronautics and Astronautics was invited to make a presentation entitled The Sun of the West Is Going Downhill; and Xie Shouguang, President of Social Sciences Academic Press, was invited to make a presentation entitled Publication and Release of the Yellow Book.

Zhang Quanjing expressed his heartfelt congratulations for the publication of The Yellow Book of World Socialism 2011-2012-Listening to the Eight Voices of the New Wave. According to him, since its establishment, the CASS World Socialism Research Center has made great achievements in theoretical studies, educational TV films Vigilance in Peace Time and The Color Revolution and works The Yellow Book of World Socialism series and History Meditates Here, etc. had substantial achievements and received a good echo from the public. In the context of the current international financial crisis, they highlight the importance and urgency to study the socialist movement. In our study of the socialist movement we must adhere to the basic theoretical views of Marxism. If we violated the basic theoretical views, it would be impossible to draw correct conclusions. The CPC Central Committee highlights that we must carry on theoretical innovation and if Marxism does not develop, it would lose its vitality. We should put forward new viewpoints according to changes in the situation and tasks. However, the basic Marxist theoretical view cannot change and changes will have taken a wrong path.

Zheng Keyang pointed out that the subprime mortgage crisis in the United States in 2008 has triggered the international financial crisis and asked what are the pillars that China can rely on to stand its impact on the world? The pillars were the leadership of the Communist party, the powerful macro-economic regulation and control of the state, a huge size of state-owned assets and the insistence on the public ownership as the mainstay of the basic economic system, enabling China to withstand the risks and stand straight. It was absolutely wrong that some people now publicly propose privatization and weakening of the public economy. If there was not a state-owned economy to develop and grow, one cannot speak of common prosperity and China could not arrive at today. The public ownership is exactly the superiority China shall uphold. It is precisely such kind of control over the economic foundation that has allowed CPC to lead the cause of socialism with Chinese characteristics to achieve one victory after another.

Li Shenming pointed out the great significance of organizing experts and scholars to make in-depth discussions on such topics as the big transformation, big adjustments in the world pattern and the changes in the social class structure, neoliberalism and financial hegemony before the 18th CPC National Congress convened. Today, when the international financial crisis is deepening, only by grasping the inner cause of the changes and adjustments in the world pattern can China correctly judge the international situation, correctly handle international issues, and uphold and develop the great cause of socialism with Chinese characteristics.

Li Shenming stressed that the world is in a big turmoil, big change and big adjustment. Today, there are two big international strategic opportunities to firmly grasp: first, the international financial crisis still continues to further deepen and even the renowned scholars in Western capitalist countries acknowledge that the capitalist system has presented major problems and the urgent need to reform, which indicate that the capitalist path is impassable. Second, the impacts of the disintegration of the Soviet Union and of the drastic changes in Eastern Europe still continue. Except Kazakhstan, the other former republics of the Soviet Union have not restored their economies to the level before the disintegration of the Soviet Union. This shows that the path of democratic socialism is also impassable. We should make full use of these two big opportunities and further strengthen our determination and confidence in taking the path of socialism with Chinese characteristics.

I. The international financial crisis has highlighted the change of class forces

1. Under the dominance of international monopoly capitalism, polarization is aggravated and social conflicts are exacerbated.

Li Shenming pointed out that the root cause of the big transformation and adjustments of the world is that the economic globalization under the dominance international monopoly capital produces a handful rich people who are getting richer and the overwhelming majority of poor, including the middle-income strata are getting poorer. The sign of the rich getting richer and the poor getting poorer is the sharp increase in sovereign debts. Therefore, the profound changes in the global capitalist social and class relations are the most important and most fundamental changes of the world today, and are deciding all the other changes.

Professor Yu Li from School of Public Management, Zhengzhou University, took the US as an example to analyze the contradictions and struggles triggered by social stratification, and thinks that, in the international financial crisis caused by the subprime mortgage crisis in the U.S. in 2008, on the one hand, the unemployment rate of ordinary American citizens as the main creators of national power grew day by day, their purchasing power decreased, and on the other hand, the bourgeoisie and especially the super financial capital oligarchy as the direct trigger of the world financial crisis and the owner of the means of production, controls the world finance, and then the world economic system for a long time, but still not obtained an effective government supervision. This class stratification in the U.S. is basically the inevitable result of the developing contradiction between the socialization of production and the private ownership of the means of production. This contradiction and conflict is unceasingly increasing in the alternation process from the old pattern to the new pattern, which is not only the root cause of the outbreak of the subprime mortgage crisis in the U.S., of the global financial crisis and of the launch of the "Occupy Wall Street" movement by the US citizens which spread to major capitalist countries, but also the root cause of the weakened world dominance of the U.S. caused by the relative decline of its comprehensive national power relative to the European Union, China and other major powers during the conversion of the world pattern in the early 21st century.

2. The current capitalist crisis highlights the importance of class analysis once again.

The viewpoint of class analysis is the basic tool of the Marxist observation and analysis of the development of the human society. In dividing classes and strata, Marxism and Western theories are essentially different. Jiang Hui, Party Secretary and researcher of the CASS Institute of Information Studies, pointed out in his thematic speech Class Polarization in Global Capitalism and Its Main Features that we must proceed from the essential level of relations of production and relations of power, make comprehensive use of the class analysis method and other social analysis methods, profoundly analyze the new changes in contemporary capitalism, and the essence, characteristics, situation and trends of its social and class relations, and profoundly analyze the class polarization and conflicts of the global capitalist. In the era of economic globalization dominated by international monopoly capitalism, a global capitalist class and a global working class are gradually taking shape in the entire world. Along with the development of global capitalism, a transnational global capitalist class is taking shape. The global transnational capitalist class is one of the many capitalist classes, which has been consciously seeking the role of the global ruling class and is controlling transnational corporations and global decision-making. In the era of globalization led by international financial monopoly capitalism, classes, class conflicts and struggles have not vanished, instead they have been manifested and expanded on a broader scale, in a much sharper and clearer form.

Cheng Enfu, the dean of the CASS Academy of Social Sciences, pointed out in his speech New Theory on Classes and Strata that Western theories advocate to divide classes according to occupation and income, which conceals ownership relations and the class relations determined them. Class is first of all a concept of the category of production relations, while stratum is the segment or subdivision within a class. Stratum division without class analysis is a non-Marxist theory. Our Marxists do not agree with the so-called "olive-shaped" social structure in the West, and should mainly use the proportion of net assets of a country's household rather than the proportion of labor remuneration (that is, the ratio of labor remuneration to GDP) to measure the social gap structure between rich and poor, while a high labor remuneration does not equal a high proportion of labor remuneration. The development of a private ownership society sometimes makes people's labor remuneration level slowly increase in a whirlpool manner, but will expand the wealth and income gap between rich and poor by ten, even dozens of times. Compared with the absolute amount of labor remuneration, the proportion of labor remuneration can even better reflect workers' social status in income distribution and economic life.

He thinks that the Western scholars set the bottom line and upper limit of the so-called middle class very low and then say what "olive-shaped" social structure is, which has no scientific sense and aims at covering up the nature of exploitation and alleviate class contradictions. The primary factor directly affecting people's income is ownership system and the primary factor for the decline in the proportion of labor remuneration is the change of the ownership structure. The demutualized privatization of a large number of existing state- and collectively owned enterprises will inevitably bring about a decline in the proportion of labor remuneration. The profit of an enterprise is created by labor and capital only provides the objective conditions for the creation. The decline in the proportion of labor remuneration means labor devaluation, capital appreciation and intensified exploitation.

Scholars attending the symposium introduced the changing conditions of the Russian economy and social classes analyzed by the Communist Party of Russian Federation. Liu Shuchun, researcher of the CASS Academy of Marxism, said that since the 21st century, the Russian Communists has analyzed the changes in the Russian economy and social classes according to the method of class analysis. They believe that the return of the capitalist system to Russia which is a top-down and unnatural retrogressive process, has led to social polarization, that is, between a handful of "strategic private owners" and the overwhelming poor, and the contradiction between capital and labor has become the main contradiction of the society. The Russian ruling class consists of the financial oligarchy, the newborn bourgeoisie and upper-level bureaucratic clique; holding the country's basic means of production and real power. The class of employed workers and the oppressed petty proprietors who account for the overwhelming majority of the Russian population are the ruled class that disposes only of 1/3 of the Russian national income, threatened by unemployment and cannot see the future. The so-called "middle class" is just a "myth" created by the ruling class in order to maintain the stability. "The contemporary proletariat" made up of employed physical and mental laborers, has a weak class consciousness as a whole. Therefore, it is an urgent task of the communists to unite various groups of workers and enhance the class consciousness of the contemporary proletariat.

II. Neoliberalism restructures the international bourgeoisie

1. International monopoly capital innovates its mode of exploitation of making excess profits.

The neoliberal current of thought in Western economics is famous for its "market fundamentalism" which excludes state intervention. Xu Chongwen, researcher of the CASS Institute of Philosophy, stressed that the cyclical economic crisis of capitalism is rooted in the basic contradiction of the capitalist society. As long as such basic contradiction continues to exist and operate, an economic crisis will break out under certain conditions. The neoliberal economic theory has caused the U.S. subprime mortgage crisis-the international financial crisis mainly from two aspects: first is to promote privatization, which intensifies the polarization between the rich and the poor and the economic imbalance and overproduction; second is to lift the control of the finance. Neoliberal practices have not only resulted in causing the U.S. subprime mortgage crisis-the international financial crisis, but also frequently caused crises and disasters all over the world in the past.

Some scholars have analyzed the characteristics and modes of manifestations of the neoliberal mode of capital accumulation. Wu Qian, a doctor of the School of Marxism, Xiamen University, talked about the three ways of neoliberal global capital accumulation: first, carrying out the neoliberal privatization wave around the globe; second, the international financial monopoly groups force other countries to accept financial liberalization policies through the IMF and the World Bank; third, expropriating other countries' strategic oil resource through the armed forces of military Keynesianism so as to maintain global capital accumulation and the unipolar global hegemony of the U.S.. Therefore, the neoliberal mode of capital accumulation is essentially an innovation in the mode of exploitation carried out for the international monopoly capital to seize excess profits. Such blatant act of imperialist plunder is more covert, deceptive, parasitic and decadent than any other previous modes of capital accumulation.

2. State monopoly capitalism has created conditions for the accelerated development into international monopoly capitalism.

Zhu Andong, the deputy secretary of the Party Committee of School of Marxism, Tsinghua University, and Cai Wanhuan, doctor of the School of Marxism, Tsinghua University, pointed out in their research report entitled Consequences of the Unchecked Spread of Neoliberalism that, in the period of neoliberalism, almost all market economy countries have experienced the phenomenon of economic financialization. Not only the financial sector expands unceasingly compared to the real economy and its proportion in the GDP continues to rise, but also the proportion of the financial capital in the capital possessed by non-financial enterprises to the industrial capital is also rising. The proportion of the financial sector profits to domestic profits and the proportion of the profits of the financial industry to business profits are both rising. After WWII, the flow of U.S. financial assets relative to GDP has maintained the upward tendency, and this proportion was 0.257 on average between 1952 and 1979, and grew rapidly to 0.418 between 1980 and 2007. The proportion of US financial industry profits to total domestic profits in the U.S. has grown bigger and bigger, increased from less than 20% in the early 1980s to about 30% at the close of the 1990s, and even reached 45% in 2002. Before the outbreak of this financial crisis, it reached 30.56% in 2006. Concurrently, the proportion of the profits in the non-financial sector including the manufacturing industry, the transportation industry and the information industry have dropped sharply, even to below 54%, showing a very significant trend of financialization of capital.

About the formation of international monopoly capitalism, Li Bingyan, professor of Jiangsu Provincial Party School, also expressed his opinions. He pointed out that the current financial crisis in the U.S. is extending to the real economy and deepened into an economic crisis. That could be proved by Citigroup, the biggest bank in the U.S., and General Motors, the representative of the U.S. manufacturing industry, which are on the ragged edge of bankruptcy. In 1989, the "Washington Consensus", concocted under the leadership of the Institute for International Economics, epitomized the political and economic theories of neoliberalism, and focused on advocating privatization and liberalization, affecting the majority of the developing countries and countries in transition. Under the circumstance that its finance, resources, market and economic lifeblood were comprehensively controlled by multinational corporations, Argentina lost most of its economic sovereignty and its economic security was seriously threatened. During 1989 and 1999, of the 100 big enterprises in Argentina, only 7 Argentinian enterprises or enterprises mainly funded by Argentina were left; till 2000, multinational corporations had controlled 90.4% of the exportation and 63.3% of the importation of Argentina. 90% of the oil and natural gas in Argentina were controlled by 8 foreign-funded oil enterprises, and 7 out of the top 10 biggest banks in Argentina were foreign-funded. Foreign-funded banks controlled 62% of all the capital in the Argentinian banking system. At the close of the 1970s, China reformed its planned economy into the market economy, and a united global market truly took shape. The above changes have all created conditions for the accelerated development of state monopoly capitalism into international monopoly capitalism. Entering the stage of international monopoly capitalism has also served as a condition for Western countries and their multinational enterprises to seek excess profits.

3. The international bourgeoisie is in a restructuring

Scholars attending the symposium pointed out that the sole purpose of neoliberalism in the three decades it manipulated the world was to restore the power of capital; push forward the integration of commercial and financial capital; and build a brand-new international bourgeoisie. The following are specific manifestations of neoliberalism.

(1) Restoring the power of capital. During 1920 and 1970, the richest 1% US people grabbed the 30%-40% of the national income, but the figure began to drop to below 25% in 1970. As neoliberalism was implemented, the share of the richest 1%, in the national income began to soar, and had been restored to about 40% as that before WWII till around 1990. The U.S. is not exceptional in this aspect. The share of the richest 1% of British people in the British national income doubled since 1982, growing from 6.5% to 13%. In the world, wealth and power were surprisingly centralized. The privatization trend in Mexico after 1992 pushed a small group of people (like Carlos Slim) onto the Forbes list of the richest people in the world almost overnight.

(2) Advancing the integration of commercial and financial capital by integrating the ownership and control of the capitalist enterprises, that is, giving the administrators (managers) stock options (title of ownership) so that the market value of stock instead of production became the indicator of economic activities and the so-called "asset management" became a sign of management performance, causing the speculation temptation thus generated to flood; and by drastically narrowing down the historical gap between financial capital and commercial capital. The gap has triggered many conflicts among financiers, producers and businessmen in history. Big companies begin to get closer to finance, and the profits from financial capital have become one of their major sources of profits.

4. The international financial monopoly capital is carrying out a new economic colonization of the Third world.

Zhou Miao, postdoctoral researcher of the CASS Academy of Marxism, held that developed countries are shifting from old colonialism to new colonialism so as to build a new colonial system. Neocolonialism is colonialism in a special form, and has the following main characteristics: They restrict the development of the Third World countries by building an international economic system which is dominated by them; and colonize the Third World countries economically, financially, commercially and industrially. All in all, the international financial monopoly capital, on the basis of US dollar hegemony, has built a new mode of capital accumulation via virtual economy-dominated globalization, which was divorced from the real economy, to exploit the vast Third World countries. At the stage of international financial monopoly capitalism, capitalism has a formal global political and economic coordination mechanism, and invisible power dynamics, forming a three-dimensional and multi-layered new type of capitalist monopoly alliance.

5. Characteristics of the international financial monopoly capital and its harms

Today, a global production system dominated by the developed capitalist countries and represented by giant multinational companies is taking shape. These huge multinational companies have monopolized the vast majority of the global market share, and have formed the global monopoly oligarchy.

Zhou Miao analyzed the characteristics and harms of international financial monopoly capital, and pointed out that the carrier of the international financial monopoly capital are huge multinational companies which all seek domestic and international monopolistic position on the basis of global development. The international financial monopoly capital has to require the world to promote financial liberalization, inevitably requires various countries of the world to open up their financial markets, implement the liberalization of capital flows, exchange rates, interest rates and banking as well as the liberalization of the financial markets. Various forms of international financial monopoly capital have already firmly occupied the dominant and leading position in all sectors of the global capitalist economy, including all aspects of investment, finance, production, sales, trading, science and technology. The mode of control of financial capital has been transformed from the traditional pyramid-shaped vertical mode of control to the network-shaped joint control of financial capital with banking capital as the core. Financial capital has controlled more economic and industrial sectors through "the participation system"

Wang Liqiang, researcher of the CASS Bureau of Scientific Research Management, pointed out that the international financial monopoly groups use their capital advantage to devour national-state wealth through financial crises in a phased way, and use their financial hegemony to frequently hype international bulk commodity prices and the profits therein. The use of neoliberalizm by international financial monopoly groups has weakened the sovereignty of various countries, and violently striking countries which don't listen to their commandments in spite of provisions of the UN Charter and strong bullying the weak have formed the new interventionism, greatly threatening world security and stability.

III. Changes in the world pattern continue to deepen

1. Emerging economies are rising meteorically and world power is shifting to the emerging economies in an accelerated way.

After the outbreak of the financial crisis, the debate on the changes in the world pattern have become more active than ever, and numerous and complicated points of view have been expressed. Amidst public opinions like "the emerging economies are towering over" and "the global character of Western influence is sliding down", "the process of the multipolarization of the world is accelerating" have become a general consensus in the international community.

Prof. Zhao Yao, from the Central Party School attached to the Central Committee of the C.P.C., pointed out that "9/11" incident and the financial crisis have devastated the Western countries so severely that the developing countries, being slightly affected, see a turnaround. Some big developing countries using their advantages such as a low starting point, abundant resources and cheap labor force and by absorbing foreign funds and introducing advanced technologies through economic globalization develop rapidly and become emerging economies, which profoundly changes the world pattern and the international economic situation. According to him, the world pattern has witnessed three major changes after WWII: The first lasted from the end of WWII in 1945 to the disintegration of Soviet Union in 1991, featuring the "bipolar" confrontation of the U.S. and the Soviet Union (a.k.a. the Yalta system) set at the Yalta conference. The second lasted from the disintegration of the Soviet Union in 1991 till the early years of the 21st century, mainly featuring the unipolar superpower of the U.S. which unswervingly pursued hegemonism and unilateralism. In the Gulf War, Bush's "New World Order" as the banner of "U.S. leadership" was formally introduced. The third lasts from the "9/11" incident in early 21st century, especially from the outbreak of the financial crisis till now. The subprime mortgage crisis in the U.S. has triggered a global financial crisis and the U.S. shows signs of decline. Some emerging economies rise meteorically, and the world pattern has shifted from a unipolar one to a multipolar one. The pattern of world multipolarization is a positive development.

Participants believe that it was first the US researcher Jim O'Neill who called Brazil, Russia, India and China as "BRICs" in his paper entitled "The World Needs Better Economic BRICs" which was published in a Goldman Sachs report in 2001. The territories of these four countries accounts for 26% of the world, their population 42% of the world and their GDP 14.6% of the world and they present great development potentials and a strong development momentum. Till the mid 21st century, the world economic pattern will be reshuffled, and the order of the world's top six biggest economies will be China, the U.S., India, Japan, Russia and Brazil. After Jim O'Neill brought forward the concept of "BRICs", the then person in charge of BRICs Economic Research Institute of Japan put forward the concept of "VISTA," meaning that Vietnam, Indonesia, South Africa, Turkey and Argentina would become the next-generation of potential emerging economies after the "BRIC" group. In 2010, at the request of South Africa, the four members agreed on South Africa's joining the group and BRIC became BRICS, including South Africa. Led by Brazil and driven by Venezuela, the third summit of the Latin America and the Caribbean region states—that convened on December 3, 2011 in Caracas, in the capital of Venezuela—announced the formal establishment of CARICOM, realizing the greatest desire of Bolivar, the hero of the national independence of the Latin American nations in the 19th century: to build a "big family" that unites all Latin American countries. Such an independent community will eventually become a regional organization of the Latin American countries, similar to the European Union, the African Union and ASEAN. The appearance of the emerging economies will deeply change the world situation and the international economic situation, symbolizing the end of the "post-colonial era" and speeding up the shift of world power to the emerging economies.

2. The world socialist movement is reviving and realizing a new transformation.

The participants analyzed and judged the revival of the world socialist movement in the international political pattern, and pointed out that, 20 years after the drastic changes in the Soviet Union, the world socialist movement had walked out of the trough and though it still remains at a low ebb, it has a rebound. As far as the communist parties in different countries of the world are concerned, they have developed from 66 million members in the past to 100 million members today. The Soviet Communist Party once had more than 20 million members, but it collapsed in a very short time, shocking the world people. However, the true Marxists, socialists and communists in those 15 countries of the region have not retreated; they have actively taken action and rapidly reorganized or restored their communist party organizations soon after the disintegration of the Soviet Union, and actively propagated the communist ideology. After 20 years of development, the communist parties in this region struggled for the legalization of their status, participated in their national and presidential elections and some even came to power through parliamentary elections, making an indelible contribution to the retention and development of Marxism and the communist ideology in the Soviet region.

Professor Nie Yunlin from the Center for Marxist Political Parties Studies of the Central China Normal University, pointed out that the contemporary world socialist movement has undergone major changes, and achieved new transformations, with the following main features: the world socialist movement transformed from a movement outside the capitalist system to a movement inside the capitalist system, from a movement to overthrow capitalism through the proletarian revolution to a movement to revolutionarily transform capitalism through a peaceful and democratic mode and developed from a movement participated by advanced social strata for the benefits of the majority to a movement participated by the majority for the benefits of the majority. According to him, the disintegration of the Soviet Union and the drastic changes in Eastern Europe has seriously damaged the international ties of the world socialist movement. However, after nearly 20 years of development, the socialist movement's international unity and cooperation presents new forms: developing bilateral relations between parties has become the main form of international ties, exchange of experiences and mutual support carried out by various communist parties; the annual "International Meeting of Communist & Workers' Parties", an important form for the various communist parties of the world to strengthen ties, exchange ideas and viewpoints and work experiences, and to promote the development of the world socialist movements, has already been held 17 times in various continents successively; the "International Communist Seminar", another form for various communist and workers' parties of the world to strengthen the ideological ties, exchange theoretical viewpoints and work experiences, conducted once a year in Brussels, has already been held for 24 times, and about 150 political parties and organizations from five continents attended it; the "International Conference of Socialist Scholars'" is also a supplementary form of mutual theoretical exchanges of the world socialist movement; the unity and cooperation of the left-wing political parties in the world, like the improvement of the relations among the communist parties and the socialist parties, have promoted the convening of international conferences of left-wing parties, the most influential of which is the Sao Paulo Forum since 1990. The Sao Paulo Forum has become an important annual meeting held by the left-wing parties in the world. In May 2004, fifteen left-wing parties from the European countries gathered in Rome and established the "Party of the European Left", promoting the unity and cooperation of the left-wing parties in Europe.

Some scholars also pointed out that, since the disintegration of the Soviet Union and the drastic changes in Eastern Europe 20 years ago, the biggest and most eye-catching change in the world is the rise of China. After holding the 3rd Plenary Session of the 11th Central Committee of the CPC in 1979, China has implemented the reform and opening-up policy, and carried out one of the most greatest economic revolutions on a world scale, a sustained and rapid development, with an average annual growth rate of 9.8%, topping the world. Its total economic capacity rose from 11th in the world before the reform and opening-up to the 7th place in 2000, surpassing the French economy in 2004, the British economy in 2005, the German economy in 2007, and the Japanese economy in 2010, becoming world's second largest economy, with its present annual output value reaching 6 trillion U.S. dollars. Till September 2011, its foreign exchange reserves has reached 3.2 trillion US dollars, and China topped the world's ten biggest countries in terms of foreign exchange reserves. Although hegemonism will not voluntarily step down from the stage of history, still cherishing and holding the "Cold War mentality", instigating troubles in the Middle East and the Asia-Pacific region, rebuilding the U.S.-led "Pacific Century", shifts the strategic focus eastward, and tightening the crescent-shaped encirclement, trying to block and contain China, it is just wishful thinking, and it is hard to stop the wheel of history rolling forward. Looking to the future, we firmly believe that socialism will certainly replace capitalism by going through a long process.

3. The world pattern presents the "polar-less" and "multi-polar" development trends

Regarding the various judgments on the multi-polarization trend in the world pattern, the current academy presented some rich "fresh" viewpoints like "polar-lessness", "collective-polarity" and "non-polarity". Liu Zhiming, associate researcher of the CASS Academy of Marxism, summarized such viewpoints. One view holds that an era of "non-polar" world order is arriving, namely that although the U.S. remains world's sole genuine big country, its decline will make the world present "an increasingly rudderless world under circumstance where the international relations are growing tense day by day" and some people call such an international order "non-polar world" order. Another view holds that a "collected-polar" world order will soon arrive, namely the world will enter a rarely-seen historical period, which is neither "uni-polar" nor "multi-polar" nor "non-polar". As a big "pole" the U.S. has lost its past strength and emerging big countries like Russia, China and India are becoming potential "poles", while there are also old big countries like Europe and Japan. Such a system would be a "collected-polar era" bringing together various small and medium-sized "pole" powers, with US as the center.

Editor of "Global Times" Wang Wenze held that the world will truly enter a "chaotic" period after 2012. It is the core content of the gaming among different countries on how to hold a relatively favorable position in the reorganized structure. In recent years, the U.S. has been gradually narrowing the challengers of its hegemony from the three major categories of terrorism, Russia and the emerging economies like China and India to China alone. In 2011, the U.S.'s preventive arrangement against China presented four new characteristics: firstly, in the military field, it made the new deployment of "approaching China with the overall strength, shift from the former following the military strength"; secondly, in terms of economy and trade, it stubbornly clinged to its dominant position in the IMF and WTO and other international economic systems, pressed RMB appreciation step by step, and tried to use unfair trade and financial rules to pass the crisis on China; thirdly, in the emerging public domains around the globe, like the sea, outer space, Internet, energy and aviation security, it played a leading role and developed new rules conducive to the U.S. interests prospectively to regulate China's expansion on global public sphere; fourthly, it initiated public criticism of China on many international occasions, sped up the penetration of its values into the Chinese society, sowed discord between China and its neighboring countries, and enticed and utilized the social forces in China, etc.. In 2012, in the situation that the global environment sees unprecedented changes, all kinds of plights and plots interweave, whether China can skillfully utilize the dialectical relationship between "keeping a low profile" and "making some contributions" seems extremely important for grasping the difficulty of step over the national power.

4. New characteristics of the world pattern and ways to deal with them

In response to the new changes and new characteristics of the world pattern, He Bingmeng, former secretary-general of the Presidium of the Academic Divisions of the CASS and CASS researcher, pointed out that under these circumstances of "multi-polarization" or "perplexed period", China's international strategic choice should be: to build the most extensive international united front to restrict the U.S. and to push forward the "multi-polaritization" of the world and the "democratization" of international relations. Concretely, it shall adopt the following tactics: (1) holding high the banner of "anti-hegemony" and "never seeking hegemony"; advocating the "democratization" of international relations, equality of world countries regardless of size, one vote for one country in dealing with international affairs, and subordination of the minority to the majority; (3) fully respecting and asserting the role of the UN in handling affairs of international relations, promoting the formulation or adjustment of the rules and regulations and mechanisms of the UN in handling international affairs in accordance with the Charter of the UN; (4) respecting the sovereignty and independence of each country and the decision of each country's affairs the people of each country, opposing interference in other countries' internal affairs, especially opposing the threat to use military force or to use military force to subvert other country's government by relying on the pretext of the so-called "human rights above sovereignty"; (5) "keeping a low profile" and "not taking the lead" do not mean idleness. At present, it is a must for China to build the most extensive international united front to restrict the U.S.: strengthen the comprehensive strategic partnership with Russia, unite with the Latin American countries represented by Brazil and West Asian and African countries represented by South Africa, striving for India and the EU, etc. so as to curb the hegemonistic behaviour of the U.S. as much as possible. These five basic tactics fundamentally target both the U.S's neorealist hegemony theory and has avoided the deficiency of the neoliberal institutionalism and has Chinese characteristics. In order to smoothly implement the above strategy and tactics, China must establish its voice in international relations.

Through discussion, the participants have reached a consensus that the outbreak of the financial crisis and the resulting new changes in the world pattern have increased the danger of global instability, and may lead to new international tensions and conflicts. Despite that, we still believe that peace and development serve the fundamental interests of each country of the world the most and will continue to be the irresistible main trend of the era.

Y. 4

"Occupy Wall Street" Movement and the Crisis of the US Capitalism

—A Deep Reflection on the Global Financial and Economic Crisis

Wang Jing[1]

Abstract: The "Occupy Wall Street" movement which began on September 17, 2011, has developed into a large anti-capitalist movement with striking left-wing colors, arguably affecting the biggest anti-system movement since 1968. The movement marks the complete bankruptcy of the neo-liberal economic order and will make the U.S. dollar hegemony, political institutions and cultural hegemony experience a shock.

Key words: "Occupy Wall Street" movement; neoliberalism; U.S. dollar hegemony; capital oligarchy

Editor's note: According to the directive of the related leaders of the CPC Central Committee and the National Planning Office of Social Sciences, the CASS World Socialism Research Center specialists have established the "International Financial Crisis Tracking Research Group" and will continue to publish research results in this area. After the disintegration of the Soviet Union, the economic globalization led by neoliberalism has dominated the global market, cleared the institutional barriers for the free

---
1 Wang Jing, Assistant Researcher at the Academy of Marxism of CASS and visiting scholar of WSRC attached to CASS.

flow of capital. The so-called "financial innovations" appearing massively in the U.S. and other capitalist countries, has laid a time bomb for the occurrence of the capitalist financial crises. Although the Asian financial crisis broke out during this period, it could not alert the world people, and almost the whole world believed that capitalism was "reborn" in financialization. In 2008, the U.S. subprime mortgage crisis broke out, after which detonated the sovereign debt crisis. In 2011, American people's "Occupy Wall Street" movement was echoed in hundreds of cities in the world. The 99% demanded justice from the 1%. The contradictions between the socialization production and the private ownership of the means of production, the unlimited expansion of production and the limited social demands are the root causes for the current international financial crisis (being essentially the crisis of the capitalist system). People have already begun to realize the problem that the capitalist system and its mode of social organization are not sustainable.

I. Rise of the "Occupy Wall Street" movement

The "Occupy Wall Street" movement which began on September 17, 2011, has developed into a large anti-capitalist movement with striking left-wing colors, arguably affecting the biggest anti-system movement since 1968.

On the first day of the start of the "Occupy Wall Street" movement, on September 17, thousands of people took part in the occupation action. Afterwards, the scale of the protesting masses got bigger and bigger and grew frequently to dozens of thousands of people, and spread from New York to the other big cities in the U.S.. The US mainstream media and Wall Street tycoons only played down and smeared this movement for the time being, hoping that it would run its course. However, faced with the growing size of the movement, the police had to take tough measures to oppress it, and had bloody clashes with the protesting masses once and again. Till early October, that is, after two weeks since the "Occupy Wall Street" movement started, in New York alone, the police arrested nearly 1,000 protesters. In the severe winter of December, the movement continued to maintain high temperatures. On December 12, the demonstrators began to attack the headquarters of Goldman Sachs, and had a violent conflict with hundreds of explosion-proof policemen, and dozens of protesters were arrested. Depicting Goldman Sachs as "vampire squid" and accusing it of "sacrificing people's rights to win the hearts of the rich", the demonstrators planned to "stick to the protest activities in winter; because only in this way can the 'Occupy Movement' break out vigorously in the coming spring once more."[2]

---

2 "Occupy Wall Street demonstrators turned their spearhead against financial tycoons", by Li Yang from China News Service, available at http://news.sina.com.cn/w/2011-12-13/065423622269.shtml.

The movement was sponsored by the Vancouver-based magazine "Adbusters", a print and online magazine famous for its sharp criticism of capitalism. On July 13, 2011, it made a call on its website, claiming Wall Street to be the capital of financial gomorrah of America, calling the people to flood into Manhattan, set up tents and kitchens, and occupy the Wall Street. Their political demand was to put an end to the influence of money over the American political establishment, for democracy not corporatocracy.[3] Later, organizations of the socialist movement, anarchists, trade unions, students, etc. joined the movement, claiming to represent the 99% to protest the 1% financial oligarchy and the US politics which served the interests of the financial oligarchy. They put forward the stand of redistribution of wealth. The overwhelming majority of the US people expressed a good opinion and support for the movement. According to the survey done by the US magazine Time, 54% of the interviewees favored the protest, and only 23% of the interviewees expressed opposition. In contrast, only 27% of the interviewees had a good opinion on the Tea Party movement.

II. "Occupy Wall Street" movement signifies the complete bankruptcy of the neoliberal economic order

The neoliberal policy, which the U.S. has been implementing for years, finally had ill effects. Since 2007, the besetting crisis in the U.S. started to appear and constantly deepen: at the economic level, the initial subprime mortgage crisis evolved into debt crisis, financial crisis and economic crisis; later, due to the improper measures taken by the elite politicians of the two major parties in the U.S., the US's political institutions were widely doubted by the people, which led to a serious political crisis. Through a series of iron facts of education, the American masses have finally seen clearly that the U.S. is a world of "rule of corporates", that the Wall Street oligarchs manipulate the US politics; that in the U.S., there is no democracy, but "corporatocracy". Thus there was the "Occupy Wall Street" movement targeting directly the crux at the heart of the U.S.

Since the era of Ronald Reagan neoliberal ideas have become a mighty stand in the U.S., even across the world. A series of capitalist reform measures initiated since Roosevelt's New Deal era were systematically liquidated. The capitalist reform measures represented by the New Deal were essentially that the American ruling clique faced with the pressure of the socialist camp like the Soviet Union and China, and of the socialist movement in the U.S. was forced to make partial concessions to the American working masses: On the one hand, more taxes were charged from the rich; on the other hand, the establishment of a social welfare and insurance system

---

3   Zhang Ni, Occupy Wall Street: We Want Democracy, Not Donors, Social Outlook (sponsored by the State Council Development Research Center), 2011 (11).

was strengthened. These reform measures—like raising workers' wages, establishing state-owned and public enterprises; increasing the taxes from on the rich and enterprises, and building a perfect social insurance system—were essentially strategic compromises made by the U.S. monopoly capital groups to prevent any protest against capitalism by the bottom-ladder people. Once domestic and foreign pressures were weakened, such reform measures were liquidated. This is the important background of the rise of neoliberalism since the 1980s. Neoliberalism does not indiscriminately oppose all government intervention in the economy. It in fact opposes intervention that is beneficial to the workers, but not beneficial to capital oligarchs. For example, the arms industry in the U.S. has long been dependent on the provision of the military expenditures. Since the 1980s, the periods of flourishing neoliberalism and reduced social welfare were usually periods of soaring military expenses. For another example, since the financial tsunami in 2007, the U.S. government has come up with trillions of dollars to aid those Wall Street financial companies stuck in the crisis.

After an analysis of the chronology of events in the last 30 years, we can see that the emergence process of neoliberalism was accompanied by the decline of socialism. For example, in 1980, the Soviet Union was up to the chin in the vortex of guerrilla warfare in Afghanistan; in 1981, Reagan suppressed workers' strike with an even tougher attitude; in 1986, Gorbachev took office to fully compromise to the United States, and also in 1986, Reagan signed the Tax Reform Act which set a precedent from the same tax rate on the rich and the poor in the U.S.; in 1989, the socialist camp began to experience a series of turmoil, and in 1990, the U.S. right-wing think tank and the International Monetary Fund officially released the "Washington Consensus;" in 1991, the Soviet Union disintegrated, and neoliberalism began to be in fashion in the world; even the Western political parties with a social democratic tendency of which advocated the so-called "third way" like the British Labor Party, the Social Democratic Party of Germany vigorously adopted neoliberal policies; in 2001, the rise to power of George W. Bush being the signal, the U.S. entered an even more thorough era of neoliberalism.

The boom of neoliberalism resulted in the great expansion of the power of capital oligarchs. The biggest beneficiaries were the dominating Wall Street financial oligarchs. From 1987 to 2005, Alan Greenspan, US citizen of Jewish origin has served as the Chairman of the Federal Reserve for 18 years. During his tenure, going through all previous presidencies of Reagan, Bush Senior, Clinton and Bush Junior, no matter from which party, they all honorifically supported the stimulation of lending low interest rates, deregulation, financial liberalization and all other policies Greenspan advocated. Most of the U.S. Secretaries of Treasury were from the Wall Street, too. For example, before taking the post as the U.S. Secretary of Treasury, William E. Simon, the U.S. Secretary of Treasury during 1974 and 1977, was a senior executive of Citibank. Donald Regan, the U.S. Secretary of Treasury during 1981 and 1985, was the CEO of Merrill Lynch, while Robert E. Rubin, the U.S. Secretary of Treasury during 1995 and 1999, was a senior partner of Goldman Sachs.

Henry Paulson, the U.S. Secretary of Treasury during 2006 and 2009 was the president and CEO of Goldman Sachs; the current U.S. Secretary of Treasury used to be the head of the Federal Reserve Bank of New York. A major event happened in 1999, that is, Clinton, Greenspan and Rubin worked together to repeal part of the Glass-Steagall Act and passed the Financial Services Modernization Act of 1999, which aimed to eliminate the barriers, supervision and control, breaking the pattern of segregated operation of the banking, securities and insurance industries in the U.S. and thus enabled the financial oligarchs to do almost everything they wanted. A whole variety of financial derivatives were developed, and the virtual economy and the bubble economy expanded rapidly.

Over years, the U.S. economy has long been stimulated by real estate mortgage, automobile mortgage business, student loans and credit card overdrafts. For example, the financiers created subprime lending and subprime bond market where houses are used as the pledge, and in turn the low-income US families could easily get bank loans for purchasing houses, which had led to widespread speculations in the real estate market, and rapidly expanded real estate bubble and subprime bubble based on the expectation of increasing real estate prices. When the gap between house prices and residents' income became really awkward, speculators would surely take opportunities to cash out; house prices dropped; the real estate bubble and the subprime bubble burst and became the first domino that has triggered this financial crisis.

Consequently, the financial industry has become more monopolistic and centralized. Of the five major investment banks in Wall Street, only Goldman Sachs has survived, a lot of SMEs in the US have gone bankruptcy, and a considerable part of the people have lost their jobs; and also the countries of the Third World were exploited in disguised forms. In the process, the culprit of the financial crisis—Wall Street financial oligarchs—would surely become the target of criticism by the lower-classes of the US and the world people.

Let's see how the U.S. neoliberal policies robbed the poor and helped the rich. The George W. Bush administration launched a tax reduction plan for the rich twice, in 2001 and again in 2003, vigorously advanced the overall privatization and marketization of the social insurance system and tried hard to maintain the interests of the rich and big companies. In 2004, according to statistics of the U.S. Congressional Budget Office, 1% of the US people each had an annual income of over 1.2 million US dollars. Benefited from Bush's tax reduction plan, this part of the US people enjoyed a total tax reduction of 230 billion US dollars in 2003 alone, that is, nearly 80,000 US dollars less per head on average. After the outbreak of the financial crisis, George W. Bush launched another economic stimulation plan about tax reduction in January 2008.[4] In his second term of office, the annual government budget plan almost massively increased military expenditures and massively reduced welfare.[5]

Before Obama came to power he tricked the American people into giving their votes. Once he came to power, he continued to adopt neoliberal policies. In December 2010, Obama comprehensively extended the Bush tax cuts; in April 2011, in the fiscal budget under negotiation with the Republicans, Obama extended tax cuts to 2013 once again. In August 2011, the U.S. saw the outbreak of a debt crisis. When negotiating about the upper limit of the debt between the Democratic and the Republic parties in the U.S., Obama once again excluded tax increase from the deficit reduction plan. He planned to collect more taxes from the rich and big enterprises each making an annual income of over 250,000 US dollars to increase government revenue and reduce the federal budget deficit, but he finally gave it up, leading to an extreme dissatisfaction of the Democratic Party voters. Even the "god of stock investing" Buffett embarrassingly wrote in a paper in the "New York Times": "My friends and I have been coddled long enough by a billionaire-friendly Congress. It's time for our government to get serious about shared sacrifice." He said that he paid a federal tax bill of 6,938,744 US dollars in 2010 and added: "That sounds like a lot of money. But what I paid was only 17.4% of my taxable income—and that's actually a lower percentage than was paid by any of the other 20 people in our office. Their tax burdens ranged from 33% to 41% and averaged 36%."[6]

As the economic bubble burst and the economic crisis went deeper, the unemployment rate and the number of poor people in the US grew rapidly. According to a new report released on November 3, 2011 by Brookings Institution, an authoritative research institute in the U.S., 46.2 million people in the US were living under the poverty line (the poverty line in the U.S. is an annual income of less than 22,300 US dollars for a family of four), of which about 20.5 million were impoverished (the impoverishment line in the U.S. refers to an annual income of less than 11,157 US dollars for a family of four) and nearly 46.2 million people lived by the government

---

4　Who benefits from the three tax reductions in 8 years by the Bush administration? by Chen Da, available in China Business News on January 19, 2009.
5　Bush's 3-trillion budget bill criticized as "ignoring the economic status" by Niu Zhen, available in Wen Wei Po on February 5, 2008.
6　Warren Buffet: Stop Coddling the Super-Rich, available athttp://www.nytimes.com/2011/08/15/opinion/stop-coddling-the-super-rich.html?_r=0, 2011.

support. In 2010, 49.9 million people did not have medical insurance. Two thirds of the university students in the U.S. have heavy debts upon graduation, each bearing a debt of 80,000 US dollars on the average (since the outbreak of the financial crisis, the U.S. government launched a plan for minifying deficits, and the fees for public universities have increased by over 15%.) Against such a background, thoughts reflecting on the capitalist system began to spread rapidly.

The "Occupy Wall Street" movement broke out just under the following circumstances: due to the neoliberal policies, the U.S. had sunk deeply in the polarization of wealth distribution and an economic crisis featuring insufficient effective demand. Financial liberalization and capital globalization further virtualized the U.S. economy and hollowed its industries; considerable amounts of industry capital went into financial speculations or were transferred to the Third World. The U.S. has been relying on finance and the service industry to achieve economic development and create new job opportunities for a decade. Its military industry and hi-tech industry could provide job opportunities to a limited population, so social wealth was even more concentrated in the hands of Wall Street financial oligarchs in the U.S. According to statistics, on December 31, 2010, the total market value of the top five financial companies in the U.S. reached 800 billion US dollars, that is, 1/20 of the GDP of the United States. After the outbreak of the financial crisis in September, 2008, the U.S. government injected 120 billion US dollars to the Bank of America and 85 billion US dollars to AIG. In early October 2008, that is, more than two months after the U.S. Congress approved the plan to save the market with 700 billion US dollars, 350 billion US dollars had been allocated to each and every major bank. A large part of the aid went into the pocket of Wall Street senior executives. In December 2011, the U.S. "Bloomberg News" agency pointed out that the Fed spent 7.7 trillion US dollars in saving Wall Street after the financial tsunami, and the number even reached 29 trillion US dollars in other analytical reports.[7] According to a survey of Los Angeles Times, of the 25 cities across the U.S., New York, a city with centralized financial industry, had the biggest gap between the rich and the poor. In 2007, the New York rich, accounting for 1% of the New York population, had 44% of the total income of the city. Besides, according to statistics of the U.S. Census Bureau, the poverty incidence in the U.S. was 15.1%, and poor Americans reached 46.2 million in 2010, being the highest ever in the past 52 years. "The richest 5% of the people have 72% of the national wealth of the U.S"[8]. After the burst of the financial bubble, all the covered institutional conflicts

---

7 Fed may spend 7.7 trillion US dollars in saving the market, far more than the official amount available in International Business Times on December 12, 2011.
8 Polarization surged "a wave of occupations", the US government is short of economic improvement measures, available in South Daily on October 11, 2011.

of capitalism broke forth, too, and the angry public pointed the spearhead of the struggle against Wall Street. The US people extensively participated in and supported the "Occupy Wall Street" movement, and that is a direct protest against the neoliberal order.

III. "Occupy Wall Street" movement shook the US dollar hegemony

The neoliberal bubble economy in the U.S. is a means adopted by the U.S. to defer and transfer its economic crisis and social contradictions, but it meanwhile aggravates the economic and social crises in the U.S.. Without the real estate and financial bubble economy in the past decade, perhaps the current economic and social crises had already broken out in 2000, when the U.S. Internet bubble burst. It is the financial bubble in this decade that drove the growth of the US industry economy and residents' consumption; eased the class conflict in the U.S. and delayed the period of bursting social conflicts. The U.S. intensified its global geopolitical strategy in the same decade and further consolidated the hegemony of the US dollar.

In general, the U.S. in the first decade of the new century was similar to the US under the Reagan administration which carried out neoliberalism domestically and militarism externally. In these ten years, the educational and medical treatment, among other social welfare, was substantially cut, but national defense expenses kept increasing to nearly 700 billion US dollars in 2010, up 81% relative to that in 2001 and accounting for more than 40% of the global national defense expenses. In fact, the general military spending of the U.S. also covers R&D funds for space weapons, medical expenses for veterans, national security expenses, etc.. It is always 80% higher than the defense budget. That is to say, the total military spending of the U.S. in 2010 was far more than 10,000 trillion U.S. dollars.

In those ten years, the U.S. worked all out to consolidate its world hegemony with military means: invading Afghanistan, invading Iraq, subverting Libya, threatening Iran, containing China and Russia…

The fundamental objective of the U.S. global strategy is to ensure the hooking of US dollar with oil trading at times when US dollar overflows and is much depreciated using its super military and geostrategic advantages, and ensure the status of US dollar as the world's top reserve currency, U.S. dollar hegemony, and the dominating position of monopoly capital in the U.S.

In terms of industry, although industries in the U.S. have become hollowed, US capital transferred to the Third World on a large scale would abstract considerable amounts of profits each year. At the financial level, as long as US dollar keeps its hegemony, some countries would continue buying U.S. treasury securities and the U.S. would be capable to provide its people with due welfare, although it may do so by borrowing money from the Third World. Therefore, resorting to military means to ensure settlement of oil transactions in US dollar so as to keep the hegemony of US dollar is the top secret of Wall Street. In 2009, the U.S. government deficits reached to a historic high, that is, 1.4 trillion US dollars, accounting for 10% of its concurrent GDP. In 2001 when George W. Bush first took office as the U.S. President, the total national debt of the country were 5.7 trillion US dollars. Till 2008 when he stepped down from office, the national debts of the U.S. had soared to 11.5 trillion US dollars. In August 2011, the total national debt of the U.S. was about 14.27 trillion US dollars, accounting for 98.3% of the concurrent GDP of the United States. According to the prediction of the Congressional Budget Office, in the next decade, the U.S. will see its total national debt growing to 25 trillion US dollars. The money will be used mainly for national defense and social welfare for the US people and for saving the big Wall Street financial companies which can't fall.

IV. "Occupy Wall Street" movement shook the U.S. political system and cultural hegemony

Besides the above means of exploiting other countries, the U.S. has also resorted to violent oppression at home.

Regarding the "Occupy Wall Street" movement, which was apparently against capitalism, CNN, Fox and other mainstream U.S. news media all kept silence at the beginning. In the first 10 days of the "Occupy" movement, all the U.S. cable news channels broadcast only one piece of related news each day on the average. Pew Research Center discovered that, in the economic news between September 25 and October 2, 2011, which accounted for 14% of all news in the same period, only 12% were about the "Occupy Wall Street" movement. Failing to block public opinions, mainstream media began to attack the "Occupy" movement for no reason at all, and tried all possible means to curb its development. The U.S. government sent a lot of riot police directly to oppress the masses with helicopters, rubber bullets, spicy water and batons. The riot police went into bloody conflicts with the protestors once and again and arrested thousands of the protestors in weeks.

What in contrast was the Tea Party movement. The "Occupy Wall Street" movement and the Tea Party movement seem to be spontaneous demonstrations and protests participated by the public, while the focal issue was the aid given to Wall Street financial giants by the Federal government. However, the Tea Party movement having the right-wing racist and neoliberal tendencies focused on protesting the government intervention in the economy instead of targeting the Wall Street. According to a survey done by weekly Times, the Tea Party movement was supported by only 27% of the US people, but "Occupy Wall Street" movement was supported by as high as 54% of the US people. Instead of being harshly suppressed like what was done to "Occupy Wall Street" movement, the Tea Party movement was greatly publicized by Fox and other mainstream media, and fully supported by the US political elite and capitalist corporations.

As can be seen, the ruling class in the U.S. is good at distinguishing contradictions of different natures: the right-wing movement supporting the capitalist system was seen as a contradiction in the class; while "Occupy Wall Street" movement was obliviously labeled as a contradiction with the enemy. That explains why the repression body suppressed it more ruthlessly than general mass movements since the beginning.

New York mayor Michael Bloomberg is at the same time the richest businessman in New York. In his youth, he worked for Solomon Brothers PLC in the Wall Street, later established Bloomberg L.P. and now has 88% of the shares of Bloomberg L.P. He got rich overnight when he served as New York mayor. His wealth mainly comes from businesses such as financial data, financial terminals and financial news, which are all directly related to Wall Street. According to the data released by Forbes, Bloomberg had a property of only 4 billion US dollars when first elected as the mayor of New York in 2001, 5.3 billion US dollars till 2007, then 11.5 billion US dollars in 2007, and then 20 billion US dollars in 2008. It's known that U.S. has one of the highest crime rates in the world. Many parks in New York are frequented by crimes, rapes and robberies; many are taken by criminals at night and it scares the ordinary citizens. Yet New York mayor has never been seen to make efforts to clear the criminals in the parks like he does to suppress "Occupy Wall Street" movement. Perhaps, to Wall Street oligarchs, the masses in "Occupy Wall Street" movement are even more formidable than criminals. Early in the morning on November 15, 2011, the headquarters of "Occupy Wall Street" movement were suddenly cleared by force, and a lot of protesters were arrested, only because the movement is distinctly against capitalism.

University students and the citizens across the U.S. stood out to support the "Occupy Wall Street" movement, and the police went into conflicts with the protesters which caused big casualties. In Auckland, California, the police used tear gas and rubber bullets to disperse protesters and arrested dozens of them; at the University of California, Berkeley, the police shot an "Occupy Wall Street" protester which was suspected of carrying a pistol. On November 15, the same year, students of the University of California, Berkeley, went on strike for the whole day to protest growing tuition and greedy big Wall Street companies. Nearly 10 thousand people took part in the protest. On November 18, the campus police of the University of California at Davis brutally suppressed student's peaceful demonstrations, triggering a protest by thousands of students. Afterwards when the principal faced with the angry public, he had to apologize.

The above facts are a clear proof that democracy, freedom and human rights above classes never exist. The state apparatus of the U.S. is a violent tool used to serve the bourgeoisie in nature.

The "Occupy Wall Street" movement and the reaction of the US ruling class to it fully proves the judgment made by Marxist classical writers more than a hundred years ago—the capitalist society is a society of bourgeois dictatorship. Over a century has passed, and the capitalist society did not see a change in its nature. Senior U.S. government officials like the U.S. Presidents, Vice Presidents, Secretaries of State and Secretaries of Treasury have been close to military enterprises, oil and financial groups. The U.S. Congress is basically a world of rich people. According to the property declaration data by the U.S. Congressmen in 2009, the U.S. Center for Responsive Politics pointed out that 46% of the U.S. senators and congressmen had each a property of more than a million US dollars, and the Capitol Hill was filled with "fat cats". In the Congress, 244 congressmen were not rich but noble, of which 138 were the Republican and 106 were the Democratic. Republican congressman Darrell Issa had a property of as high as 451 million US dollars, ranking the first; Democratic congressman Kerry ranked the second with 294 million US dollars.

In 1891, Engels wrote, "Nowhere do 'politicians' form a more separate, powerful section of the nation than in North America. There, each of the two great parties which alternately succeed each other in power is itself in turn controlled by people who make a business of politics, who speculate on seats in the legislative assemblies of the Union as well as of the separate states, or who make a living by carrying on agitation for their party and on its victory are rewarded with positions…and nevertheless we find here two great gangs of political speculators, who alternately take possession of the state power and exploit it by the most corrupt means and for the most corrupt ends – and the nation is powerless against these two great cartels of politicians, who are ostensibly its servants, but in reality exploit and plunder it."[9] Just look at how Wall Street executives have kidnapped the U.S. government, how the mayor of New York has got rich by acting in collusion with Wall Street, how the mayor of New York has brutally suppressed a peaceful protest of the public, and how the judges in the U.S. favor capital oligarchs. We see that the remarks of Engels are not outdated at all. The

---

9 Collected Works of Marx and Engels, Vol. 2, People's Publishing House, 1972.

so-called separation of the three powers actually enables the three powers to serve capital oligarchs. In the U.S., there is no democracy, human rights or freedom, but "corporatocracy", "rule of corporates" and freedom of capital. The history of the U.S., which is longer than 200 years, has fully proved that the U.S. economic, political and cultural systems are in nature tools used by capital oligarchs to exploit, carry out autocracy and brainwash the American masses.

Y. 5

Class Division of Global Capitalism and Its Main Features

Jiang Hui[1]

Abstract: Under the conditions of globalization, the exploitation of labor by capital has expanded rapidly and intensified. The spread of economic crisis unceasingly intensifies and the class contradictions sharpen again. Under such circumstances, the class analysis method seems even more prominent and important. The class of capitalists and working class have overstepped the scope of national boundaries, forming the global class of capitalists and the global working class, which display different characteristics. On the one hand, the global capitalist class unites and its aggressivity and greediness are even more prominent, gradually forming a distinctive class consciousness. On the other hand, the global working class is objectively forming and its class consciousness is gradually awakening and forming, but is in a relatively divided and dispersed state.

Key words: global capitalism; class analysis; global capitalist class; global working class

---

[1] Jiang Hui, deputy director of the CASS World Socialism Research Center, and secretary of the Party committee and researcher of the CASS Institute of Information Studies.

In the rapid development process of capitalism around the globe, the objective fact of social changes and development once again highlights the relevance and importance of the class issue. Well then, how should we understand the class structure and class relations of contemporary capitalism? How to re-evaluate the role and significance of class division and class analyses in such a rapidly changing era? How to understand the class division and conflicts of the global capitalism? All these are major questions to be urgently studied.

I. The capitalist crisis once again highlights the importance of class division and class analyses

At present, the economic globalization is developing rapidly, and the exploitation relationship of capital and the wage labor is expanding and spreading even more unscrupulously. Meanwhile, capitalism is undergoing a new economic and social crisis, being a time which demands to apply the method of class analysis to analyze contemporary capitalism and modern Western society. However, for a long time, even some theorists who claimed to be left-wing have adopted an eclectic and pragmatism attitude and evaded talking about the class issue. Just like the Spanish scholar Camillo Cahis commented, "They are afraid of using the Marxist theories for analysis... and some intellectuals are even more interested to evade the universal contradiction between capital and labor, that is to evade that socialism is the third path to replace capitalism." "Here, social classes, class struggles, capitalism, capital accumulation, surplus value, imperialism, state and other realities do not exist at all, because they all have been evaporated within the simple abstraction of man, people and citizens."[2]

However, in the first decade of the 21st century, capitalism saw the outbreak of a new economic crisis and serious social polarization, the unbridled greedy pursuit of excess profits by the class of transnational capitalists, and an even more naked exploitation of workers in different countries and the specter of the "middle class" gradually gave way to the harsh reality of "re-proletarianization", which all genuinely and urgently demand to explain the modern capitalist society by a class analysis that reflects the true economic and power relations. The whole world can no longer evade the issue of capital-wage labor relationship, which is the issue of fundamental class oppositon and conflict.

At such a historic moment, viewpoints such as "classes have died out", "class politics has ended", "class analysis has no meaning at all" started to look pale and powerless. The reason is that, if ideological prejudices are

---

2 Camilo Cahis: Criticizing the Ideology of "Globalization" with the Viewpoint of Class Struggle, El genocidio transgénico, June 11, 2006.

put aside, they replace the essence of the capitalist class relations with the representation of the capitalist social structure of a particular period, or just as in the past, consider the changes in the social structure and life relations in the scope of a single country in an isolated way rather than focusing on the expansion of capitalist relations of production and class relations in a globe scale.

Some men of insight in the Western society have clearly realized this. For example, the German scholar Ekkehard Lieberam believed, "Capitalist neoliberalism is closely related to class issues. It is clear that along with the social polarization and the intensification of the class struggle, considering the concepts of society, politics and the state from the class perspective is strengthening. Even the bourgeois press is talking about the class society, the dissolution of the middle class, class differences, etc.."[3]

According to the data released by the British National Center for Social Research in January 2007, in Britain, 57% of the British people consider themselves as working class. The National Center for Social Research was very "astonished" by this figure, because for a long time both politicians and the mainstream media had been telling everybody that "we are the middle class". Of course, the standard of the "middle class" exaggerated by them has a mortgaged real estate and a compact car. Of the wage earners who had avoided the "working class" title and were proud of being included to the "middle class" since long, 57% went so far as to position themselves as "working class" in the face of the grim social reality, which was a truly "astonishing" phenomenon, although this figure was 10% lower than that during the 1960s.[4] In February 2010, "New York Times" published an article, in which it was claimed that the financial crisis has caused "a division in the middle class". Millions of people were who were once tacked on "the middle class label" now have to rely on public relief to make ends meet. These "new poor" will possibly "not be able to return to the middle class life". In Japan, there is a bestseller entitled *Disappearance of the Middle Class in 2010*. Its author Katsuhiro Tanaka thought that in 2010, Japan with "a total mid-stream (middle class) of 100 million people" will "see a great split between the %10 rich and the rest 90% poor, and the middle class will disappear".[5]

---

3 Class Analysis, Social Polarization and Class Formation by Ekkehard Lieberam in German journal Marxistische Blaetter, Issue 5, 2004, edited by Huang Rujie, published in Foreign Theoretical Trends, Issue 7, 2006.
4 Refer to "Has working-class consciousness collapsed?" by Phil Hearse, Studies on Marxism, Issue 10, 2009.
5 Refer to "The fear of the West: The middle class may be the 'root of unrest'" by Mu Chunshan, Ji Shuangcheng, etc., Global Times, March 15, 2010.

How do we see the class division and class conflicts in the global scale today? Historically, the two major classes in the capitalist society have gone through three different historical periods with three different characteristics.

Before the 1930s, it was arguably the stage dominated by the laissez-faire capitalism. The class contradiction was very sharp; the capital-labor relationship assumed a fierce confrontation trend and class struggles were launched on a large scale, which even led to violent revolutions and directly threatened the capitalist system itself.

From the 1930s to 70s were the so-called "golden years" of capitalist development. Under the impetus of the long struggles of the working class, the class of capitalists adjusted the production relations and ruling policies, alleviated the class contradictions, implemented welfare state policies and formed the "tripartite system" of the employers, the employees and the state. The posture of class relations turned from fierce confrontation beyond the system to "compromise and cooperation" within the system. It was the period of great development of the so-called "middle class," and a period when the Western society declared to "bid farewell to the working class".

Since the mid-1970s, especially since the 1980s, it has been the period of capitalism dominated by neoliberalism. The capitalist production relations were once again adjusted in order to deal with the economic "stagflation" crisis, remove the burden of social welfare, lower labor costs and increase profits. The capitalist class has unceasingly destroyed the previous welfare achievements and the rights obtained by the laborers, deprived them of their union power and the working class retreated and unceasingly suffered frustration and weakening. The myth of "the middle class" has been shattered, and the phenomenon of "re-proletarianization" has appeared. The posture of the capital-labor relationship has turned from "compromise and cooperation" in the system in the previous stage to "estrangement and confrontation" in the system. Moreover, the capitalist relations of production and class relations spread throughout the world with the global expansion of capital.

All in all, since the 21st century, when class contradiction in the Western society gradually intensify again and the nature and characteristics of each class gradually come to light, discussions about these issues are gradually increasing, too. For example, discussion topics such as "persistent class boundaries", "useless 'middle class' myth", "elegy of the middle class", "poverty-stricken, helpless middle class without any choice", "'middle class anger' worries the West", and "class confrontation" is bound to appear in the Western society, etc. are increasing. In this situation, the global development of capitalism has made the past class analyses confined to the scope of national states narrow and incomplete, which requires us to adjust the premise and horizon of class analyses, go beyond the limit of the scope of national states to examine the formation and development of global class relations as well as the formation and development of class relations of concrete national states in the scope and against background of the entire world.

II. Formation of the global class of capitalists: A more aggressive and more greedy class that is gradually forming a distinct class consciousness

The process of expansion and reconstruction of the capitalist relations of production at the global level is at the same time the process of formation and development of transnational classes and class relations. It also proves Marx's judgment, "when capital has reached this point, then wage labor itself reaches the point."[6] Over 160 years ago, Marx and Engels said, in the era of capitalism, "Society as a whole is more and more splitting up into two great hostile camps, into two great classes directly facing each other —bourgeoisie and proletariat."[7] Today, in the era of economic globalization dominated by international monopoly capitalism, the whole world is splitting up into the global class of capitalists and the global class of wage laborers.

Along with the development of global capitalism, a transnational global capitalist class is taking shape, indicating that the capitalist society has entered a new stage after centuries of development. The transnational class of capitalists is one group of many capitalist classes. Although it has not totally substituted the capitalist class that is formed and developed within the scope of national state, part of the latter is gradually transforming into the former and the class of national capitalists does not have its past advantages, and it is more and more difficult for it to keep its independence. The national capitalist class is bound to relocate itself in the globalization trend. Although the transnational capital, national capital and local capital mix and conflict with one another and the capitalist class groups at different levels overlap and merge in the differentiated reorganization, we more and more clearly see that a transnational capitalist class group is emerging and increasingly obtains a dominant status in the capitalist class group with increasing superiority. Foreign scholars have asserted, "The transnational capitalist class is the new global ruling class."[8] All in all, a transnational capitalist class has sought the role of

---

6 Collected Works of Marx and Engels, first part of Vol. 46 (Grundrisse), People's Publishing House, p. 237.
7 Selected Works of Marx and Engels, Vol.1, People's Publishing House, 1995, p. 273.
8 William I. Robinson, A Theory of Global Capitalism: Production, Class, and State in a Transnational World, Social Science Academic Press, 2009, p. 60.

the global ruling class, controlling the formation of transnational state institutions and global decision-making which are taking shape. Its economic, political and ideological agents have also gradually developed at the global level.

Well then, what are the distinctive features of this forming global transnational capitalist class as compared with the previous capitalist class? What groups or classes is it composed of? In short, the global capitalist class is a new capitalist group which has gradually formed in the period of rapid development of economic globalization since the 1980s and which takes the operation transnational capital as its main activity, the pursuit of global excess monopoly profits as its goal, transnational companies as its main pillar and platform, large-scale international economic organizations and financial institutions as its main tool of control and the exploitation and rule of the whole world as its main aim. As for composition, it consists of capital oligarchs and the senior "management elite" that control transnational companies, transnational financial institutes and international economic organizations, economic, political and ideological agents who serve the rule of transnational capital within each and every country. To define and classify the global capitalist class this way, we have to make clear the following several points:

First, the global capitalist class accumulates capital and carries out production beyond the scope of national states and attempts to go beyond the control of national states or regional political entities in the global system. But such class uses the mightiest capitalist state organs in the world as leverage to achieve its global aims and tries to get rid of the limitation by the power of national states, which is not equal to say that it does not use state power. The parent companies of transnational companies are usually located in developed capitalist countries or regions, from which they radiate to the whole world. Meanwhile, it increasingly uses large-scale international institutes like the IMF and the World Bank as tools.

Second, members of the global capitalist class group are not just capitalists and various agents in developed capitalist countries, but cover the capitalists and various agents in other countries who serve global capital accumulation and production. They are in different countries and regions in the world, including the poorest areas, cooperate and compete with one another, but pursue and realize the overall interests of the transnational capitalist class on the whole.

Third, fundamentally, the global capitalist class takes shape and develops in order to pursue excess economic profits and global economic interests. However, to achieve such aim, it has to not only hold the dominant position and lifeline of the global economy, and set the direction of world production, but also pursue domination over the political, cultural and social forces and fields in the world. Just like the previous capitalist class pursued to obtain domination over the economic, political, cultural and social fields in the scope of national state, it now gradually becomes a "global capitalist class for itself" in a global scale.

III. Global working class: even more complicated and scattered class with a graudally awakening class consciousness

What accompanies the global capitalist class is the gradual formation of the global working class (the global wage laborers class). Along with the formation of the global labor market, features of confrontation between the two major classes become more and more prominent in the global capital-labor relationship which has reflected more clearly the capitalists and the workers as the two poles of the relations of production revealed by Marx. Compared to the formation and strong position of the global capitalist class, the formation of the global working class can be described as a passive and unconscious process.

Economic globalization led by international monopoly capital oligarchs will involve billions of wage laborers in different world countries into a unified world labor force market and though they are from different countries, they are inevitably suffer the exploitation and control by the global capitalist class together. If the global capitalist class is gradually transforming from a "class-in-itself" into a "class-for-itself," the global working class is transforming relatively more slowly and more complicatedly. Some foreign scholars studying the working class have noticed the issue. For example, the US scholar William Tabb held that, "along with the reorganization and reconstitution of the capitalist class caused by increased international economic penetration and the corresponding reorganization and reconstitution of the working class, its members, despite their diverse locations and cultural identities, now more than ever need to unite. So far, the capitalists, through mediating tools such as the IMF, have done far better than the working class in reorganizing and acting on their class interests to restructure the way the economic, political and social spheres function."[9] However, the fact that the global working class is still in a state of "in-itself" and a global working class consciousness has not yet clearly formed cannot deny the fact that a huge global working class is gradually forming and developing and that the global working class is at a stage of the development of various protests.

---

9 William K. Tabb, "Neoliberalism and Anticorporate Globalization as Class Struggle" in: Michael Zweig (ed.), What's Class Got to Do with It? American Society in the 21st Century, Cornell University Press, 2004, p. 63.

The formation process of the global working class is mainly influenced and conditioned by the following factors:

First, under the conditions of economic globalization, the strengths of "strong" capital and "weak" labor are even more unbalanced and the global capitalist class has been strengthening its free hand and direct control of labor. Workers of different countries are losing protection from governments and trade unions, so they cannot effectively resist or fight against the attacks of global capital.

Second, workers of different countries are having more contradictions and conflicts, and are scattered in the face of combining global capital. They compete against and exclude one another for their respective interests, so it is hard for them to unify. For example, the contradictions between workers in the developed countries and those in the developing countries are extremely prominent. In order to maintain their employment rates and wage levels, the workers and trade unions in developed countries support trade protectionism and oppose the labor force of other countries to enter their domestic labor markets and oppose migrant workers.

Third, the subjectivity and class consciousness of the working class still deficient. If we look at the history, from the early period of capitalism to the current period of global capitalism, the working class has gone through three stages: "class in itself"—"class for itself"—"global class in itself". In the early stage of the formation of the working class, it lacked class consciousness and carried out only spontaneous economic struggles to fight against capital exploitation. By the mid and late 19th century and the first half of the 20th century, under the guidance of scientific theories and the leadership of the working class parties, it formed a strong class consciousness and carried organized and conscious economic, political and social struggles, then struggled for socialist revolutions and aiming at overthrowing the capitalist system. Since WWII, especially in the "golden years" of the Western capitalism, along with the adjustments and changes in the capitalist development and mode of rule, the working class has gradually lost its class consciousness once again, approved for the capitalist system and mainly carried out economic struggle within the capitalist system. In the period of the globalization of the rule of international capital, although the exploitation of transnational capital was even more direct and ruthless, the gap between the rich and the poor and various inequalities got even more serious; the capital-labor confrontation and conflict in the global scale became even more significant; and the workers in different countries have begun to realize their class status and class interests, but their consciousness as a global working class has not yet been formed, and they have not still gained the subjectivity and self-consciousness to confront the rule of capital around the globe, so they are still at the state of being "a class in itself"

Under the neoliberal economic and social policies, trade unions are greatly paralyzed and weakened. They fight by themselves, and do not have the tactics or strategies for walking out of the plight. They are unable to organize the working class to mount large-scale economic and social struggle. Some left-wing political parties, including the social democratic parties and some communist parties which have been the political organizations representing the working class in the past, now claim that they are not political parties of a class. As can be seen, political party organizations deficiently representing their interests is an important factor why the working class is still at the state of "class in itself".

All in all, in the era of global capitalism, classes and class conflicts and class struggles instead of disappearing have been manifested and expanded in a sharper and more clear way in a bigger global scale. Today, it is impossible to correctly understand the contemporary capitalist society without class discourse and class analysis and it is impossible to correctly analyze the social relations and class relations of contemporary capitalism without studying the class issue of contemporary capitalism from a global perspective.

Y. 6

Capitalism is like the Sun in the West

—World Situation and Prospects after 9/11

Zhang Wenmu[1]

Abstract: World capitalism following Karl Marx's life time did not contribute to a sustainable mode of development of mankind. World capitalism following Lenin's life time even lost its ability to self-reform. In the past century, it simply maintained the existing pattern it had: unceasingly experiencing the same kind of crises, facing the same kind of contradictions and solving the contradictions with the same kind of high-cost way, namely crisis plus war. Meanwhile, there was only the repetition of technical renewal and crisis, but no renewal of its existing mode. The innovation accomplishments of the world lags far behind its scale of destruction. Lenin, once put forward the judgment that "imperialism is the highest stage of capitalism", but this cannot be vulgarly misinterpreted as capitalism is to perish immediately. At present, the Western countries, in terms of the governance of the world, have no edge and use nothing but fists. The sun in the West is about to set and capitalism has no way out.

Key words: globalization; capitalism; socialism

---

[1] Prof. Zhang Wenmu, visiting researcher of the CASS World Socialism Research Center, researcher at the Center for Strategic Studies, Beihang University.

Around the world in 2011, especially in the U.S. and Europe, there were upheavals of varying degrees. The absolute infiniteness of development and the absolute scarcity of resources is the basic contradiction of international politics under the condition of market economy. Faced with such contradiction, the capitalist modes of solution fall into the embarrassment of self-denial.

I. The "periphery supplies center" model is difficult to succeed

Globalization is essentially the globalization of the industrial capital, the capital with high potential spreads to the periphery market with low potential to extract high-quality resources, get high profits and incessantly create new peripheral markets and hereby incessantly form new advantages to oppress the periphery market.

Since the 18th century, capital globalization has gone through several waves of development and resistance processes. Britain is the "motherland of capital", and also the first source of capital globalization process. Capital must seize surplus value from the laborers, press labor force income up to the level they can maintain their basic subsistence, or even up to a lower level, and finally cause the labor force to revolt against capital. The laborers are the most elementary domestic consumer group. While incessantly providing profits for capital, their income gets less and less, causing a continuous shrinkage of the domestic consumer market. In Britain, the antagonism between the working class and the capitalist class has appeared very early. In the 1840s, the British working class was seriously impoverished, and strikes and demonstrations were the direct consequences of capital squeeze and shrinkage of the domestic consumer market. Laborers' revolts caused the unsustainability of capitalist production. Therefore, the British capital could do nothing but expand outward, resulting in the shift of the contradiction between the British domestic capital and labor to Europe, which created a polarization in Europe. While resisting the impact of British capital, Europe was entirely involved in the capitalist mode of production and suffered the consequences of domestic polarization. In order to get rid of the contradiction of polarization, Europe then began world expansion driven by and together with Britain, got high profit return from the periphery areas, in order to provide a massive primitive for the early development of European capitalism. Thus the world was divided into capital-central countries and capital-periphery countries, which then led to the emergence of the oppressing and the opposed nations. The contradiction between the central and the periphery countries is the relocated form of the contradiction between the oppressing class (i.e., the capitalist class) and the opposed class (i.e., the working class) existing in capitalist countries. Its result is that while the capital-central countries develop, the integrity of capital-periphery countries falls into destruction.

On the surface, the process of global expansion of capital seemed to be a pastoral process of free trade, but this expansion was actually accompanied by an extremely bloody and violent plunder. In the mid 19th century, capitalism expanded to Asia. In several wars of aggression, the British conquered China and India. Since then, the enormous wealth of China and India flew from the East to Europe. This external wealth greatly increased the consumption level of the European working class and gradually alleviated the problem of polarization in Europe. After the Paris Commune failed in 1871, the struggles of the workers fell into a silence. Although the European labor movement once ran high during the 1880s under the leadership of the Second International, the mass base of the class struggle had a certain weakening and presenting Bernstein's revisionism. In a sense, the originally oppressed part of the working class turned into "labor aristocracy" enjoying high welfare under the nourishment of profits from the East. Europe entered the "Victorian era" of seeming "peace and development".

The same was true of the US. After the Civil War, the capitalist market economy developed rapidly, leading to polarization and intensified labor-capital contradiction in the U.S. In the second half of the 19th century, the American labor movement has been quite active. For example, the big Chicago parade in October 1884 was magnificent, it was more influential than the "Occupy Wall Street" movement. In order to alleviate the domestic social contradictions, the US government began to vigorously develop overseas market since the end of the 19th century just like Europe had done in the past in order to get rid of the inherent and domestic contradictions of capitalism. In 1898, the U.S. occupied Hawaii, Cuba and Philippines, joined the European imperialism's war in the East and obtained a massive profit backflow. In the early 20th century, the labor-capital contradiction in the U.S. was largely mitigated.

However, the capital-periphery countries, if their expropriation went to extremes, would rise up in rebellion, too. The earlier American War of Independence (1776-1783) and the Napoleonic Wars (1799-1815) were the first massive resistances of American and French peoples against British capital. The war of 1812 between US and UK in the early 19th century (1812-1814) and the great Revolutions of 1848 in Europe were the second massive resistance against the British capital-center by the capital of the periphery areas. These two resistances gave birth to the ideologies of nationalism and democratism in North America and Europe.

The socialist camp led by the Soviet Union has blocked the process of globalization where the Western capital expropriated the Third World for half a century. The Cold War was essentially was to block the expropriation of the periphery areas by the central capitalist countries, at least the socialist countries. After the disintegration of the Soviet Union, after the fence against Western capitalism built by the Soviet Union and former socialist countries in Eastern Europe collapsed, Eastern Europe has fully opened up its resources, markets and labor force, and became the periphery market for of Western Europe once again, thus the wave of capital globalization saw a great upsurge. The disintegration of the Soviet Union provided new periphery markets for the central-capital countries, and U.S. capital swept away all obstacles around the world, so that the US gave up the production of material goods, which gave birth to the so-called "new economy" and thought that it could dominate the world only by relying on finance, new technologies and new concepts.

The constant squeeze of the periphery countries by the central countries has resulted in a continuous decline of income and spending power of the overwhelming majority of laborers in the world, while the capital in central countries was accumulated in the hands of a handful rich, and intensified the polarization between the rich and the poor as well as the social contradictions. The "9/11" incident against the U.S. in 2001 was the result of the intensified contradiction between capital-center and capital-periphery in the period of globalization. In order to suppress the revolts of periphery areas against international capital, the U.S. waged a war against "terror" which has lasted for nearly a decade. Today, it withdraws troops from Afghanistan and Iraq, indicating that capital-central countries have failed to control the periphery countries. Besides, the rise of the emerging economies and the multi-polarization trend of the whole world which force the Western capital to shrink back from the periphery countries, will reverse the inherent crisis of capitalism to press their own laborers—laying off employees and cutting salaries and welfare, which will lead to intensified domestic contradictions. All sorts of "Occupy" movements that are taking place in the West today are the result of the intensification of the labor-capital contradiction in capitalist countries.

II. The theory of "free competition" falls into an embarrassing situation

Andy Stern, a famous correspondent, published a commentary in the website of Wall Street Journal on December 1, 2011, in which he said, "The conservative-preferred, free-market fundamentalist, shareholder-only model—so successful in the 20th century—is being thrown onto the trash heap of history in the 21st century. In an era when countries need to become economic teams, Team USA's results—a jobless decade, 30 years of flat median wages, a trade deficit, a shrinking middle class and phenomenal gains in wealth but only for the top 1%—are pathetic."[2]

---

2 Andy Stern: China's Superior Economic Model, available at http://www.wsj.com/articles/SB10001424052970204630904577056490023451980.

Capitalist development has been caught in a plight of two minds: first realize capital augmentation by exploiting domestic laborers, resulting in causing domestic revolution; in order to avoid domestic revolution, capital then turned to outward expansion and achieved augmentation through external exploitation so as to mitigate domestic contradictions, which then intensified the contradictions between capital-central countries and capital-periphery countries. Now this model did not work, so the pressure of capital augmentation returns inwards, leading to the revolt of domestic labor and capital.

To break out of the current crisis, the capital-central countries have to do more than just self-adjustments, because they have lost the ability to self-renewal. If they cannot find a new periphery space like that following the dissolution of the Soviet Union, they will inevitably decline. Currently they have targeted the Middle East and China, looking upon the former's resources and the latter's market. US's war "against terrorism" in Afghanistan was only nominal, its essence was to control capital-periphery areas with abundant resources. In his State of the Union Address in 2002, former US President George W. Bush said, "We have clear priorities and we must act at home with the same purpose and resolve we have shown overseas: We'll prevail in the war, and we will defeat this recession."[3] Europe initiated a war in Libya also because it needed a lot of external resources to solve its own crisis. The other target is China. If China falls, almost the entire Asia will become dependent to an obstacle-less market for Western capitalism. Like the consequence of the dissolution of the Soviet Union, this will contribute to a new recovery of Western capitalism. Therefore, Europe has begun to make overall arrangements in its policies along the southern shores of the Mediterranean, and the U.S. has also announced the policy of "Pivot to East Asia".

Security issues remain there even if China gets rich. On the contrary, China has to be sober and alert, and never gets wildly optimistic. Although capitalism today is smeared with the gold powder of "globalization", it is not different from the capitalism in the eras of Marx and Lenin at all. Capitalism has to always expand to the periphery for subsistence. Without the periphery, capitalism will have nothing left, but domestic social revolutions. The world of capital is a world of jungles. The West today will never be China's true "partner" because of its "entry into the WTO" and participation in globalization.

It's been a decade since China entered the WTO, but joining the WTO does not mean prospering and getting developed naturally. France at the close of the 18th century believed that it would become a member of the

---

3 George W. Bush: January 29, 2002 State of the Union Address by George W. Bush, available at https://www.ssa.gov/history/gwbushstmts2.html.

civilized and a rich country as long as it joined the center-capital system. It was not that simple. In 1786, France and the U.K. signed Eden Treaty, wishfully thinking that as long as it consciously "integrated into globalization", it would benefit from the industry of the U.K. and develop as fast as the U.K. However, France did not think that the British capital has a quite high potential power and a quite high added value to products and the British industrial production system has a superior competitive position, which made the French economy unable to withstand the impact of British capital, caused farmers to lose their lands and flood into the city, dragged the workers to general poverty, and intensified social contradictions, finally leading to the outbreak of the French Great Revolution in 1789. From the experience of France, we can see that China has to be objective regarding the advantages, disadvantages and consequences of "integration into globalization", and analyze them calmly instead of treating them simply.

The focus of international struggles is not the right to labor, but the right of wealth distribution. The world of capital is like two triangles, upright and inverted, which are overlapping in the same place, with the inverted triangle is capital and the upright one is labor force, resources, etc.. The place with the least share of capital is the place with most labor force and the place with the least labor force is the place with the highest share of capital. A small number of financial groups occupy most of the capital shares, but the overwhelming majority, especially laborers supplying physical labor and backward countries supplying raw materials obtain a few shares in international capital distribution. Raw materials and labor force are always the weak side in the exchange for capital. That's also why currently China supplies a lot of labor force to the world market, but receives few.

The U.K. is often said to be a country of free trade. As a matter of fact, it absolutely monopolized technologies in the early period. Friedrich List, an economist of the German Historical School, once said that economically backward countries could not directly copy the principle of free trade. Backward countries would be shattered, if they did not properly implement state monopoly in the face of the impact from high potential capital.[4] German Prime Minister Bismarck adopted List's method and brought Germany to rise very quickly.

---

4 Friedrich List made a critical evaluation of the nature of the American Civil War. He said, "It is one of the primary reasons for the American revolution that all industries were monopolized by the state. The tea tax just provided a spark for the outbreak of the revolution." By studying the American economy, List criticized the then prevailing free trade theory by Adam Smith. He said, "the earlier and the most recent experience of the U.S. has proven that periods with the most frequent and serious (economic) crises were just periods when the intercourse with the U.K. was less restricted." The National System of Political Economy by Friedrich List, translated by Chen Wanxu, the Commercial Press, 1961, p. 89, p. 97.

When the U.S. started its first industrialization, it protected its industries even more strictly. After the Civil War, the U.S. established a centralized control power of the central government, and built a universal national market by collecting high custom tariffs. From 1820 to 1902, the average rate of tariff on products in the manufacturing industry surged from 40% to 73% in the U.S., being far higher than that in the other emerging industrialized countries. In 1913, the U.S. set its advantageous position in the world economic system, and substantially reduced its rate of tariff to 44%.[5]

Therefore, we can't blindly believe in and worship "free competition". Any country in the lower reaches of the capital chain would inevitably face a complete collapse, if it carries out free competition. Achieving independent development and stability are the most important matters for China. There would be no way out for China, if it took the path of colonization and dependency, or comprised to the Western capital. Deng Xiaoping got right down to the heart of it, "Because if we did not uphold socialism, we would eventually become, at best, a dependency of other countries, and it would be even more difficult for us to develop. The international market has already been fully occupied, and it will be very hard for us to get in. Only socialism can save China, and only socialism can develop China."[6]

III. History is in a return to Marx and Lenin

After the Cold War ended in the 1980s, the Western governments have intoxicated itself with the joy of "victory without fight". The Japanese-American scholar Fukuyama put forward "the end of history" theory, arguing that the ideological struggle has come to an end, when Western freedom and democracy have "become the universal ultimate form of all human governments." When the U.S. army was stuck in the mud of the Iraq war, Fukuyama reflected on his theory of "the end of history" and thought that the establishment of a stable and effective ideal-type system of freedom and democracy was not a historical necessity, but a dumb luck.[7]

Since it is "dumb luck," it cannot be history. History can only be the unity of necessity and contingency. Fukuyama, who once became popular in the Western world with "the end of history" apparently lost its persuasive ability facing today's history.

---

5 Data from 1820-1913 Average Rate of Custom Tariffs on Imported Products in the Manufacturing Industry in Industrialized Countries in Stand Straight, China: Shocks of Globalization and China's Strategic Industry by Gao Liang, Petroleum Industry Press, 2001, p. 12.
6 Selected Works of Deng Xiaoping, Vol. 3, People's Publishing House, 1993, p.311.
7 Liu Shan: Fukuyama—From his theory of "the end of history" to a historical observation of the Chinese model, journal of Chinese Social Sciences Today.

After the "Occupy Wall Street" movement broke out in 2011, the eyes of the world began to notice Marx and Lenin. From the "Occupy Wall Street" movement, people understand the correctness of Marx's judgment "the death knell of capitalist private ownership has been sounded"[8] and Lenin's judgment "imperialism is the highest stage of capitalism"[9]. According to reports, in 2011, the sales of Marx's *Capital* in Germany doubled compared with 2005, and was 100 times as great as the sales of it in 1990. The statue of Marx returned to the campus of the University of Leipzig.

It is discovered that world capitalism after Marx did not contribute to the sustainable development of mankind and that world capitalism after Lenin has even lost the ability to self-reform. For almost a century, it has maintained its existing mode of existence: facing the same kind of crises, facing the same kind of contradictions, and solving the contradictions with the same kind of high-cost way, namely crisis plus war. Meanwhile, there was only the repetition of technical renewal and crisis, but no renewal of its existing mode. The innovation speed of the world lags far behind its scale of destruction. In *The Philosophy of History*, Hegel criticized the Oriental medieval history as being "repetition of the same majestic ruin", so it was "unhistorical history".[10] He said that in the ancient Orient, "subsidence is therefore not really such, for through all this restless change no advance is made."[11] Isn't the subsidence of contemporary capitalism not exactly the repetition of the features of Oriental "subsidence" depicted by Hegel?

The judgment made by Lenin—"imperialism is the highest stage of capitalism"—can't be vulgarly interpreted as capitalism is coming to an end soon. At present, in world governance, Western countries have nothing but fists. The sun in the West is setting, and there is no way out for capitalism. Such a judgment does not mean that capitalism will die soon, but means that capitalism in the U.S. will see inexorable doom in the near future— very possibly in the first half of this century. In order to get rid of the current crisis, the Western world will lead its internal troubles to the periphery areas of capital. Although the West is economically declining now, it still possesses a massive military strength. Comprehensive national strength, primarily military strength, is everything in the world. War is not far away from us, and what the West just lacks is a "reason". The problem for China now is that a fairly large number of the Chinese people, including some intellectuals, lack self-confidence and self-consciousness in the great success of the socialist political system and in the excellent Chinese national

---

8 Marx: Capital, Vol. 1, People's Publishing House, 1975, pp.831-832.
9 Lenin: Imperialism, the Final Stage of Capitalism, Selected Works of Lenin, Vol. 2, People's Publishing House, 1960.
10 Georg Wilhelm Friedrich Hegel: The Philosophy of History, trans. by Wang Zaoshi, Shanghai Book Store Press, 2001, p. 108.
11 Ibid., p.109.

culture. They acknowledge that the socialist path taken by China is correct and they have seen the dawn ahead, but they actually doubt whether it is "universal" enough and have first laid down their arms psychologically. If this situation continues for a long time in the future, real risks will grow gradually.

Y. 7

Where are the "Dangers" of Capitalism?

Jiang Hui[1]

Abstract: The analysis of the economic crisis is a very important way and means to observe and study capitalism. The currently developing crisis of capitalism demonstrates that the capitalist mode of production is gradually losing its historical rationality and its capability and space of self-adjustment and innovation are unceasingly weakening. At the same time the diversity that capitalism once developed is tending to uniformity. The current crisis of capitalism, which has exposed the "curse" that capitalism cannot get rid of and the "incurable disease" it does not want to admit, will have a profound impact on the fate of capitalism. On the one hand, we must scientifically understand capitalism, especially its parasitic, decaying and moribund features. On the other hand, we must also dialectically analyze the development of the world socialist movement, realize the new opportunities and challenges brought about by the crisis of capitalism and also see the new issues and challenges that socialism faces.

Key words: capitalist crisis; basic contradictions; destiny of capitalism

---

1   Jiang Hui, deputy director of the CASS World Socialism Research Center, Party Secretary and researcher of the CASS Institute of Information Studies.

The current capitalist crisis reminds people of Lenin's humorous and profound remarks, "History likes irony and likes to play tricks on people. One meant to walk into one room, but got into another."[2] When Eastern Europe saw drastic changes and the Soviet Union disintegrated more than 20 years ago, the world was discussing the "crisis of socialism" everywhere, some people were jubilantly celebrating it, some were busy writing "socialism's obituary", and some were confidently preoccupied to declare "the end of history". What a vigorous, hoarse anti-socialist "chorus" it was at that time! However, 20 years later, a period shorter than "a blink of the eyes" in history, history played a trick once again pushing the "crisis" into the "room" of capitalism. However, history is by no means so simple. Behind the vivid metaphor of "playing tricks", there are the laws of history that are playing their role objectively, strictly and severely. Historical necessity always paves its way through all kinds of contingencies.

The economic crisis is a very important way and method to observe and study capitalism. Today, figures around the world and in various fields are discussing about the "crisis of capitalism", even heavy-weights of capitalism, including state leaders like French Sarkozy, former head of the Federal Reserve, Mr. Greenspan, financial magnate Soros and the originator of "Washington Consensus" Williamson, high-end conferences like the Davos World Economic Forum, the top newspapers like "The Economist" and "Time" are all openly discussing about the "crisis", "rescue", "adjustment" and "reform" of capitalism, not to mention the left-ring figures who are fiercely attacking and angrily denouncing it. This crisis of capitalism has the same expressions and mechanism as in the past crises, but quite different contents, features and forms, with different implications, impacts and trends. Therefore, now, many figures, including defenders of capitalism are talking about "it is different this time". Well then, where are the "dangers" of the current capitalism? Does capitalism have a chance to escape once more? What kind of historical logic does the crisis contain? What does such crisis mean to the socialism?

I. The "curse" that cannot be get rid of and the "incurable disease" that is not admitted willingly

Since the first comprehensive economic crisis in Britain in 1825, periodical crises of capitalism occur every several years, and capitalist figures have always thought that capitalism itself can cope with the crisis. That's why capitalists always call such crises usual "cyclic adjustments" of capitalism. They hope people believe that prosperity—recession—depression—recovery form an inevitable cycle of capitalist economy, as natural as

---

2 Collected Works of Lenin, 2nd edition, vol. 20, 1972, Progress Publishers, p. 456.

the succession of the seasons and the rise and fall of the tides. They appeal to the people to live simply and frugally, tighten their belts, to endure and sacrifice, and to give up some of the interests and life conditions they have enjoyed when capitalism was prosperous, ride out of the storm so as to usher in new prosperity. Some even proclaim that each crisis will make capitalism "turn over a new leaf" and "recreate and regenerate". Today there are still defenders of capitalism saying that the crisis will let capitalism to "rise from its ashes". For example, the "British Financial Times" published an editorial on January 4, 2012, entitled "Let capitalism advance with the times", holding that the 1980s, when Reagan in the U.S. and Margaret Thatcher in the U.K. were in power, presented that to regenerate capitalism it had to be reformed, because such capitalism proved to be not stable enough and, more importantly, unfair, and caused catastrophic crises. However, the editorial also pointed out that "capitalism would be able to continue to exist by reform, and that past experience applies today."

In order to mitigate the impacts and consequences of the crisis, economists have invented a wide range of anti-crisis theories and measures, such as fiscal policy, monetary policy, state intervention, macro regulation and control, stimulation of consumption, balance of supply and demand, etc.. However, the "curse" that capitalism can't get rid of is: on the one hand, capitalism always gets through the hardships in the crisis it is involved time and again, escapes the disasters thereafter and reforms its form of existence, continuing to expand recklessly; on the other hand, no matter how many cosmetic changes it has, or how madly it expands, capitalism gets caught in the devil's net of crisis time and again.

In fact, by piercing the fog of the history of capitalism and by removing the mystical shell of capitalism, Marx revealed the basic contradiction of the capitalist society, that is, the contradiction between the socialization of production and the private ownership of the means of production, which is the "curse" that can't be dispelled. This basic contradiction is always presented through the outbreak of crises. To capitalism, economic crises always play two roles: on the one hand, attempts and adjustments made to solve the crisis can temporarily recover the productive forces, and lets it obtain a greater development than that before the crisis; on the other hand, since being determined and restrained by the basic contradiction, the doom of capitalism is a necessary trend, that is, the inborn "incurable disease" always demonstrates its historical fate of inevitable doom with more serious syndromes. As Marx pointed out, in the crisis, "Capitalist production seeks continually to overcome these immanent barriers, but overcomes them only by means which again place these barriers in its way and on a more formidable scale."[3]

---

3 Collected Works of Marx and Engels, 2nd Edition, Vol. 46, 2003, pp. 278-279.

However, the capitalist economists, historians and politicians always evade and write off this contradiction of capitalism, intentionally or unconsciously. Some of them believe that crises are not necessary, but are caused by the "failure" of capitalism from time to time. The most representative figure of such a "failure theory" is the American economist and the inventor of the "Okun theorem" Arthur M. Okun. More than forty years ago, in his book entitled *The Political Economy of Prosperity*, he wrote, "Recessions are now generally considered to be fundamentally avoidable, like air plane crashes and unlike hurricanes. But we have not banished air crashes from the land and it is not clear that we have the wisdom or the ability to eliminate recessions. The danger has not disappeared. The forces that produce recurrent recessions are still in the wings, merely waiting for their cue". When expressing reasons for this crisis, a variety of figures have introduced various reasons: ineffective supervision, financial fraud, excessive speculations, a handful of greedy people, etc. And what most interesting and thought-provoking was the doubt cast by the heads or titular heads of the U.K. and the U.S. on the "collective intelligence" of the capitalist economists and political scientists. First, at the end of 2008, British queen Elizabeth II asked some top economists during her visit at London School of Economics why none of them noticed or predicted the arrival of the crisis. It was reported that the economists on the spot were sitting in collective silence and speechlessness. A few days after, some of the top economists wrote a collectively signed letter to the Queen, saying, "Your Majesty, we are so sorry that we failed to see the international financial crisis coming." "In summary, Your Majesty, the failure to foresee the timing, extent and severity of the crisis and to head it off, while it had many causes, was principally a failure of the collective imagination of many bright people, both in this country and internationally, to understand the risks to the system as a whole."[4] Please note that it was an excellent replication of the "failure theory" that Okun expressed more than 40 years ago. Second, the US President Barack Obama has the same "excellent" doubt and helplessness. In his words, "…Our economy is badly weakened, a consequence of greed and irresponsibility on the part of some, but also our collective failure to make hard choices and prepare the nation for a new age."

What "risks to the system"! What "hard choices for a new age"! These terms are extremely ironic: it is another "collective cheat" and "overall perfunctoriness" before the big exam of crisis by the top capitalist politicians and economists. The most outstanding "elites" are still fooling the people and the world with such cunning technical terms. However, both terms contain "regarded as a whole," which actually indicate the re-seizure of the

---

4 How can the Western economists be so far off the beam? available at http://news.xinhuanet.com/world/2009-10/18/content_12247221.htmlon October 18, 2009.

inherent stubborn illness and the "incurable disease" of the entire capitalist system. Such deceiving explanations have also indicated the helplessness, avoidance and concealment of the basic contradiction of capitalism by its defenders! However, leaving the essence and core of the issue, all efforts made to solve the crisis are nothing but Don Quixote's tilting at windmills depicted by Cervantes!

II. What are the "differences" of this crisis, then?

History is by no means a simple recurring cycle. In the three or more centuries since its establishment, although the capitalist system seems to have always experienced a constant and unchanging cycle in which prosperity alternates with crisis, the dialectic of historical development is ruthlessly pushing forward substantial changes, the realization of necessary laws and phased qualitative changes amidst the seeming unchanging representations, sudden accidents and continuous quantitative changes. The periodical nature that capitalism presents as a result of the alternation of prosperity and crisis is exactly what Marx profoundly revealed: "The world trade crises must be regarded as the real concentration and forcible adjustment of all the contradictions of bourgeois economy."[5] This is precisely because "it cannot produce any real solution so long as it does not break in pieces the capitalist mode of production, the collisions become periodic."[6] Each crisis adds new insights into the examination of the fate of capitalism, and adds new meaning to the historical solutions which go beyond the capitalist system itself. Well then, what exactly is this "different" in this crisis? What does it mean regarding capitalism and socialism?

This crisis has been lasting for nearly 5 years, and there have been numerous elaborations on its causes, manifestations and trends. I believe that at least the following three aspects deserve in-depth thinking and studies in reflecting on the fate of capitalism.

1. The current capitalist crisis demonstrates more prominently that the capitalist mode of production is gradually losing its historical rationality.

The capitalist mode of production is in the final analysis unlimited accumulation of capital and unlimited demand for profit driven by its basic contradiction. Its basic features are: the pursuit of capital augmentation at all costs, capital expansion and production enlargement completely divorced from social demand, and ignorance of human lives as long as there are conditions for reducing wage costs. All in all, it is a production model which pursues private profits regardless of all consequences. In *Capital*,

---

5 Marx: Theories of Surplus-value, Vol.2, People's Publishing House, 1978, pp. 569-570.
6 Selected Works of Marx and Engels, Vol.3, People's Publishing House, 1995, p. 626.

Marx once quoted British trade union activist Thomas Dunning: "Capital eschews no profit, or very small profit, just as Nature was formerly said to abhor a vacuum. With adequate profit, capital is very bold. A certain 10 per cent. will ensure its employment anywhere; 20 per cent. certain will produce eagerness; 50 per cent., positive audacity; 100 per cent. will make it ready to trample on all human laws; 300 per cent., and there is not a crime at which it will scruple, nor a risk it will not run, even to the chance of its owner being hanged. If turbulence and strife will bring a profit, it will freely encourage both."[7] Today, for the pursuit of greater profits, this mode of production has replaced organized production with gambling and speculation, destroyed the real economy with virtual economy, replaced "civilized governance" with naked plundering and replaced "selling short" the whole national state with exploiting individuals or groups. It has gone far beyond trampling the law and encouraging dispute, while one percent is destroying the whole world for the pursuit of high profits is! Of course, it also destroys the capitalist system itself. No wonder the US investment guru Grantham sighed that "capitalism threatens our existence", that "the policy of 'growth at any cost' is a recipe for planetary suicide" and that "globalization would offer the capitalists more rope to hang themselves".[8] No wonder that the old arch-hawk capitalist strategist Brzezinski writes in his new book that "the financial catastrophe ... jolted America and much of the West into a sudden recognition of their systemic vulnerability to unregulated greed."[9] No wonder that Klaus Schwab, Chairman of the World Economic Forum, said that "the capitalist system does not fit into the world anymore".[10]

2. The current capitalist crisis demonstrates more prominently that the capitalist mode of production is gradually losing its capability and space of self-adjustment and innovation.

Taking an overall look at the history of capitalism, capitalists have always made the capitalist system constantly change and update in order to escape crises one after another and seek new development and higher profits. As Marx has asserted: "The bourgeoisie cannot exist without constantly revolutionizing the instruments of production, and thereby the relations of production, and with them the whole relations of society".[11] All such rescue and adjustment methods include strategies such as the strategy of technical innovation, the strategy of geo-spatial expansion, the strategy of industrial

---

7 Marx and Engels, Selected works Vol. 5, People's Publishing House, 2009, p. 871.
8 Available on March 5 at http://www.marketwatch.com/story/grantham-wonders-if-marx-was-right-after-all-2012-02-29 .
9 Brzezinski: Strategic Vision: America and the Crisis of Global Power, Basic Books, 2013, p. 4.
10 Klaus Schwab: Das kapitalistische System passt nicht mehr in die Welt, Financial Times Deutschland, January 25, 2012.
11 Selected Works of Marx and Engels, Vol. 1, People's Publishing House, 1995, p. 275.

upgrading, etc. Capitalists also deserve to be called "excellent innovators", and each of their strategies has arguably reached the extreme in terms of driving capital and profits. Technical innovations lets capital always seize the most advanced sciences and innovations of mankind; geographic expansion lets capital fully control the pulse of globalization and spread to each corner of the world; industrial adjustments allow capital to always occupy industrial sectors where it most possibly gets excess profits in the fastest way. It is precisely because capital tends to reach the limit of the movement that capitalism is always made escape the crises one after another and develop rapidly, historically. However, it is also precisely such capital movement that causes comprehensive and fiercer crises occur and makes its methods to prevent crises get fewer and fewer. Each weapon to deal with crises turns against it. As Marx said half a century before, "Modern bourgeois society, with its relations of production, of exchange and of property, a society that has conjured up such gigantic means of production and of exchange, is like the sorcerer who is no longer able to control the powers of the nether world whom he has called up by his spells."[12] For example, the constant technical innovation leads to the constant rise of the organic composition of capital and the law decline of the profit margins became more significant, therefore capital is forced to run after profits like crazy through financialization, the virtual economy gets seriously divorced from the real economy and turns to the uncontrollable "powers of the nether world". Such "powers of the nether world" called up by the spell of "financial innovation" make it "seize the life powers", making capitalism hard to dominate and control. Along with the unconstrained expansion of capital in a global scale, its basic contradiction and various other contradictions are also intensified in an international scale and the developed countries' "transfer of crisis" to abroad is now resisted by global boykott. Thus, the contradictions then turn back home, so that the West encounters fierce resistances such as the "Occupy Wall Street". As can be seen, capitalism's capability and space of self-adjustment and innovation has become a serious issue.

3. The current capitalist crisis demonstrates more prominently that capitalism is losing development diversity.

Taking another overall look at the history of capitalism in the past centuries, it can be said that capitalism has been a unity of diversity, as much as other social forms. Different models of capitalism have emerged in different countries and regions at different historical periods, like the "Anglo-Saxon model" characterized by holding up free market in the U.K. and the U.S., the "Rhine model" characterized by social market economy in Germany and other countries of Continental Europe, and the "Swedish model" characterized by emphasizing capital-labor coordination and social security in

---

12 Selected Works of Marx and Engels, Vol. 1, People's Publishing House, 1995, p. 277.

Sweden and other Skandinavian countries. However, after more than 30 years of global expansion of international monopoly capitalism, neoliberalism has become rampant, and entire capitalism inclined to its primitive mode of accumulation and rule as a whole. Especially in this crisis a serious evil of capitalism has been exposed—its evolvement to a single development model. The neoliberal model was discredited, and besides a handful of extreme defenders, also other bourgeois supporters shunned it for being inferior. Even former French President Sarkozy and Fukuyama, the preacher of the theory of "the end of history" think that it is a must to change such capitalism taking freedom above all else. As for the other modes of capitalism, we can say that they have lost their unique foundation, unique philosophy and advantages due to their erosion and assimilation by neoliberalism in the past more than 30 years. For example, the social democratic model, which proposed the so-called "third way" innovation, gradually adapted to, accepted and moved closer to neoliberalism, and bet its development method and destiny on the neoliberal path. After neoliberalism has gone bankrupt in the crisis and the mainstream Western economics has lost its credibility, it is still hazy where capitalism will actually go and towards which direction it will adjust. It is an evil consequence of the prevailing single capitalist model and the gradual loss of the development diversity of capitalism, while loss of diversity means fade of vigor and vitality.

III. What is the destiny of capitalism?

When reflecting on capitalism, many people, including the left-wing figures against capitalism and the right-wing figures supporting capitalism, have made judgments and prediction over the future destiny of capitalism. Here are some representative viewpoints.

Left-wing figures: Immanuel Wallerstein, the founder of the famous world-system theory, argues that the development of capitalism has reached its limits and the impetus for further expansion has exhausted. He predicts that the capitalist world system will live for another 40 to 50 years before seeing a split and having two possible development directions: a world system featuring more stringent hierarchy and oppression; or a world system more inclined to equality and justice. He expressed that he prefers the latter.

Moderate right-wing figures: US senior journalist Michael Schuman thinks that capitalism after the "great recession" will get a makeover. From Los Angeles to London, and then to Athens, the outbreak of public discontent is absolutely unneglectable. However, no matter how loud the call for change is, capitalism will not die away. The challenge we face now is how to reform capitalism, the result of which will determine the fate of capitalism in the following 20 to 30 years.

Of course, some of these figures have a stronger sense of urgency. David M. Rubenstein, co-founder and co-CEO of the Carlyle Group, warned that "we have another 3 to 4 years to reform our economic model, otherwise our system will come to an end."

Conservative right-wing figures: Alan Greenspan, former chairman of the Federal Reserve, published an article entitled "Meddle with the market at your peril", thinking that whatever the flaws exist in the free-market capitalism, among the systems being tried as a substitute for it—ranging from Fabian socialism to the Soviet model of communism—there is no system that can successfully meet the demands of the people of the country. Now capitalism needs to be adjusted, but it should not "reform" its model at will.

Lawrence Summers, Harvard University professor, wrote a paper to deny that capitalism must be reformed. He said that, once the macroeconomic policy adjustment is done, today's worries will vanish into thin air. The part that needs to be reformed the most in contemporary economy is not the part with the thickest color of capitalism, but the lightest one.

This crisis makes capitalism as an entire social system subject to a worldwide and massive doubt or resistance for the first time after WWII. The "Occupy Wall Street" movement is the first large-scale mass movement in the past more than half a century to make capitalism the main target of mass criticism. This makes the various contradictions of capitalism tend to sharpen and makes the inherent evils of capitalism, especially the most deep-rooted ones come to light. Therefore, the parasitic, decaying and moribund features of capitalism, as revealed by Lenin 100 years ago, strongly manifest once again in the current era of global capitalism.

Here we need to highlight how to scientifically understand the parasitic, decaying and moribund features of capitalism. It firstly requires us to have a historical vision, a world scale and dialectical thinking. That capitalism is parasitic and decaying can't be simply understood as it can't develop at all but, just as how imperialism was understood by Lenin 100 years ago, as the co-existence of the trend of stagnation and that of rapid development. Applying a world scale to measure its degree of decay is not judging a dying patient in everyday life, that is if he dies today or will die tomorrow, either. It should be correctly understood as: Capitalism is gradually losing its historical rationality and the vitality of life. Its historical limitation and temporariness as that of a social formation are more than often presented in concentration by the historical phenomenon of overall crises. Its perfectness and eternality preached by its supporters are shattered in the tests of history one after another.

Regarding the world socialist movement, the crisis creates a new situation and new conditions beneficial for socialist development, but the crisis does not necessarily bring the revival of socialism. It is just like the crisis of capitalism in the 1970s, after which not the development of world socialism came closer, but, on the contrary, the decline of the world socialist movement, while capitalism did its best to break out and adjust after that crisis, and created its global expansion in the following 30 years. The dialectics of history is such: the two trends—capitalist crisis and development—co-exist; in the history, the forfeiture of historical rationality and the still very strong capability of self-adjustment and restoration also coexist. Which period, which trend and which forces predominate, depends on the combined effect of various conditions. But, the law of history that socialism will ultimately replace capitalism cannot change. We hope that socialism will have new achievements and development after the crisis and that socialism will seize the initiative and advantages in the new round of historical competition with capitalism. Hegel said, the owl of Minerva does not fly to the blue sky when the sun is rising, but takes its flight only when the shades of night are gathering. Hopefully, socialism will spread its wings to rise toward the sky of history, more powerfully and confidently, after a new baptism and vicissitudes of history.

Y. 8

On the Increasing Risk of Economic Turmoil: U.S. and Europe's Transfer of Losses of Economic Crises, Domestic and External Transfer

Yang Bin[1]

Abstract: In 2012, the economies of the 17 countries in the Euro zone are expected to shrink by 0.3%, and Greece and Spain will see a deep recession. However, the stock markets in the European countries in the Spring of 2012 also saw a significant rebound similar to that of the U.S., which on the one hand reflects that the stock market is no longer the barometer of the national economy, that the stock market is more and more detached from the real economic operation; on the other hand reflects that the international financial capital has formed a new-type of high-degree monopoly pattern, which can manipulate the global stock market by setting traps for carrying out a unified arrangement, casting a net of hunting using the close interaction among the stock markets of various countries formed by the globalization of stock markets. The U.S. also provokes the Philippines and other countries in the region to create tensions in the South China Sea, and launches political, economic, diplomatic and public opinion offensives against the state-owned countries of China, resorts to special means to curb the rise of China and to transfer the economic crisis. In the face of the above, China must make a proper plan to deal with the possibility that the U.S. may create an emergency.

Key words: U.S. and EU economies, stock market, transfer of crisis, reform of the state-owned enterprises

---

1 Yang Bin, researcher of the Academy of Marxism attached to CASS.

I. Recognizing the misleading public opinion preached by the U.S. that the economy is recovering in an accelerated way

In March 2012, the Western media ballyhooed the good news of the rebound of the U.S. and European stock markets, even of the soar of the Greek stock market which had been stuck in a debt crisis, to make the public believe that the debt crisis in the U.S. and Europe has begun to ease, and that the U.S. and European economies had seen the return of spring after a cold winter. However, in early April 2012, the global economic rebound situation suddenly suffered a heavy blow, when Spain reported the news that a bond market and sovereign debt crisis has occurred, urging people to realize that the European debt crisis has not disappeared, but all the more proliferated. On April 23, the U.S. and the European stock markets commonly suffered a panicky selloff pressure and even the German stock market, which was always the most stable one, plunged by 3.4%. Spain also plunged into the vortex of a vicious economic circle like Greece: The more the government implemented austerity and reduced fiscal deficit, the more the shrinkage of social demand, causing economic recession; the more the decline of the government tax revenue, the more the expansion of fiscal deficit, the more international financial corporations have new pretexts to plunder wealth, that is, they would exert pressure on Spain through the IMF and the World Bank to force Spain to privatize its monopolistic industries and carry out further austerity.

In 2011, Spain's ratio of sovereign debt to its GDP accounted for 35.8%, which later soared to 79.8% in 2012 along with the domestic economic recession. According to the estimation of international experts, as Spain is implementing the second-round of fiscal austerity, the virtuous economic cycle could be accelerated and cause this ratio increase to 100%. Like Greece, Spain has experienced large-scale social protests. In early April 2012, Spanish workers started a 24-hour nationwide general strike to protest the surge in unemployment, the cuts in social security and government's austerity policy. Spanish police forces blocked the streets around the central plaza of Barcelona (where government office is located), while the protesters built barricades to back up the traffic arteries of Barcelona. The merry atmosphere caused by the U.S. and European stock markets data suddenly evaporated and was replaced by a thick haze. The continuous slump indicates the risk of an even greater turmoil. All the international investors know that the scale of the Spanish economy is more than 5 times as great as that of Greece, so an economic crisis in Spain would have even worse impacts and more serious consequences than those in Greece.

The rebound in the U.S. and European stock markets is by no means a sign of economic recovery, but an overblown illusion created by the international financial corporations in order to plunder the wealth of world people. Due to the slack transactions in the U.S. stock market speculations and public indifference, Wall Street financial corporations were forced to inject more financial resources in this wave of bubbles in the stock market. In March 2012, most media in the West widely publicized the new historical high hit by the U.S. stock market since the crisis, and the stock markets in Europe and Greece also rose sharply under the stimulation of loose monetary policy. Many people began to believe that there is really a rebound in the U.S. economy and stock market and that the global economy and stock market indeed show a trend of recovery. If the investors from various countries lack vigilance and blindly follow them, they could fall into the trap of bubbles.

In early 2012, the real economy in the U.S. and Europe did not improve. In spring, the U.S. construction market had a rebound, and some construction indexes presented an annulus growth over the recent several months, but continued the deterioration trend over the same period in the previous year. In February 2012, the sales of new houses in the U.S. dropped by 1.6%, being far away from the growth of 1.3% forecasted by the economists; housing prices dropped for the 5th consecutive month, and the S&P/Case-Shiller Home Price Index dropped to the lowest point in 12 years. In March the same year, the sales of new houses dropped by 7.1%; the falling speed was surprisingly accelerated; the sales of second-hand houses also declined by 2.6%; and there was a corresponding decline in the confidence index in the builders and the buyers. Housing construction is a pillar industry in the U.S. national economy. If it is yet to get rid of the sluggish state, it would be naïve to hope for overall economic recovery, indicating that the recovery of the real estate industry was falsely propagated by the US media using exaggerated annual growth indicators. The indexes in the other economic fields in the U.S. have also exposed hidden hazards. The Consumer Confidence Index (CCI) released by the US Chamber of Commerce dropped from 71.6 in February to 70.2 in March; the Dallas Fed Manufacturing Index was 17.8 in February, but dropped to 10.8 in March; the Richard Mander Manufacturing Index was 20 in February, but declined to 7 in March. The orders of durable goods in the manufacturing industry in the U.S. dropped by 4.2% in March—the biggest single-month decline since January 2009.

The manufacturing industry consumes the most energy in the U.S. national economy, but since the outbreak of the financial crisis in the U.S. in 2008, total energy consumption has been sliding down, and has not yet recovered to the level before the outbreak of this financial crisis. Therefore, besides replenishing inventory consumption and experiencing short-term growth during seasonal adjustments, it is impossible for the U.S. manufacturing industry to promote overall economic recovery or ameliorate employment. In 2007, the U.S. experienced the "bottleneck" of being incapable of extracting or processing energy, which was blamed by the U.S. media to be an important factor for the soaring prices of natural gas that year. However, in 2010, that is, more than a year after the U.S. officially declared that its economy had begun recovery, energy extraction and processing in the U.S. saw severe overcapacity, and the U.S. had to reduce production to adapt to the decline in demand for energy by the U.S. national economy. Till 2012, according to the reports of Wall Street Journal, the U.S. found itself still unable to meet the sharp decline in domestic demand for energy, even after its energy extraction and processing enterprises reduced their capacity, so they had to turn to the international market to expand energy exportation, changing the U.S. from a net energy importing country into a net energy exporting country. As can be seen, the so-called statement that the growth of the U.S. manufacturing industry has advanced economic recovery is false. There is another statement that the U.S. manufacturing industry has become informationalized and energy-saving, but according to the statistics released by the U.S. Commerce Department, the orders for the information industry from the manufacturing industry also saw a significant decline, and reduced from 28 billion US dollars in 2008 to 24 billion US dollars in 2011. It reflects that the overall decline of the manufacturing industry has even affected the information industry.

There is another saying in the U.S.—that it was the service industry instead of the manufacturing industry that pushed forward economic recovery. Ironically, just when the U.S. government declared that the U.S. economy and employment situation had been improved in spring 2012, big retail chains in the U.S. staged massive lay-offs. A big electronic product retail chain enterprise in the U.S. declared that, due to market downturn, it had suffered a loss of 1.7 billion US dollars in a single quarter, so it would have to close 50 shopping centers nationwide; another large-scale chain department store in Seattle also declared that it suffered a loss of 2.4 billion US dollars, and would close more than 1,200 chain stores and lay off employees by 10,000 to 20,000 across the U.S. The latest statistics in the U.S. also show that the vacancy rate of shopping centers has made a historical record. The above facts show that, like the manufacturing industry, the U.S. service industry has been on the decline instead of recovering since the crisis broke out; the industry has not got rid of the plight of loss or cutbacks in personnel, let alone pushing forward economic recovery. The statistics of the U.S. Department of Labor show, although the working age population in the U.S. has been growing, more and more US people are unwilling to participate in the labor market, dropping the labor market participation rate from 66% in 2008 to 64% in 2012. Besides, in the officially announced period of economic rebound, the falling speed was even greater than that during economic recession, indicating that more and more people have to leave the labor market because they could not find a job, and that the employment situation in the U.S. has been deteriorated instead of ameliorated.

II. The gap in the trap laid by Goldman Sachs seen from the abnormal peak of the European and Greek stock markets

The economic recovery claimed by the U.S. government and the media covers the deterioration of the U.S. economic situation, but the official statistics of the European countries can't hide the accelerated deterioration of the economic situation. As early as in the fourth quarter of 2011, economies of the European countries have begun to be stuck in economic recession, in which the British economy shrank by 0.3%, and the French economy 0.2%. According to the prediction of Eurostat, the economies of the 17 countries in the Euro-zone are expected to shrink by 0.3%, and both Greece and Spain will see profound economic recession in 2012. However, why did the stock markets in the European countries also see a significant rebound like that of the U.S. in the spring of 2012? On the one hand, it reflects that shareholders are no longer barometer of the national economy, that the stock market is more and more out of touch with real economic operations; while on the other, it reflects the new-type high-degree monopoly of the international financial capital, which can manipulate the global stock market, set overall traps, and cast a hunting net with the closely associated stock markets of different countries thanks to globalization. The capacity and appetite of the international financial capital for coveting after and devouring the wealth of global shareholders has been expanded as never before. Although the U.S. and Europe are in fact stuck in severe economic sluggishness, the international financial monopoly capital, for being unable to profit from normal economic growth, is eager to trigger a financial war to plunder great wealth and have the crises transferred. Ignoring the contradictions between stock market manipulation and the operation of the real economy, the international financial monopoly capital pushes all economies, sluggish or vibrant, into the trap of the stock market bubble.

In 2011, the Greek economy saw a deep recession of 6.5%. In the spring of 2012, the Greek economic situation kept deteriorating, and the overall economic and fiscal situation in Greece slumped drastically, and all big cities in Greece witnessed continuous protests and riots. In this situation, general investors were far too shy to rashly push up the stock market; general international financial corporations dared not to take risks, either, in the face of the dangers of the Greek economy. Behind the hype could only be the huge international financial monopoly corporations, which grasp adequate profit from it. They must have huge financial resources and influence to coerce the financial capital in various countries to cooperate; they must predict accurately and be capable of manipulating the specific times of the burst of the stock market bubbles. When no one dared to hype the Greek stock market when the Greek society was amidst social riots rashly, it was Goldman Sachs, which is called "world dominator" and "winner take all", a huge international financial monopoly corporation having the capacity to manipulate the global stock market to revert the hype. In 2007 when the global price of oil skyrocketed to 200 US dollars/barrel, it was Goldman Sachs which dared to sign contracts with Chinese enterprises, to drop the oil price to 60 US dollars/barrel in order to attain sudden and huge profits from. It is precisely because Goldman Sachs knew in advance and manipulated the accurate time of the outbreak of the financial crisis, that it dared to publicly advocate U.S. economic recovery in the public opinion, while secretly selling short in the global subprime derivative bonds market, in the global stock market and in the global oil market, thus reaped huge profits from the heavy loss of the global investors caused by the financial crisis. If one is aware and vigilant to guard against wealth plunder occurring in the new-type of financial wars, he can see the cat or the gap in the trap laid by Goldman Sachs in the abnormal boom of the Greek stock market.

Goldman Sachs dared to blow bigger the stock market bubble when Europe and Greece were stuck in economic recession, because it has an especially high degree of monopoly power, which other international financial magnates do not have. By placing agents in proper positions and buying off senior government officials, it directly controls important political figures in the European countries. Mario Draghi, now President of the European Central Bank, used to be Goldman Sachs' president in Europe. Greek Premier Lucas Papademos and national debts director Pedro have close ties with Goldman Sachs—they were the instigators assisting Goldman Sachs in luring Greece into the trap of debts, and they were the ones who developed macro fiscal and financial policies collaborating closely with Goldman Sachs in the latter's financial war and helped the latter to plunder wealth. At the end of 2011 and in the spring of 2012, inspired by Goldman Sachs, the central banks of the U.S. and European countries pumped money into their respective private banks. Although the FED did not publicly introduce quantitative easing policy, it was forced by the U.S. Congress to reveal the documents of some transactions, and the scandalous event of secrete injection of funds (total 16 trillion US dollars) was revealed, thus it was seen that the US government had secretly attempted to save the markets. Today, in the face of the "Occupy Wall Street" movement and due to intensified social contradictions, the U.S. government feels the urgency to pacify its people, pretend that everything is going well, and help Obama in his presidential campaign. Without any doubt, it will continue its usual bailout policy under which it secretly injects money into the Wall Street. To save Greece and the other countries heavily suffering from debts crisis, the European Central Bank has been injecting trillions of Euros to private banks through various available European financial stability mechanisms. However, such money instead of being injected into the real economy, was used for financial speculations, and the loans from private banks to small and medium-sized enterprises have diminished instead of growing, which is exactly the true reason why Europe and Greece are stuck in economic recession, whereas their stock markets upsurge.

The negative effects of the heavy capital injection into private banks by the central banks in the U.S. and Europe have appeared. According to the economic data released by the UN Food and Agriculture Organization, as of March 2012, the global food prices had been growing for three months in a roll, pushing the world countries into a more severe socioeconomic situation since 2011. The rise in the global food prices in early 2011 triggered the political unrest in the Middle East, when many countries including those in Europe still maintained a growing momentum. However, in 2012, many European countries and Japan have stuck in economic recession where growing commodity prices, rising unemployment and wage stagnation more easily caused social turmoil. Fueled inflation may probably force the U.S. and Europe to slow down reckless issuance of currency, about which the international investors feel panic. They worry that it would burst the stock market bubble. Now even a slight change in the words of the US and European government officials would cause intense turbulence in the global stock market. Over the years, the quantitative easing policy, under which currency is issued recklessly, has failed to save the U.S. and European countries from the crisis, and will lead to even severe economic recession or inflation if it is to be continued. In order to protect its own national interests, the interests of the people of other countries, as well as the security of its foreign exchange reserves, China shall stick to the Marxist crisis theory and the theory that finance serves the real economy; be bold enough to point out the harms of the economic policies—like reckless issuance of currency, stimulation of speculations and ignorance of the real economy—that are adopted by the U.S. and Europe; join hands with people in other countries to exert pressure together to force the U.S. and European governments to correct such mistake.

III. Being alert to U.S.'s resorting to special measures for transferring the economic crisis

1. Revealing the main intention of the U.S. to create regional tensions and attempt to transfer the economic crisis; and principles for properly handling the dispute over South China Sea

At present, the U.S. is facing a critical situation where an even bigger financial crisis may break out, so it feels urgent to loot great wealth to transfuse blood to the financial bubble, which is to burst. It is strengthening control over the global natural resources and natural monopolistic industries through various means so as to get super profits even when the global economy is stuck in a crisis. In order to grab and control the natural resources around the globe, the international financial monopoly capital would first resort to provoking international and tribe conflicts and domestic wars in general, and then propose harsh conditions to both sides therein to force them to remise resources for weapons. If it fails to buy off the government of some country or stir a domestic war or conflict, it would plan brutal assassination, military coup or agitate the neighboring countries to invade such country. If it fails in all these attempts, the U.S. may do it on itself, claim that some country has weapons of mass destruction or it backs up terrorism, thus threatens the U.S. national security and then invade and occupy such country with its own troops or mercenary troops of private corporate organizations, or even by mustering the military strengths of its NATO allies. Since rich mineral deposits, including special metals needed to develop high technologies, were found in North Africa, this region has been involved in endless tribe conflicts, domestic wars and invasions. Over the past decades, at least 5 million people lost their lives in wars and conflicts.

Seen from the disgusting conducts of the U.S. of provoking international conflicts in order to plunder natural resources, we can see why it instigates Philippine and some other countries to stir up a dispute with China over South China Sea. With all kinds of bait, the U.S. lures Philippine and some other countries to disturb the stability over the past years in South China Sea. It may even plot unexpected events like cocking off accidentally during gun cleaning to intensify the tension in South China Sea, to which China has to be fully alert and develop proper plans to deal with unexpected events. Considering that the countries surrounding South China See all seek long-term interests of stability and development, and that only the U.S. attempts to create regional tension and transfer crises, China should not fall into the trap set by the U.S. or let the U.S. succeed in its strategic attempt; but should make relevant countries' idea of gaining from conflict-building which benefits the U.S. fail and let them understand that it's far more beneficial to cooperate with China to jointly promote regional stability and development than getting benefits from the U.S.

2. Correctly handling the offensives of the U.S. monopolistic financial corporations against the Chinese state-owned enterprises

Compared with the declining trend of transnational enterprises and banks since the outbreak of the crises in the U.S. and Europe, the state-owned enterprises and banks of China better adapt to the shocks of the crises and present a vigorous development momentum. Fifty-nine of the world's top 500 enterprises released by U.S. magazine Fortune in 2011 were Chinese state-owned enterprises, of which China Petroleum and Chemical Corporation (Sinopec), China National Petroleum Corporation (CNPC) and State Grid Corporation of China (State Grid) were among the top ten. Of particular concern is the fact that more than ten of the Chinese state-owned enterprises among the top 500 enterprises in the world were newly added, showing a strong growth momentum. Central enterprises, the core of the state-owned enterprises, displayed greater market vitality and competitiveness, and saw their total assets, revenues and taxes paid doubled within five years; the annual maintenance and appreciation rate of state-owned assets reached 115%. It is exactly for that reason that the U.S. international enterprises, banks, the U.S. government and Chamber of Commerce have seen Chinese state-owned enterprises as "thorns". As early as in May 2011, that is, on the eve of the Sino-U.S. strategic talks, leader of the U.S. Chamber of Commerce announced that it was "dangerous" to focus on the exchange rate of RMB, and that the Chinese state-owned enterprises were the "biggest threat" to the U.S. Chairman of the U.S. Chamber of Commerce Ted Dean claims that many state-owned enterprises in China have been big enough to support their overseas expansion; they get programs in China, even compete with the US companies and companies from other countries for programs in overseas business. In particular, in a series of fields like electric cars, clean energy and express railways, China has developed a series of industrial policies to support local enterprises, which exert great market competition pressure on the U.S. international enterprises.

Against such international background, the U.S. monopolistic financial corporations launch political, economic, diplomatic and public opinion offensives against the state-owned enterprises of China to exert pressures on the Chinese government, media publicity, etc. Senior U.S. government officials accuse China of violating "competition neutralism" because the latter supports its state-owned enterprises. But why not read the critiques, by all walks of life in the U.S., of the U.S. government for its support to Wall Street oligarchs in the "Occupy Wall Street" movement? Since the outbreak of the financial crisis in 2008, the U.S. government and Fed have invested huge amounts of money in saving the US's financial oligarchs, which are accused as culprits of the financial crisis. Senior U.S. government officials do not have the right or title to criticize the Chinese government for the latter's policy of supporting the real economy, but not financial speculations, but shall first correct their mistake of "playing preference in competitions," which is much criticized by the public, and stop the policy of reckless issuance of currency, which may trigger global inflation and threaten the foreign exchange reserves of China. The ratio of the taxes paid by state-owned enterprises to their sales revenues in China is 5 to 10 times as high as that in foreign-invested and private enterprises, which enables China to give super national treatment of tax preference to international companies. The U.S. does not mention its own policy of inject huge amounts of money to support speculations in Wall Street, or thank the Chinese government for giving special tax preference to its international companies, but blames the Chinese government for carrying out economic policies beneficial to the interests of the whole society. That's a biased behavior of ignoring the competitiveness of the Chinese state-owned enterprises by taking a non-market approach.

When making the policy suggestion to China, the U.S. claimed that China would invite crises if it did not follow the U.S. reform plan. China has to soberly realize that the U.S. is exactly the one who wants China to be stuck in crises, because that would remove China's to the U.S. global hegemony as a rising economy and eliminate the "biggest threat," of the Chinese state-owned enterprises, against the market monopoly of the U.S. international enterprises. China should always firmly bear in mind to follow its own path; be self-confident, firm and sober and avoid self-inflicted setbacks. It must also be highly alert against unexpected events plotted by the U.S. to tarnish the reputation of the Chinese state-owned enterprises so as to create pressure with public opinions and cooperate to collapse the competitive threat of the Chinese state-owned enterprises. When the secret strategy was implemented under the Reagan administration in order to dissolute the Soviet Union, U.S. president Reagan, in order to curb energy exportation which was of crucial significance to the earning of foreign exchange by the Soviet Union, used counterplot to purposefully deliver to the Soviet Union false technical information on oil exploitation, triggering industrial explosions which were second to nuclear explosions and causing huge damages. China shall stay alert to similar unexpected events and public opinion offensives the U.S. may concoct with similar means to defame the Chinese state-owned enterprises. In March 2004, At the Abyss: An Insider's History of the Cold War was published in the U.S. Its writer Thomas Reed, former Secretary of the U.S. Air Force and a member of the U.S. National Security Council, revealed in the book that, during the Reagan administration, CIA under the leadership of William Casey launched a "brutal and ruthless economic war" against the Soviet Union, including manipulating a big explosion of a natural gas pipe in Siberia. It is surprising that the plot which was normally seen in thrilling spy movies really had happened in the "soft warfare" hatched by the U.S. Using the economic difficulty caused by the reduction of the Soviet Union's foreign exchange reserves, the U.S. sapped the confidence of the leaders of the Soviet Union, exerted pressure on the Soviet Union to make it scruple at the opposition of the West and not dare to say no to separation or defend its unity, which led the Soviet Union into disintegration and national humiliation.

3. The state-owned enterprises should be courageous enough to fulfill their social responsibilities and work hard to cope with the pressure of growing costs instead of speculating in the trend of price increase in the international market to seek super profits and to shift the burden of the growing international prices to the vast consumers and down-stream enterprises.

Only by mastering hard skills, well coping with the growing costs and improving efficiency can the long-term development of enterprises be better facilitated, or it would trigger political turmoil and cause greater losses to the whole society and relevant enterprises. China shall resolutely detach its domestic pricing mechanism from the speculations in the international market; encourage its state-owned enterprises engaged in foreign trade to detour the commodity futures market manipulated by Western financial capital, and to directly discuss about long-term trade with the producers and consumers in the real economic fields. Minimizing the obstruction of speculations is conducive to a better price reflection of real value; helps lighten the consumers' burden, and allows the enterprises to make plans on long-term production and investment. The economic circles have to soberly realize that the international market is heavily manipulated by the financial venture capital, that integrating into it is not conducive to effective distribution of resources and normal operation of the real economy. China shall build a mechanism for commodity price stability and reserves of strategic materials; buy low and sell high, which is opposite to international speculations, to stabilize prices and prevent volatile market prices from damaging the interests of the enterprises and the consumers. Egypt and Tunisia canceled government's price subsidies and got integrated into the world market, which allowed smooth delivery, into Egypt and Tunisia, of the ups and downs of the prices of agricultural products and energy speculated on by the international financial capital, greatly shocking the life of their people and creating conditions for the U.S. to export inflation and political turmoil and manipulate "color revolutions".

4. China's attempt to encourage state-owned enterprises to share out bonuses (to return equity investors) is a correct reform that conforms to the Marxist theory of socialized property rights.

With this reform, state-owned enterprises should get rid of the narrow thinking of conducting enterprise reforms according to Western enterprise system, give full play to their function of social responsibility and employ the spirit of serving the people wholeheartedly, utilize their human resources, material and financial resources they possess to actively solve various socioeconomic problems which cause social discontent among the people, including providing good and reliable products for the vast people at low costs, eliminating the wide-spread concerns caused by frequent vicious incidents like fake food, vigorously build low-cost, fairly qualified affordable housing in a planned way and to fully satisfy the demand of the medium- and low-income families which account for 80% of all (according to latest population data), support public welfare undertakings like poverty alleviation, education, employee training, medical care, and S&T researches; establish new-type public-owned enterprises which can offer a larger number of stable job opportunities and ideological education in those areas harassed by frequent mass events and rampant separatist activities, thus eliminate the soil for social unrest, national secession and Western interference. With the effect these policies, the overwhelming majority of the Chinese people will, like the Venezuelan people, stand out to protect the security of the Chinese state-owned enterprises and the country at critical moments without being influenced by the anti-state-owned enterprises opinions designed by the United States.

Y. 9

The Domination of Financial Monopoly Capital and the Formation of the Global Rentier Empire

Chen Renjiang[1]

Abstract: The parasitism and speculation are the essential attributes of financial capital. Its social domination is based on the money capital monopoly, and its domination and control over the social as well as the economic spheres have eventually led to the generation of monopoly-finance capital. Monopoly-finance capital during its accumulation and expansion process, has increasingly detached from the industrial capital on one hand, while it is increasingly dependent on the non-industrial fields on the other. These two trends of monopoly-finance capital have become obvious since the mid and late 20th century, which has aggravated its parasitism and decay. The control and possession of other countries' industries and resources plus the plunder of values and wealth of the rest of the world by the monopoly-finance capital, being enforced globally have formed the "global empire".

Key words: financial monopoly capital, financial speculation, parasitism, imperialism

---

[1] Chen Renjiang, visiting researcher of the CASS World Socialism Research Center and assistant researcher of the CASS Academy of Marxism

I. Parasitism and speculation are the essential attributes of financial capital

Money capital holds a dominant position in the current capitalist society. It is not only the direct and real form of value and surplus value, the measure of capitalist social wealth, but can generate new values. The circuit of commodity production starts with the purchase of the means of production and labor force by the capitalists, and ends with the realization of the exchange value in money form, and this exchange value is proliferated. The emergence of loan capital has changed such value proliferation logic of production. With the money ownership, money owner gets the remuneration (interests) by transferring his use right, and obtains the right to carve up surplus value, which fully demonstrates the pure capital logic of "making money with money."

In the form of interest-bearing capital, every definite and regular (universal) money revenues seen as interest on some capital, regardless of whether the income is indeed generated from such capital or not.

Marx believed that the monetary capital circuit of "making money with money" "...expresses most graphically the compelling motive of capitalist production—money-making. The process of production appears merely as an unavoidable intermediate link, as a necessary evil for the same of money-making. All nations with a capitalist mode of production are therefore seized periodically by a feverish attempt to make money without the intervention of process of production."[2]

Once capital is invested in production, it is tied and fixed to such forms as the machinery, plants and labor force, and can't be reclaimed freely or cashed immediately; capital in the form of money is extremely flexible and discretionary, and can be cashed more quickly. However, it is a must that money capital changes into virtual capital—a certificate of profits or capital ownership—in order to enable capital to keep the form of money capital for its owner so that capital owner can recall its capital as monetary capital at any time by selling owner's claim to profits. To constantly convert monetary capital into virtual capital, the latter has to be constantly converted into monetary capital, and differential profits must be realized by trading virtual capital so as to constantly stimulate transactions. In other words, being speculative is the natural attribute of virtual capital transactions. By now, we have demonstrated the dominant logic of parasitism and speculative natures of money capital proliferation via virtual capital transactions.

Production and exchange in the capitalist society are essentially unstable. The greater the economic scale, the more dependent the economic subjects on credit relations. In the modern capitalist society, monetary

---
2 Marx: Capital, Vol.2, People's Publishing House, 2004, p.68.

capital is mainly held by banks and financial institutions such as the stock exchange-centered capital market, funds and trust companies, which, as agents of social capital, collect, manage and distribute capital, and get interests, commissions and other capital gain by providing credence, managing and operating monetary capital. With the development of credence, it has become more and more popular that capital ownership gets separated from capital functions. With credence, people do not use their own money, but others' money to make industrial investment and engage in financial speculation. On the one hand, financial speculation emerges, because joint social capital is occupied through capital ownership certificate, which in itself represents the virtualization of monetary capital. Then, through gambling transactions (that is, transfers of the certificate ownership) on the secondary market, the same property would be much virtualized. Stimulated by credence expansion, virtual capital, namely financial derivatives, would be mass-produced along the same path so as to expand speculation dividends. That's exactly what's happening in today's financial market.

On the other hand, based on production concentration, industrial organizations see a new change in form—the joint-stock system appears, indicating the emergence of a new ownership structure. Under the joint-stock system, capital owners do not participate in corporate production, but ask for the corresponding part of the surplus value realized with such capital with capital ownership certificates (stocks, bonds, etc.) Concrete corporate operation and management are done by their agents (managers of enterprises). The control power and interest distribution power of capitalists (shareholders), who are beyond enterprise production and operation, can be realized through banks and other financial institutions, which then connect capital owners with financial institutions.[3] The powers of both are demonstrated as partition and extortion of profits (in such forms as interests, dividends and rents) deviating from simple ownership of currency capital, and exercise the power as big capital, that is, "finance power" through the process of capitalization. Capital used to realize such power is finance capital.[4]

Although financial capital gets its profits fundamentally from the surplus value brought about by industrial capital, it does not mean that the accumulation of financial capital and that of industrial capital are a completely overlapping process. Financial capital is accumulated in two ways: by directly combining with industrial capital, where it occupies part of the

---

3 Gérard Duménil and Dominique Lévy: Second Phase of Financial Hegemony: Neoliberalism, Foreign Theoretical Trends, Issue 10, 2005.
4 The concept of finance capital employed here is partially from the interpretation of "financial capital" by Gérard Duménil and Dominique Lévy, but also different from the "finance capital" and "financial industrial capital" as defined by them, I believe that finance capital should also involve financial industrial capital, or it would be impossible to comprehensively grasp the increasing economic speculation and gambling since the early 1980s.

surplus value created in the production process in such forms as dividends and bonuses through the agency movement of commodity production cycle, and plays the role in promoting industrial investment; and by bearing interests purely, without getting combined with industrial capital, where it detours the production process, and invests in virtual capital, which is irrelevant to the requirements industrial investments, and is completely speculative. Under such circumstances, proliferation is realized not because of the surplus value in the production sector, but because of the fictive expansion of value. Meanwhile, beneath the fluctuation in virtual capital prices, big capitalists exploit small capitalists, speculative lucky dogs exploit the unlucky ones, and social wealth is not increased at all, but only transferred.

In the early 1970s, developed capitalist countries witnessed a general decline in profit margins, a slow down of industrial capital accumulation and production stagnation. Therefore, a lot of capital surplus, due to the lack of profitable investment spheres, left the industrial sector and flooded into the financial sector. Therefore, since the 1970s, financial capital has accumulated in the latter form, that is, self-cycle of virtual capital which is completely divorced from industry, indicating that financial capital has become more speculative.

II. Financial monopoly capital and the growth of rentier economy

The credit system and the joint-stock system accelerate the centralization of monetary capital into the hands of a handful of people. A small group of private owners can dominate enterprise wealth and social wealth with a block of shares, causing big capital to elbow small and medium-sized capital and leading to the expansion and monopolization of financial capital. On the contrary, the monopoly of financial capital further expands and accelerates the accumulation of financial capital. In order to control the capitalist social wealth in its direct form (money), financial capitalists can always intervene in all socioeconomic sectors—aim to control banks, purchase factories and enterprises, participate in infrastructure investment, gobbling up businesses, speculate on state debts, seizing lands and natural resources, and control the distribution of consumers goods. Monetary capital is like a magic wand, which enables financial capitalists to seize highly profitable sectors one after another in a more flexible, freer and effective way, and enables them to freely withdraw from those sectors having a profit margin lower than the general. Through these processes, financial monopoly capital "seizes a large part of the actual accumulation"

Since the era of neo-liberalism, the overall economy of the developed countries in the West has begun to change into a speculative and rentier economic mode, greatly strengthening the power of financial monopoly.

1. The policy of "relaxing or eliminating financial controls" has greatly pushed the virtual capital in developed countries such as the U.S. to expand; financial institutions have invented numerous high risk financial derivatives to reap higher profits.

Financial derivatives have been far too many, the financial assets around the globe are in a pyramid structure, of which, 80% are financial derivatives; 10% are financial bonds, and the rest 10% are the supply of money[5] In the global circulation, financial derivatives constitute the overwhelming majority. In 2009, financial derivatives have contributed to 82% of the global circulation, that is, 1048% of the entire world's annual GDP! [6]Transactions of derivatives grew fast, too. From 2002 to 2008, transactions of derivatives have quadrupled, reaching more than 25 times greater than the U.S. GDP.[7]

2. Under the conditions of continuous depression of the real economy and excess liquidity of the financial system, household dept has become an important way of stimulating consumer demand and investment demand, and a way of expanding accumulation.

After the bubble burst in the U.S. stock market in 2000, real estate mortgage loans market became the core of the consumption in the debt-driven economy. Spurred by inexpensive loans, real estate consumption kept growing, so did the house prices, which also stimulated the speculation in the capital market. The wealth effect caused by the rise in the real estate prices supported debt financing. Debts became an important means adopted by financial institutions to plunder the profits of the enterprises and incomes of households. On the one hand, individuals, families and enterprises were allowed to mortgage anything to borrow from the banks or from other mortgage based lending companies. Once house prices fell, the borrowers had to continue to bear high-cost repayments, and were faced with the danger of foreclose. On the other hand, banks viewed mortgage loans as assets which can bring further interests, so they securitized their mortgage loans, and received commissions from issuing and selling mortgage-backed securities. Funds and investor agencies buying such securities benefited from asset price inflation. Therefore, since the 1970s, the U.S. gradually turned from the production-driven stock monopoly economy to debt securitization-based gambling arbitrage economy. By creating artificial asset price

---

5   Zhang Youwen et al.: The World Economy after the Financial Crisis: Major Themes and Development Trends, People's Publishing House, July 2011, p. 178.
6   Ibid, p. 68.
7   World Bank: Global Economic Prospects 2010, China Financial & Economic Publishing House, 2010, p. 42.

bubbles, banks have attracted more people to invest into the market, thus a growing part of individual income was converted into loan capital capable of bringing interests. Repeated collateral financing operations further led to accumulation of the debts. Meanwhile, virtual credit was extremely amplified. When banks started to lend to those people who were unable to repay, a landmine that would trigger crises was buried.

3. Pension funds, insurance companies, mutual funds and investment companies, among other institutional investors have gradually replaced the traditional banks and family relatives and become the most important financing and investing entities in the financial market.

Institutional investors raise monetary capital from depositors and private investors by borrowing money from the latter. In their hands, such monetary capital becomes a considerable and centralized amount of investment capital. To a large extent, a small number of institutional investors holding considerable amounts of investment capital are determining the direction of investments, and control the distribution of economic surplus before they become new financial monopoly capital groups. Statistics show that shares held by the US families account for 42% of the total, and those held by institutional investors account for 46% of the total.[8]

During 1987 and 2000, the average %age of shares held by institutional investors in the 1,000 US enterprises rose from 46.6% of all to 61.4% of the total. Till the end of 2007, such percentage had reached unprecedented 76.4%. In enterprises where institutional investors held the most shares, ownership was unprecedentedly centralized. In 1985, institutional investors held less than 60% of shares in all enterprises. Till 2007, their ownership had reached or exceeded 60% in 17 companies; in 6 companies, their ownership had even reached or exceeded 70%. It indicates that institutional investors have become monopolist owners of big US enterprises. In wealth distribution, institutional investors also hold a lion's share. According to statistics, from 1995 to 2005, the total assets of institutional investors have become more than double. In 2005, financial capital reached 46 trillion US dollars. As of the end of 2006, the total amount of assets held by all institutional investors, including pension funds, investment companies, insurance companies, banks and foundations, had reached 27.1 trillion US dollars, that is, 9 times greater than the total amount in 1980; and the ratio of market value of all the shares held by them to the total value of the US stock market grew from 37.2% in 1980 to 66.3% in 2006.[9]

---

8 James Crotty: Nonfinancial Corporations in the Neoliberal Era in Financialization of Capitalism and the International Financial Crisis edited by Liu Yuanqi, Economic Science Press, 2009, p. 99.
9 Data from Institutional Investment Report 2008 of the Conference Board.

Today, "the sum of the annual net income of any two of the world's major Private Equity dealer companies, like Blackstone Group, Texas Pacific Group or KKR, would exceed the total annual net income of majority of the US companies"[10]

Most institutional investors are not supervised by the government or not transparent. They are obsessed with making speculative risk investment with all investment capital being externally raised. For example, capital for pension funds comes from residents' deposits. Due to the lack of stable national social welfare, such investment is the only guarantee for the future life of low-income earners. However, financial monopoly capital groups make residents' income and deposits an important source of their pursuit of huge speculative profits.

Meanwhile, under the conditions of neo-liberalism, financial monopoly capital has strengthened erosion of the profits of industrial enterprises. More than a century ago, Marx profoundly revealed the essence of the activities ates Crédit Mobilier, a French company established in the era of Louis Bonaparte, pointing out that its aim was not to encourage or subsidize industries and business, like it publicly claimed, but to make use of business and commercial enterprises to speculate in stock issuance and pursuit for maximum profits. This example by Marx revealed the coming sign that financial oligarchs would force industrial enterprises to succumb to its wealth accumulation. Today, the idea that "industrial feudalism (stock companies—note by the author) is made into a contributor to agiotage" is the guiding principle of investment banking and securities companies. Take the U.S. for example, the fall in profit margins and the vicious competition caused by the high interest rate shock caused by the policies of Fed Chairman Paul Volcker in the 1980s forced industrial enterprises (including large-scale monopoly enterprises) to surrender to vicious M&As supported by garbage securities (which went to a climax in the mid 1980s). While debt-supported enterprise mergers and acquisitions have aggravated interest burden. Throughout the 1980s the actual interest rate was two or three times higher than that in the first 30 years after 1950. Till 2008, that is, after the outbreak of the financial crisis, interest rates fell to the lowest level since the 1950s. Accordingly, the interest burden of the industrial sector has been rising since the 1970s. The share of interest payment in after-tax profits have soared from 11% in 1966 to nearly 34% in 1970, and remained higher than 29% till around 2008. In 1980, 1990 and 2002, it even reached to the level of 45%. [11]

---

10 C.P. Chandrasekhar: The U.S. Subprime Crisis against the Background of the Contemporary Capitalist Economic Crisis in Financialization of Capitalism and the International Financial Crisis edited by Liu Yuanqi, Economic Science Press, 2009, p..51.
11 Data from Neoliberalism, the Rate of Profit and the Rate of Accumulation by Erdogan Bakir and Al Campbell, see figure 5 on the p. 333 and figure 7 on the p 335, Science and Society, Issue 3, 2010, published in USA

On the other hand, under the pressure of short-term capital gain pursuit, enterprises were forced to ignore the objective of long-term steady development, instead they started to aim "shareholders' interest supremacy" with high stock prices and high dividend returns. The dividend returns paid by non-financial enterprises to shareholders accounted for more than 60% of their distributable profits (after the deduction of interest expenses) in the 1970s, but today dividend returns are more than 80%. At about 2001 and 2008, the %age even increased to 100%![12] Hence, most of the economic surplus created by the industrial sector was seized by the financial sector; the cash flow of industrial enterprises shrank, which caused the rate of investment to continue to fall. Besides, target enterprises are not viewed as fixed and stable entities , but as entities which can be easily divided and re-arranged. For the institutional investors which invest in and acquire other enterprises or other financial group, the quality of the enterprise capital is important, the best case would be if it is more liquid and easier to be transacted. Soon after the acquisition they make plans to split and rearrange their assets, peel off their non-performing assets so as to drive up its stock prices.They also trigger asset price bubbles in order to get maximum profits by trading their assets.

Challenged by the decline in profits and affected by the continuous rise of financial earnings, industrial enterprises tend to the same thing—they withdrew their capital from production activities and invested more and more in the financial sector—thus they increasingly became inherently financialized. All these trends have transformed the whole economy to be more rentier-based and speculative, and enabled financial institutions to increasingly strengthen their control over the investments by the industrial enterprises and asset management companies.

From the following economical statistics in the US, we can see the increase of profits seized by financial capital. By the financial industry alone, the proportion to GDP of the added value created by the financial sector in its broad sense, —including banks, investment funds, insurance companies and real estate firms—has been growing since the 1960s. The proportion of such added value was 14.2% in 1960, increased up to 18% in 1986, that is, higher than that of the manufacturing industry, and to 21.5% till 2009. By contrast, the proportion of the financial industry profits[13] compared to the total profits of all industries saw an even more dramatic increase. In 1960, the profits of the financial industry accounted for 17.3%

12　Data from Neoliberalism, the Rate of Profit and the Rate of Accumulation by Erdogan Bakir and Al Campbell, see figure 5 on the p333 and figure 7 on the p. 335, Science and Society, Issue 3, 2010, published in USA
13　The financial industry here refers to the financial industry in the narrow sense, involving simply banking and insurance branches.

of the whole sectors. After a period of more than 20 years of fluctuation in a narrow range, it has increase to 20.8% till 1985. Throughout the 1990s, it fluctuated between 25 to 35%, thus transcended the highest level after the WWII. It has grown rapidly to 41.3% till 2001, even to 43.8% in 2003, the highest ever in its history. In a few years after that, influenced by the growing interest rates in the U.S., the proportion of the financial industry profits compared with the whole industries, fell to 26.6% in 2007, saw slight increases during 2008 and 2009. But its fall was basically lower than the fall we observe in the manufacturing industry.[14] When we take into consideration the current trend of financialization of industrial enterprises, the boundary between the industrial sector and the financial sector regarding their respective profits becomes hard to trace. But, it is an iron fact that the financial capital gets the lion's share of profits.

Evidence shows that financial capital plays a leading role in economy, and holds to its monopoly. Financial oligarchs holding financial property and plus the rentier class are plundering and controlling social wealth on an extremely big scale. Among the 1% richest men in the US, most are from the financial sector. "The upper 1% is now grabbing nearly a quarter of the nation's income every year. In terms of wealth rather than income, the top 1% controls the 40%. Their lot in life has improved considerably. Twenty-five years ago, the corresponding figures were 12% and 33%"[15] Another study shows that, during the 1980s and 90s, in most OECD member states, the ratio of the income of financial institutions to national income and that of the income of financial capital owners to national income both were greater than that during the 1970s.[16]

III. Rentier empire under the control of financial monopoly capital

Since the close of the 1970s, world economy has seen a major change, that is, the external expansion and plunder of financial monopoly capital has reached an unprecedented scale in both width and depth in the name of economic globalization. The US-centered financial monopoly capital has not only controlled domestic industrial and financial sectors, but strengthened the penetration and domination of the vast developing countries. The dissolution of the socialist camp caused by the disintegration of the Soviet Union and the drastic changes in Eastern Europe has put a large number of the former socialist countries under the control system of international capital.

---

14 The data above is from The Economic Report of the President 2010, see Table 91.
15 Stiglitz: Of the1%, by the 1%, for the 1%, available at http://wen.org.ai/modules/article/view.article.php/2545.
16 Gerald A. Epstein: Financialization and World Economy, Foreign Theoretical Trends, Issue 7, 2007.

The US-centered international control system of financial monopoly capital is based on two pillars—the global industry system and US's monopoly over the world monetary system. Through the global industrial restructuring since the 1980s, the existent international industry system has intensified the tendency of global monetary speculation. Developed countries have seen varying degrees of decline in the proportion of their manufacturing industry in their national industries; industrial sectors have been more active to participate in financial activities, and this trend is most significant in the U.S.

In sharp contrast, some Western countries maintain only the service industry, some hi-tech industries and military strategic industries domestically; and move capital and production abroad on a large scale with the intent to form low-end industries and change developing countries into the terminal platform for their manufacturing industry in the global industrial chain. This helps them to make full use of the inexpensive labor force and raw materials in the developing countries, and intensifies competitions of small and medium-sized capital groups in the developing countries, which reduces their profits but instead increase the profit shares of Western multinational capital groups in the manufacturing industry.

More than that, the export of inexpensive consumer goods manufactured by developing countries to developed countries like the U.S., also supports the consumption-on-debt economy in these countries. Eastern Asia and southeastern Asia have become major production bases providing consumer goods to rich financial nations and groups which never get involved in production. For example, China, the world's biggest manufacturing nation, sees over 60% of its GDP originating from foreign-invested enterprises. In China, foreign trade is led and composed by low-profit processing trade, of which more than 50% of the volume of trade exports is contributed by foreign-invested enterprises. Inexpensive and high-quality consumer goods made in China are mainly exported to the U.S. and Europe. Being made in China and consumed in the U.S. has been the major driving force for the entire world economy. On the other side, the U.S. and other rich financial nations, with their leading position in technical S&T and IP protection, charge high patent fees for the new technologies used by the developing countries. They not only get high rents margins by monopolizing technologies, but also restrain the industrial upgrading in developing countries, and continue to keep these countries' position as industrial "contributors". Domestic industries in developing countries become further hollowed, but surplus value increase sharply in these rich financial nations, and capital surplus becomes even more serious. All these factors push the rich financial nations to get further financialized, make their monopoly capital more parasitic and decayed.

Financial monopoly capital groups, dominating and sitting at top of the international industrial system, are greedier to suck profits and interests that are endlessly transfused to them both at home and abroad. The contradiction between industrial capitalism and financial capitalism at the global level then becomes the contradiction between the vast developing countries and a small number of US-centered rich financial countries at certain levels.

The U.S. monopoly of the world monetary system constitutes another big pillar of the global domination of financial monopoly capital. Since U.S. dollar was disconnected with gold in 1973, the gold standard system has been abolished from the world monetary system, and U.S. dollar is used as the currency for international circulation and settlement. That U.S. dollar becoming world currency means that the U.S. can purchase commodities, services and resources in other world regions illegally, gain big profits with a small amount of capital simply by printing US currency which is alone in itself worthless. That's the basis of the US dollar hegemony, and the basis for the domination of the U.S. financial monopoly groups, which monopolize currency issuance, to loot wealth from all over the world. The special status of US dollar as the world currency has not only deepened the exchange of unequal values between the US and other countries in the international labor division system, but also allowed the U.S. to transfer crises to the other countries through such labor division status.

For example, when the US economy is in its expansion period, in order to curb its inflation and avoid any sharp increase in its foreign deficits due to economic overheating and to intensify economic overheating in the countries exporting to US, the U.S. substantially reduces foreign trade deficits during economic recession and intensifies overproduction in the countries exporting to U.S.

Besides, as US dollar is the reserve currency held by the most countries in the world, the U.S. gets a lot of royalty earnings, and major countries with US dollar reserve (except Japan, mainly undeveloped countries like China, Russia, India and South Korea) buy considerable amounts of low-interest US Treasury bonds, securities, which injects US dollar back to U.S. again, mending its domestic financing gaps, and helping it to curb inflation. Such loop of US dollar has tied those countries holding US dollar reserves tightly to the war chariot of the US economy. These countries see that their dividends on investments being closely linked to maintaining the currency value of US dollar, and they therefore willingly become parasitic "capital contributors" of the U.S. indebted consumption mode of US dollar hegemony. More importantly, the U.S. is the biggest debtor nation in the world, but a major creditor country for many developing countries. Some countries having poor foreign exchange reserves and having to use US dollar in their foreign trade settlements (usually undeveloped countries at the stage of accelerated industrialization) have to borrow money from the U.S. which, opportunistically can exploit these countries with the latter's debts in US dollar, and then control their national economy. At the turn of the 1970s and 1980s, a debt crisis broke out in the developing countries, especially in Latin America , fundamentally because the U.S. commercial banks wantonly granted loans to Latin America and the East Asian countries, and made these countries unable to bear their debts in US dollar under the pressure of substantial increases in the interest rate in the U.S.

International financial institutions, especially the International Monetary Fund (IMF) and the World Bank, serve as forceful tools in the global expansion and domination of financial monopoly capital. The U.S. holds an absolute dominant position in these two organizations, making them the tools of the U.S. national interests and those of the U.S. financial interest groups to a large extent. IMF is always on the stage as an international creditor (mainly the creditor of the U.S.) which takes advantage of the original debt crises in the developing countries or the debt crises in these countries after financial storms. With the pretext of capital aid, IMF forces the debtor nations to accept its harsh lending requirements. Classical IMF prescription is to ask the debtor nations to apply deflation policy, cut the state budget expenses, and carry out industrial reforms (that is, selling state-owned assets of SOEs and carrying out privatization) so as to increase the government funds of the deptor, ensure their debt repayment, and further require the debtor nations to open their domestic market and financial market to foreign capital. Provided that the debtor nations accept to apply these measures, it will lead to a series of serious socioeconomic consequences and they may completely become vassals of international monopoly capital. The deflationist policy would not only deteriorate people's living conditions, lead to and intensify social injustice, but will also increase national debts. Thus governments are forced to privatization and open up their domestic market under external pressure, which gives the international monopoly capital a chance to invade them on a large scale—either acquiring and taking over the state-owned enterprises or public sector service industries of these countries. Thus gain a monopolistic position and monopolistic rights regarding these industries before breaking down the national capital of these countries; or they purchase local banks, manipulate the exchange rates and the local stock market indexes, get control of their financial systems, which all leads to one well known consequence: the economic lifeline of these countries being under total control of the international financial monopoly groups. Utilizing the wave of privatization in the debtor countries or developing countries since the 1990s, the US based international investors (transnational enterprises) have local public resources such as land, ores, water and electricity, the transportation system, and state-owned enterprises of the Third World at extremely low prices. However, they felt no interest to expanding the production of these enterprises to gain profits from their actual operations, but instead they have triggered financial bubbles through a series of speculative operations such as pushing up the prices of corporate stocks or assets (especially related to real estate and natural resources); or collecting monopoly rent and profits, which was more than often preconditioned with certain requirements such as layoff of employees, diminish department sizes and rearrange assets. Such investment and privatization strategy closely combined with financial speculation, naturally hinders the development of the local industries, creates lesser job opportunities, or host country cannot benefit form the achievements of economic globalization. Moreover, such investment and privatization strategy causes the industries of the host country to shrink and be by the international financial monopoly capital groups.

Controlling and monopolizing the world's energy sources and other bulk commodities like oil, natural gas and grains also constitute important fields utilized by the financial monopoly capital to dominate the world. Financial monopoly capital grabs the pricing right of the bulk commodities around the globe and makes high monopoly profits, which means that it controls the lifeline of the world economy. In order to achieve this objective, it is very necessary to control the regions where these sources (energy sources or bulk commodities), even by resorting to such extreme means of war. After the end of the Cold War, utilizing the perishing of the biggest direct rival, the Soviet Union and pushed by the logic of securing economic control, the U.S. still maintains militarist policies and even intensifies them and wantonly engages in military aggression in order to hold the monopoly of the right to allocate world's scarce resources with its geopolitical superiority.

It indicates that imperialism, although it assumed several new forms in its development and encountered various changes since the end of the 19th century, its essence remains as the pursuit of capital accumulation . After WWII, almost all other former imperialist countries were subordinated to the uni-polar military hegemony of the U.S., and US-imperialism had gained unprecedented strength. Today, against the background of globalization, financial monopoly capital still needs imperialism to maintain and open territories in order to build a rentier empire, and has even become more decayed and parasitic than in the period at the turn of the 19th century and during 20th century. The interests of such empire, to some extent, are the national interests of the U.S., the overlord of the world system.

However, can the financial monopoly capital-dominated world empire, in which a small group controls and monopolizes all social capital and world capital in a rentier and speculative way, and which aims to plunder the unpaid labor of most people, be maintained eternally? The fact that the international financial crisis that broke out 5 years ago, has not been yet overcome shows that the empire contains many contradictions and flaws in itself. And the movement against the domination of the financial monopoly capital in world countries, like the most influential one "The Occupy Wall Street" movement, reflects that more and more people are awakening. The fact that the global financial monopoly capital groups led by Wall Street are toppling after the crisis and the resistance of the masses indicates the rise of the progressive movement in the world against the global domination of financial monopoly capital, and sounds the knell of capitalism.

Y. 10

The Crisis of the Capitalist System and the Future of Socialism

—A Research Report on "Foreign Communist Parties' Theory and Practice"

Song Lidan[1]

Abstract: The foreign Communist parties argue that the current crisis of capitalism is still the result of the fundamental contradiction of capitalism—the contradiction between the socialization production and the capitalist private ownership—having universal and overall characteristics. Capitalism cannot eliminate its own contradiction, by itself. It can only transfer it on to the shoulders of others internally and externally. The crisis highlights the aggressiveness of imperialism and the world may enter a new era of crisis and revolution. The only way out of the capitalist crisis is the struggle of the working class and other masses against the rule of capital: Socialism is the future of mankind.

Key words: communist parties; crisis of the capitalist system; socialism

---

1 Song Lidan, visiting researcher of CASS World Socialism Research and associate researcher of CASS Institute of Marxism Studies.

Since the outbreak of the global economic crisis in 2008, communist and workers' parties abroad have been paying close attention to the world situation, while studying and analyzing the chances and challenges faced by the socialist movement. They release their research findings and views to the world mainly in the form of conference speeches at the annual "International Meeting of Communist and Workers' Parties". During December 9 to 11, 2011, the 13th "International Meeting of Communist and Workers' Parties" was held in Athens by the Greek Communist Party. Over 100 representatives from 78 political parties in 59 countries attended the meeting. "Socialism is the future!" being the theme, the following topics were discussed at the meeting: the international situation 20 years after the Soviet counterrevolution and the communists' experience; the task to launch class struggles and develop current mass struggles and uprisings under the capitalist crisis and imperialist war conditions; the task to struggle for the rights of the working class and the people and to strengthen the proletarian internationalism and anti-imperialist front and the task to overthrow capitalism and build socialism. The communist and workers' parties abroad confirm that the current capitalist crisis is the most serious crisis of the capitalist system since the Great Depression starting in 1929. It is the intensification of the contradiction between socialized production and the capitalist private ownership, and the antagonistic contradiction between capital and labor is where the crisis is centered with.[2] The communist and workers' parties abroad introduced the new characteristics of this crisis based on the situations in their respective countries, and the ways of developing to the future of socialism in the face of the challenges and chances provided by the capitalist system. This paper analyses and summarizes related views, held by the communist and workers' parties abroad, on the current crisis and the world pattern based on the documents of the 10th to the 13th International Meeting of Communist and Workers' Parties (especially nearly 70 papers at the 13th International Meeting of Communist and Workers' Parties).

I. New characteristics of the current crisis

1. Crisis of the capitalist system is accompanied by multiple crises

The crisis of the capitalist democratic system

The introduction by various communist parties on how the respective governments deal with the crisis situation shows that the monopoly capital, especially financial monopoly capital tries to shift the burden of the crisis away through various means. Firstly, it infringes laborers' rights and interests. The bourgeoisie tries hard to abolish the social achievements obtained

---

2 Song Lidan: Summary of the 11th International Meeting of Communist and Workers' Parties, Studies on Marxism, Issue 2, 2010.

by the workers through centuries of struggle, including the right to collective bargaining and the right to labor and social security and forces the workers to accept poor work conditions. "As a result of the austerity policy of our government all the working people in Luxembourg have lost 12.5% of one monthly salary in the period from the month of May till October."[3] In 2011, the real incomes of the British families dropped at a speed of 11%, that is, the biggest drop in the past 34 years.[4] Second, private capital losses are socialized and internationalized. Socialization of private capital losses is "to promote the process of neoliberalism, especially the privatization of basic public services (like healthcare, welfare and education departments)" through economic cries so as to continue to transfer public funds to a handful of powerful individuals. A typical example of the internationalization of private capital losses is the US which "…solves its deficit by means of printing money and depreciating the US government bonds and treasury bonds held by the other countries."[5] It is actually internationalizing the losses of the economic crisis through the hegemony of US dollar. Third, the welfare system is abolished. It is claimed that the welfare society is raising lazybones and producing social injustice. So "'welfare society' is disintegrating. People must fend for themselves". "And 20 years after the dismantling of the Soviet Union, the Swedish welfare society still is dismantled and has soon reached the end of the road."[6]

The crisis of the capitalist ideology

The measures to deal with crises taken by the bourgeoisie operate with the working people, which discredits the prestige of capitalism and makes capitalist "democracy, equality, freedom" much doubted. In the "Occupy Wall Street" movement people shouted out slogans such as "No more crimes in the name of democracy!" "Power to the people," "Nazi Bank Wall Street," "Rich get richer, poor get poorer,"[7] and the capitalist ideology encountered an unprecedented crisis.

---

3 Communist Party of Luxembourg: Uli Brockmeyer, 13 IMCWF, Contribution of CP of Luxembourg, available at http://www.solidnet.org/luxembourg-communist-party-of-luxembourg/13-imcwp-contribution-of-cp-of-luxembourg-kpl-en - on September 1, 2016.
4 Building up a popular, democratic anti-monopoly alliance led by the working class—Secretary-general of the British Communist Party on the current international financial crisis, translated by Zhang Shunhong, Hongqi Wengao, Issue 5, 2012.
5 Song Lidan: Summary of the 12th International Meeting of Communist and Workers' Parties, Studies on Marxism, Issue 3, 2011.
6 Swedish Communist Party: Kjell Bygden, 13 IMCWF, Contribution of CP of Sweden, available at http://www.solidnet.org/sweden-communist-party-of-sweden/13-imcwp-contribution-of-cp-of-sweden-en - on September 1, 2016.
7 Tan Yangfang: "Occupy Wall Street" ignites anger of the American people, World Socialism Research, internal material of CASS World Socialism Research, Issue 12, 2011.

The crisis of international relations

"There is also an attempt to put the cost of recovery onto 'developing' countries, in particular in the Doha round at the WTO and in relation to climate change talks."[8] The former is in nature to advance trade liberalization, cancel export subsidies and utilize the industrial advantages of developed countries to obtain a trade advantage; the latter is in nature to create new sources of profits through carbon emission trading, and suppress industrial development in the third world, which will surely deepen the conflicts between the south and north hemispheres, and exacerbate the gap between the south and north hemispheres so as to make the world situation more volatile.

Most communist and workers' parties abroad believe that the current crisis started in the 1970s. It should have occurred already at an earlier time if the opening up of the Eastern European economies did not allow the developed countries to ease the contradiction of overproduction through transferring the crisis. The imperialist bloc led by the US later kept expanding its control over strategic areas and energy sources through a number of wars including those in Kosovo and Libya. While its influence are getting stronger and stronger, the revolts and struggle also get more and more fierce, which has virtually accumulated factors for geopolitical transformations. "The crisis of capitalism impacts upon and has strong consequences over the correlation of forces in an international scale. It accelerates the tendency to relative decline of the United States on one side, and the ascension of other countries, China in special, on the other hand."[9] The international situation has entered a new round of turmoil.

Therefore, "We witness an economic and financial crisis but also a crisis of democracy, international relations and ideology. ...In the upcoming years, this crisis will be aggravated by the environmental crisis, another intractable problem inherent to capitalist production."[10]

---

8 Communist Party of Australia: 13. IMCWP, Anna Pha, Contribution of the Communist Party of Australia, available at http://www.solidnet.org/australia-communist-party-of-australia/13-imcwp-contribution-of-cp-of-australia-en - on September 1, 2016.
9 Brazil Communist Party: 13. IMCWP, Contribution of CP of Brazil (PCdoB), available at http://solidnet.org/brazil-communist-party-of-brazil/13-imcwp-contribution-of-cp-of-brazil-pcdob-en-sp-pt - on September 1, 2016.
10 Workers' Party of Belgium: 13. IMCWP, Herwig Lerouge, Contribution of the Workers' Party of Belgium, available at http://www.solidnet.org/belgium-workers-party-of-belgium/13-imcwp-contribution-of-the-workers-party-of-belgium-en-it - on September 1, 2016.

2. International financial monopoly capital gets further strengthened.

Seen from the object of crisis relief, although industrial capital is as affected as financial capital, what we see is that the government rescuing banks and the other financial institutions by cutting social spending, but barely investing anything in the industry.

Seen from the consequences of the crisis, "The capitalist crises also help enormously the central monopoly capital with support from the Monopoly State apparatus to get rid of a lot of big and small monopolistic competitors, and take over their eventual assets for free, which also enhance profits."[11]

Seen from controlling forces, "The present economic and financial crisis has a number of components including currency wars; inter-imperialist rivalries; and strengthening the domination of monopoly capital, in particular establishing a more direct and open dictatorship by the banks and financial institutions over governments."[12]

Seen from the magnitude, "Finance capital has since the start of the overproduction crises in the 1970s developed very strong. By the end of 1980s finance services was about 55% of the GNP in the OECD countries. By 2009 derivates and instruments of debt in the unregulated international finance markets amounted to 1500 billion US dollars, which was 30 times larger than the GNPs of all the countries in the world together."[13] That is to say, more than one year after the crisis broke out, international financial capital was actually enhanced instead of shrinking.

This indicates that the monopoly status of financial capital has been further enhanced, domestically or internationally.

3. Neoliberalism lingers, and socialism re-enters people's vision.

"It should be noted that during the absolute reign of neoliberalism and the unipolar world in the 1990s, the words 'socialism' and 'imperialism' almost disappeared from the public language of almost all left parties and leaders, and even more of the centre-left. The crisis of the neoliberal model imposed during the 1990s by the so called Consensus of Washington on Latin America and the Caribbean region brought about the emergence of several popular governments and uprisings, as well as the proliferation of

---

11 The Communist Party of Norway: 13. IMCWP, Svend Haakon Jacobsen, Contribution of CP of Norway, available at http://solidnet.org/norway-communist-party-of-norway/13-imcwp-contribution-of-cp-of-norway-en - on September 1, 2016.
12 Communist Party of Australia: 13. IMCWP, Anna Pha, Contribution of the Communist Party of Australia, available at http://www.solidnet.org/australia-communist-party-of-australia/13-imcwp-contribution-of-cp-of-australia-en - on September 1, 2016.
13 The Communist Party of Norway: 13. IMCWP, Svend Haakon Jacobsen, Contribution of CP of Norway, available at http://solidnet.org/norway-communist-party-of-norway/13-imcwp-contribution-of-cp-of-norway-en - on September 1, 2016.

militant social movements, among which we have to highlight the indigenous people, the students, the working sectors and unemployed people. ... on the basis of... the debate in this context on the socialism of the 21st century...the issue of socialism has started to be raised again in a minority, but increasing, group of parties and leaders."[14] The return of "socialism" to the mainstream political discourse in South America and the establishment of Community of Latin American plus Caribbean Region States (CELAC), the first Latin American regional organization without the US and Canada at the end of 2011 demonstrate that Latin American region seeks to completely remove the influences of neoliberalism and tries to find a development path to get rid of the control of imperialism in the socialist inspiration.

In the United States, "Financialization-neo-liberal policies over the past 30 years spurred the rise to dominance of parasitic finance capital, more and more concentrated through mergers and acquisitions...has created an epidemic of foreclosures (people losing their homes) and increased joblessness and state and local budget crises."[15] The "Occupy Wall Street" movement of "We are the 99%", which broke out in the second half of 2011 before spreading to around the globe, clearly and correctly shows that neoliberalism is also cast aside in the US.

In Europe, the strikes in Greece, France and Spain and the riots in Britain all indicate that "Capitalism has not been asserted like a definitive model. Neo-liberalistic market ideology, after thirty years of hegemony, stops to be perceived as a common sense."[16]

In Asia, the neoliberal "Washington Consensus" has caused greater damages. In Bangladesh, at present, "...the unemployment to the tune of more than 30 million, poverty and pauperization due to the capitalist path dictated by the World Bank, IMF, WTO and the so called donors is creating grave unrest amongst people."[17]

---

14 Communist Party of Cuba: Speech of the Representative of the Communist Party of Cuba at the Meeting of Communist and Workers Parties, available at http://www.solidnet.org/cuba-communist-party-of-cuba/13-imcwp-contribution-of-cp-of-cuba-en-it - on September 1, 2016.
15 US Communist Party: 13. IMCWP, Susan Ebb, Contribution of the CP USA, available at http://www.solidnet.org/usa-communist-party-usa/13-imcwp-contribution-of-the-cp-usa-en - on September 1, 2016.
16 Party of Italian Communists: 13. IMCWP, Fausto Sorini, Contribution of the Party of the Italian Communists, available at http://www.solidnet.org/italy-party-of-the-italian-communists/13-imcwp-contribution-of-party-of-the-italian-communists-pdci-en-it - on September 1, 2016.
17 Communist Party of Bangladesh: 13. IMCWP, Ruhin Hossain Prince, Contribution of CP of Bangladesh, available at http://www.solidnet.org/bangladesh-communist-party-of-bangladesh/13-imcwp-contribution-of-cp-of-bangladesh-en - on September 1, 2016.

The comparison of Chinese path and Western path surprises the world. The Workers' Party of Belgium believed, "...globally there is no doubt that the economic relations of China with Asia, Africa and Latin America allowed tens of countries to develop more independently from western imperialism, which inevitably means a weakening of the latter."[18] The Communist Party of Italy pointed out, "If we consider the success of China and CPC, how could it be possible to affirm that communism has been defeated by history? We don't agree with the idea that the powerful rise of China is due to an alleged conversion to neo-liberalism."[19]

In the Arab region, although the official regimes mostly reverse to imperialism, the Arab Left Forum which aims to strengthen the unity of forces against imperialism was established in the second half of 2010, aiming to "...allow for a radical change in the issue of development in the Arab world along the lines of breaking away from dependency modes of production and dependency on imperialism."[20]

This crisis brings socialism back to people's vision, and the contest between socialism and neoliberalism, namely international financial monopoly capitalism, has been highlighted.

II. Latest dynamics of the crisis

1. The crisis of capitalism is still worsening.

Such worsening is reflected by the continuous recession and growing unemployment rate (especially that in the young people) in each and every country. "There is a recessionary situation, with a forecast drop in GDP of 3% next year. Portugal is a small country of little more than 10 million inhabitants and is now the European Union's most unequal country. There are about 1 million unemployed (30% of which are young people between the ages of 15 and 30), 1.2 million workers with precarious jobs, over 2 million people living below the poverty line. And the situation is getting worse."[21] "Now, unemployment in Bangladesh has been to the tune of more than

---

18 Workers' Party of Belgium: 12. IMCWP, Intervention by WP of Belgium, available at http://www.solidnet.org/belgium-workers-party-of-belgium/13-imcwp-contribution-of-the-workers-party-of-belgium-en-it - on 09 December 2010.
19 Party of Italian Communists: 13. IMCWP, Fausto Sorini, Contribution of the Party of the Italian Communists, available at http://www.solidnet.org/italy-party-of-the-italian-communists/13-imcwp-contribution-of-party-of-the-italian-communists-pdci-en-it - on September 1, 2016.
20 Lebanese Communist Party: 13. IMCWP, Dr. Marie Nassif Debs, 13. IMCWP, Contribution of Lebanese CP, available at http://solidnet.org/lebanon-lebanese-communist-party/13-imcwp-contribution-of-lebanese-cp-en-it-ar - on September 1, 2016.
21 Portuguese Communist Party: 13. IMCWP, Contribution of the Portuguese CP, available at http://www.solidnet.org/portugal-portuguese-communist-party/13-imcwp-contribution-of-the-portuguese-cp-en-pt-it - on September 1, 2016.

30 million."[22] "In Germany, more than half of the working youth under 25 work in unsafe jobs. Two thirds of young people under 35 work in precarious employments or are unemployed."[23]

2. Capitalism is bound to transfer its crisis, it cannot fundamentally cure it.

There are no more than two ways of solving the capitalist crisis: inward transfer, that is, adopting austerity measures, and outward transfer, which may be carried out in two ways—controlling oil, strategic channels among other resources and getting reconstruction contracts through wars like the war in Iraq and that in Libya in order to get profits or constructing "a structured debt relationship between the core states and the heavily indebted peripheral countries, which will result in massive transfers of wealth from the periphery to the centre.."[24] For example, the Latin American and other big countries with huge foreign debts have to repay substantial loan interest and capital each year. It may also be that debtor countries such as the US—in order to achieve wealth transfer—issue excessive currency by using the hegemonic position of US dollar to dilute the value of the huge amounts of claims (creditor's rights) China and other countries.

3. Germany and France speed up advancing EU integration.

Swedish Communist Party pointed out that 80% of the Swedish laws today are up to the decision of Brussels. Communist Party of Luxembourg believed that "the ruling forces of Germany and France are about to construct a European Union on the basis of their ideas. 66 years after its military defeat in World War II the German imperialism is again on the way to dominate other countries. With the aim to maximize the profits of German capitalists, the German government is imposing its model of ruling the society and the economy to other countries."[25] The Workers' Party of Belgium held that, "at the European level, we witness a silent 'coup d'État' of Business Europe who imposes on all the so-called German model, the export world champion based on compression of direct and

---

22 Communist Party of Bangladesh: 13. IMCWP, Ruhin llossain Prince, Contribution of CP of Bangladesh, available at http://www.solidnet.org/bangladesh-workers-party-of-bangladesh/13-imcwp-contribution-of-the-workers-party-of-bangladesh-en - on September 1, 2016.
23 Communist Party of Germany: 13. IMCWP, Bettina Jürgensen, Contribution of German CP, http://www.solidnet.org/germany-german-communist-party/13-imcwp-contribution-of-german-cp-en - on September 1, 2016.
24 The Communist Party of Ireland: 13. IMCWP, Eugene McCartan, Contribution of CP of Ireland, available at http://www.solidnet.org/ireland-communist-party-of-ireland/13-imcwp-contribution-of-cp-of-irelanden-it - on September 1, 2016.
25 The Communist Party of Luxemburg: 13. IMCWP, Uli Brockmeyer, Contribution of CP of Luxembourg, available at: http://www.solidnet.org/luxembourg-communist-party-of-luxembourg/13-imcwp-contribution-of-cp-of-luxembourg-kpl-en - on September 1, 2016.

indirect wages."²⁶ Two EU big powers, namely Germany and France are now stepping up to promote the EU integration.

III. The world may very possibly enter a new era of crises and revolutions

The communist and workers' parties generally believe that human beings are experiencing the hardest and most complicated and changing moment in history. In order to get rid of the overall economic and political crisis, imperialism, besides transferring the crises to the laboring people, steps up to create a tense international situation for but one purpose, that is, to "eliminate" the crisis at no matter what cost, seriously threatening world peace. The Communist Party of Denmark believed that the world was on the verge of a new era of crises and revolutions.²⁷ According to the Communist Party of Norway, "The Israeli government has decided to give Prime Minister Netanyahu the permission to attack Iran, even with atomic rockets. This could easily escalate into a large conflict of a global magnitude, a World War III."²⁸

The US carefully crafts the interference strategy. The Obama-Clinton line tries to make the EU, the UN and NATO to participate more in the North Atlantic multilateralism. It is not an abandonment of direct military interventio, a miniature country, "The military budget now is times higher than that in the worst period of the Cold War."²⁹ Each and every NATO member state "will be asked to increase their military spending".³⁰

The US war preparations are in full swing. In October 2008, the US established its 6th headquarters in Africa for directing global operations, and in Latin America the backyard of the US, "rebooted the 4th fleet, strengthened the US military bases in Columbia, staged a coup in Honduras and an attempted coup in Ecuador, and placed Cuba under growing pressures".³¹

26　The Workers' Party of Belgium: 13. IMCWP, Herwig Lerouge, Contribution of the Workers' Party of Belgium, available at http://www.solidnet.org/belgium-workers-party-of-belgium/13-imcwp-contribution-of-the-workers-party-of-belgium-en-it - on September 1, 2016.
27　The Communist Party of Denmark: 13. IMCWP, Henrik Stamer Hedin, Contribution of CP of Denmark, available at http://www.solidnet.org/denmark-communist-party-of-denmark/13-imcwp-contribution-of-cp-of-denmark-en - on September 1, 2016.
28　The Communist Party of Norway: 13. IMCWP, Svend Haakon Jacobsen, Contribution of CP of Norway, available at http://www.solidnet.org/norway-communist-party-of-norway/13-imcwp-contribution-of-cp-of-norway-en - on September 1, 2016.
29　Song Lidan: Summary of the 12th International Meeting of Communist and Workers' Parties, Studies on Marxism, Issue 3, 2011.
30　Ibid.
31　Ibid.

Efforts are made to accelerate the building of the PRO missile defense system in Europe in order to make the Russian nuclear deterrence fail and gradually encircle Russia by force, which threatens world peace and security.

The "Greater Middle East Initiative"—"a project which we all know aims to acquire the natural oil and gas resources in the region (including the triangle of waters between Palestine, Lebanon and Cyprus), the waters and the waterways and geostrategic locations in the Arab world"[32]—has been carried out.

The US is implementing its plan to encircle or curb China. "US President Barack Obama has repeatedly stressed that a genuine and long-term threat to the leadership of the US...is China."[33] Because China's development threatens the US's absolute control of the world arena, especially in Asia, Africa and Latin America. The US's rapprochement with Burma is one part of the US's strategic encirclement of China. The US wars in Afghanistan and Pakistan, wooing of India and Burma, and efforts to install compliant regimes in Uzbekistan, Turkmenistan and Kyrgyzstan cover the west flank of China. On the east flank, the US has recently escalated tensions in the Korean peninsula, with the aim of setting up bases near China's border, in South Korea. It has military bases in South Korea, Japan, Guam and Diego Garcia. The US was forced to remove its bases from the Philippines, but this country still remains a close ally, hosting regular visits of the US war ships. The US is preparing for war in the Asia-Pacific region, and it may possibly be a nuclear war.[34]

IV. Socialism is the future

1. The right time for the struggle in the ideological field

This crisis is like a sudden wild storm which beats the masquerading of the capitalist ideology into pieces. "The reality that bourgeois democracy will be truncated to meet the needs of capital when it is in crisis is becoming more open and visible. This is an important ideological strategic weakness of theirs... Capitalism's lack of democracy and its efforts to corral and to narrow the people's options is its Achilles heel."[35]

32　Lebanese Communist Party: 13. IMCWP, Dr. Marie Nassif Debs, Contribution of Lebanese CP, available at http://www.solidnet.org/lebanon-lebanese-communist-party/13-imcwp-contribution-of-lebanese-cp-en-it-ar - on September 1, 2016.
33　Song Lidan: Summary of the 12th International Meeting of Communist and Workers' Parties, Studies on Marxism, Issue 3, 2011.
34　The Communist Party of Australia: 13. IMCWP, Anna Pha, Contribution of the Communist Party of Australia, available at http://www.solidnet.org/australia-communist-party-of-australia/13-imcwp-contribution-of-cp-of-australia-en - on September 1, 2016.
35　The Communist Party of Ireland: 13. IMCWP, Herwig Lerouge, Contribution of the Workers' Party of Belgium, available at http://www.solidnet.org/ireland-communist-party-of-ireland/13-imcwp-contribution-of-cp-of-irelanden-it - on September 1, 2016.

The communist and workers' parties have "to further develop class consciousness through struggles in all areas."³⁶ "There are times when an intermediate position can't be adopted, since this intermediate position does not demonstrate the autonomy of the working class party, but on the contrary, shows the fear of openly contradicting the dominant ideological position, which is none other than the position of the ruling class"³⁷ "We need to undertake a far more rigorous study of the problem of the formation of social and class consciousness in the current conditions, and most importantly, how best to counteract bourgeois ideological influences on our class, and make a more skilful and compelling case for socialism as the only alternative to capitalism, as the necessary and desirable alternative to capitalism. And we need to develop new and creative ways to make that case. Simply repeating over and over again slogans about the 'superiority of socialism' just won't suffice."³⁸

The Communist Party of Denmark pointed out that the wheels of history once again turned left, and the turn once again happened in Europe. The accumulation of the internal contradictions of capitalism led to the outbreak of a severe world economic crisis, "Communists had predicted this, but were not noticed; now, more and more people are able to see that our analysis was correct and that the world is on the verge of a new era of crises and revolutions."³⁹

2. How to move towards socialism

Although the crisis is in general an opportunity for the struggles for socialism, the communist and workers' parties abroad mostly maintained a sober judgment on the situation. They believe, "Whilst all the objective conditions are maturing for an assault on capitalism in one of its worst crises, the subjective forces and the motive forces for an alternative socialist struggle are indeed extremely weak."⁴⁰ Firstly, class consciousness is at a low level. Although people have a certain sober understanding of capitalism, "the policy of so-called 'social partnership' in our country has led to the result wanted by the ruling class… An analysis of the situation

---

36 Ibid.
37 The Communist Party of the Peoples of Spain: 13. IMCWP, Carmelo Suárez available at http://www.solidnet.org/spain-communist-party-of-the-peoples-of-spain/13-imcwp-contribution-of-cp-of-the-peoples-of-spain-en-sp-it - on September 1, 2016.
38 The Communist Party of Canada: 13. IMCWP, Miguel Figueroa, Contribution of CP of Canada, available at http://www.solidnet.org/canada-communist-party-of-canada/2419-13-imcwp-contribution-of-cp-of-canada-en - on September 1, 2016.
39 The Communist Party of Denmark: 13. IMCWP, Henrik Stamer Hedin, Contribution of CP of Denmark, available at http://www.solidnet.org/denmark-communist-party-of-denmark/2302-13-imcwp-contribution-of-cp-of-denmark-en - on September 1, 2016.
40 South African Communist Party: 13. IMCWP, Contribution of South African CP, available at http://www.solidnet.org/south-africa-south-african-communist-party/13-imcwp-contribution-of-south-african-cp-en - on September 1, 2016.

in Luxemburg by the CPL came to the conclusion that the consciousness of the working class in our country is on the lowest level since the end of the Second World War". Fortunately, "the labor-capital contradiction in the imperialist countries is getting sharper and sharper. The so-called era of 'social partnership' has ended."[41] The communist and workers' parties should take the chance to declare the bankruptcy of the path of social reform to the masses, and that only socialism can give workers real economic and political democracy and freedom. Secondly, the relationship between the party and the working class is very weak. "By the weakness in the subjective factor what we first and foremost mean or allude to is the nonexistence of the revolutionary parties of the working class in most of the countries and in the countries where such parties exist their link with the working class is weak."[42] Such weakness is also reflected by the reality that most trade unions in terms of theory accept social democracy, and are intimate with social democratic parties or the government in terms of organization. The communist and workers' parties either do not have the right to form a trade union or, even if they do, have negligible influence (which is the direct consequence of the dissolution of the Soviet Union) and are unable to lead the trade union movement.[43]

Allying with the poor strata. The communist and workers' parties held similar opinions on this issue. The Communist Party of Greece has pointed out time and again that "left-wing parties" such as the European Left, the German Left Party and the Swedish Left Party, are all pseudo-left-wing, so they have to be fought against uncompromisingly. The Communist Party of Greece insisted on the stance of keeping a distance from the bourgeoisie. "The solution for the people is not to align with a section of the domestic bourgeois class, not to align with one of the imperialist centers fighting another one at a time when their contradictions have sharpened. Neither is it a solution to support new bourgeois parties against the old ones, coalition governments instead of one-party governments," but to build "a sociopolitical alliance of the working class with the poor petty bourgeois popular strata in the city and the countryside."[44]

---

41 Communist Party of Luxembourg: 13. IMCWP, Uli Brockmeyer, Contribution of CP of Luxembourg, available at http://www.solidnet.org/luxembourg-communist-party-of-luxembourg/13-imcwp-contribution-of-cp-of-luxembourg-kpl-en- on September 1, 2016.
42 Turkish Labor Party: 13. IMCWP, Contribution of EMEP, Turkey, available at http://www.solidnet.org/turkey-labour-party-emep/13-imcwp-contribution-of-emep-turkey-en - on September 1, 2016.
43 The Communist Party of Luxemburg: 13. IMCWP, Uli Brockmeyer, Contribution of CP of Luxembourg, available at http://www.solidnet.org/luxembourg-communist-party-of-luxembourg/13-imcwp-contribution-of-cp-of-luxembourg-kpl-en, - on September 1, 2016.
44 The Communist Party of Greece: 13. IMCWP, A. Papariga, Contribution of CP of Greece, available at http://www.solidnet.org/greece-communist-party-of-greece/13-imcwp-contribution-of-cp-of-greece-en-ru-sp-pt-it-ar - on September 1, 2016.

The way out is to strengthen the parties' fighting strength. The "Occupy" movement is not the way out, though it is undoubtedly advanced. The Jordanian Communist Party even believed, "'Rise Up Europe'…'Social Justice'…What links both movements together with the worldwide movement 'Occupy Wall Street'? The answer is definitely: Moving towards socialism"[45]. But the "Occupy" movement will not move towards socialism automatically, it has limits in that "without a common goal, without socialism as an alternative, nothing will change, and the movement will die quietly like the Attack movement did some years ago."[46] It also lies in that "without working class leadership, without the leadership of the communist and workers' parties, these movements remain handicapped and limited in policy direction and what they can achieve."[47] The Communist Party of Brazil pointed out that it has to prevent the "Occupy" movement from becoming a way of paralyzing the working class. "The way out lies in struggles organized around workplaces and trade unions,"[48] and it is necessary "to rally forces on a social-class basis, to widely enlighten the people concerning the crisis, its character and the way out, to organize and escalate the class struggle in all its forms from top to bottom and inversely so as to draw in new working class and popular masses."[49] For this purpose, the Workers' Party of Belgium believed it to be a must to strengthen its fighting strength. First, it would be well build the party, "We want to educate our party about the strategic role of the working class in the struggle for socialism," and maintain the advanced nature of the vanguard of the working class; second, it would be to reinforce the party and pay attention to finding new members at workplaces in developed countries, "we want to focus on recruiting union organisers and workers from the main factories. We want to multiply and reinforce our party groups in the factories. We want to create a new generation of communist working class organizers."[50] But the working

---

45 Jordanian Communist Party: 13. IMCWP, Layla Naffa, Contribution of Jordanian CP, available at http://www.solidnet.org/jordan-jordanian-communist-party/13-imcwp-contribution-of-jordanian-cp-en - on September 1, 2016.
46 The Communist Party of Denmark: 13. IMCWP, Betty Frydensbjerg Carlsson, available at http://www.solidnet.org/denmark-communist-party-in-denmark/13-imcwp-contribution-of-cp-in-denmark-en - on September 1, 2016
47 The Communist Party of Australia: 13. IMCWP, Anna Pha, Contribution of the Communist Party of Australia, available at http://www.solidnet.org/australia-communist-party-of-australia/13-imcwp-contribution-of-cp-of-australia-en- on September 1, 2016.
48 The Brazilian Communist Party: 13. IMCWP, Contribution of Brazilian CP (PCB), available at http://www.solidnet.org/brazil-brazilian-communist-party/13-imcwp-contribution-of-brazilian-cppcb-en-sp-pt-it - on September 1, 2016.
49 The Communist Party of Greece: 13. IMCWP, A. Papariga, Contribution of CP of Greece, available at http://www.solidnet.org/greece-communist-party-of-greece/13-imcwp-contribution-of-cp-of-greece-en-ru-sp-pt-it-ar - on September 1, 2016.
50 The Workers' Party of Belgium: 13. IMCWP, Herwig Lerouge, Contribution of the Workers' Party of Belgium, available at http://www.solidnet.org/belgium-workers-party-of-belgium/13-imcwp-contribution-of-the-workers-party-of-belgium-en-it - on September 1, 2016.

class in the third world has a small number of members, so the communist and workers' parties can't simply rely on the working class for its class source, but "shake the capitalist world has worsened the life conditions of the workers, of small peasants, of the marginalized youth."[51]

Upholding the banner of militancy. "…If we do not possess a material force for change, we will not change anything at all. We want to put in the centre of attention at all levels the question of strengthening the ties between the party and the working class."[52] The focus of the work is to "recapture the rights to the trade union". It is a must "to fight to defeat the right-wing class collaborators in the unions and the social democratic movements while building the revolutionary party dedicated to the struggle that can unite and mobilise the working class behind the banner of socialism"[53] The Communist Party of Brazil has put armed struggle on a real agenda, "The struggle of masses, in all its forms, adjusted to local realities, is and always will be the only arm of the proletariat… We make clear that our Party considers all forms of action. We can't opportunistically have a blind eye to the right of peoples to rebellion and armed resistance. In many cases, it is the only way to face the violence of capital and overcome it. The peoples can count only with their own forces."[54]

Looking ahead to the international communist movement, and setting clear struggle targets. "We talk openly to the people…about the regrouping of the workers' and people's movement with a clear anti-imperialist antimonopoly orientation, anti-capitalist in the final analysis."[55] Building a more extensive unified front. "…it seems important to create a wide-ranging international front with a clear anti-imperialist character, embracing progressive individualities and political forces identified with the struggles for self determination of peoples; peace among them; preservation of eco-environment and natural resources; social, political and worker's

---

51 Algerian Party for Democracy and Socialism: 13. IMCWP, Contribution of Algerian Party for Democracy and Socialism, available at http://www.solidnet.org/algeria-algerian-party-for-democracy-and-socialism/13-imcwp-contribution-of-algerian-party-for-democracy-and-socialism-en-fr-it - on September 1, 2016.
52 The Workers' Party of Belgium: 13. IMCWP, Herwig Lerouge, Contribution of the Workers' Party of Belgium, available at http://www.solidnet.org/belgium-workers-party-of-belgium/13-imcwp-contribution-of-the-workers-party-of-belgium-en-it December 2011.
53 New Communist Party of Britain: Andy Brooks, 13. IMCWP, Contribution of New CP of Britain, available at http://www.solidnet.org/britain-new-communist-party-of-britain/13-imcwp-contribution-of-new-cp-of-britain-en - on September 1, 2016.
54 Brazilian Communist Party: 13. IMCWP, Contribution of Brazilian CP (PCB), available at http://www.solidnet.org/brazil-brazilian-communist-party/13-imcwp-contribution-of-brazilian-cppcb-en-sp-pt-it - on September 1, 2016.
55 The Communist Party of Greece: A. Papariga, 13. IMCWP, Contribution of CP of Greece, available at http://www.solidnet.org/greece-communist-party-of-greece/13-imcwp-contribution-of-cp-of-greece-en-ru-sp-pt-it-ar - on September 1, 2016.

rights; against imperialist wars and fascistization of societies."[56] Special attention has to be paid to youth movements. In the mass movements in the developed countries, slogans of democracy and national sovereignty can be used to win the people. "From our viewpoint we see democracy and national sovereignty as central struggles."[57] In the third world, it is also necessary to attract the people to participate in the struggle with the slogan of democratic state by "the establishment of a democratic popular and progressive State which expresses the interests of the workers class and of laborious layers."[58] Different strategies shall be adopted in different countries and regions. "This was the deep cause of the emergence of an ascending movement of popular resistance that led the way to the rise of an unprecedented and peculiar progressive cycle, of patriotic anti-imperialist and democratic character, in Latin America and the Caribbean."[59] In South America the communist and workers' parties are not as strong as the other left-wing forces, so it is necessary to propagandize themselves through extensive participation and establishing ties and expand their influence before strengthening themselves. The foundation of a new international communist movement center was mentioned once again. "In order to improve the potential of a protagonist role of communists and workers in world level it is necessary and urgent to constitute a political coordination not intending to work as a new International but to assume a role of organizing international and regional solidarity campaigns, contribute to the debate of ideas and distribute information on the struggle of peoples."[60] In Europe, it is an urgent need to build exchange bodies among the communist and workers' parties. In fact, the communists in Belgium, Holland, Luxemburg and Germany have already established such a coordination center.

Currently, the international financial monopoly capital is strengthening its rule of the world, during which people in each country suffer most severe deprivation, and people's resistance is accumulating; Between Europe

---

56 The Brazilian Communist Party: 13. IMCWP, Contribution of Brazilian CP (PCB), available at http://www.solidnet.org/brazil-brazilian-communist-party/13-imcwp-contribution-of-brazilian-cppcb-en-sp-pt-it - on September 1, 2016.
57 The Communist Party of Ireland: 13. IMCWP, Eugene McCartan, Contribution of the Communist Party of Ireland, available at http://www.solidnet.org/belgium-workers-party-of-belgium/13-imcwp-contribution-of-the-workers-party-of-belgium-en-it- on September 1, 2016.
58 The Algerian Party for Democracy and Socialism: 13. IMCWP, Contribution of Algerian Party for Democracy and Socialism, available at http://www.solidnet.org/algeria-algerian-party-for-democracy-and-socialism/13-imcwp-contribution-of-algerian-party-for-democracy-and-socialism-en-fr-it - on September 1, 2016.
59 The Communist Party of Brazil: 13. IMCWP, Contribution of CP of Brazil (PCB), available at http://www.solidnet.org/brazil-brazilian-communist-party/13-imcwp-contribution-of-brazilian-cppcb-en-sp-pt-it - on September 1, 2016.
60 The Communist Party of Brazil: 13. IMCWP, Contribution of CP of Brazil (PCB), available at http://www.solidnet.org/brazil-brazilian-communist-party/13-imcwp-contribution-of-brazilian-cppcb-en-sp-pt-it - on September 1, 2016.

and the US, the two international financial monopoly capitals, there is not only conspirative cooperation to transfer the crisis, a fierce competition in all fields will also begin. This situation is a tough test but also a rare opportunity for the communist and workers' parties of each country. Communist and workers' parties of each country should pay attention to arm themselves with revolutionary Marxist theories in order to lead the workers and oppressed nations of the whole world, in order to unite them and to surge to another high tide of the international communist movement after the October Revolution in the struggle!

Y. 11

A Preliminary Exploration on the Early Warning System of the Financial Crisis

—Three Reflections on the Global Financial Economic Crisis

Wang Liqiang[1]

Abstract: The scale of capital controlled by international financial groups has far exceeded the financial market scope of any single country. The joint acts of entry-exit and pursuit of excess profits of such capital groups led by a handful of investment banks constitute the immediate cause for the financial crisis. The financial crisis has not caused the evaporation of wealth, but has changed the ownership of wealth in a quick and massive way. The essence of the financial crisis is the massive swallow of people's wealth by international monopoly capital. Under the dollar-standard currency system, the classic procedure of such swallow of people's wealth works as follows: (1) expanding the money supply so that the state of monetary supply shift from abundance to excess; (2) using ultra-low interest rates as a tool to make investment earnings far exceed the cost of funds, to stimulate of financial speculation bubbles, and cause asset prices rise sharply; and (3) unify the mobilization of funds at a high cash out and capital realizes profit target. Therefore, the historical lows of the US Fed's interest rates are the precursor of the outbreak of the financial crisis; the great excess of investment earnings over the cost of funds and the rampant financial speculations are the warnings of the outbreak of the financial crisis; and the simultaneous record highs of stock market, real estate market and foreign exchange market are a critical signal for the outbreak of financial crisis.

Key words: international financial monopoly; financial crisis; warning

---

[1] Wang Liqiang, deputy director of CASS World Socialism Research, academic secretary (deputy director level) and researcher of CASS Bureau of Scientific Research Management

I. High degree of monopoly is the origin of financial crises

The top 10 U.S. financial institutions are entrusted with a total amount of funds of 93.9 trillion US dollars; the top 10 asset management companies in the world are managing 16.7 trillion US dollars; the top 10 hedge fund managements have an amount of assets of 1.7 trillion US dollars. The above 30 financial institutions alone have controlled a wealth over 112 trillion US dollars. In the US, the biggest economy in the world, "being as rich as the world" is exactly a true portrayal of these 30 financial groups. For these financial groups, assets are the capital to be invested in various projects to make more profits, and the means of operating capital to seek sudden huge profits. When they invest massive funds to various kinds of capital markets in order to maximize the benefits, especially when they work hand in hand under the guidance of a handful of big investment banks, what will be the consequences of that?

In its "Evening Peak News" on February 25, 2011, China National Radio reported, "The Korean brokerage subsidiary of Deutsche Bank is faced with a fine of 1 billion South Korean Won. According to the transaction records, when the South Korean stock market crashed on November 11, the sell orders of overseas investors holding 2.4 trillion South Korean Won were executed, and 1.6 trillion of it was executed through the Korea Stock Exchange under Deutsche Bank. Deutsche Bank got 45 billion South Korean Won from it." In this case, the investment advisory report of the international investment banks actually played the role of scheduling and commanding capital in general.

Why would it cause a stock market crash in other countries when the customers of Goldman Sachs withdrew their money from the stock market? In the gaming, the party with decentralized funds and decision-making may accidentally make profits, but inevitably loss. Goldman Sachs has a team of dedicated economic researchers with more than 3,000 members. Supported by such a huge professional team, the international monopoly capital takes unified actions, to sell or to buy, so earning more and seldom losing becomes a norm. The international capital accounts, although separated, do far better than local investment agencies to advance or retreat along under the overall command and dispatch of the international investment banking. It is no wonder they can make waves in, even dominate the capital market. From one small clue one can see what is coming. Massive capital cashing out of and fleeing various markets will surely lead to a financial crisis.

II. Re-dechiphering some habitual wordings on the financial crisis in the era of financial hegemony

1. Is it wealth evaporation or wealth transfer?

When describing the stock market crash, the media more frequently use "wealth evaporation" which misleads the shareholders the most. The influence of and losses caused by the financial crisis are nothing less than a massive hot war. But the biggest difference between a financial crisis and a hot war is that the former will not destroy wealth or cause the evaporation of wealth, but change the ownership of wealth in a sharp and significant way.

2. Is it the outbreak of a crisis or the end of illegal and unfair wealth accumulation?

The media often announce to the public that "a financial crisis is coming" after a stock market crash, and view the crash as the starting point of a crisis. According to a report by the South Korean government, stock market crash is the result of the international capital cashing out and fleeing at a high level, and a sign of wealth being looted as well. We believe it to be inaccurate to say that stock market crash is where an overall social crisis starts. Firstly, for international capital, a stock market crash marks the ending, not the beginning of the period of making money with money. Secondly, the stock market slump is only the initial sufferings of small shareholders, and the monopolistic financial groups have earned a lot and see no crisis at all, making it inaccurate to say that the whole society has been stuck in a crisis by "financial crisis". Thirdly, investors' investment in the stock market is all sucked by financial monopolies; the market is starving for cash; and socioeconomic life is in the danger of being paused. On the surface, it seems to be a social crisis, but in nature, it is a means adopted by the financial capital to force the government to pay the social costs of their profit-seeking behaviors. The truth behind the "financial crisis"—international monopoly capital devours people's wealth—has to be clearly recognized.

3. One "crisis" and two "plunders"

It is the first loot of wealth that the international monopoly capital cashes out of and flees the stock market at a high level, and puts the shareholders' investment in its pocket. It is the second time of looting wealth that the international monopoly capital, with the "financial crisis" featuring cash squeeze, forces the government to pay the social costs for it with people's hard-earned money in order to save the market. According to the documents left behind the 800-year-long history of financial crises, the social costs of a financial crisis cover at least the following three items: free government relief funds to the banking; reduction or exemption of taxes by the government for at least 3 years; an expansion of the government's public indebtedness by 186.3% on the average.

The sovereign debt crisis today pushes the scale of the second time of wealth loot to a historical peak. Xinhuanet.com reported on December 7, 2011 that, according to US magazine "Bloomberg Markets", the US Federal Reserve made the biggest capital injection ever to the big banks in the US in secrecy. From August 2001 to March 2009, the Fed had injected 7.77 trillion US dollars to the US financial system. During the financial crisis, the Fed's emergency lending rate was lower than one can imagine. For example, it even dropped to 0.01% in December 2008. It is only one item of the relief funds the US government offered to the US banks. The public indebtedness in the US has been raised once and again to a historical high of 15.2 trillion US dollars. The massive government funds for saving the market have to be repaid by future income, which is the focal issue of sovereign debt.

III. Capital operation context and the financial crisis early warning system

It is the mode of existence and sole purpose of capital to make money with money. The classic procedure of its operating capital and massively misappropriating people's wealth works as follows: expanding the currency supply so that the state of monetary supply changes from abundance to excess; using ultra-low interest rates as a tool so that investment income far exceeds the cost of funds, that the bubbles of financial speculation are stimulated, and that asset price rises sharply; and manipulating funds so that they can cash out and flee at a high level.

Therefore, the historical lows of the US Fed's interest rates hint at the outbreak of the financial crisis; the great excess of investment income over the cost of funds and the rampant financial speculations forebode the outbreak of a financial crisis; and the simultaneous record highs of stock market, real estate market and foreign exchange market is a critical signal for a forthcoming financial crisis.

1. Under the premise that the US dollar is the predominant international currency, the Fed wheels currency supply so that the state of monetary supply changes from abundance to excess basically by reducing the US dollar interest rates.

When the US dollar standard system was first introduced, it rapidly improved the investment capability and promoted accelerated economic development. The rapid development of economic globalization soon transferred the manufacturing industry from the developed countries to the developing countries where manpower cost was low, which further boosted economic financialization in the developed countries; brought out salient features of economic financialization, that is, the contraction of the real economy; an increased proportion of financial services; financial revenues exceeding sales profits in national income; complete mismatch and disproportion of the investment capacity and the needs of the real economy. Against such background, the international financial cartels are no longer satisfied with raking in the profits from commodities, but make use of its advantage in controlling capital and currency to devour global wealth in the range.

In this game, currency is the medium used by the monopolistic financial groups to concentrate wealth. Therefore, to gather the wealth held by the public, it is a must to provide a loose monetary environment. The so-called ample monetary supply is for the real economy. Currency supply which goes far beyond the absorptive capacity of the real economy shall be excessive supply. The following is an analysis of the big international financial crises in the past 80 years.

The financial turmoil in the US in 1929. During 1921 and 1929, besides reducing the federal funds rate, the Fed made another important policy choice—to increase currency supply. In 1928 alone, it issued 60 billion US dollars of currency to its favored member banks, which used their bank checks on mortgage of 15 days. If all the money was converted into gold, it was 6 times as much as all the gold in circulation in the world then! US dollars issued in this way were 33 times more than the currency issued by the Federal Reserve Bank by B/B in the open market!

The financial crisis in Japan in the 1980s. After signing the "Plaza Accord" with the US, Japan began to adopt loose monetary and fiscal policies in order to expand domestic demand and reduce the pressure of further appreciation of Japanese yen. The Bank of Japan cut the interest rate five times, and reduced the discount rate from 5% to 2.5% during January 1986 and February 1987. In order to prevent the yen-US dollar exchange rate from rising continuously, the Bank of Japan bought US dollars and sold Japanese yen in a large scale at the foreign exchange market, leading to a rapid expansion of money supply—by over 10%—in 1987.

The financial crisis in Southeast Asia in 1997. Since Southeast Asian countries had achieved financial liberalization, the international capital could directly shock the financial systems of these countries. In the financial crisis in Southeast Asia, liquidity was not caused by lowering the interest rates or issuing additional currencies by the local currency policy authority, but by buying US dollars on a large scale. The root cause that the investment agencies holding US dollars could put out a lot of money to the Southeast Asian countries on interest was the Fed's low interest rate policy. The growth rate of foreign debts became an external sign of liquidity growth.

The US subprime crisis in 2008. In 2001, the IT bubble deflated and the US economy began to decline. In order to stimulate the economy, the Fed adopted a highly expansionary monetary policy. After cutting the interest rate on 13 occasions, till June 25, 2003, the Fed had reduced the Federal Funds Rate to 1%, the lowest level in the recent 45 years.

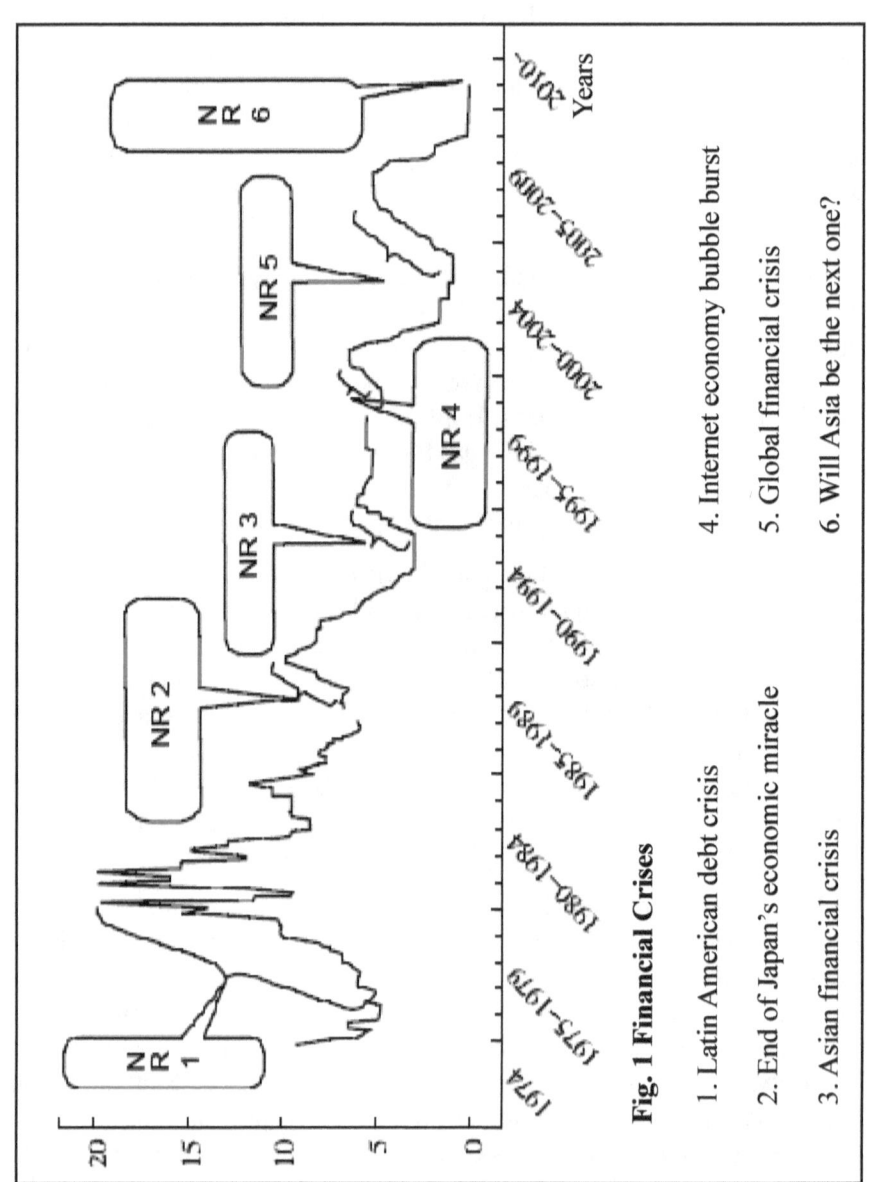

Fig. 1 Financial Crises

1. Latin American debt crisis
2. End of Japan's economic miracle
3. Asian financial crisis
4. Internet economy bubble burst
5. Global financial crisis
6. Will Asia be the next one?

The above historical data show that a crisis would come shortly after each historical low of the Fed's interest rate. Therefore, each time when the Fed reduces the interest rate till it reaches a historical low, it will mean the entry into the embryonic stage of a financial crisis. Records on low interest rates became the first early warning sign against the outbreak of a financial crisis.

2. Allowing the investment earnings far exceed the cost of funds to push up the asset prices sharply

Since the investment that could be absorbed by the real economy is limited by capacity and the market conditions, the real economy was unable to fully absorb the massive capital inflows in the era of financialization. Therefore, the excessive funds had to find a way out, so they flooded into the speculative financial market. Driven by profits, financial institutions competed with one another to give preferential loans to the borrowers, and the speculative gains in the financial market soon exceeded the loan costs, which soon activated profiteering. The prices of stock or real estate assets saw a rapid and continuous growth beyond the support of economic fundamentals, and then the formation of a bubble. Also with the examples of the above big international financial crises, let's reveal how the financial institutions provide cheap money for stocks and other asset investment and speculation behaviors, which then adds fuel to the expansion of asset bubbles.

The US 1929 financial turmoil. The margin could be 10% in the securities market, that is, using 1,000 US dollars of discretionary funds, one could buy shares worth 10,000 US dollars, and borrow the rest, which greatly facilitated the investment and speculative behaviors in the stock market. The size of loans to stockbrokers was about 1-1.5 billion US dollars in the early 1920s, but it grew to 2-2.5 billion US dollars in early 1926, 3.48 billion at the end of 1927, and then as high as 6 billion till the end of 1928.

The financial crisis in Japan in the 1980s. According to the statistical comparison made by the Japanese Planning Agency, from 1984 to 1989, the net fixed assets grew by 35.4%, land assets grew by 129.2%, and stock assets grew by 93.4% in Japan. In the late 1980s, the stock prices in Japan began to soar. In 1985, the total stock market price in Japan was 196 trillion Japanese yen, being 60% of the concurrent GNP. Till the end of 1987, Japan, with a population half of the US population and GNP only 60% of the US GNP, saw its stock market jumping to the world's first; and the Japanese total stock market price accounted for 41.7% of the world total. The ICIW grew by 2.7 times in the four years from 1986 to 1989.

The financial crisis in 1997 in Southeast Asia. The domestic financial market was opened far too early when conditions were not yet ripe, creating conditions for the international capital of tens of billions, even hundreds of billions of US dollars to directly shock the financial systems of these countries. Instead of flowing to the real economy as expected by the governments of the Southeast Asian countries, foreign capital flew to the securities and real estate markets, which are highly speculative, leading to soaring asset prices.

The housing loans in Thailand were 145.9 billion Thai Baht in 1989, but had already grown to 793.4 billion Thai Baht till 1996, being 5 times greater. During 1988 and 1992, land price grew at an annual speed of 20% to 30%. From 1992 to July 1997, the average growth rate of land price was as high as 40%.

The US subprime crisis in 2008. Driven by innovative real estate mortgage products, the real estate financial institutions in the US kept lowering the loan threshold against subprime borrowers, soon expanding the scale of subprime housing loans to 400 billion US dollars in 2003, over 1 trillion US dollars in 2004, and 1.4 trillion in 2005. In 2006, the growth of housing loans slowed down. The ratio of subprime housing loans to housing mortgages grew from 2% in 1999 to nearly 15% in 2006. As the scale of subprime housing mortgages kept expanding, mortgage-backed securities and related credit derivatives like GDO, GDO square, CDO cubic, CDS grew rapidly, too. Till the end of the 1st quarter in 2007, the MBS balance was about 5.984 trillion US dollars, and the ratio of the MBS balance to the balance of housing mortgages (about 10.4 trillion US dollars) reached about 57%. Since 2002, the real estate prices in the US had been growing at an annual speed of over 10%. Till the end of 2005 when the bubble of the real estate was the most prevalent, the growth rate of real estate prices soared to 17%, and the S&P/Case-Shiller U.S. National Home Price Index, which reflects the changes in the housing prices in 10 major cities, grew from 114.58 points in January 2001 to 226.29 points in June 2006, up 97.5%. Therefore, financial bubbles are the second phase early warning sign of the outbreak of a financial crisis.

3. "Capital movement order" is the evil backstage manipulator that mobilizes funds to cash out and flee at a high level and leads to the collapse of asset prices.

It is the nature of financial crises that the international monopoly capital loots others' wealth with its capital advantage. "Liberalization" and "legitimacy" are the shield amulet used by the international monopoly capital to get rid of criminal suspect. Since the legitimacy of making money with money is protected and recognized by law, people have to focus on the complicated appearance of the financial and economic crises and study the transmission mechanism and interaction of the crises instead of investigating the guilt of monopoly capital under the protection of "liberalism" and "legitimacy" That's also the reason why people have been unable to explain or forecast financial crises for 800 years.

When efforts were made to find the backstage market manipulator and the culprit of the financial crises, people found that it did not appear after the stock market crashed, but was the "capital movement order" (investment advice report) or the "adjustment order" (a sudden significant change in bank rate) before the "financial turmoil".

In the US financial turmoil in 1929, the Fed raised the interest rate to 6% on August 9, 1929. Soon the Federal Reserve Bank of New York raised the interest rate on securities dealers from 5% to 20%. After the sudden rise in the interest rates by the Fed, the banks were unable to effectively give credit. The United States, a robust fat sheep, suffered from a shock caused by severe blood loss. International bankers rushed in and bought lots of blue chips and other high-quality assets at super low prices equivalent to small percentages of the normal prices. In these unprecedented economic disasters, a handful of people in the central circle had known that the speculative game would end soon. They therefore were able to timely sell the stocks in their hands and buy government bonds, and then achieved the leap of personal wealth. For example, Henry Morgenthau went to Bankers Trust days before the "Black Tuesday" (October 29, 1929), ordering his company to sell all the stocks within three days. His men were much confused and suggested him to gradually sell them out in several weeks, which they believed might bring in RMB5 million more. He shouted angrily, "I am not here to discuss with you all. Just do it as I said!"

Japan's lost decade. After singing the "Plaza Accord" with the United States, the Japanese yen appreciated by 57% in February 1987. During 1987 and 1989, stock price grew by 94%; the urban land price grew by 103% on the average in Japan, and the land price in Tokyo doubled. At the end of 1989, the US Secretary of the Treasury first announced in a high-profile that the Japanese bubble economy was on the brink of collapse. Then the financial monopoly groups led by the US financial institutions shorted the Nikkei index. The Nikkei 225 dropped by 63% from 38,915 points on December 31, 1989; and the Japanese stock market price dropped from 630 trillion Japanese yen at the close of 1989 to 299 trillion Japanese yen in 1992, being 331 trillion Japanese yen less in three years. In 1990, the land price of the Tokyo Imperial Palace was equivalent to the total sum of all real estates in California, the US. After the bubble burst, the real estates in Japan shrank by 70%. Japan lost 6 trillion US dollars due to the stock market crash and the slump in the real estate market. The wealth of the whole country shrank by nearly 50%.

South Korea caught the backstage manipulator—the Deutsche Bank. In the last ten minutes before the South Korea stock market closed on November 11, 2010, the South Korea Kospi index fell 48 points, mainly because of the arbitrage between futures and the stock index. During the period, foreign investors issued an order of about 2.4 trillion South Korean Won, of which about 2 trillion South Korean Won were operated by the securities department of the Deutsche Bank in South Korea. It directly caused the stock market plunge in South Korea. After a three-month investigation, South Korea caught the capital "adjustment order" from the Deutsche Bank and got other evidence: Firstly, all the orders came from abroad, mostly from the Deutsche Bank. Secondly, the huge orders were issued in the very last 10 minutes before the stock market closed that day, that is, at a time when others were unable to respond to it. Thirdly, the Deutsche Bank practiced arbitrage between futures and the stock index.

The capital movement order issued by Goldman Sachs in China. On November 10, 2010, major clients of Goldman Sachs received from Goldman Sachs the order to sell China-related shares. After that, they fled secretly, with munificent profits. The Chinese stock market soon saw a continuous sharp decline. This time, China found the "capital movement order" of Goldman Sachs which helped recover the three stages of its capital manipulation. First, given the lowness of the Chinese stock market, many securities dealers suggested their clients to sell China-related shares they held, but the international financial groups took actions in the opposite way—they bought China-related shares and highlighted the grounds and reasons for buying such shares. Secondly, the Chinese stock market soon saw a sudden rise by 24%, and many investors began to buy China-related shares. Almost all the Chinese securities dealers issued the order to their clients suggesting the latter to buy China-related shares. Thirdly, on November 10, Goldman Sachs suddenly issued an order to its main clients, suggesting them to sell the China-related shares they held. The stock asset loss of the Chinese investors accounted for 13.4% of all the stock asset loss that time. The above case indicates that international financial groups are the backstage manipulator which issues the "capital movement order" or decides to issue the "adjustment order" to manipulate the stock market. As can be seen, information is the core of financial wars.

4. "Three peak values" are the external signs of the maximization of capital profits.

Seen from the pursuit of capital, it is simple and straightforward—profits. The above-mentioned cases show that capital in the form of currency typically has no change, except changes in its value in the foreign exchange market. What's unpredictable is the substitute of capital—various marketable securities. Capital firstly hides in its substitute to deal with the holders of marketable securities. At the peak of its market value, its real face would flee in silence with the gold and silver used by the investors to buy its substitute.

The two norms of conduct—first, capital will never show its real face before it reaches the "peak value," that is, climbing to the "peak value" is the precondition for the appearance of capital; second, capital must get rid of its substitute and become currency again in order to convert its substitute's market value into real profits—followed by capital in all cases of financial crises allow people to find clues for warning any crisis in advance. It is an absolutely secret process to cash the market value of capital substitute. It would be hard for capital to get out of the game once information was leaked. In real life, the "peak value" of the financial assets would be the historical high of the stock market, the real estate market and the foreign exchange market. When the market value of these marketable securities reaches the historical high, it would be the moment the theoretical investment income achieves the maximization, or the moment capital should cash out of the market and flee. Realizing the precondition for capital appearance, we would find the critical sign of the outbreak of a financial crisis.

Why would people say that a financial crisis is not looming only when the stock market, the real estate market and the foreign exchange market reach their "peak values" simultaneously? International capital never puts money in the same basket when making investment. It is sure that it will invest part of some fund to the stock market and part of it to the real estate market. If one market grows to the peak value, but the other is weak, it can't meet the preset profit target of the capital, so it won't cash out or flee. As for national capital, it has the same goal as international capital, that is, wealth accumulation, but plays a different role in the national macro economy. National capital usually continues to be in "the blood circulation," does not influence the total amount of state funds, but international capital enters the local financial market for profits and usually repatriates the profits, which is "drawing blood" in nature.

Financial liberalization and the system where US dollar is the standard currency damage the monetary sovereignty of different countries. Marketization of the exchange rate inevitably makes the foreign exchange market an important place for profiteering. Although China does not apply financial liberalization, exchange rate still plays a pivotal role in the flow of international capital. In the special environment in China, international speculators have to conduct arbitrage operations in the form of RMB. They would eventually repatriate their financial profits, so they always pay attention to the changes in the exchange rate. When the stock market and the real estate market have already reached the historical high, further rise in the exchange rate would be another profit lever for the international financial speculators, and an opportunity for them to flee. The exchange rate then will inevitably detonate capital outflows. Therefore, it is totally feasible to use "the three peak values" as the critical signs of an incoming financial crisis.

IV. Avoiding simultaneous appearance of "the three peak values" to prevent severe loss of blood of the national economy

The contest between a country and the international speculators is not after, but before the stock market plunge of the same country. According to the aforesaid critical signs of a financial crisis, the government may take effective countermeasures to prevent the situation from being deteriorated. After the rate for the US dollar reaches a new historical low, the financial management authorities must take measures to tighten up the country's monetary policy and prevent the development of ample liquidity to excessive liquidity. If the first line does not work, and the speculative gains in the market go far beyond the capital costs, the government must take comprehensive measures to eliminate the bubbles in the financial market.

When "the three peak values" are faintly visible, the government has but one chance to game with the financial giants—to take all necessary measures to make the peak values of the stock market, the real estate market and the exchange rate bubble and burst, rise and decline alternatively to try to avoid the simultaneous appearance of "the three peak values" In so doing, it can effectively stagger the time international capital cashes out of the market and flees. Once the time the international capital cashes out of the market is linearly dispersed, the phenomenon of huge losses of national wealth in a short time, that is, severe financial shocks, would be avoided, and the state would avoid suffering huge losses.

Y. 12

Suggested Research and Formulating Long-term Strategy in China– Some Observations about Capitalism

Li Changjiu[1]

Abstract: Leaders of the US and UK have vigorously promoted liberalization, privatization and financial deregulation since the end of the 1970s. As a result, numerous financial derivatives have expanded viciously and the virtual economy has detached itself from the real economy. Western countries' monopoly capitalism gradually extends to the international financial monopoly capitalism. Western countries reap excessive profits from the rest of the world especially from the developing countries by occupying the dominant international currency advantage and through multinational companies. The global income gap between the rich and the poor is widening. Most countries in the Western world have sovereign debt crisis or financial distress since the outbreak of the global financial crisis in 2008. However, Western countries still have a strong pressure-resistant capacity and flexibility. China and other developing countries have to develop a long-term development strategy to prevent or mitigate the crisis and the challenges transferred from Western countries. At the same time, China and other developing countries need to keep pace with the update cycle of the technological revolution and strive to be in the forefront.

Key words: state monopoly capitalism; international financial monopoly capitalism; virtual economy

---

[1] Li Changjiu, visiting researcher of CASS World Socialism Research and researcher of World Studies Center of Xinhua News Agency.

About 3 to 3.5 million years from now, human reproduction and development appeared on earth, and 99 percent of human history was in the stage of primitive society. Till around 10,000 years from now, men entered the Neolithic Period and started to engage in agriculture and animal husbandry, and had more and more surplus products, which then led to private properties. However, it was not until nearly 5,000 years later that men entered the class society, and then another 5,000 years later the slavery and feudal societies.[2] The American sociologist William Robinson published a book entitled *A Theory of Global Capitalism: Production, Class, and State in a Transnational World*, in which he held that capitalism had begun to develop in Europe as a new system 500 years ago. But from the British parliamentary struggle in 1640 to "the Revolution of 1688" during 1688-1689, new aristocracy being the representative, the masses were relied on to overthrow feudal ruling and build the capitalist system. The capitalist society lasted for only 367 years since the triumph of the British bourgeois revolution over the feudal rule. The evolution of human history is influenced by many factors including the development of the productive forces and changes in production relations. It is complicated and slow to transit from one social system to another. This paper will focus on some viewpoints on capitalism.

I. Human history is still in an era where capitalism holds a dominant position

The US financial crisis since 2008 has not only triggered the most serious global financial tsunami since the Great Depression in the 1930s but also led the world economy to the severest recession since the end of WWII in 1945.

The year 2012 is not one that witnesses "radical changes" in the global financial and economic situation. German Chancellor Angela Merkel delivered a speech at the German lower house of parliament on May 9, 2010 and warned that Euro was in great danger; that Europe was facing the toughest test in the past 12 years, which concerned the existence and continuation of "Europe" the concept, so it was a historic challenge and task faced by Europe; and that "if euro fails, Europe fails" She believed that it would take another decade to solve the European debt problem. Some researchers hold that the European debt problem will not see any new turning point until the year 2030. Japanese government bonds have been two times greater than its GDP. Researchers worry if Japan is losing another decade after losing the first two. Till 2011, the debts of the US federal government had exceeded 15 trillion US dollars, which was also beyond the US GDP. Some economists point out if the US government fails to take effective countermeasures, the

---

2 World History (1st volume of "Modern History") edited by Wu Yujin and Qi Shirong, Higher Education Press, 1992, pp13-14.

US will similarly experience "the lost decade" like Japan did. Harassed by the national debt problem in the West, the world economy will continue the low-speed growth for another 5 years in a roll or an even longer period.

This global financial crisis and world economic recession once again break the myth of the so-called omnipotence of the "invisible hand" in laissez-faire free market economy; sharply widen the gap between the rich and the poor; cause social contradictions and conflicts to be even sharper and exacerbated, shaking the capitalist liberal and democratic system in the West. However, history does not end, so does capitalism. Major capitalist countries remain very capable of self-adjustments, and of easing social contradictions and conflicts by adjusting the production relations, distribution relations and social relations. In particular, these countries still have advantages in technical innovations. Human beings are welcoming the 4th technological revolution led by the development and effective utilization of energy resources—information technology has entered a large-scale data era. Smart production will be the first structural revolution since Henry Ford combined standard production of parts with line production to achieve "mass production" at the beginning of the 20th century; emerging materials science will bring revolutionary reforms to materials production; and the revolution of the communications technology will connect most of the 7 billion villagers of the "global village" wirelessly. Western developed countries led by the US will still dominate this technological revolution. These countries still have the potential for developing productive forces and achieving economic growth. Therefore, we are still in an era where capitalism holds a dominant position. As for how long such dominant position will be held, in a certain sense, it will depend on various conditions, including the initiative of each strategic force.

II. State monopoly capitalism is developing to the stage of international monopoly capitalism.

The accelerated development of state monopoly capitalism to the stage of international monopoly capitalism started at the end of the 1970s. After Margaret Thatcher served as the British Prime Minister in 1979 and Reagan took office as the US President in 1981, the two tough right-wing political figures on both sides of the Atlantic worked together to advance liberalization and privatization, influencing the world. In developed countries, numerous financial derivatives expand viciously; the virtual economy has separated itself from the real economy; national industrial monopoly capitalism soon turns to international financial monopoly capitalism; more and more wealth is held by a handful of financial oligarchs; and the gap between the rich and the poor is being sharply widened. According to the data released by Finance and Development, a quarterly magazine published by the International Monetary Fund, the wealthiest 1% of the US held only 10% of the total national wealth in the 1970s, 23.5% in 2007 before the outbreak of the subprime crisis, and as high as 40% in 2009, while the lower-middle class The US, accounting for 80% of all the USs, held only 7% of the national wealth in the same year (2009).[3] Nobel Prize winner in economics and former Vice President of the World Bank Stiglitz published an article entitled Of the 1%, by the 1%, for the 1% in US magazine Vanity Fair in May 2011 to lash out at the comprehensive control of the economic, political and social life by financial oligarchs. Alain Touraine, 86-year-old researcher of the School for Advanced Studies in the Social Sciences, pointed out in an interview on November 22, 2011 that growing inequalities occurred everywhere and were especially significant in the US; that at the end of the 19th century, the income gap between CEOs and ordinary workers was 25 times, but now it was 400 times, which was more than crazy; that the sharp change between the rich and the poor allowed people in the front to continue to go forward and those lagged behind to be left behind farther and farther; that similar phenomena existed in Europe, though they were not as serious as they were in the US.[4]

At the turn of the 1980s and 90s, after the dramatic changes in Eastern Europe and the dissolution of the Soviet Union, two balanced markets no longer existed. On December 19, 1991, Yeltsin issued a presidential decree to approve 1992 Basic Principles of the Outline of Privatization of State-owned and City-owned Enterprises. A "shock therapy"-style "reform" became in full swing in Russia. Chubais, who is known as "Father of Privatization" in Russia, once served as Russian Deputy Prime Minister and chaired Russian Government Privatization Commission, said, "Properties can be given to anyone, even pirates, as long as they are taken back from the state." After the dissolution of the Soviet Union, the Russian economy was stuck in chaos for lack of regulatory control and privatization. A few people became millionaires, but the overwhelming majority of the public became poorer and poorer. In 2005, the then Russian President Vladimir Putin pointed out in the annual state of the nation address, "the collapse of the Soviet Union was a major geopolitical disaster of the century. As for the Russian nation, it became a genuine drama"[5]

The "Washington Consensus" concocted under the leadership of the US-based Institute of International Economics in 1989 demonstrated the political and economic theories of neoliberalism, the core of which was advocating privatization and liberalization. It influenced most developing countries

---

3 Qiao Jihong: Divide between the rich and the poor—Pain of the 99% Americans, Xinhua Daily Telegraph, November 12, 2011.
4 Wen Hui Pao, November 23, 2011.
5 20th anniversary of the ruin of the Soviet Communist Party and the Soviet Union—Russians are complaining, World Socialism Dynamics, December 31, 2011.

and countries in transition. For example, during 1989 and 1999, 93 out of 100 big enterprises in Argentina became foreign-owned. Till 2000, multinational companies had controlled 90.4% of the export and 63.3% of the import of Argentina. 90% of the production of oil and natural gas in Argentina had been controlled by 8 oil companies, and 7 out of the 10 biggest banks in Argentina had become foreign-invested; and foreign-invested banks had controlled 62% of all the capital in the Argentina banking system. The neoliberal "reforms", especially comprehensive privatization, excessive opening up and marketization, caused Argentina to lose its economic sovereignty largely and placed its economic security under great threat, under the circumstance that multinational companies had controlled the finance, resources, market and economic lifelines of Argentina.[6]

Since the end of the 1970s, China has implemented the reform and opening-up policy, and was integrated into the global market, and the shift from the planned economy to the market economy has truly taken shape.

The above changes created conditions for the accelerated development of state monopoly capitalism to international monopoly capitalism, and then for Western countries and their multinational companies to seek excess profits at the stage of international monopoly capitalism.

1. Multinational companies get excess profits from all around the globe.

Multinational companies optimize and reorganize their production factors and resources on the stage of the global market, use the inexpensive labor force and resources in the developing countries to seek excess profits. According to the studies of Dai Xianglong, director of the National Council for Social Security Fund, most of the currencies earned by the developing countries by supplying commodities to the developed countries are used to buy bonds in the developed countries or deposited in the banks of these countries for a rate of return of 3% to 4% only; while the developed countries centralize their domestic capital and capital inflows before using them to make direct investment in the developing countries and get a rate of return of 10% to 20%. Japanese weekly Economist published an article entitled The World Has Entered An Unprecedented Era Of Excess Profits on May 8, 2007 which held, "The world economy has entered an era of integration. Even though, there are still huge wage gaps between the developed countries like Japan, the US and Europe and the developing countries like China and India. If the developed countries make full use of the cheap labor force in the developing countries, they will surely get significant excess profits, which, through multinational companies, will benefit the economies and financial markets of the developed countries more."

---

6 Shen'an, Reviewing and Thinking about the Argentina Crisis, World Affairs Press, 2009.

Competitions among countries are increasingly demonstrated as competitions among enterprises. In the Fortune Global 500 companies in 2010, 325 enterprises on the list were from 7 big Western countries, accounting for 65% of all, of which 139 were from the US and achieved total annual sales of 6,977.2 billion US dollars, that is, 2 times greater than the total volume of foreign trade and 9 times greater than the total volume of the trade deficits of the US. It indicates that the US did not have any trade deficits at all. Experts of Swiss Federal Institute of Technology in Zurich analyzed the data of 43,000 companies before getting the conclusion that nearly half of the world's wealth was held by 147 inextricably linked multinational companies.[7] It was introduced on the website of US magazine Forbes on September 21, 2011 that the top 400 wealthiest The US had total assets of 1.53 trillion US dollars, exceeding 1.46 trillion US dollars, that is, the sum of the GDP of 1,466 million people in India, Pakistan and Bangladesh in 2008.

2. Patents are used as the weapon and marketing channel to get excess profits.

Most of the developing countries are still at the low end of the international industrial chain, and they mainly assemble and process products and provide labor-intensive products for the developed countries. Although China has become a big manufacturing country, it remains a "world factory" getting meager processing fees. According to statistics, patents first issued by the US account for 60% of all, and patents first issued by China account for less than one percent. For example, media player iPod developed by US Apple Inc. costs 299 US dollars each. Although Apple Inc. does not have the production line nor consumes the domestic resources of the US, the US gets an income of 163 US dollars for designing, patent and marketing, and 132 US dollars for parts and transportation (of which 93.39 US dollars go to Toshiba and other companies); China gets only 4 US dollars (of which 3 US dollars are for assembling) for producing one iPod, accounting for only 1%.

However, according to the rules of origin, for each iPod "exported" from China to the US, the US deficit against China would be 150 US dollars more.[8] For another example, each year, China produces 38 billion ballpoint pens, each of which is sold at the price of 1.99 US dollars in the US market, but since 90% of the nib head cores are imported, Chinese factories earn only 0.1 yuan for producing one ballpoint pen.

---

7 147 multinational companies control the global economy, Russian newspaper network, October 20, 2011.
8 Deconstruct the cost of iPod—Apple benefits the most by designing, Business Weekly, Taiwan, July 29, 2007

3. International reserve currency is utilized to seek excess profits.

According to statistics, in December 2006, that is, before the subprime crisis broke out in the US, US dollar, euro, yen and pound sterling accounted for 65%, 25%, 6% and 3%, respectively, of the international reserve currencies, and other currencies accounted for 1% of all; till the end of the third quarter in 2011, US dollar, euro, yen and pound sterling accounted for 61.7%, 25.7%, 3.8% and 3.9%, respectively, of the international reserve currencies, and other currencies accounted for 4.8% of all. From the subprime crisis, the financial crisis to economic recession, the currencies of these countries are little impacted. These countries get enormous profits with the statuses of their currencies as international reserve currencies. In 2010, US seigniorage[9] income accounted for 0.5% of its GDP. Famous American historian Francis wrote in his book Gold, Dollars & Power: The Politics of International Monetary Relations, 1958-1971 that the collapse of the Bretton Woods system was a watershed. Before that, US dollar was an assertive political tool, but after that, it became mild, secretly dominating everything. In the process of globalization, the US gets maximum interests; and the controlling power of US dollar over the world market is strengthened instead of weakened. After shaking off the yoke of gold, it freely inflates. In the decades since the 1970s when US dollar was decoupled with gold, world paper wealth has been growing several times faster than entity wealth, and the difference between the two is basically harvested by the US.[10]

In order to protect the hegemony position of US dollar and for huge profits, the US once ruthlessly suppressed yen and euro. In particular, under the suppression of the US, Japan failed to take correct countermeasures, so it suffered terrible losses. The US will by no means let pass RMB, so the Sino-US currency war and war of exchange rate will come one after another, to which China must adopt effective countermeasures.

Voluminous facts indicate that state monopoly capitalism is developing to the stage of international monopoly capitalism in an accelerated way. The point is that major developed capitalist countries and their multinational companies will get more and more excess profits from around the globe at the stage of international financial monopoly capitalism.

---

9 Seigniorage, the government's revenue from the creation of money.
10 He Yongxin, Gaming between great powers behind the soaring gold price, Shanghai Securities News, September 14, 2011.

III. Reasons for the eastward shift of the US global strategic focus, its goals and prospects

The eastward shift of the US global strategic focus is a major adjustment of the US global strategy and foreign policies when the US power and hegemony status are on the decline. The overall trends of the global deployment of the US are global contraction and attack against key sectors. The US global strategic focus shifted from Europe to Eurasia, and then from Asia to the Asia-Pacific region, because there is no war in Europe, and NATO and the European Union can be used to continue to suppress some countries in the Middle East; urge political alternation in these countries; and protect the strategic and economic interests of the US in the Middle East.

As the world's economic center of gravity returns to Asia, Asia is becoming the world's biggest investment and trade market. The US has invested a lot of political, economic, military and diplomatic resources in the Asia-Pacific region for the following objectives: To vigorously advance "Trans-Pacific Strategic Economic Partnership Agreement" (TPP) and protect its dominant position in the Asia-Pacific region; to protect and expand its economic interests in the Asia-Pacific region through multinational companies; and to confederate with others, sow seeds of discord, and contain and curb China and Russia. Since more and more countries in the Asia-Pacific region are having increasingly intimate economic and trade relations with China, it is hard to achieve the above objectives. On December 1, 2011, Indian newspaper The Telegraph published an article entitled "New Delhi rebuffs the anti-China axis" on its website. The article wrote, "A security pact with the US and India is worth exploring...Australian foreign minister Kevin Rudd claimed..., because... the response from the Indian government has really been quite positive...,'" but a spokesperson for the foreign ministry in Delhi denied knowledge of the proposed treaty. Foreign secretary Ranjan Mathai emphasized that New Delhi would persist with its policy of engaging with both China and the US without antagonising one or the other. French newspaper Le Monde published an article on November 20, 2011, in which it introduced that Indonesia established the "strategic partnership" with the US in 2010, but was worried recently. After U.S. President Barack Obama delivered a speech in Australia, Indonesian Foreign Minister warned that Indonesia did not want the situation to develop to the level of setting up a chain of reactions. Singapore Foreign Minister warned that being stuck in the "divergence of interests" between opposing powers would lead to a threat.

On November 19, 2011, after the East Asia Summit ended, Japanese Prime Minister Yoshihiko Noda was "satisfied," as reported by Yomiuri Shimbun daily on November 21, because the "Network to Encircle China," which had been fabricated a year before finally surfaced. Yoshihiko Noda not only followed the US to intervene in the dispute over South China Sea and promote the so-called "maritime cooperation and discussion," but announced that Japan would participate in TPP multilateral negotiation. However, since China has become Japan's biggest trade partner with the most investment from Japan, Japanese politicians, especially Japanese researchers have quite different opinions on whether Japan should continue to strengthen the Japan-US alliance and completely follow the US, or expand the cooperation with China and other Asian countries. Japanese monthly World published, in its 2nd issue in 2012, To must transform the understanding of the world—Determination that should be made by Japan in 2012, an article written by Jitsuro Terashima, director of the Japan Research Institute. It was pointed out in the article that Japan was still clinging to the "Cold War mentality," the diplomatic idea of "solitary freedom and prosperity" ("democratic countries" encircled China and Russia) in the period of Taro Aso and the old idea of "deepening the Japan-US alliance" when world countries were all making efforts to build a "participatory global order" Japan should get rid of the shallow idea about "relying on the US to fight against China's threat" It should seek self-respect and independence on the issue of "Trans-Pacific Strategic Economic Partnership Agreement;" get an equal status with the US; and play a main role in building a stable situation in the Asia-Pacific region. Japanese monthly Voice published in its 2nd issue in 2012 An interpretation of the future direction of the international monetary system chaos, an article written by Gyohten Toyoo, Japan's former treasurer and director of the International Currency Institute. In the article, the author wrote, "The unipolar leadership of the US as a hegemonic country has become weakened. Japan has been considering its relations with the US only since WWII, but that will not work in the future. Even if Japan is to participate in the TPP negotiation, it can never destroy the Japan-China relations. While participating in the TPP negotiation, Japan shall advance the negotiation with China about concluding a free trade agreement"

A wise man submits to circumstances. The US has to know its enemy and itself instead of continuing to go against the historical trends. U.S. Secretary of State Hillary Clinton published an article entitled The US's Pacific Century in Foreign Policy in November 2011. Indonesian President Susilo Bambang Yudhoyono points out, "It is no longer possible that the Asia-Pacific region would be dominated by a single super power" Former Malaysian Prime Minister Najib Razak published in The Jakarta Post an article entitled "ASEAN and global power shift," and wrote in the article, "If the 19th century belonged to the British Empire and the 20th century to the United States, the 21st century is going to belong to Asia" It is the correct choice of the US to participate in maintaining peace and stability in the

Asia-Pacific region; push forward the coordinated development of different countries and regions; and achieve win-win and mutual benefit.

IV. China is suggested to develop a long-term strategy

In November 2008, the U.S. National Intelligence Council published a research report entitled "Global Trends 2025: A Revamped World," in which it predicted "Anchored by the US and EU in the West, Russia and the GCC states in Central Asia and the Middle East, and China and eventually India in the East, the financial landscape for the first time will be genuinely global and multipolar". The report predicted, "Tensions between the principal actors in the multipolar world are high as states seek energy security and strengthened spheres of influence".

The Institute of World Economy and International Relations (IMEMO) of the Russian Academy of Sciences, an important think tank in Russia, released Strategic Global Outlook: 2030, in which it analyzed the main trends of global changes, "International efforts will be oriented towards achieving stronger coordination between institutions of global and regional governance. They should have wider credentials in solving issues of financial stability, social development, innovations and security." "However, it is difficult to expect that fundamentally new international mechanisms will be created in next twenty-year perspective," "cooperation of global and regional powers in the maintenance of international security" will be increased; "the existing and creation of new institutions of regional integration in Europe, Pacific Asia" will be consolidated; the world will see "gradual democratic reforms in China," "increasing number of democratic countries combined with a growth of nationalism".

It is suggested that China studies and develops a long-term strategy of "World Pattern and China: 2050" to study what the world pattern will be like and what position China will be in at the 100th anniversary of New China. Internationally, China is suggested to study the international environment for its development in a profound way, study and judge the economic development trends of the developed countries such as the US, those in Europe and Japan and their relations, while focusing on the future trend of the US—will it decline or revive and its influences; study the grand trends of the developing countries, especially emerging economies and their cooperation prospects, and reduce the reliance on developed countries; study the changes in the political and economic security situation in neighboring countries and regions, their influences on China, and possible countermeasures.

Domestically, China is suggested to profoundly study the ways to proper deal with and optimize five major relationships—between the optimization of foreign capital and better use of domestic capital, introduction of technologies and independent innovations, expansion of external demand and expansion of domestic demand, the virtual economy and the real economy, and between wealth increase and just and fair distribution of wealth; firmly take the development path of socialism with Chinese characteristics; and achieve the great rejuvenation of the Chinese nation. A strong socialist China erecting in the world will contribute more to the gradual revival of socialism in the world, world peace, as well as the advancement of harmonious development of the world economy and common prosperity.

Y. 13

Reflections on the Predicaments of Capitalism in the West Today

Zhao Minghao[1]

Abstract: The Western elites has been assessing and analyzing the predicaments of capitalism in a profound and far-flung manner. Their reflections are not only related to the economic, fiscal and social welfare policies but also include the weakening of the middle class, the political dysfunction and the crisis of democracy. It seems that the Western countries are increasing their awareness of underlying challenges and making efforts to seek exit strategies, enforce required reforms, and improve the political-economic institutions. Most Western capitalist countries including the U.S. confront a threefold predicament in terms of achieving a stable recovery in the short run, and are faced with challenges to revitalize growth and competiveness in the medium term. And in the long term, it seems hard that they can justify and secure the hegemonic position or domination in global governance.

Key words: the financial crisis; capitalism; state capitalism; re-globalization

---

[1] Zhao Minghao, visiting researcher of CASS World Socialism Research Center and research associate in China Center for Contemporary World Studies, International Department of the Central Committee of CPC.

Themed with "The Great Transformation: Shaping New Models," the World Economic Forum held in Davos at the beginning of 2012 has encouraged the Western political and business circles to make more profound and comprehensive critiques of capitalism on whether 20th-century capitalism is failing the 21st-century society. Many mainstream media in the West were surprised, because it was absolutely unthinkable in the past that such discussions would be held in the World Economic Forum in Davos, an occasion which was once devoted to promoting neoliberal policies. Now, the new round of reflections by the West on capitalism starts with secular trends and long-term issues, extends from improving financial, fiscal, welfare and other peripheral policies to analyzing the free market model, especially the profound defects of "neo-liberalism," and deals more with problems concerning the core elements of the capitalist system like the fate of the middle class and the predicament of democratic politics, showing a further enhanced sense of crisis to seek reforms, get rid of the predicaments and save themselves by the capitalist countries in the West. But meanwhile, they vigorously speculate topics like "state capitalism", trying to set more obstacles and restraints against the development of the emerging enemies under the cloak of protecting international rules.

I. "Capitalism's business license" is doubted

At present, the reflections of capitalism by the West can be generalized into the following several.

1. Capitalism has lost the "moral compass", thus it is hard to honor its promise to the ordinary people, and its legality is much doubted.

British Chancellor of the Exchequer George Osborne published an article, in which he pointed out that capitalism is in danger of losing its "business license" The legitimacy crisis of capitalism is mainly manifested in the following three aspects: Firstly, the capitalist economy is severely unbalanced; laborers' value is underestimated; labor relations are deteriorating; and "unemployment has become a black hole of capitalism" On the one hand, workers are no longer viewed as human capital, but pure costs, on the other, the excessive bonus system closely links managers' income with capitalists' interests, and profligate and excessive high salaries and benefits have ruined managers' practicing atmosphere. In 2010, under the circumstance that the U.S. had not got rid of the financial crisis, the CEOs of its big corporations received an average annual income of 10.8 million US dollars, up 28% over 2009, but the average annual wages of ordinary workers were 33,121 US dollars, up only 3%. The income of the CEOs was 325 times greater than that of the average workers. Besides, unemployment is becoming more and more severe. It was pointed out in the ILO pointed out in its World of Work Report 2012 that one of three workers on the average is unemployed or in poverty (approximately 1.1 billion in total) around the globe, and 600 million jobs will have to be created over the next decade. Secondly, economic inequality is becoming aggravated; social mobility is reduced; and the living standards of the ordinary people sink down significantly; and social contradictions are further intensified. The "Occupy Wall Street" movement since 2009 is a prominent demonstration of the phenomena. According to its latest survey results released by the US Pew Research Center in early 2012, the US is becoming more and more aware of class conflict; 66% of those interviewed, that is, 19% up over 2009, believe there is a "very sharp" or "sharp" conflict between the rich and the poor. Thirdly, free market becomes a tool for a handful of the elite and elite alliances to seek profits and private gains. "People's faith in the free market becomes shaky". People used to believe that free market could offer roughly equal opportunities and that anyone, regardless of his background, could succeed and win social respect and status with his own efforts, only that the myths seem to have shattered. Financial elite and the elite in other social sectors form a strong coalition of interests. They are greedy for and "only responsible for profits," ignore their social responsibilities and public interests, use political power to hinder reforms so that the public have to pay bills for "big and never-failing" businesses engaging in financial speculations, and to bear the impacts of the crisis and the cut of public expenditure by the government. Like a review in British newspaper "Daily Mail", the crisis and the social unrest caused by the crisis seem to be the contrast between a few of the financial elite or financial monopoly capital and the ordinary people on the surface, but indicate that the cornerstone of free market capitalism is shaking if one takes a deeper look.

2. Capitalism remains the winner of "the competition of imperfect systems," and it will be twice-born with a few self-improvements.

Former Federal Reserve Board Chairman Alan Greenspan explained that capitalism has been making successes in human history and created huge wealth for the human society; that corruption, greed and inequality are not traits of capitalism; and that aggravated income inequality is even more a result of globalization and technical innovation. Harvard University professor Summers, who once chaired the White House National Economic Council in the Obama administration, claimed it to be only an engine breakdown of capitalism which can be solved with proper fiscal and currency policies instead of bold structural reforms. Alcatel-Lucent CEO Ben J. Verwaayan believed that capitalism creates wealth, opportunities and freedom for the middle class in the world, so it remains a desirable system for most people. Besides, someone believes it better to attribute the current crisis not to the defects of the capitalist system, but to government incompetence. Therefore, the setbacks and difficulties of capitalism are just partial and temporary, and capitalism will become vital again with good repair. British Prime Minister David Cameron calls on solving the present predicament of capitalism with "responsible capitalism" and "moral capitalism of the market" Chairman of the World Economic Forum Schwab points out that economic competitions today do not rely solely on capital investment, but more on innovation and non-material services, talent doctrine where talented people and innovations are core elements shall be used to improve capitalism so that capitalism can continue to lead economic and social progresses. Secretary-general of the International Trade Union Confederation Shalan Burrow said that governments of Western countries fail to sufficiently invest in social protection; and that social unrest will continue. She called on global companies to invest in creating jobs and developing "productive economy" Many of the influential business elite have expressed their opinions on how to improve capitalism. Microsoft Corp. founder Bill Gates claims that capitalism remains a great system, but pure selfish capitalism has ended; in the future, technical innovation and welfare pricing should be used to build "altruistic capitalism". Deloitte CEO Joe Echevarria advocates developing "sympathetic capitalism," that is, regaining balance between economic growth and public demand for social protection. The Carlyle Group co-founder David Rubenstein believes that capitalism is not perfect, but as long as it can overcome its two big disadvantages—unrestrained pursuit of wealth and social inequality, it could revive.

3. The vitality of capitalism is shifting from the West to the East, and emerging economies are becoming the advocators and supporters of capitalism.

Desai, senior professor of London School of Economics, believes that capitalism full of vitality—vibrant and innovative capitalism which single-mindedly pursues economic growth—has been transferred to the East, though capitalism in the West is suffering geriatrics. Rubenstein claims that former communist and socialist countries have become the most skillful controllers of capitalism. The US magazine Times comments that China and India are hugging capitalism without any hesitation; taking reform measures to speed up the flow of capital and loosen national control of the banks, interest rates and currency, and their people are using the market to accumulate wealth rapidly, when the capitalist countries in the West are stuck in crises. Associate editor of British newspaper The Times Kaletsky brings up that capitalism is always full of new vigor in crises; that the current crisis will help transform capitalism from free trade capitalism in the 19th century, state welfare capitalism in the 1930s and neo-liberalism in the 1980s into "capitalism version 4.0" which is more mild and equality-based.

4. Although Chinese model is thought to constitute a big challenge against capitalism, no system or model can completely substitute capitalism.

The US-Japanese scholar Fukuyama says that many people are optimistic about China's system, not only because China's record of economic successes, but because China is able to always make big and complicated decisions very quickly, which forms a sharp contrast with the worrisome decision-making paralysis having been harassing the U.S. and Europe in the past several years. Chinese model and the growing inequality are two big crucial challenges faced by capitalism, but Chinese model is backed by its special political culture and historical traditions, and has a number of disadvantages. It is difficult to be copied by the other countries. British journal The Economist claims that the state capitalism of China creates "seemingly prosperity;" and that in the long run, economic growth and social stability can't be achieved along in China. British newspaper Financial Times believes that the mixed model of China where public ownership is the basis and market economy is introduced will cause corruption and inequality; the authoritarian mode of Singapore has been losing public trust and support though it once brought high-speed economic growth. These models can't be substitutes of the Western free market capitalism.

II. "State capitalism": the enemy of free-market capitalism?

In the reflections by the West of the predicament of capitalism, the so-called "state capitalism" becomes a focal topic, indicating that "what role should the state play in economic development?" is actually one of the core issues for the future development of capitalism. The West labels China and Russia "state capitalism", and claims that state capitalism is a big challenge and threat of free market capitalism. The argument is becoming a basic consensus of in the elite political and business figures and a topic heated by leading public opinions in the West, and producing substantial policy influences.

At the Davos 2012 World Economic Forum, Rubenstein said, "You now have two types of capitalism competing with one another. You have laissez-faire and state capitalism, which has been creating more jobs at a greater rate than we are in the West. If the West doesn't solve its debt problems and make government more efficient, the state capitalism model could prevail" His view was approved by a lot of attendees to the forum. In this January, British journal "The Economist" published a special report on state capitalism, in which it claimed that state capitalism is the most powerful enemy met by laissez-faire capitalism so far. In fact, the debate on the state capitalism model continues to heat up in the West since the outbreak of the financial crisis. In October 2009, Soros, a well-known financier in the world, said that the global order before the outbreak of the financial crisis was the Washington Consensus-centered "multilateral mechanism of international capitalism," but the financial crisis severely wounded "international capitalism," and was challenged by "state capitalism" led by the Chinese model. The President of Eurasia Group Ian Bremmer also published a monograph—The End of the Free Market: Who Wins the War Between States and Corporations?—to discuss the issue.

In this debate, the state capitalism model is thought to integrate national power with the power of capitalism. Specifically, the ultimate objective of state-owned enterprises (as defined by the UN Conference on Trade and Development, an enterprise where the government holds more than 10% of its shares is a state-owned enterprise) and sovereign wealth funds is to maximize the government's political strength. State capitalism worries the West because it now has significant features such as "being large-scale, emerging fast, having diverse means, and being increasingly internationalized". It is developing vigorously, and its global influence keeps growing. …governments, particular in the emerging world, are learning how to use the market to promote political ends". "The invisible hand of the market is giving way to the visible, and often authoritarian, hand of state capitalism" State capitalism may become "the future trend". According to the data cited by "The Economist", state companies make up 80% of the value of the stock market in China, 62% in Russia and 38% in Brazil. They accounted for one-third of the emerging world's foreign direct investment between 2003 and 2010. Sovereign wealth funds now control 4.8 trillion US dollars of capital, which will grow to 10 trillion US dollars by 2020.

Westerners understand state capitalism from the angle of the antithesis of free market capitalism, and compete to doubt state capitalism, thinking that state capitalism use capital far less efficiently than private companies, so it is not conducive to improving corporate innovativeness and labor productivity, though it indeed can get an upper hand and succeed in infrastructure construction; that state capitalism connives at the rent-seeking behavior of company elite, leading to corruption; and that state capitalism can't well operate only under the control of an elite government, so it is much influenced by political factors. Even if state capitalism has so many weaknesses to the West as mentioned above, it still has adverse effects on the world economy and the free market capitalism model that can't be ignored, because "the crisis of liberal capitalism has been rendered more serious by the rise of a potent alternative: state capitalism"

Firstly, state capitalism will shock the global trade system, especially the principle of fair trade, and then trigger trade wars. Charlene Barshefsky, former U.S. trade representative, says the rise of powerful state-led economies like China and Russia is undermining the established post-WWII trading system; the lavish investment of these countries in strategic emerging industries will place private companies at an extremely unfavorable position. Secondly, countries implementing state capitalism are developing with "concerted efforts," and quite a number of countries are considering following this model. For example, for the decision, made by the French Sarkozy administration, to build up a sovereign wealth fund, officials of the French Finance Ministry attributed such government intervention fervor to China's influence. Japan's trade ministry viewed the emergence of state capitalism as one of the most important drivers for its development of a new interventionist industrial strategy in 2010.

In the debate on state capitalism in the West, China becomes a representative in the emergence of state capitalism around the globe. Soros and the others generalize features of China's state capitalism in the following three aspects: First, economic decision-making and behaviors are fundamentally driven by political rather than commercial motives; second, it gets resources and energy around the globe relying on the state-owned enterprises and sovereign wealth fund, despite the nature of the regime of the target countries and the interests of these countries' ordinary people; third, more attention is paid to bilateral relations rather than actively participating in the international multilateral system, like it did not join the Extractive Industries Transparency Initiative. Obviously, the West labels China state capitalism and hypes up the so-called confrontation between two types of capitalism, mainly to shift the focus and conflicts; transfer responsibilities; seize the commanding height of morals and public opinions; use the so-called international rules to constrain, limit and suppress competitors, and establish a new system for the new round of economic globalization so as to protect its global hegemony. Now, the doubt of and attack against state capitalism by the West go completely along with the economic strategies and policies of the Western countries. They are mutually supported. The trend will go deeper in the foreseeable future, and then challenge the future development of China. In October 2011, the US Secretary of State Hillary Clinton in article The US's Pacific Century requested China to remove preferential treatment for the Chinese enterprises and huge subsidies allocated to its state-own enterprises, and to stop policy discrimination against the US, other foreign countries and foreign-funded enterprises. She accused that China's behaviors were not conductive to healthy economic competitions required to be open, free, transparent and fair in general. While promising to set up a trade law enforcement department to investigate "unfair trade practices" in China and other countries, the Obama administration made great efforts to carry forward highly exclusive "Trans-Pacific Partnership Agreement" (TPP), attempting to consolidate the established advantages of the US in the region, even around the globe (like its global strategic layout of advanced manufacturing) with high thresholds in IP protection, environment protection and laborers' rights, and reshape the international economic mechanism and trade rules favorable to the US in the American way and with American standards.

III. The threefold predicament of capitalism

1. Seen from historical development, in the 20 or more years after the end of the Cold War, capitalism is facing new challenges.

It is the first comprehensive and profound crisis in the West in the context of globalization. On the one hand, in the era of globalization, capitalism develops from state monopoly capitalism to international monopoly capitalism; economic activities go beyond national boundaries; and monopoly capital is not controlled by the state. On the other hand, the cyclical crisis of capitalism has not disappeared yet and the economic crisis in the era of globalization is even more complicated. It is difficult for traditional nation-state structure and governance model to effectively deal with such systematic crises. Meanwhile, along with the mass rise of the emerging world and the enhancement of various non-governmental forces, the West has become less dominant over the international order, and globalization "dividends" obtained by them by controlling the international order have reduced, making it more difficult for them to get rid of the crisis, to some extent. It is safe to say that economic globalization brings an increasingly prominent double-edge effect to the West. After getting great benefits, the developed countries have to pay for industrial hollowing, economic bubbles and weakened technical advantages. Nobel laureate in Economics and Stanford University professor Michael Spence published an article in Foreign Policy in July 2011, in which he pointed out that along with globalization in the recent decade, the emerging world has achieved sustained and irreversible improvements in the international industrial chain. The U.S. advantages in information technology and biomedicine have been threatened, and the U.S. achieves economic growth mainly on "non-traded goods" Globalization splits economic growth and employment in the US, and the problems like unemployment and income inequality have become increasingly intensified.

2. Seen from the present predicament of capitalism, the US, Europe and Japan—the three major pillars of the capitalist world—are greatly shocked. Besides, the three major core elements of the capitalist system, namely the market economy, democratic politics and social contract, have faced problems of varying degrees.

First, it is market failure. Resources are excessively centralized in the financial sector, "the reasonable proportion between speculation using fictitious capital and the real economy-based investment activities has been seriously broken, even out of control" The US among similar countries, due to excessive consumption, lending excesses and excessive import and welfare, will find it difficult to mitigate and adjust unbalanced domestic economic structure in a short term, and their long-term and sustained economic growth is not guaranteed and fully motivated. Second, it is the disability of their democratic institution. "Polarization" is prevailing in party politics. Deficit policy is abused to excessively please the voters. Political parties blame one another and have intensified struggles. They therefore can't develop before implementing policies for long-term national interests and overall social interests, leaving room for market speculations. Since the financial crisis, many Western countries have been stuck in the policy dilemma of austerity and restoration of economic growth, and had so few appropriate fiscal and currency policies. Third, it is the failure of social contract. The public are in the dilemma of having no income increase; the middle class see reduced incomes and living standards; the costs of welfare society are hard to bear; the social values system that respects diversified cultures is doubted; and the society is becoming more and more conservative. According to a report of the Royal Institute of International Affairs, since the financial crisis broke out, the right-wing populist trend has obviously ascended in many European countries; anti-immigration and anti-Muslim sentiment, denial of equality, rejection of openness and political discontent interact; and the situation is very likely to be further exacerbated. Therefore, the current plight of capitalism is the result of problems and their resonance in major links like the market economic system, the political system, the social welfare system and the values system. It is hard for the Western capitalist countries to develop and carry out systematic solutions.

3. Analyzing the prospects and the way out of the plight of capitalism, capitalist countries are in a vulnerable period of development in general. Even if they finally set to walk out of the plight, it will be hard for them to return to the "good old days" of the post-Cold War period, before the outbreak of financial crisis.

British weekly magazine "The Economist" published comments which bluntly pointed out: "the system is walking to a crossroad, where there are neither reform paths domestically nor alternatives externally." On the one hand, there are critics everywhere, but no real reformers in the West, and the elite in various sectors can't reach an agreement on how to solve the plight of capitalism and can't overcome the psychological disorder against learning from other development models, while on the other, the world economy will enter a period of "high inflation, low growth" in the following years, and the external economic environment on the whole is not conducive to the efforts made by the Western countries to promote their domestic economic adjustments. The Western monopoly on the global market, resources and technologies is declining, and the credibility and efficiency of the Western development model is being doubted by more and more countries. Developing countries are paying more and more attention to learning from the emerging economies. In line with the above, most Western capitalist countries including the U.S. confront a threefold predicament in terms of soon achieving settled recovery, revitalizing the growth and competiveness in the medium term, as well as justifying and securing the hegemonic position or domination in global government in the long run.

The reflections of capitalism by the West now should be treated objectively, calmly and dialectically. On the one hand, we have to be always alert to the capitalist countries because they always transfer conflicts by exerting political pressures on other countries through financial means, trade means or using the international rules and mechanisms, but on the other, we have to study the lessons and experience in the development of capitalism; seize the opportunity that the say and institutional hegemony of neo-liberalism is being severely shocked; make good use of the institutional plight in the West and the "retroaction" of various system offensives against China; promote the development of sciences; and advance institutional innovations so as to always keep the vigor and vitality of the socialist system of China.

Y. 14

Some Thoughts on the International Strategy

He Bingmeng[1]

Abstract: The start of the international financial crisis in the United States and the outbreak of the subsequent social unrest in the U.S. and Europe, the Middle East and Africa marked the bankruptcy of the neo-liberalism model. The Status of the US, "the sole superpower", is shaking and human society is going into another epoch of "social turbulence." At present, China's international strategic choice should be: adhering to the five "holding highs": establishing the widest international front to restrict the US hegemonism; promoting world multi-polarization and democratization of international relations. I think there should be three keywords in China's diplomacy: anti-hegemony, democracy and institutional approach. China should focus to develop a richer international relations discourse in order to have a say in the field of international relations theory at the earliest convenience.

Key words: U.S. financial crisis; bankruptcy of neo-liberalism; US hegemony; international strategies

---

1 He Bingmeng, executive director of World Socialism Research Center attached to CASS, former secretary-general of CASS, member of Presidium of the Academic Divisions.

Introduction

Materialist dialectics holds, "The nature of a thing is determined mainly by the principle aspect of a contradiction, namely the principle aspect which has gained the dominant position. The principal and the non-principal aspects of a contradiction transform themselves into each other and the nature of the thing changes accordingly"[2] It tells us that, in the contemporary era, it is the world capitalism—which has dominance in the political and military strengths and even cultural soft strength—that determines the nature and basic characteristic of the current times. The changes in capitalism, especially the changes in the U.S. will directly influence the transformations in the world pattern. Therefore, to observe the grand trends in the world, certain attention has to be paid to examine contemporary capitalism, especially the development of the US—the capitalist hegemon. Only after a proper examination of contemporary capitalism and the US, can we better study and determine China's international strategy.

In the first ten years of the 21st century, the U.S. has encountered too much trouble: Soon after entering the 21st century, it was stuck in the 11th cyclical economic recession after the WWII; it could start economic recovery till around 2004, and then saw the outbreak of the "subprime mortgage crisis" in 2007. The so-called "subprime mortgage crisis" was nothing but a "cover-up" of the financial crisis in nature. Unexpectedly, things got worse and worse. In less than a year, the crisis was intensified and assumed a comprehensive character. Wall Street financial magnates like Lehman Brothers, Fannie Mae, Freddie Mac, Merrill Lynch & Co. and the American International Group (AIG) have collapsed one by one. Due to its position as the hegemon of the current international financial and monetary system, the financial crisis rapidly swept the whole world like a plague. The most severe international financial crisis in nearly a century broke out, and the human society began to suffer another economic catastrophe after the Great Depression in the 1930s. The US is finally becoming "the originator of human disasters"

It has been five years since the outbreak of the financial crisis in the U.S. and the subsequent international financial crisis, and the human society is still struggling desperately. The US and the developed capitalist countries of the Europe are witnessing an in-depth growth of the financial crisis, and the sovereign debt crisis has pushed many countries to the verge of bankruptcy. It never rains but it pours. What's especially fatal is the social crisis coming immediately after the financial crisis—international financial capital cartels and their political agents are trying hard to shift the losses caused by the financial crisis on to ordinary people by laying off employees in large scales

---

2 Selected Readings of Mao Zedong, People's Publishing House, 1986, p.163.

and pushing tens of thousands of them to the ranks of the unemployed; significantly lowering the wages to exert super economic exploitation on tens of thousands of laborers; substantially reducing social welfare which secured the welfare and social security, namely pushing them to the streets.

Since September 17, 2011, "Occupy Wall Street" movement which spoke for "the 99 %" has begun to shake the base of the US international financial monopoly capital and was supported by the majority Americans. It soon spread from New York to all big and medium-cities of the US. Although it was brutally repressed by the US police and authorities; although unarmed peaceful protesters were expulsed brutally and violently and even thousands of them were prisoned, the "Occupy" movement still grew vigorously. It is a miracle that the "Occupy" resistance movement could continue for years in the US, a country filled with policemen and prisons! Europe has not been quiet, either. From Britain to France, Italy, Greece, Spain, even Germany, workers, teachers, students, citizens, even public servants have joined strikes, held walkouts and protest marches. Even armed struggles have occurred from time to time.

Since the 1980s and 90s, the US has been promoting neo-liberalism in the world. For developing countries, neo-liberalism is the proximate *source of trouble*. A direct consequence of adapting to and promoting neo-liberalism is the collapse of national economy, and then the formation of "economic dependence" to the US and British international financial monopoly capital, leading to severe polarization where the poor—the vast majority of the people—are poorer and the rich—a handful of people—are richer, and sowing the seeds of social unrest. The large-scale unrest in the Middle East and Africa offers enough evidence to explain this. Egypt in the Middle East is the most typical example among the unrests in the region. In 1991, the US sold its "Washington Consensus" to Egypt. Its loyal companion in the Middle East, namely President Mubarak signed a restructuring agreement with the IMF (International Monetary Fund)which is still under the protection of the US international financial monopoly capital. In the agreement, both agreed to mandatorily promote financial liberalism, privatization, deregulation, open market regime, privileged treatment to foreign investors so as to make Egypt model country following and applying the US's neoliberal reforms in the Middle East. The result was that the national economic lifelines of Egypt like banks were held by the international financial monopoly capital; national wealth of Egypt went into the hands of international financial monopoly capital and a handful of people in Egypt; social polarization was severe; 90% of the Egyptian people did not have any share from the GDP growth and the achievements of economic growth; 40 % of the Egyptian people lived under the poverty line. The international financial crisis made the situation worse for the Egyptian people, victims of neoliberal reforms. Manipulated by the international financial monopoly capital and the comprador capital in Egypt, prices lost control and rose sharply; inflation went up like crazy; the unemployment rate kept growing; and the real wages of the ordinary workers and people continued to decline...All these inevitably led to the riot on January 25, 2011 and triggered the so-called "Arab Spring," and soon spread to Tunisia, Yemen and Libya. Despite quite different causes, the unrests in these countries were more or less relevant to the expansion of neo-liberalism. Accordingly Samir Amin, the famous Egyptian scholar and thinker, pointed out, "'Egyptian revolution' symbolizing 'Arab Spring' points to the possible end of the neoliberal system which has been shaken at all levels, political, economic and social."

Thus in line with the above, the US financial crisis and the international financial has caused, the debt crisis in the US and Europe and the subsequent continuous social unrest in Western developed countries including the US and European countries, the violent social unrest in Africa and the Middle East being the symbol, human beings have entered another "unrest situation" or "period of social agitation" In such context, the international strategy to be adopted by China is of great significance to China's administering and controlling the international situation in the future, to continue in to advancing China's socialist modernization, and for pushing forward the world socialist cause.

II. Characteristics of the present world pattern and its causes

In the recent 20 years, the world has been full of ups and downs. Events which have occurred during this period and greatly influenced the changes in the world pattern are the following four:

1. The dissolution of the Soviet Union and the dramatic changes in Eastern Europe at the turn of the 1980s and 90s

This was a huge incident in the human history in the 20th century, which had three impacts on the world pattern: Firstly, the dissolution of the Soviet Union put an end to the Cold War where the world's two superpowers, namely the Soviet Union and the US, struggled for world hegemony. The US became the sole superpower of the world. "The only major power" supremacy pattern took shape. Secondly, the dissolution of the Soviet Union and the dramatic changes in Eastern Europe were not only results of continuous "peaceful evolution" strategy targeting the Soviet Union and the socialist countries in Eastern Europe by the US- and Europe-led international monopoly capitalist class, but also caused by the subversion and collapse of the socialist cause from inside, namely the communist parties in the Soviet Union and Eastern European countries, mainly the

Khrushchev—Gorbachev traitorous clique inside the Communist Party of the Soviet Union. Due to their acts, the socialist camp was formally disintegrated and the world's socialist movements worldwide has entered low ebb. The reality also warns the communists, especially members of the victorious communist parties, that it is a must to be always alert to any possible traitorous cliques emerging inside the party. Thirdly, the contradictions and struggles between the two systems and two roads still exist in the world, but their strengths are greatly unbalanced. The capitalist camp led by the US is holding an absolute superiority.

2. The introduction of the "Washington Consensus" being the symbol, and the troika of neoliberalism, the international financial currency system where US dollar is the sole hegemon, and IT revolution being the driving force, the US and Britain are transiting to the stage of international financial monopoly capitalism mainly featured by the neoliberal model.

The "Washington Consensus" has made huge impacts on the world pattern: Firstly, the international financial monopoly capitalism is extremely predatory, parasitic and decadent. Some British scholars like Peter Nolan call it wild capitalism. Introduced in 1990, the "Washington Consensus" promotes neoliberal capitalism around the globe, bringing great disasters to the US and British people and the whole peoples of the world. Secondly, the neoliberal model, typically represented by the US and Britain, policies promotes the so-called "efficiency first"—which is featured by "capital rights first". It domestically exacerbates polarization, and intensifies the social contradictions in these countries. The international propagation of hegemony featured by neoconservatism or neorealism continues to deepen the domestic and foreign rancor against the US in the current stage of international financial monopoly capitalism.

3. The spectacular rise of the developing countries: China, Russia, Brazil and India

When the US, Britain among other Western countries were stuck in the war in Afghanistan and that in Iraq and had no leisure to think about others, instead the developing countries like China and Russia focused on developing modernization and achieved great progress. That was another major event in the world at the turn of the 20th and 21st centuries. It has very profound influences on the world pattern mainly in the following three aspects: Firstly, thanks to their increased economic strength, especially China and Russia and other rapidly developing countries have gained greater say in international affairs. In particular, the development path of China has been more and more influential in the vast developing countries. Secondly, the influence and position of the US have weakened relatively. On the international stage, a country's influence and status depends on two points: enjoying a dominant position of morals—as the Chinese saying goes: "A just cause gains great support, an unjust one gains little," secondly, if its status is sufficiently supported by this economic, political and military strength.

In the recent decade or more, the US often employed threats to use force in the international relations. It even utilized ridiculous lies and manipulation. It waged armed invasion of Iraq and some other sovereign states alleging them having weapons of mass destruction; massacred Islamic believers; completely tore off the hypocritical mask of the so-called "democracy" and "guardian of humanitarianism" exposed the ugly face of state terror; and was morally denounced by the world people who love peace and freedom. Besides, the long-term stationing of the US troops abroad has greatly consumed the economic and military strength of the US and gradually demonstrated its powerlessness to continue to dominate the world. Thirdly, the above two points create conditions for the economic and political multi-polarization.

4. In the first decade of the 21st century, the US has been suffering from economic recession, financial crisis, debt crisis, overall economic crisis, which has finally led to a global financial crisis and debt crisis and made the US "originator of human disasters"

The financial crisis and economic recession in the US have three impacts on the world pattern: firstly, the economic crisis and financial crisis, which have continued for a decade, has become the last straw that overwhelms the supremacy of the US, "the sole major power", and have further shaken the US hegemony. Secondly, the ongoing financial crisis announces the complete bankruptcy of neo-liberalism, of the mainstream ideology in the US, and symbolizes the incoming end of the historical transition of capitalism, —represented by the US and Britain—to the stage of international monopoly financial capital. Thirdly, the world performs the prelude from the supremacy of "the sole major power" to multi-polarity.

All in all, in some sense, the present world pattern seems to reproduce the "Warring States" period of China. In the era of Warring States, some dreamed to be the overlord, but was powerless; more and more parties fought for their respective interests, which was the so-called "multi-polarity" But we can say that there are too many unknowns where the world pattern will go. Therefore, the world today is in a "chaotic period" or in a transitional phase. Scientifically grasping this feature of the present world pattern should be the logical starting point of China when developing its international strategy.

III. China's choice of current international strategy

When human beings are in such a "chaotic period" or transitional phase, China's choice of current international strategy should be: building the broadest international united front against hegemonism to restrain the US, and promoting the trend of "multi-polarization" and "democratization" of the international relations. Specifically, China should adopt the following strategies:

1. Holding high the banner of "anti-hegemonism" and "seeking no hegemony"

Hegemony and political repression and economic plunder go hand in hand. A country's hegemony or rule will inevitably be accompanied by political suppression and economic plunder of other countries or nations. Socialist China must hold high the banner of fighting against all forms hegemonism, that is, while fighting against other countries' attempt to seek hegemony we should always stick to the principle of never seeking hegemony.

2. Holding high the banner of "democratization" of the international relations

All countries, big or small, should be equal. In international affairs, China must oppose the final say monopoly held by a few powers, and advocate soliciting of opinions from various countries big or small and handle international relations and conflicts on the basis of comprehensive communication and negotiation.

3. Holding high the banner of the UN's leading role when handling the issues related to international relations

China must respect and give full play to the leading role of the UN in handling international relations; and assist the UN in developing or adjusting regulations, systems and mechanisms for dealing with international affairs according to the UN Charter.

4. Holding high the banner of respecting other countries' sovereignty and national independence

The affairs of each country should be left to the decision of the people of that country. China must oppose interference in the internal affairs of other countries with the so-called excuse of "human rights above sovereignty" In particular, China has to oppose the threat of force and subversion targeting other states.

The above four "hold highs" should be the five basic principles of diplomacy to be followed by China in a fairly long time in the future. There are three keywords: anti-hegemony, democracy and institutional approach. The four "hold highs" and three "keywords" seem to be capable of being the basic framework of China's international strategy in the foreseeable future. China has to gradually occupy the commanding height of morals in the international community by carrying out its international strategy within such basic framework.

IV. Building up China's say in the field of international relations theory

In order to successfully implement the above tactics and strategies, China must first build up its say in the fields of international relations theories or international relations science.

Since the 1970s and 80s, in the fields of international relations theories or international relations science, there have been two most influential theories: neo-realism (sometimes known as structural realism) and neoliberal institutionalism (sometimes shortened as neo-liberalism in the books written by Western scholars. In order to avoid confusion between neoliberal institutionalism and the mainstream economic theory of neo-liberalism in the West, this paper specifically calls it neoliberal institutionalism.)

Neo-realism is relative to traditional realism. Traditional realism is a theory of traditional international relations in the West. It is based on the thinking of philosophy of history, namely the principle of humanity. In the 1950s and 60s, it was challenged by behaviorism and other theories for its defects. Some realists like Kenneth Waltz, in order to defend realism and adapt to the needs of global expansion of international financial monopoly capital, reviewed the theories of traditional realism, and gradually developed theories of neo-realism in the 1970s and 80s. Neo-realism replaces the principle of humanity followed by traditional realism with the principle of system theory, holding that the factor that continuously plays a role in international relations is the international architecture. The architecture they mean includes two aspects: the fundamental organizational principle of the international system is anarchy; and the distribution of abilities (position of strength) among states. To put it simple, it emphasizes power without any constraints in international relations, that is, the hegemon should have the final say. It is a hegemony theory that speaks for the interests military groups, within the international financial monopoly capital of the US.

Neoliberal institutionalism as the antithesis of neo-realism took shape in the 1970s and 80s. Representatives of neoliberal institutionalism include Robert Keohane. Neoliberal institutionalism believes that the state (strength)-centered international relations theory advocated by neo-realism ignores the mutual dependence of countries and the role of international institutions; and that it has to go beyond nations or countries; pay attention to the international system and institutions; and value international cooperation, international economic exchanges, and mutual communication when handling international relations. As theory of international relations, it represents the interests pursued by the middle and petty bourgeois or the bourgeois left wing.

The say in the international community is an important component of a country's soft power. Building up China's say in the theoretical field of international relations is an important link to improve China's international status and influence. In this aspect, the community of social sciences of China, especially the Chinese social scientists studying issues and theories of international relations shoulder an important historical mission. In a sence the study of the theories of international relations is an arduous basic theoretical study. For that reason, we expect determined researchers to do painstaking researches and fill the blanks or areas of weaknesses of China's social sciences in this field.

Y. 15

Social Crisis Induces the Resurgence of French Left-wing Thoughts

Shen Xiaoquan[1]

Abstract: Repeatedly shaken by severe economic and social crisis, the French society has seen a rise of various social thoughts that reflect the emotions and voices of the French people, which seems to change the French political landscape profoundly. Mainstream conservatism has lost its appeal among the public, and various extremist and radical right wing thoughts have emerged. One of the prominent trends in the aftermath of the 2012 French presidential election is the continued expansion of the ultra-Right forces, coupled by a comeback of the left-wing thoughts that regained support from the public. The main manifestations are as follows: the Socialist Party's return to power after 17 years, the biggest left-wing party of France; the unexpected rise of the radical left-wing forces; the attempts by the traditional left-wing force, the French Communist Party, shows signs of leaving behind its slump period, and finally the vivid rise of "anti-globalization" movement that is sweeping across the French society.

Key words: French presidential election; left wing thoughts; anti-globalization

---

[1] Shen Xiaoquan, visiting scholar of the World Socialism Research Center attached to CASS, researcher in Xinhua News Agency World Research Center.

Severely shocked by severe economic and social crises, the French society has seen a vivid rise of various social thoughts that reflect the emotions and voices of the French people. Mainstream conservatism has lost its appeal among the public; and various extremist and radical thoughts have emerged. The ultra-Right forces continue to expand, coupled by a comeback of the left-wing thoughts that have regained support from the public. During the French presidential election last year, these new trends and changes in social thoughts could be seen even clearer.

I. Two extremes among the French people in terms of political orientation

The results of the first-round voting was held in April 22, 2012 have not only produced candidates for the second-round voting but also tested the strength of political forces represented by the other candidates. Right wing president Sarkozy seeking re-election and Francois Hollande, the socialist candidate, both received the majority votes, the votes they obtained being 27.08% and 28.63%, respectively. They were not high, instead even lower than expected. The votes received by both candidates accounted for less than 56% of total votes and the rest votes which were more than 44 went to the other candidates. In France the strength and influence of the traditional left-wing and right-wing parties tend to diminish.

Besides the left-wing Socialist Party and the right-wing Union for a Popular Movement, the other three of the top five parties in this election were ultra right-wing National Front, Left Front and centrist Democratic Movement. The five parties constituted a full political spectrum of "ultra right-wing—right-wing—centrist—left-wing—ultra left-wing" The votes obtained by ultra right-wing National Front surged from 10.44% five years ago to 18.01% this time; that of votes obtained by Left Front, the French Communist Party being its core, surged from 1.93% five years ago to 11.13% this time. The centrist Democratic Movement saw a reverse change. In 2007, centrist candidate Francois Bayrou obtained as high as % 18.3 of all votes, but this time votes received by him has fallen to 9.11%. The change in votes showed the rise of the two extreme parties and the decline of the center parties, and the votes for the traditional left-wing and right-wing parties were about up to the average. If the trend in 2007 French presidential election was votes going from both ends to the centrist, 2012 French presidential election would reveal the political orientation of the ordinary French people from the centrist party and traditional left-wing and right-wing camps to the two extremes. The phenomenon of "polarization and going to extremes" reflects French people's resentfulness and confusion amidst deep economic and social crises.

After the WWII, France experienced "glorious thirty years"—its economy developed rapidly; France reemerged as one major industrially-developed countries of the West; a whole set of social security systems were built in succession; and France became the template and model admired by other world countries. However, it did not last long. The 1970s witnessed the outbreak of the first oil crisis in the world, which dragged the French economy to a downward course. Since 1981, either the left-wing Socialist Party or the right-wing Conservative Party succeeded in effectively halting the decline of the national economy, nor could lead France to rejuvenation. Especially, in recent years, strongly shocked by the international financial crisis and the sovereign debt crisis in Europe, the French economy fell into recession, become less competitive, with severe debts and serious unemployment, and has seen a widening gap between the rich and the poor. Excessive social welfare emphasis had become unsustainable, and the French people were complaining. Social discontent grew sharply.

In this context, traditional conservatism was questioned and criticized for failing to govern the country properly. President Sarkozy encountered a miserable failure in his attempt to win a new term after his 5-year term of office; and the conservative Union for a Popular Movement, which had been in power since 1995, has now lost control over the supreme power of the state. Extremist political thoughts rose gradually, among which the first were extremist right-wing thoughts led by National Front. National Front is racist, advocates narrow nationalism, discriminates the immigrants, and its leader has even touted Nazi fascists. Since the 1980s, it has become increasingly influential. In the previous elections that reflect the strength of ultra right-wing political forces, National Front was supported by about 15% of the voters, and the figure rose to 18% in the 2012 presidential campaign, once again shocking France and the entire Europe. The ultra right-wing thoughts and forces keep growing, which has become a normality in French politics in the recent 30 or more years. Many voters vote for National Front in the election not necessarily because they agree with ethnic xenophobia, but mainly because they want to express their protest against various social ills and government incompetence.

II. Socialist Party returns to power due to deepened social crises

In this presidential campaign, the most notable thing was the re-emergence of various thoughts representing left-wing politics. The Socialist Party is the strongest left-wing party in France. In 1981, Mitterrand was elected French President and the Socialist Party got the ruling position. In the following 14 years of Mitterrand's administration, the French government advocated social democratic model of development, which became the mainstream leading the French society. Later, Chirac, leader of the conservative Gaullist party, succeeded Mitterrand as the French President. In the 17 years since 1995, the Socialist Party has always been the opposition party, and defeated by the conservative party in the two presidential campaigns during this period. In the presidential campaign in 2002, Jospin, the Socialist Party candidate, has even lost to the National Front candidate and was eliminated from the election in the first-round voting.

In the 2012 presidential campaign, the Socialist Party had been favored since the very beginning. Former secretary of the Socialist Party Hollande was elected as the presidential candidate in October 2011. Despite the fact that he was not an experienced statesman or and always kept a low-profile, his support rate in the public opinion polls grew all the way. In the second-round voting in the presidential campaign on May 6, he defeated Nicolas Sarkozy who was seeking another term of office; and the Socialist Party regained the country's supreme authority. Hollande had won easily because Sarkozy did not have any good performance record and his way of behaviors was disgusting in the five years when he was in office. However, seen from social causes, in the face of growing social crises, the vast majority of the public were very discontented, so they had pinned their hope for the future with the left-wing. That was the root cause for the victory of the Socialist Party. It was just this such social atmosphere where "people wanted a change" and the same social discontent determining the opinions of the public that pushed the Socialist Party back to power. Washington Post pointed out that the crisis of capitalism had created opportunities for the European left-wing parties for climbing to power. France has offered as a typical example of that.

III. "Melenchon phenomenon" — was not a contingency

This French presidential campaign saw the emergence of a new political organization, the Left Front. Jean-Luc Melenchon, 61 years old, had joined the Socialist Party in 1977, in the presidential campaign, he led as the representative of the Left Front, and became hot and popular. In 2000, he had served as the minister in charge of vocational education in the French cabinet. In 2008, he left the Socialist Party and established the Left Party. In 2011, his Left Party formed a left-wing coalition with French Communist Party. He was elected as the candidate representing the Left Front (Communist Party of France, Left Party, Unitarian Left) in the 2012 French presidential election At the beginning, he was not even noticed by the public, and was only supported by less than 5% of the French people. As the campaign proceeded, his popularity surged. His support rate poll forecast on the eve of the election reached above 15%, and he was expected to be in the third rank winner following Hollande and Sarkozy. According to the results of the first-round voting, although the votes he obtained was lower than expected, it was indeed "a miracle" that he exceeded many other candidates, who had run the presidential campaign for many times, and got a support rate of 11.13%, the fourth rank.

The "Melenchon phenomenon" was by no means accidental, but an outbreak of the social discontent nurtured in the hearts of the French society for years. March 18, 2012 was the 142nd anniversary of the Paris Commune, and Melenchon addressed the rally on Bastille Square, symbol of the French Revolution. In his speech, Melenchon strongly criticized social polarization and regress in social welfare and security; advocated an immediate substantial increase in the minimum wage; called for a "civil rebel" to defend mass interests; and requested the amendment of the constitution and building "the Sixth Republic of France" The campaign meetings he spoke attracted more than 100,000 audiences, demonstrating that his ability of mobilization was much better than Sarkozy and Hollande who had administrative resources and donors. It caused a sensation in the society, and can be called another "Occupy Wall Street" movement in France.

Melenchon's actions had great appeal to the grassroots. He therefore was supported by a considerable number of traditional left-wing voters, which not only shocked the right-wing conservative parties but also threatened the left-wing Socialist Party. If the votes obtained by Hollande in the first-round voting was lower than expected, it was directly related to Melenchon's winning part of the votes.

1. Attempt by the French Communist Party to leave behind the slump period

Founded in 1920, the French Communist Party has a glorious history, and is the backbone force in the left-wing camp of France. During the WWII, it played a key role in the anti-Fascist resistance movement against the traitor Vichy government. After the WWII, it had as many as 500,000 members and became the biggest left-wing political party in France. After the founding of "the Fifth Republic of France," it became one of the main forces of the French politics. In 1969, it ran the presidential campaign and received 21.27% of the votes, hitting a historical record. As the international environment had changed and the French Communist Party was unable to adapt to the external changes, it became less and less influential and public support for it saw continued declining trend. In the 2007 presidential elections, the votes it obtained was only 1.93% which demonstrated that it had indeed become an insignificant party.

When preparing for the 2012 presidential elections, the French Communist Party revitalized itself by allying with some other left-wing parties to form a Left Front and decided to propose the Left Party founder Melenchon, a more popular candidate, to run the presidential election as the representative of the Left Front . Mechenlon's campaign slogans also represented its left-wing radical ideas. The charming and attracting campaign activities held by Melenchon stimulated the past political enthusiasm of the majority of the French Communist Party supporters. Many old French Communist Party members enthusiastically participated in Melenchon's campaign rallies and cheered for him. A middle-aged French Communist Party member, excitedly commented about the 100,000-person rally on Bastille Square: "I have not seen such a passionate rally for years" 72-year-old French Communist Party member Daniellec has made a long and arduous journey in order to participate the mass rally held in Marseilles, a port city in Southern France, on April 14. She was so excited and said, "His (Melenchon's) speech touches our heart, and is full of human touch. The economic conditions have become too hard these days. We need a touch of loving care."

Brossa, a 32-year-old young French Communist Party member, expressed, "All my generation has only seen failures. In this year's campaign activities, we finally have the sweet taste of revenge" Pierre Laurent, leader and the National Secretary of the French Communist Party, refuted the National Front saying: "National Front claims to prevent communism from resurrection, but I have to tell them that it is just the beginning" The General Confederation of Labor (CGT)—the workers'union-- has been a traditional ally of the French Communist Party. A member of the union said, "We need a left political party that opposes capitalism instead of remaining passive and doing nothing".

Melenchon was able to get %11.13 of all votes certainly due to the strong mass base which was nurtured long by the French Communist Party. The campaign ignited the political enthusiasm of left-wing masses, and gave the French Communist Party expectation and resumed to confidence for fighting back, namely now the party began to believe in the possibility of resurgence. It seems that the French Communist Party with its glorious history will continue to increase its efforts to win a more advantageous position in the current political stage of France.

2. "Anti-globalism" sweeping the French society

The rise of left-wing movement is inseparable from the current "anti-globalization" social thought trend which is sweeping France now. France is the world's fifth biggest economy, but it has become significantly less competitive in the world in the recent 10 or more years due to major changes in the world pattern and the rise of emerging countries. It is also undergoing a domestic economic downturn with a fairly high rate of chronic unemployment; serious social polarization; decline in the living standards of the people and regress of social security for people. Observing all these serious social problems, the French public has embraced "globalization"

As early as in 1999, the strong voice of "anti-globalization" was heard in France. It was most strongly voiced by the farmers. Due to the fall of agricultural prices, farmers' income continued to decline, arousing strong opposition to the import of agricultural products from the US. "McDonald's" as a symbol of American products became their target of venting anger and frustration. A farmer was prosecuted by the judiciary as a criminal because he led a group act aiming to destroy a "McDonald's" chain store, and was sentenced. The final judgment of the court was quite controversial, thus the farmer himself became a hero of "anti-globalization" movement in France.

Currently, the wave of "anti-globalization" has become more obvious and sweeps the French society. Some put forward weird slogans like "free trade causes people starve", "Production and import of cheap goods destroyed the employment in France" However, ultra right-wing and radical left-wing hold different opinions on the issue of "globalization"—the former advocates to resist against globalization in extreme ways of exclusion, separation, hatred and shutting the doors to outside, while the latter advocates combining or correcting globalization to enable the goals of social justice, solidarity and sustainable and rational economic and social development. Socialist Hollande has advocated "patriotic economism" slogans such as "re-industrialization" and "purchase local commodities " in the campaign, which obviously have left-leaning colors.

Objectively speaking, globalization has both positive and negative influences on France. It largely benefits large-scale multi-national enterprises of France, while introducing a lot of disadvantages to France. Large-scale enterprises may have benefited from globalization, but not the whole France economy. In the recent three years, France's shares in world trade has seen a dramatic decline. The 40 biggest listed French companies have cut their France based employees by 4%, but increased their employees by 50 % in the other regions of the world. A lot of enterprises and talented people have left France, consequently some traditionally strong industries of France have lost global competitiveness, and even closed down and went bankrupt. Lots of workers with low and middle level skills, or those with minimum special skills have lost their jobs, resulting in a significant increase in the unemployment rate.

From the aspect of ordinary people, globalization brings an economic downturn, reduces purchasing power, loss of jobs and polarization. Since the 1980s, neither right-wing nor left-wing government has taken effective measures to fundamentally solve these social problems. Increasing employment, improving the purchasing power, halting wealth disparity deterioration and expanding social welfare used to be the duties of governments, but faced with the voracious tide of globalization, successive governments of France and their measures have failed in these problem fields caused by globalization. The vast public has lost trust in governments, and the expectation to improve governance by changing the ruling parties. Therefore, the extreme trend of anti-globalization has become popular. In a deeper sense, "anti-globalization" wave is a result of the strong blows or shocks given by globalization to the current political institution of France.

There are also scholars who compare France with German. They believe that the problem of France is not globalization, but its closed economy and stagnant social issues. The way out of solving the so-called "globalization" problem is to give play to its innovative edge and revive its competitiveness instead of resorting to trade protectionism and the like. So the future of France will depend on how it adapts to globalization.

Another wave related to the "anti-globalization" trend is the spread of "anti-EU" sentiment. Successive French governments have been the major force for advancing the cause of European integration, but the "anti-EU" sentiment is spreading in the French people, who believe that the integration goal developed and advanced by Europe is the root cause for the economic and social crises of France. In the referendum of 2005, French people rejected the EU Constitutional Treaty, which is just the demonstration of such sentiment. In those days Melenchon was in the Socialist Party and he resolutely advocated casting negative vote. In the campaign, Hollande, during his campaign in early 2012 also strongly questioned the Financial Contract signed by 25 EU member countries, and resolutely requested a re-negotiations, which also reflects the "anti-EU" trend in the society to a large extent.

VI."Return" of Marxist studies

On the one side those ultra right-wing thoughts cored with discrimination an xenophobia has for long been observed and rejected by the people, on the other side the negative consequences of laissez-faire capitalism in France, under the shock of the latest international financial storm and the sovereign debt crisis in Europe, have rendered positive theoretical reflection and explorations in left-wing movement.

Left-wing scholars believe that the new financial capitalism has changed the political ecology of France. In the past, the parliament decided to pass laws and regulations to protect laborers' rights and interests, but today it is almost replaced by banks and financial funds, additionally people and the national parliament has become ineffective to control international capital by legislation they are supra-national and globalized. Therefore, some left-wing scholars suggest that socialist strategy must be updated. First, social groups represented by left-wing parties have greater demands. Left-wing parties have the tradition of struggling for the rights of laborers, and they should protect the rights of the majority from all walks of life including the unemployed, new university graduates, retirees, consumers, freelancers, small business owners and housewives. Second, they suggest that ways of actions or struggles led by the movement must be updated. In the past, rights and interests were defended by strikes and mass demonstrations, but today new means and ways are needed to restrict and exert pressure on the "invisible force" of financial capitalism. It is a brand-new topic. The resurgence of the left-wing thoughts and conceptual renewal has ignited the interest in re-studying Marxism among the French scholars. A recent article published in the French newspaper "Le Monde" pointed out that the "return" of Marxist studies is likely to be expected in France, a country with a strong communist culture, in the background of the severest capitalist crisis since 1929. Currently, French intellectuals have become very active, they organizing seminars, expressing and debating their ideas in the newspapers, books and papers, and usher in a new phase to maintain and ameliorate Marxist and "communist thoughts." If we recall the 1960s and 70s when a trend had emerged arguing that some Marxist theories had become obsolescent, it is interesting to see that today many French scholars argue the opposite view and propose another analysis. This analysis by French scholars point out that in the face of surfacing ills and drawbacks of liberalism, Marxist theory serves as the guiding thought for the left-wing studies in France.

Y. 16

From Iran to Xinjiang—
The Swirl in the "Oval-shaped" Zone under the Shadow of the U.S. Middle East Strategy

Ma Zhongcheng[1]

Abstract: During the 20 years after the end of the Cold War, the hot spots around the world are almost always associated with the "Islamist political revival or awakening". In view of the United States, the same violence acts by radical Islamist forces, when targets the United States, is labeled as "terrorism"; but when targets the countries such as China and Russia, is named as "fight for freedom" The US strategy in the Middle East began at the end of the Bush era in 1993. In order to confront Iran, the United States decided to trigger and promote the sectarian conflict between the Shia and Sunni Muslims, and the Sunni extremist groups represented by al Qaeda got support from the United States. After, Obama came to power, this policy was further carried on and deepened. In 2011 the United States created the "Libya model", the cooperation between the United States and al Qaeda to overthrow anti-US regimes. All signs indicate that the "terrorist fire" instigated by the United States will spread to China's Xinjiang, and become more intense as the US strategy is shifted from the West to the East.

Key words: Libya; Syria; Iran; China's Xinjiang; terrorist; Al Qaeda; Brezinski; Bin Laden; East Turkistan

---

1 Ma Zhongcheng, visiting scholar in the World Socialism Research Center attached to CASS and senior researcher at Marine Institute for Security and Cooperation in Beijing.

Shortly after the end of the Cold War in 1993, Brzezinski, the best brain of the US monopoly financial groups, "predicted": "The political awakening of Islam is generating not only a collision with the residual Russian imperialism in the North but, in the near future it is also likely that this Islam will contest the Western domination in the South"[2] He also depicted an "oval-shaped" zone in Eurasia, covering the Balkans, the Middle East, Central Asia, the southern region of former Soviet Union and which includes China's Xinjiang. He believed that the "oval-shaped" zone would be filled with "turbulent swirls"[3] Brzezinski's "prophecies" have always been correct, fundamentally because he has made great impacts on the foreign policies of the U.S. government. It is safe to say that all "hot spot" issues—like the Iraq issue, the issue of Kosovo, the issue of Afghanistan, the issue of Chechnya and Russia, the issue of China's Xinjiang and the Middle East upheaval which began in 2011—in the world in the 20 years after the end of the Cold War are almost all in the "oval-shaped" zone "prediction" made by Brzezinski.

I. Islamic fundamentalism—a sharp weapon of the U.S. to dismember the Soviet Union, Russia and China

After the WWII, the U.S. lost heavily in the Korean War and the Vietnam War successively, and fell into a historical low. In the 1970s, it was forced to carry out a diplomatic strategy restructuring and succeeded: on the one hand, it eased the relations its with China and focused on dealing with the Soviet Union; on the other, it fostered a large number of radical forces of Islamic fundamentalism, and fought hard to infiltrate the Soviet sphere of influence and also the territory of the Soviet Union was the target of this infiltration . The development and implementation of these two policies were closely related to Brzezinski's "predictions".

In the early 1970s, four different forces were apparent in the Islamic countries: Sunni fundamentalists—the Wahhabism movement related to Saudi Royal family and the Muslim Brotherhood movement); Shia fundamentalists who established the Islamic Republic of Iran at the close of the 1970s; the Islamic socialist forces represented by Nasser; and the Westernized liberal democrats. During the Cold War, Saudi Arabia and other Sunni fundamentalists had intimate relations with the U.S., while Iran opposed both the U.S. and the Soviet Union, and rather targeted the U.S. on the whole.

---

2 Brzezinski, Great Chaos Era Big (formerly published as Out of Control: Global Turmoil on the Eve of the 21st Century), China Social Sciences Publishing House, 1994, p.175.
3 Brzezinski, Big out of control and chaos, China Social Sciences Publishing House, 1994, p.176.

At the end of the 1970s, the U.S. made an important decision to generously aid the radical forces of Sunni fundamentalism so as to fight against the anti-U.S. forces in the Soviet controlled regions and the Middle East. Brzezinski wrote: "It was July 3, 1979 that President Carter signed the first directive for covert aid to the opponents of the pro-Soviet regime in Kabul" That rendered the Soviet Union to invade Afghanistan—"Moscow had to carry on a war unsupportable by the government, a conflict that brought about the demoralization in the Soviet Union and finally the breakup of the Soviet empire"[4]

The Soviet Union failed to successfully stop the revival and expansion of Islamic fundamentalism in its the periphery. In the late 1980s, utilizing the opportunity offered by Gorbachev's "reforms" including "openness" and "new thinking," the radical forces of Islamic fundamentalism aggressively expanded in the constituent republics of the Soviet Union. Together with local nationalism, they became one major power that caused the dissolution of the Soviet Union.

After the dissolution of the Soviet Union, the Islamic fundamentalists supported by the U.S. were divided. Wahhabism movement attached to Saudi royal family and the Muslim Brotherhood continued their pro-US policies, but Bin Laden, opposed the stationing of the US troops in Saudi Arabia, his Holy Land, gradually viewed the U.S. as the biggest enemy. It was exactly like what Brzezinski predicted in 1993—the Islamist radical forces might continue to confront Russia or struggle against the U.S. Therefore, according to him, the strategy towards such a force to be adopted by the U.S. could only be taming it, and then try to transform it to a controllable force and use it. The "war on terror" started by the U.S. since 2001 is by no means to eliminate the so-called terrorism, but to continue to coach and lead terrorism to a course fighting against Russia and China.

In terms of China's Xinjiang, after the founding of New China, Xinjiang saw rapid progresses in politics, economy and social construction, and ethnic separatist forces had basically disappeared till the 1970s. Into the 1990s, religious extremism, violence terrorism and ethnic separatism became ever more rampant in the background of international context. Consequently, terrorism, extremism and separatism, the "three evil forces" have expanded rapidly with the support of the U.S. after the dissolution of the Soviet Union. Former U.S. President Clinton and Vice President Al Gore, among other important political figures have secretly met with ethnic separatists from Xinjiang, China for many times. The U.S. Central Intelligence Agency designated staff from specialized departments to train ethnic separatists from

---

4　The CIA's Intervention in Afghanistan, Interview with Zbigniew Brzezinski, available at http://www.globalresearch.ca/articles/BRZ110A.html.

Xinjiang, China. Clinton even publicly met the chairman of the executive committee of the "East Turkestan National Congress"[5].[6]

In view of the United States, the same violence acts by radical Islamist forces, when targets the United States, is labeled as "terrorism"; but when targets the countries such as China and Russia, is named as "fight for freedom." It has been experienced by China: After President Bush launched the "war against terrorism" war and also during the Obama Era, the three forces "terrorism, extremism and separatism" in Xinjiang remained close allies of the CIA; Rebiya Kadeer who fled abroad lives as a distinguished guest of the U.S. It has also been experienced by Russian Federation: Chechen terrorists and separatists are even more violent than Bin Laden, but Chechen independence is supported by the Western intelligence agencies because the latter, after dismembering the Soviet Union, intended to dismember Russia; intelligence agencies of Western countries gave generous support to secessionist Chechen forces, "Ichkeria passport" was printed in France, "Ichkeria currency" was allowed to circulate in Germany, and delivered weapons to Chechen rebels.[7]

It has been also experienced by Yugoslavian State : the so-called "Kosovo Liberation Army"—which triggered the Kosovo crisis and finally led to the dismemberment of Yugoslav—is exactly the Islamic radical force supported by the U.S....

II. "Sharp Turn" in Bush's Policy, Obama's "policy of reconciliation" and Bin Laden's "death"

The U.S. strategy in the Middle East began to change at the close of the Bush Era in 1993. In 2003, with the pretext of the war against terror, the U.S. accused Saddam's regime of colluding with al Qaeda, and waged the war of invasion against Iraq. In fact, in the Middle East, the Saddam and Gaddafi regimes suppressed al Qaeda the most. After Saddam's regime was overthrown by the U.S., Shiites with the most members rose in Iraq, while Iraqi Shiites were closely related to Iran and Syria. Once Iraq was dominated by anti-US forces and joined the Iran-Syria-Lebanon anti-US and anti-Israel alliance, Bush's Middle East war would fail at the last stroke. Therefore, the next move of the U.S. in the Middle East war would be overthrowing the Iran-centered alliance of anti-US regimes and transforming Iran into a pro-Shiite Islamic country. So a major change was seen in the U.S. Middle East policy at the close of the Bush administration.

---

5 An organ of Uyghur separatist movement, based mainly in New York, Munich and Istanbul.
6 Guo Xiaobin, External Factors for the Breeding of "East Turkistan" Terrorism, available at http://www.china.com.cn/zhuanti2005/txt/2002-10/29/content_5224398.htm
7 Unrecognised secessionist Chechen Republic of Ichkeria. See article "The Caucasus Project," A documentary broadcasted in the First Channel of the Russian State Television, March 22, 2008. Ifeng. Com / mil / history / 200804 / 0423_1567_505227. Shtml.

On March 5, 2007, senior U.S. reporter Seymour M. Hersh published an article "The Redirection—Is The Administration's New Policy Which Benefits Our Enemies in The War on Terrorism?" in the famous magazine, "The New Yorker". In his article, Seymour wrote, "In the past few months, since the situation in Iraq has deteriorated, the Bush Administration, in both its public diplomacy and its covert operations, has significantly changed the Middle East strategy. This 'Redirection,' as some people close to the White House have called the new strategy, has brought the United States closer to an open confrontation with Iran and, in several regions of the region, propelled a sharper sectarian fight between Shiite and Sunni Muslims. To undermine Iran, which is predominantly Shiite, the Bush Administration has decided, in effect, to reconfigure its priorities in the Middle East. ...The U.S. has also taken part in clandestine operations aimed at Iran and Iran's ally Syria. A by-product of these activities has been the bolstering of Sunni extremist groups that espouse a militant vision of Islam and are hostile to the US and sympathetic to al Qaeda".

Seymour also pointed out, "One contradictory aspect of the new strategy is that, in Iraq, most of the insurgent violence targeting the US military facilities has come from Sunni forces, and not from Shiites. But, from the Administration's perspective, the most profound—and unintended—strategic consequence of the Iraq war is the empowerment of Iran"[8]

After Obama took office, this policy was further deepened and implemented. Faced with a prevalent anti-US sentiment in the Islamic world, Obama had to add a policy of "conciliation" to the former policy. He declared to never engage with Islamic countries, trying to establish friendly and harmonious bilateral relations with the Islamic world as much as possible. On May 1, 2011, the U.S. President Obama declared to the world that Bin Laden had been shot by the U.S. Special Forces in his house located in Pakistan, and claimed it to be a major achievement of the U.S. counter-terrorism operations. Soon, on June 29, the White House took the advantage to launch a new version of National Strategy for Combating Terrorism, in which it contracted the anti-terrorism front and stressed to shift the focus of the anti-terrorism war to terrorist attacks against the United States.[9] It lays a foundation for the cooperation between the less radical anti-US forces of Islamic fundamentalism.

From the war against terror in the early days of the Bush administration to the strategic shift at the end of the Bush era, and to Obama's "following established rules," we can see that the U.S. worldwide layout is continuous and

---

8 The Redirection Is the Administration's new policy benefitting our enemies in the war on terrorism?, available at http://www.newyorker.com/reporting/2007/03/05/070305fa_fact_hersh#ixzz22TNnr3S4.
9 The National Strategy for Counterterrorism, available at http://www.whitehouse.gov/sites/default/files/counterterrorism_strategy.pdf.

complementary instead of broken or mutually negative. Some socialist countries including the former Soviet Union were completely different—their domestic and foreign policies changed hither and thither. After the old-generation leaders passed away, the new-generation leaders completely negated the former and carried out thorough reforms till these countries finally collapsed.

On January 5, 2012, Obama and the Pentagon released a new military strategy report Sustaining U.S. Global Leadership: Priorities for 21st Century Defense which held that "The demise of Osama bin Laden and the capturing or killing of many other senior al Qaeda leaders have rendered the group far less capable," "Over the long term, China's emergence as a regional power will have the potential to affect the U.S. economy and our security in a variety of ways."[10]

Therefore, the U.S. chose to gradually end the wars in Afghanistan and Iraq (but designate agents and special forces there for strategic deterrence) to "rebalance toward the Asia-Pacific region"[11] The report for the first time lists China and Iran as "potential adversaries" of the U.S., so the U.S. has to "credibly deter" them.

It is still unknown how much the killing of Osama bin Laden and the capturing or killing of many other senior al Qaeda leaders have weakened the capability of this organization. In Afghanistan, although a puppet regime has been established under the occupation of the U.S. army in the central region of this country, Taliban and al Qaeda still control large regions in this country and have built regional local governments. In Iraq, during the Saddam era, Saddam had iron-fistedly oppressed al Qaeda for long, but after the regime was toppled, Iraq falling in chaos became a fertile ground for the al Qaeda. It is in such context that Obama announced the withdrawal of troops from Iraq and Afghanistan.

Sometimes, retreat means attack. In the year of 2011, political turmoil spread in the Arab world. During the Bush administration, the U.S. army was deeply stuck in Afghanistan and Iraq, and Iran had somewhat benefited the situation. After taking office, Obama's policy gained sympathy in the Middle East even if he substantially withdrew troops from these regions. Why?

---

10 See the full text of Sustaining U. S. Global Leadership: Priorities for 21st Century Defense at http://graphics8.nytimes.com/packages/pdf/us/20120106–PENTAGON.PDF.
11 Ibid.

III. From "Iraq model" to "Libya model": an analysis of the new situation in the "oval-shaped" zone

Concerning the Libya war, the first shot in this war came after a statement made by al Qaeda to condemn Libyan President Muammar Gaddafi and appeal to all Muslims to support Libyan people to overthrow the rule of tyrant Gaddafi.[12]

In the Libya war, NATO air strikes and NATO special forces on the ground first defeated the Gaddafi troops, but those truly playing as the backbone force of the attack and that played the major role on the ground were an affiliate of al Qaeda—the jihadist Libyan Islamic Fighting Group. This organization formally had joined al Qaeda in Southern Asia in 2007.[13]

In 2007, West Point Combating Terrorism Center of the USA prepared a report titled as Al-Qaida's Foreign Fighters in Iraq in which said: "a large part of the terrorists in Iraq come from Benghazi—Darna—Tobruk of Libya". This was exactly the force that was used to overthrew the Gaddafi government in 2011.[14]

According to the reports of the BBC and other media, Libya rebel commander Abdelhakim Belhadj was also a leader of a terrorist organization in Benghazi. As one leader of the Libyan Islamic Fighting Group, he was once banished from Libya by Gaddafi. In 2004 Belhadj was arrested by the CIA and harshly tortured in Thailand. He then spent 7 years in the Abu Selim Prison before being freed in 2010.[15]

It is strange that in early 2011, he flew to Benghazi in an aircraft of Qatar, a U.S. ally, under the arrangement of British and US intelligence agencies. He was assigned to lead rebels backed by the terrorist organizations of al Qaeda. By cooperating with the British and the US agents and special forces, they defeated Gaddafi.

Abdel Hakim al-Hasady—another important figure among the Libyan rebel fighters and an Islamic cleric who occupied Darna and was intimate with Bin Laden—was arrested by the Pakistani government after the war in Afghanistan started by the U.S. in 2001 and put into the famous prison of Guantánamo. In 2011, after the Libya War was launched by the U.S. and the Western forces, he chose to work with British and US special agents to fight

---

12 Reuters report available at http://cn.reuters.com/article/CNTopGenNews/idCNCHINA-3857920110224?sp=true.
13 The Enemies of Our Enemy, Foreign Policy online, available at http://www.foreignpolicy.com/articles/2011/03/30/the_enemies_of_our_enemy?page=full.
14 Al-Qaida's Foreign Fighters in Iraq, available at http://kms1.isn.ethz.ch/serviceengine/files/ISN/45910/ipublicationdocument_singledocument/a211881e-3c49-455b-b4b9-7f6196ae78f8/en/CTCForeignFighter.19.Dec07.pdf.
15 Profile: Libyan rebel commander Abdelhakim Belhadj, available at http://www.bbc.co.uk/news/world-africa-14786753.

against Gaddafi. His speeches were obviously pro-US. In an interview with Wall Street Journal, he said, "If we hated the Americans %100 in the past, I can say today it is diminished to less than 50%. Because they have started to redeem themselves for their past mistakes by helping us to preserve the blood of our children"[16]

In 2011, the U.S. created the "Libya model" on the precondition that the US troops would be withdrawn from the Arab world, leaving behind only a few special forces and special agents for strategic deterrence; and the U.S. decided to cooperate with al Qaeda to overthrow those anti-US regimes. The U.S. and Saudi Arabian government offered money, weapons, equipment and intelligence, and al Qaeda offered manpower. The former policy was the premise of the latter policy, because the U.S. was well aware that the Islamic radical forces and Gaddafi would join hands to fight against the invading U.S. troops if the latter directly and massively invaded Libya like it did in the war in Afghanistan and that in Iraq.

What is on earth is the essence behind Gaddafi's tragedy? After the U.S. invaded Iraq in 2003, Gaddafi began anew policy against the Western major forces. However, instead of completely deserting to the West, Gaddafi just intended to use and benefit from the contradictions between the Western powers.

For example, he gave Italy most of the Libyan oil, which severely frustrated the U.S., Britain and France. At the end of 2007, French President Sarkozy tried hard to "please" Gaddafi, and grandly welcomed the latter to visit France. However, after returning home, Gaddafi cooperated with the U.S. to oppose the "Mediterranean Union" plan supported by France—which was highly valued by Sarkozy. Gaddafi, openly and in a high-profile, criticized Sarkozy, which ridiculed the latter by his domestic political rivals. On the one hand, Gaddafi showed friendliness to the U.S., but on the other he tried to play the role of the Islamic world leader, criticized Israel and attacked the war in the Middle East waged by the U.S. Finally, the Gaddafi regime was destroyed by the cooperation of Sarkozy and Obama administration. Unlike George W. Bush administration who resisted against the "Mediterranean Union" plan of major European powers by its unilateral approach, Obama followed a multilateral approach which aimed to increase the support of Europe to the U.S. That explains why Gaddafi, was easily sacrificed by the Obama administration. Well, there was only one way out for the Gaddafi regime, which had entered into Western economic globalization, that is, being a puppet regime, that acts "wisely and honestly" without annoying the U.S. and satisfy its interests, like what the dictator-like leaders of Saudi Arabia, Qatar and UAE has been doing.

---

16 Ex-Mujahedeen Help Lead Libyan Rebels, available at http://online.wsj.com/article/SB10001424052748703712504576237042432212406.html.

IV. Why did Bin Laden die on the eve the Syria crisis which emerged in 2011 March?

After the end of the Cold War, Sunni radical organization led by Bin Laden viewed the U.S. and the West as its biggest enemies. However, Bin Laden had conflicts with the other anti-US regimes in the region, and among them Saddam and Gaddafi suppressed Bin Laden's al Qaeda the most. Iran also fought against Bin Laden and al Qaeda, but Iran did not spit with Bin Laden and al Qaeda, trying to form a united anti-US front with Sunni fundamentalist anti-US forces.

In such a context, it is easy to understand why the U.S. shot Bin Laden or "announced" the death of Bin Laden in May 2011. It completely coincided with the time the U.S. decided to start its plan in Syria. Try to recall the facts, if Bin Laden was still alive, or if we consider "Bin Laden's political line and sentiments" which targeted the U.S. as its main enemy continued to lead al Qaeda's political line, would this organization choose to cooperate with the U.S. to attack Syria and Iran? We know that it was just after May 2011 that Syrian crisis has emerged.

In February 2012, al Qaeda's new leader Ayman al-Zawahiri released a new video clip titled Go Forward, O Lions of Sham, in which he criticized the Syrian regime for the latter's crimes against the Syrian people, called on the Muslims in Turkey, Iraq, Jordan and Lebanon to support the uprising and overthrow the current Syrian government. Since 2011, large-scale violence and terrorist attacks and explosions appeared in Syria, causing more than 10,000 casualties. Russia, the UN and the U.S. all pointed out that these violent terrorist activities were mostly done by al Qaeda,[17] that CIA officials were helping the so-called "freedom fighters" with weapons to topple the Syrian regime.[18] Barring any unforeseen incident, Syria case was planned to repeat the Libya model.

V. The Bargain between al Qaeda and the U.S.

On September 10, 2012, the brother of the al Qaeda leader Ayman al-Zawahiri (who once spent 14 years in an Egyptian prisons for his participation in terrorist activities) proposed to mediate a peace deal between the West and Islamists on behalf of al Qaeda in an exclusive interview with CNN. He pointed out that he and his brother were ideologically inseparable, so he was the one to convince his brother to make a deal with the West.[19]

---

17 Reuters report available at http://cn.reuters.com/article/CNTopGenNews/idCNCNE84H01R20120518.
18 CIA Helps Syrian Opposition with Weapons, available at http://finance.ifeng.com/money/roll/20120622/6643801.html.
19 Exclusive: Al Qaeda leader's brother offers peace plan, available at http://edition.cnn.com/2012/09/10/world/meast/zawahiri-peace-plan/index.html.

It is easy to get burnt while trying to command the fire of terror. Soon after Ayman al-Zawahiri offered the above peace plan, Innocence of Muslims—a movie shot by the US, which seriously slanders the prophet of Islam Muhammad—triggered an anti-US storm in the Islamic world, during which the US ambassador to Libya was attacked and killed. It is worth noting that clips of such movie had been uploaded to the Internet in July 2012, but had caused no big sensation. Exactly at the time when the U.S. and al Qaeda made public the peace plan, it received a widespread concern in the Islamic world and expectedly caused an anti-US storm. Was it just a coincidence? There are probably two reasons behind: first, Zawahiri and the other al Qaeda leaders were bargaining with the US; second, the radical leaders inside the al Qaeda did not want a concession with the US, so they made a fuss of the movie to destroy the peace negotiation. No matter what occurred, it could not change the grand trend that al Qaeda was approaching to the US day by day.

VI. The obstacles faced by the U.S. to "settle" the issues of Syria and Iran

Today, defending against the superior air forces power of the US-led NATO plus the destructiveness of al Qaeda on the ground becomes very hard for Syria, and even for Iran. Around August 2012, Syrian opposition and al Qaeda as the backbone of this Syrian opposition was in a situation of a stalemate with Syrian government forces. If NATO had started air strikes against the Syrian government forces, the Syrian regime would soon and undoubtedly be toppled. Today the only barrier for NATO is the resistant attitude of the Russian President Vladimir Putin. If Russia strongly supports the Syrian government in order to keep its naval base in Syria, NATO would surely hesitate to wage air strikes against Syria, and that may also postpone the settlement of the conflict between the West and the Iran.

Both Moscow and Vladimir Putin are well aware of the situation in Syria today. On September 6, 2012, in an interview with Russia Today, a famous TV canal in Russia, when the reporter mentioned that free Syrian army backed by the West was hiring al Qaeda fighters, Putin said, "...when someone aspires to attain an end they see as optimal, any means will do. As a rule, they will try and do that by hook or by crook... Today some want to use militants from Al Qaeda or some other organizations with equally radical views to accomplish their goals in Syria. This policy is dangerous and very short-sighted. In that case, one should unlock Guantanamo, arm all of its inmates and bring them to Syria to do the fighting—it's practically the same kind of people"[20] Since Putin has pried out the covert grand strategy of the US in the Middle East, Russia will not easily give up in the Syria issue, even Iran is aware of this strategy, because

---

20 Putin: Using Al-Qaeda in Syria like sending Gitmo inmates to fight, available at http://rt.com/news/vladimirputin-exclusive-interview-481.

once it is achieved, it means complete loss of the strategic interests of Russia in the Middle East, the return of the fire of terror to the peripheries of Russia, and the re-intensification of Chechen problem.

However, if the anti-US Iran could overcome the containment of the US and exist for long, al Qaeda and the other Sunni radical forces would very possibly turn their weapons against the US and form a united anti-US front with Iran for their own expansion. That is and can be the most terrible nightmare for the US.

VII. The "terrorist fire" will become ever hotter and spread from West to East and reach China's Xinjiang

Till 2012, taking an overall look at the "oval-shaped" zone "predicted" by Brzezinski, from Afghanistan to Iraq, from Yemen to Egypt and from Libya to Syria, the radical Islamic fundamentalist forces have all seen an unprecedented expansion. In the past, the terrorist organizations in Libya were unable to threat Gaddafi, but under the command of al Qaeda leaders, all terrorist forces in Afghanistan, Iraq, Yemen and Egypt gathered in Libya. This coupled with air strikes, the cooperation between the British and the US special agents, weapons and technical supports made it so easy to defeat Gaddafi. In the Commonwealth of Independent States led by Russia in the northeastern part of Brzezinski's "oval-shaped" zone and in Central Asia, after years of repeated "color revolution-style" operations, Westernized forces supported by the US have become mature, and Islamic fundamentalism has grown rapidly. Once the anti-US regimes like Syria and Iran were completely toppled by the West, this fire of terror will inevitably, rapidly and fiercely sweep Central Asia region, which has been soaked in years of efforts of the US, to the last corner of the oval-shaped zone—China's Xinjiang.

As the US is adjusting its strategy, the three hostile forces in China's Xinjiang including "Eastern Turkistan" extremist organization are getting more and more close towards integration . According to a report of The Long War Journal, a magazine which has long focused on the issues of anti-terrorism war, shortly before Bin Laden was shot, Abdul Shakoor Turkistani, the current chief of the Turkistan Islamic Party, was appointed by al Qaeda as the new commander of the armed forces and training camps in Pakistan. His predecessor was Saif al-Adel, one major mastermind and planner of al Qaeda. It indicates that "Eastern Turkistan" organization has attached itself to the core leadership of al Qaeda, making both much more undistinguishable, and that "Eastern Turkistan" is playing an increasing role in al Qaeda's core decision-making.[21]

21　See Al Qaeda appoints new leader of forces in Pakistan's tribal areas, available at http://www.longwarjournal.org/archives/2011/05/alqaedaappointsne2.php　and China in Al Qaida's sights again?, The Times Of India, available at http://articles.timesofindia.indiatimes.com/2011-05-11/china/29532133 1al-qaida-pakistan-s-fata-al-rashid-trust for more details.

It is predicable that if the US will be able to subvert the Iranian regime in the future several years, more and more members of the three forces from China's Xinjiang who are fighting against the US troops beyond the territories of China will come back, and those terrorist forces which are based in the Middle East countries will gradually gather in Xinjiang. By then, the perilous situation of Xinjiang will surely escalate. In this context, the eastward shift of the US strategy (or the shift of its strategic focus to the Asia-Pacific region) is by no means simply withdrawing its troops from Afghanistan and Iraq and deploying them to the eastern coastal areas of China, but it is rather an insidious act, to attack and siege China from both sides, which includes a covert cooperation with the radical Islamic forces.

Y. 17

The US-Style Oligarchy: Paul Krugman's Critique of Social Inequality in the United States

—An analysis of the dilemmas of capitalist ideology

Yu Haiqing[1]

Abstract: Among Western academic circles, in the discussion of the inequality issue, Paul Krugman has always advocated the 'political decision theory' and praised the role of some traditional institutions and norms, such as return to strong trade unions and higher progressive taxation from high-income earners. In his many articles he published recently on the issue of inequality of wealth and income in the United States, he analyzed several important phenomena such as the lower inter-generational mobility and oligarchy, and presented some important viewpoints that can help us in grasping the polarization between the rich and the poor and social conflicts in contemporary Western societies.

Key words: Paul Krugman; American society; inequality issue

---

1 Yu Qinghai, visiting scholar of the World Socialism Research Center attached to CASS and research associate in the Academy of Marxism attached to CASS Academy.

Since the outbreak of the international financial crisis, the problem of inequality, along with the ever widening divide between the rich and the poor, and increasingly prominent social contradiction and conflicts, has returned to the field of vision of the US scholars and theorists. In particular, the outbreak and spread of "Occupy Wall Street" movement, the release of a series of the latest research data by big institutes, and the sharp confrontation between the Democratic Party and the Republican Party on "Buffet rule"—a rule about increasing taxes on the rich—even push the debates among the theorists, which continue to heat up, to the cusp of waves.

As a resolute New Keynesian, Paul Krugman, 2008 Nobel laureate in economics and professor of Princeton University, has long been sticking to the theory of market failures and defending the necessity of government intervention. His stance has run through his critique of social inequality in contemporary US. Recently, he wrote some articles to elaborate on wealth and income inequality in the U.S., and made some profound discussions on the inequality phenomena prevalent in the American society today.

I. Antagonism between the 99.9% and the 0.1%

Krugman speaks highly of the idea behind "We are the 99.9%" —one of the political slogans widely used and coined by the Occupy movement, thinking it to be quite bright, because it correctly defines the problem as the antagonism between the middle class and the elite instead of the antagonism between the elite and the poor, and tells people that, in this new gilded era, the big winner is a handful of rich people. If this slogan has to be improper, it would be the target set too low. Most of the profits held by the top 1% people are actually in the hands of fewer people, that is, the topmost 0.1% of the top 1% people, the wealthiest 0.1%. Krugman has pointed out that few in the 0.1% are innovators like Steve Jobs, and most of them are corporate bigwigs and profit suitors in the financial sector.

One recent analysis found that 43% of the super-elite are executives at nonfinancial companies, 18% are in the finance sector and another 12% lawyers or do real estate business. And these are not, to put it mildly, professions in which there is a clear relationship between someone's income and his economic contribution. Executive pay, which has skyrocketed over the past decades, is generally set by boards of directors appointed by the very people whose pay they determine; poorly performing CEO's still get lavish paychecks, and even unsuccessful and fired executives often receive millions as they go out the door. The economic crisis has shown that a lot of the face value created by modern finance is nothing more than mirage. However, most financial crises are not borne by the profit suitors themselves, but naïve investors or taxpayers. To the 99.9%, it is not important to hate the 0.1%, but to demand that the super-elite pay substantially more in taxes.[2]

II. Income inequality and the US-style oligarchy

Krugman holds that the growth of social inequality in the US society is reflected in the rise of oligarchy, the less and less wealth possessed by lower-income earners, the growing centralization of income and wealth in the hands of a few privileged elite. He quotes data in a recent report of the US Congressional Budget Office (CBO) and points out that the share of total income going to lower- and middle-income Americans saw a sharp decline, that with the bottom 80% of households now receive less than half of the total income, but nearly two thirds of the income of the elite flows to a handful of people accounting for 0.1% of all.

Since the end of the 1970s, the richest %0.1 of the Americans have seen their real incomes rise more than 400%. Krugman therefore doubts if the US still remains to be a "middle class" society made up of two classes—the upper class and the middle class. Today, the employment situation of workers who have received higher education is better than that of poorly-educated ordinary workers, but similarly they are faced with stagnant incomes and an increased risk of economic security.

In fact, wage increases for most college-educated workers have been non-existent since 2000, while even the well-educated can no longer count on getting jobs with good pay. The U.S. today shows such a landscape: A smaller wealthy social class is becoming dominant in the country. They intervene in politics and influence the ruling power. The US political system is being warped by the influence of big money group. The extreme concentration of income is incompatible with real democracy, and "the whole nature of our society is at stake"[3]

III. The US is not a fair arena

Krugman points out that American citizens are much more inclined to believe that they live in a meritocracy, compared to citizens of other nations. But this self-image is a fantasy. The US actually stands out as the advanced country in which one's family background matters most, the country in which those born on one of society's lower rungs have the least chance of climbing to the top or even to the middle. He contends that the root cause of such class-bound nature is the loopholes in the US social security network, or the US government's inefficacy in creating equal job opportunities.

---

2 Paul Krugman, "We Are the 99.9%," New York Times, Nov.24, 2011, http://www.nytimes.com/2011/11/25/opinion/we-are-the-99-9.html.
3 Paul Krugman, "Oligarchy, American Style," New York Times, Nov.3, 2011, http://www.nytimes.com/2011/11/04/ opinion/ oligarchy-american-style.html.

To him, if children from lower social rungs of US society do manage to enter into a good college, the lack of financial support makes them far more likely to drop out than the children of the affluent, even if they have as much or more native abilities. He has argued: "It's no wonder, then, that Horatio Alger stories, tales of poor kids who make good, are much less common in reality than they are in the legends…"[4] He agrees with Alan Krueger, chairman of the president's Council of Economic Advisers, that intergenerational mobility in the US society is a "Great Gatsby curve," that is, "highly unequal countries, have low mobility: the more unequal a society is, the greater the extent to which an individual's economic status is determined by his or her parents' status" "…The US in the year 2035 will have even less mobility than it has now …it will be a place in which the economic prospects of children will largely reflect the class status into which they were born"[5]

He also holds that the myth of a classless US society has already been exposed: Among rich countries, the US stands out as the place where economic and social status is most likely to be inherited.[6]

IV. Unequal growth is the root of polarization in the US's political landscape

Krugman believes that the US politics has presented a trend of bi-polarization since the 1970s. Specifically, the split between the Republican Party and the Democratic Party in the political spectrum has become increasingly evident. Even the most conservative Democrats and the most enlightened Republican left wing are not intersected. Political polarization in the current the US society is strikingly similar to that before the WWII, especially before the Great Depression. Besides, the growing gap between the two parties is not a reflection of the Democratic Party turning more left, but the Republic Party turning more right. For example, Obama's health care reform plan was once envisaged and suggested by the "Heritage Foundation" of the Republican Party, but now it is criticized as a "socialist" plan by the same party.

To Krugman, such political polarization in the US society today is closely related to the growth of inequality, and to the increasingly bigger share of income of the top %1 Americans. The growing income and wealth of a few Americans "can buy the loyalty of a major political party". The Republican Party is turning to a right-wing stance, which it had adopted a century ago,

---

4 Paul Krugman, "America's Unlevel Field," New York Times, Jan. 8, 2012, http://www.nytimes.com/2012/01/09/ opinion/ krugman-americas-unlevel-field.html.
5 Paul Krugman, "How Fares the Dream?" New York Times, Jan.16, 2012, http://www.nytimes.com/2012/01/16/ opinion/ krugman-how-fares-the-dream.html.
6 Paul Krugman, "Money and Moral," New York Times, Feb.9, 2012, http://www.nytimes.com/2012/02/10/ opinion/ krugman-money-and-morals.html.

because benefiters of such stance, with their economic strength, can provide campaign funds and some kind of security network for politicians. In the current economic crisis, the intense political conflicts between both parties are not conductive to the formation of effective anti-crisis policies. For example, the Obama administration made so much painstaking effort to get, in the Senate, the 60 votes of support necessary for the pass of the stimulus package. Obviously, extreme income inequality has led to extreme political polarization, which, in turn, greatly hindered policy responses and measures against the crisis. It means that inequality issues can't be separated from economic recovery, and that only by controlling inequality and its anomalous influence on policy debates can the US have benign macroeconomic policies.[7]

V. Social inequality is about money rather than morals

Conservatives claim what's behind the Occupy movement are morals, and that the collapse of the middle class family values should be seen as being responsible for the growing inequality. In his new book *Coming Apart: The State of White Americans 1960-2010*, Charles Murray has pointed out that the main reason for the phenomenon of polarization in The US is not income, but the quite different behaviors of the educated upper tribe (accounting for 20% of the American population) and the lower tribe (accounting for the %30). He claims that the decline in the marriage rate of poorly-educated white Americans and that in the labor participation rate of male laborers, the rise in non-marital birthrate, and the decline of other traditional family values lead to the division of the whole society.[8] Krugman objects this view and insists that social inequality is about money rather than morals. He points out that although traditional family values have been losing their position, some indicators symbolizing social dysfunctions like teenage pregnancy rate and the rate of violent crimes in different races have been greatly improved. The change that traditional working-class families are experiencing is really about "money", like a drastic reduction in the work opportunities, good benefits and medical insurance available to less-educated men. Leaving inflation aside, the entry-level wages for working men of high school education have fallen to 23% since 1973. Meanwhile, employment benefits have collapsed. 65% of the high school graduates who just began to work in the private sector of the economy in 1980 got medical benefits, but till 2009, this rate has dropped to 29%.

7　Paul Krugman, "Income Inequality, Political Polarization and Economic Crisis," May 2, 2012, http://www.classwarfareexists.com/krugman-inequality-is-a-major-reason-the-economy-is-still-sodepressed/#axzz22WDzZVzF.
8　Charles Murray, Coming Apart: The State of White America, 1960-2010, Crown Forum, 2012.

As can be seen, the influence of traditional values on inequality is not as significant as it is said by the conservatives. The social change happening in the US working-class is not an issue of "moral failings of those Americans being left behind," but rather the result of factors that soar inequality.[9]

VI. "Blue inequality" is more important than "red inequality"

David Brooks, a conservative column writer of "New York Times", wrote an article, in which he claimed there are "two inequalities" in the current US society: one being what one might call Blue Inequality—the kind experienced in New York City, Los Angeles, Boston, etc.—which represents the income inequality between the 1% and the 99%; the other being what one might call Red Inequality—the kind experienced in Scranton, Des Moines and other inland areas—which exists mainly between people of higher education and people who did not receive higher education. People of higher education are obviously better than people who did not receive higher education supported by a stable family structure, child bearing patterns and lower social communication network. Brooks believes that "red inequality" is obviously more important. Although the rising wealth of the richest 1% Americans is a problem to face, it is far less serious than the dropout of tens of millions of people, %40 children born to unmarried parents, stagnant human capital, its stagnant social mobility and the disorganized social fabric in the bottom 50%.[10]

Krugman disagrees with him. He pointed out that the rise of a so-called fairly broad class of knowledge workers was a misreading of the US society, also an "80-20" fallacy which believed 20% of the US workers who had the skills could gradually distance themselves from the rest 80% of the US workers who did not have the skills to use the advantages of new technology and globalization. Many people of insight bought such fallacy not because it was correct, but because it was comforting. It boils all problems down to education and consider inequality as a result of the supply-demand relationship. So the way of settling the problem of inequality became improving the educational system. Nobody was to be blamed for rising inequality, because better education was a value to which just about every politician in the US paid at least lip service. Krugman said that it was necessary to correct the US education system, especially the problem of inequality at the starting line, but some problems can't be solved by

---

9 Paul Krugman, "Money and Moral," New York Times, Feb.9, 2012, http://www.nytimes.com/2012/02/10/ opinion/ krugman-money-and-morals.html.
10 David Brooks, "The Wrong Inequality," New York Times, Oct.31, 2011, http://www.nytimes.com/2011/11/01/ opinion/ brooks-the-wrong-inequality.html.

education. In particular, he believed it to be a wishful thinking to let more children receive higher education so as to recover the middle class society of the past US. According to him, the answer to building a society whose prosperity was shared more extensively was not education, but the resumption of laborers' bargaining power which was lost in the past 30 years, the provision of basic insurances, the most important of which was health insurance, for each and every US citizen.

Krugman also doubted why Brooks excluded the hinterland and limited oligarchy to coastal areas. He stresses that the US economy is highly integrated, and that securities, futures and other major financial industries—although they clustered in New York—were making money all across the US. Even if oligarchs obviously got profits from the so-called inland areas of "red inequality," they liked oil tycoons Koch Brothers mainly live in New York. Videlicet, the wealth created by one state flew to "absentee landlords" and became the statistics of another state—that can't demonstrate equal income distribution in the former. "Oligarchy" is much disturbing, but it is what happens today.[11]

VII. Income inequality is the new flywheel of racial inequality

Krugman pointed out that the grip of racism was far weaker than once it was while it had by no means been banished from the hearts of the Americans. Widening income inequality was going beyond racial issue and becoming a primary problem in the US society today. People were no longer judged by the color of their skin but by the size of their wealth. It was the time to say goodbye to racial discrimination and return to the class society system. Economic inequality wasn't inherently a racial issue in the US but the American society being what it was, there were racial implications to the way incomes had been pulling apart. During the 1960s and 70s, it was widely assumed that ending overt discrimination would improve the economic as well as legal status of minority groups. Over the course of the 1960s and 70s, substantial numbers of black families climbed up to the middle class, and even into the upper middle class; the proportion of black households in the top 20% of the income distribution has nearly doubled. But around 1980, the relative economic position of blacks in the US stopped improving, an important part of the answer to which, surely, was that circa around 1980s, income disparities in the United States began to widen dramatically. Krugman encouraged people to never stay quiet in the face of rising income inequality, but work hard to reverse the trend of income inequality and preserve both the American

---

11 Paul Krugman, "Graduates versus Oligarchs," Nov.1, 2011, http://krugman.blogs.nytimes.com/2011/11/01/ graduates-versus-oligarchs/.

values and the dreams of black Martin Luther King who refused to stay quiet about racial discrimination.[12]

Today, Western theorists are debating fiercely on issues like social inequality, of whom many are supports of Krugman. Conservatives also suggest some diametrically opposed views. For example, some refuse to recognize the significance of "oligarchy" proposed by Krugman, and doubt if the political influence of a better redistribution will really make the United States a non-oligarchy country once the upper 5% richest families are imposed upon 100% heavy taxes; and doubt if criticizing the rich would really ameliorate relative poverty of children in single-parent families.[13]

Some conservatives directly point out that the anger against inequality should never be directed against the rich, and the rich should not be blamed for inequality; they suggest the real income problem in this country is not a question of who is rich, but rather of who is poor; that making the poor more economically mobile has nothing to do with taxing the rich and everything to do with finding and implementing ways to encourage parental marriage, teach the poor useful marketable skills and induce them to join the legitimate workforce. Raising taxes on the rich would provide more money to help the poor. But the problem facing the poor is not little incomes, instead they have too few skills and opportunities to advance themselves.[14]

Regardless what kind of opposing ideas employed to criticize Krugman, he is still too concerned about to the effect of institutions and policies in the inequality growth, and his critique has "dangerously" caught people's attention in the US. However, in the flooding of neoliberalism in contemporary West, Krugman's interpretation of inequality constitutes an important warning. He has focused on the inevitable inner relations between social polarization and high centralization of wealth and oligarchy; awakens people about the destructive consequences of laissez-faire market economy; and calls on the US government to take more active measures in protecting social justice and in maintaining social stability, which is of great significance for the Western developed societies where social contradictions and conflicts have become prominent and for China which is also faced with a great challenge of a widening gap between the rich and the poor.

---

12   Paul Krugman, "How Fares the Dream?" New York Times, Jan.16, 2012, http://www.nytimes.com/2012/01/16/ opinion/ krugman-how-fares-the-dream.html.
13   Will Wilkinson, "Paul Krugman Gets Distracted," Nov.1, 2011, http://www.economist.com/blogs/ democracyinamerica/2011/11/ inequalities? page =1.
14   James Q. Wilson, "Angry about Inequality? Don't Blame the Rich," Washington Post, Jan.27, 2012, http://www.washingtonpost.com/opinions/angry-about-inequality-dont-blame-the-rich/2012/01/03/gIQA9S2fTQ_story.html.

Y. 18

Pursuit of "Universal Values" as Part of the US Foreign Strategy

Xie Xiaoguang[1]

Abstract: The pursuit of "universal values" are the realization of the US's ideological hegemony in essence, a tool used by the US to promote cultural imperialism, as well as one means utilized by the United States to overthrow the regimes of the socialist countries, including China. The United States uses double standards when promoting "universal values" because, in fact "universal values" have obvious class characteristics and functions in the U.S.-led capitalist countries. "Universal values" is used to support its hard power with cultural "soft power" as the part and logic of its basic strategy to transform globalization to Americanization.

Key words: "Universal values", the U.S. strategy; mode of implementation

---

1 Xie Xiaoguang, visiting scholar in the World Socialism Research Center attached to CASS; Professor of Liaoning University School of International Studies.

The deep political implication of the debates on the "universal values" reflects the intensification of the struggles between China and the U.S.-led Western countries in the ideological field. It indicates that the U.S.-led Western countries have never slackened the "peaceful evolution (transformation)" strategy targeting the socialist countries. "Universal values" fundamentally deny the democratic politics aspect of socialism with Chinese characteristics; completely separates the inherent connection between economic system reform and political system reform in the course of China's reform and opening-up; and try to misguide China's political reform towards to the trap of Western "democratization". This erroneous trend of thought has made a great impact and damaged the leading role of socialist core value system in the construction of China's cultural soft power. The essence of clarifying the issue of "universal values", means to refute the U.S.-centered "universal values;" reveal the U.S.'s political attempt to "Westernize" and "split apart" China and expounding the basic direction of socialism with Chinese characteristics. Therefore, in the current ideological construction of our country, it is an urgent task to defend against the infiltration of Western ideology.

I. A Review of the relevant studies on the "universal values" debate

Some Chinese scholars, in their debate on the "universal values," propose the "absolute value theory," arguing that "universal values"—which are absolutely permanent in time and space—really exist, and that freedom, equality, human rights and democracy, among other concepts, fall within this category. These people advocate that "universal values" are values that are universally applicable and will exist eternally, they are received by all people under heaven, and penetrate the development of human society from beginning to end. They believe that "universal values" have universal applicability, eternality and universal necessity. But most Chinese scholars agree about "the theory of relativity of values" holding that no universally applicable "universal values" truly exist, that concepts such as freedom, democracy, equality and human rights are class-based, historical and regional, and that different groups and countries have dramatically different interests and demands, thus such "universal values" —which are universally applicable—hardly exist.[2]

There is also a comprising view which opposes taking the Western values as "universal values" but also argues that the concept of Chinese characteristics is incompatible with the "universal values" of the humanity.

---

2 Zhen Yan, Several Questions on the Understanding of the "Universal Values", Beijing Daily, June 16, 2008, p.3.

The concept of "universal values" obscures the complexity of the problem of values, and misleads people's understanding of values.[3] The fundamental difference between values and truths is that truths are always unitary, while values are always diversified. The variety character of subject differences between subjects inevitably determine the heterogenity, particularity and diversity of values. People, humankind is universal, abstract and have commonalities, but individual person is concrete, specific and historical, and the social nature of men determines that there will never be "universal values" that apply to all times and to all men.[4]

An argument of strategy is at work, to "universalize" the unique values of Western civilization, by completely equalizing Western civilization to "universal values" and viewing the non-Western civilization as having separate unique values.[5] No values in the world are universally applicable or eternal, and the West is whipping up public opinions by advocating "universal values" in order to frustrate or overthrow the socialist system.[6]

The theory of the end of history proposed by the US scholar Fukuyama propagated for the final victory of American liberal democracy, claiming that the American style is the "universal value" and it is final and full fledged form of governance. Huntington's "Clash of Civilizations" held that the fundamental root cause of conflicts in the new world order of the future will be cultural, —instead of being "ideological or primarily economic", and that major divisions among humankind and international conflicts after the Cold War will originate from "the fault lines between different civilizations or cultures." His argument highlights the diversity of conflicts and the differences among different nations. Besides, Huntington viewed Confucian civilization represented by China as a threat to Western civilization. German scholar Hans Kung advocated "the global ethics," that is, "commensuration" among different cultures for the purpose of "universal values" In 1990, he imagined building universal ethics in the world through dialogues, trying to seek some universal values that can be followed by all parties in a conflict amidst the diversified conflicts occurring in the world. The U.S. government has been taking the promotion of "universal values" as one of its foreign strategies. Since taking power, Obama has held that ideological soft power—the strength of compassion and hope—is more important than military strength even economic strength. He proposed to

---

3 Ma Depu, Complexity of the Value Problem and Misleading Concept of "Universal Values", CASS Journal of Political Science, Issue 1, 2009.
4 Wang Tingyou, Untenable Basis for Proposing the "Universal Values", Journal of Ideological & Theoretical Education, Issue 3, 2009.
5 Zhou Xincheng, Random Thoughts on the "Universal Values", Studies on Marxism, Issue 9, 2008.
6 Zhong Zheming, Thoughts on the Issue of "Universal Values", Journal of Ideological & Theoretical Education, Issue 3, 2009.

develop and employ the foreign strategies of the US with "smart power" to re-design the world with universal human rights, social institutions and open economies.

The 2010 US Quadrennial Defense Review for the first time expounded the definition of US security interests of the administration: "America's interests are inextricably linked to the integrity and resilience of the international system. Chief among these interests are security, prosperity, broad respect for universal values, and an international order that promotes cooperative action." An inherent concept in this policy paper was to make the American culture, policy or values more appealing, and persuade other countries to follow, understand and identify themselves with the views of the US in the international community so as to defend the national interests of the US. 2010 National Security Strategy of the USA clearly advocated that: "respect for universal values at home and around the globe" and defined it as an important "lasting benefit for the United States."[7] The "new imperialism theory" promoted by the US advocates transforming the world with American values and exporting the so-called democracy and freedom to other countries by use of force, its advantages and military strength, in an attempt to establish a US-centered world order. The Iraq war and the "Latin American Trap" are the evil consequences of the US's promotion of the so-called "universal" and "modern social values and institutions"

II. The essence of "universal values" pursued by the U.S.

1. A demonstration of the U.S's ideological hegemony

Western civilization is in a dominant position in the world, which has inherited the achievements of mankind and formed the contemporary modern civilization, so the advocates, advises and voices of the U.S. and other Western countries occupy a mainstream position in world politics, even world's development issues. In the debate on "universal values," and regarding development China and the U.S. and other Western countries have different understandings, identity and different practical approach. The U.S. insists on promoting and popularizing its mainstream ideology—"universal values"—throughout the globe, "freedom, democracy and human rights" being the core of it, and which both ignores the diversity of world cultures, and the historical and class-based nature of values, —as an ideological and theoretical weapon—so as to claim the moral high ground globally, to pursue its national interests and world hegemony. We also know that this hegemonic behavior that pursues national strategic interests is sold as one that maintains international justice.

---

7   The White House, The National Security Strategy of the USA, May 2010, p.7; http://www.Whitehouse.gov/default/files/rssviewer/national security/strategy.pdf.

According to the American standards, only the multiparty political system, government in the form of separation of three powers and the general election system to determine the ruling government can be regarded as democracy, but in fact, we can comfortably say that the representative government system is only one way of achieving democracy, and if the representative government system is equalized with democracy, it is like equalizing the US-style democracy, just one of the democratic models in the world, with democracy as a whole, which obviously means substituting the general or abstract with the concrete and particular. It is clear that this logic not only simply misleads people but causes a one-sided understanding of democracy more easily. This means that this view does not take into consideration the political ideology of democracy, social and political institutions of a certain country, the social consciousness democratic ideas of its people, their democratic behaviors and lifestyles when evaluating and debating the issues of democracy, freedom, equality, human rights. Instead this view narrowly focuses on the democratic rights granted to people by the constitution or state and incorporates this approach when discussing the above issue, and the judgments arrived are purely abstracted. In fact, behind the "universal democratic values" promoted by the U.S. is the parochial mentality aiming to serve the bourgeois interests. Therefore, the U.S's intention to promote "universal values" is not about "democracy, freedom, human rights," per se, but only about the social system behind "democracy, freedom and human rights".

2. A tool used by the U.S. in the pursuit of cultural imperialism

"Universal values" is the latest version of "Pride and Prejudice" of the American culture. The U.S. promotes its own values as "universal values", and views other cultures as the opposite of "universal values," which can easily lead to the flooding of extreme nationalism. The US advocates "universal values" firstly to suppress its strategic rivals, design and manipulate the public opinions of them, and then to export the so-called "freedom, democracy and human rights," so as to suppress civilizations and values it disagrees about, and even employs us of force, political subversion, diplomatic blockade and economic sanctions, to achieve these ends. In so doing, it is not to lead these countries smoothly to a broad road, but to weaken the leading capability of the supreme leading power system of these countries so as to enhance its ability to control the power structures of these countries. As a strategic tool to promote its cultural imperialism, "universal values" plays a very important role, and has achieved very significant results in such aspects as competing for the right of ideological discourse, beautifying its hegemonic acts as behaviors of maintaining human justice, weakening the leading capability of the supreme power of the rival countries it opposes, and supporting the formation of puppet governments through "color revolutions" Some people propagate "universal values" in order to advocate pluralism in the guiding ideology of our country; promote Western bourgeois values; frustrate the guiding position of Marxist ideology; and disturb the building of our socialist core value system. Politically, they attempt to coach the development of our democratic politics and our efforts to deepen the reform of our political system, by the Western model of democracy, and finally aim to fundamentally change the development direction of China's socialist democratic political construction.

3. A means resorted to by the U.S. to overthrow the regimes of the socialist countries including China

The US has a very clear objective when propagating the "universal values"—that is to lead China to develop along the established orbit of capitalism, to subvert the fundamental political system of China and to put an end to the state power led by the Communist Party of China, which is a concentrated expression of the Westernization plot schemed now by the hostile capitalist forces against China through infiltration of Western values. The dissolution of the Soviet Union and the upheaval in Eastern Europe serve us as grave lessons, which reveals the true color of "universal values" advocated by Gorbachev (namely his "common human values"). Gorbachev abandoned the Marxist approach of class analysis and class views, and worshipped "common human values" that "are above all" which do not exist at all, which has objectively disarmed the Soviet Communist Party ideologically, and catered for the requirements of the Western "peaceful evolutionary transformation" strategy. Guided by the so-called "common human values" he was singing praises, that the Soviet Union should gradually abandoned the socialist system and the leadership of the communist party[8] before he finally embarked the road of no return leading to the the destruction of the party and the state.

All in all, not only should we reveal the political intentions of the Western countries, in their pursuit of "universal values" but also recognize the positive achievements of the progress of human civilization, and pursue to reach a value consensus in a certain range through international cooperation and cultural communication.

III. The role of "universal values" in the U.S foreign strategies

Upholding the banner of "universal values," the U.S. is actually seeking a pretext for promoting hegemony so as to establish its ultimate world hegemony, thus complete the substitution of "global democratization" with "global Americanization".

---

8 Wang Tingyou, Untenable Basis for Proposing the "Universal Values", Journal of Ideological & Theoretical Education, Issue 3, 2009.

1. Historical origin of the establishment of "universal values" strategy by the U.S

After the WWII, in order to get an upper hand in its gaming with the rest countries, the U.S. shifted from free trade to protectionism, and after it became stronger, it shifted from protectionism to free trade for world hegemony. In the 1980s, in order to expand its established hegemony, the U.S. made "universal values" an ideological weapon in the struggle for cultural leadership around the globe, attempted to involve the whole world into a U.S.-centered global order so as to complete its global strategic deployments. After the Cold War, in order to maintain its status as the world's sole superpower, the U.S. developed a brand-new strategic framework, under which maintaining security deployments, economic expansion and promoting democracy would be advanced simultaneously. To meet the requirements of maintaining its hegemonism and power politics, "human rights" was further promoted so as to become one of the important tools used by the U.S's global democratization strategy.

New conservative forces of US believed that concepts such as "democracy" and "freedom" should be spread to the whole world, so they proposed to put excessive emphasis on the role of ideology in foreign diplomacy and formulated the doctrine of building a "free world" through "global democratization" process. In the first term of George W. Bush which started in 2001, priority was given to promoting unilateralism and the "preemptive defense strategy." The George W. Bush administration claimed that the United States is locked in a global war; a war of ideology, in which its enemies are bound together by a common ideology and a common hatred of democracy. At the beginning, the U.S. stressed the reshaping of the international order by its development model and by its strength. The 9/11 terrorist attack has made the U.S. to feel gravely threatened, and this fact also demonstrated the failure of its foreign strategy which mainly relied on its "hard power" It rendered George W. Bush, return to putting emphasis on "soft power" like "universal values" in his second term, that is, to lessen the external security threats by promoting democratic regime changes i.e reforms, around the globe by propagating American democratic values and political institutions and advancing democratic reforms around the globe. In 2008, after Obama took power, he adopted policy to establish a broader coalition which pinned hope of promoting "universal values" "with the power of model, not as a model of power".

2. Double standards in the U.S's foreign strategy of "universal values"

The U.S. ignores the reality that diversified values exist in the current world, and employs the wrapped "universal values" as a diplomatic tool; and believes that its values far exceed others' values; and exports its values worldwide unscrupulously so as to seek its own national interests and become world's dominant hegemon. What's even worse is that it constantly maintains double standards on "universal values" to suppress its strategic rivals and defend its interests. For example, in the face of political unrest and turmoil in the Middle East and North African countries, the policies U.S. adopted towards Libya, Syria and Bahrain, Yemen were self-contradictory.

On April 8, 2011, the US Department of State released its 2010 Country Reports on Human Rights, and 2 days later the State Council Information Office of China issued the Human Rights Record of the United States in 2010, which has shown that US's human rights record is so bad that it does not qualify to be the world's "human rights judge"; yet US kept releasing reports on human rights practices of others every year to criticize and blame the human rights situation in other countries and regions. Though neglecting to improve its serious human rights problem, the U.S. is keen to promote its so-called "human rights diplomacy," which fully exposes its use of hypocritical double standards on the issue of human rights and "universal values;" besides reveals its pursuit of hegemony under the pretext of human rights and "universal values". It is obvious that it uses human rights as a political tool to defame other countries' images and pursue its own strategic interests.

3. Class essence of "universal values" in the U.S foreign strategy

Since class antagonisms and superiority of sovereign interests still exists in the current world,"universal values" cannot qualify to be the "universal truth", by no means.

Marx once pointed out that "the ruling ideas of each age have ever been is the ideas of its ruling class."

Today, the capitalist class remains to be the ruling class in the international community, consequently the so-called "universal values"—like freedom, democracy, human rights, rule of law, equality and fraternity—serve the interests and needs of the capitalist class, therefore these lofty sounding slogans can only be pretexts for big countries to bully small countries and strong countries oppressing weak countries.

In order to carry out ideological and political infiltration around the globe, the U.S. under the guise of defending "freedom, democracy, human rights"; organizes the so-called "dissidents" to engage in street politics; subverts regimes that do not meet the interests of the United States through "color revolutions;" even achieves its objectives directly by force under the banner of "universal values" These are the functions of "universal values" In the post-Cold War era, the U.S. has instigated "color revolutions" in Ukraine, Georgia and Central Asian countries; cleared the way for its Greater Middle East Initiative by force; and interfered in China's internal affairs under the pretexts of human rights, democracy and Tibet issue. All these facts prove that the vigorous promotion of "universal values" by the United States is nothing more than a trap. Therefore, it would be absurd to discuss on the "universal values" in an abstract way. Only when abstract value concepts like freedom, democracy, human rights, the rule of law, equality and fraternity are combined with specific nations and ethnic groups in a specific way of implementation can concrete values be truly developed.

IV. Procedure in the promotion of "universal values" as the part of the U.S. foreign strategy

Currently, the U.S. adopts the "soft power" approach when including the promotion of "universal values" as one component part of its global foreign strategy, thus the promotion of "universal values" has become the main form of its ideological diplomacy as well as an important part of its grand strategy of liberalism.

1. The strategic logic of the U.S. of promoting "universal values" is shifting from globalization to Americanization

Globalization which implies worldwide competitions, is actually combined with the process of economic globalization and gradual formation of a unified world market- i.e, the process global integration. The U.S. is aware that, in the current age of globalization, and since the world is divided as center and periphery power structure, in the process global integration, only the countries which have access to ideological hegemony can maintain their dominant position and become the rule-makers.

Therefore, although continuing to strengthen its military and economic competitiveness as its primary target, the U.S aims to raise the competition in the ideological, cultural and core values spheres, to an important strategic height, making it convenient to promote the US-style democratic politics around the globe so as to ultimately achieve the political globalization. To a large extent, globalization has been Americanized under the cloak of "universal values" From economic integration to cultural homogeneity and then to the "democratization" of politics, this is the procedure, i.e game plan of the so-called "global modernization" pursued by the U.S.[9]

---

9 Zhong Ping, Motives Behind "Universal Values", Daily of Chinese Academy of Social Sciences, Jan. 13, 2009.

2. "Hard power" as the backing and "soft power" as the means

In order to achieve its strategic goals, the U.S., relying on its formidable material and military power, promotes liberalism and the US-style democracy under the banner of "universal values;" and forces different countries to follow the American-style democratic institutions, as an important part of its "soft power." The U.S. has abundant material resources for spreading "universal values" including language, cable TV network, the Internet and financial aids for the supported countries. With such basic strength, it can carry out vigorous cultural wars to spread "universal values" especially by interminably using modern media and global propaganda broadcasts; promoting the American ideology and values; conducting secret cultural penetration under the cover of cultural communication through non-governmental organizations and private foundations; exporting the American cultural products through international trade, and spreading the American values and ways of life, through developing media diplomacy by establishing a variety of global media networks, such as cable TV network, the Internet; and promoting its democratic systems and political values through public political socialization channels and propagating mass consumer culture.

(This paper is an intermediate research result of a key research project—Studies on the Export of American Democracy and Ideological Security of China—supported by the Social Science Planning Project of Liaoning Provincial administration in 2012.)

Y. 19

How Has "State Capitalism" Become the "New Pet" of the West?

Cheng Enfu and Hou Weimin[1]

Abstract: Focusing on the reprimand by Western academia that the emerging economies advocate "state capitalism", this paper discusses the consequences of neoliberal policies, the development paths chosen by the emerging economies, and the content of socialist market economy in China. The article attempts to reveal the exploitation of the notion of "state capitalism" in the Western media and by some critical academy, discusses their intention to cover up domestic failures and shift attention. Authors offer a brief comparison between "socialism with Chinese characteristics" and "state capitalism", refute the distortions about the former.

Key words: state capitalism; new emerging economies; neoliberalism; Socialism with Chinese Characteristics

---

[1] Cheng Enfu, Deputy Director of the CASS World Socialism Research Center, Dean and researcher of the CASS Academy of Marxism; Hou Weimin, deputy researcher in the Academy of Marxism attached to CASS.

Each and every great crisis in the capitalist world trigger debates on the future and destiny of the capitalist system. Amidst the prescriptions written out by the Western public in order to defend the crisis, conceal contradictions and shift attention, "state capitalism" has become "a new favorite" this time. British weekly "The Economist" published a group of columns themed as "state capitalism" on January 21, 2012, including "The Rise of State Capitalism: The spread of a new sort of business in the emerging world will cause increasing problems", "State Capitalism's Global Reach: New Masters of the Universe", "The World in Their Hands, Going Abroad: State capitalism looks outward as well as inward", "Something Old, Something New: A Brief History of State Capitalism" and another six articles. In the same month, during the World Economic Forum in Davos, a debate on capitalism was organized.

All the articles and debates revolve around one basic point, that is, "the state capitalism" especially in China, Russia, Brazil, India and Singapore—made up of solely state-owned companies, state-held companies, companies where the state holds some of the shares, sovereign wealth funds and private companies supported by the state—is developing rapidly around the globe. In its economic activities, state capitalism actively makes deals of mergers and acquisitions foreign enterprises, struggles for international resources, makes independent innovations, thus severely threatens the development of "liberal capitalism" in the West.

The public in the West who have long made neoliberalism the criterion now change their belief in the myth claiming the free-market system to be invincible, and associate the current capitalist crisis with state capitalism. The reasons behind are just intriguing.

I. Defending neoliberalism in the name of "state capitalism"

1. "State capitalism" theorists ascribe the crisis partially to the so-called state capitalism of the emerging economies, trying to divert people's attention from the financial crisis, debt crisis and continuous economic crisis in the West.

The outbreak of the financial crisis has fully demonstrated that the laisser-faire market economy has come to its end, and private ownership- and profit-seeking-based monopoly capitalism has lost the ability to handle the healthy development of economic globalization in the 21st century.

In October 2008 when the crisis first started, a column titled Capitalism at bay published in "The Economist" avowed, "In the short term defending capitalism means, paradoxically, state intervention. Over the past century and a half capitalism has proved its value for billions of people. The parts of the world where it has flourished have prospered, the parts where it has shriveled have suffered."

However, we think the reality has ruthlessly broken this view. In fact, it is hard to fundamentally ease the crisis in the Western society if the government intervention to capitalist private ownership is not reformed.

In recent years, Greece, Portugal, Italy, Spain and Ireland, known as the "Pigs" in the international community, have witnessed serious debt crises in succession, indicating the great difficulty in maintaining fiscal austerity implemented by EU. However, "state capitalism" theorists of the West hold the following: "The crisis of Western liberal capitalism has coincided with the rise of a powerful new form of state capitalism in emerging markets, the crisis of liberal capitalism has been rendered more severe by the rise of a potent alternative: state capitalism. State capitalism is on the rise, overflowed with cash and emboldened by the crisis in the West."

We think this is just an envy of other countries' development while framing these countries, so as to conceal their inability to ease the crisis. It has already been confirmed that China and the rest fast-growing BRICS countries do not cause or exacerbate the crisis in the Western countries. On the contrary, emerging economies, especially China have boosted the world's economic recovery and eased various crises in the West, to a certain extent.

2. "State capitalism" is wielded in the West also because Western countries intend to ascribe the crises they face to laissez-faire capitalism in the West instead of the capitalist economic system where private ownership is the mainstay.

This above superficial view is denied by some sober Western scholars. Below is an example: Niall Ferguson argued in an article he wrote for the "Times" entitled "We Are All State Capitalists Now" the following: "Ultimately, it is an unhelpful oversimplification to divide the world into 'market capitalism' and 'state capitalism' camps;…But is it in fact correct to ascribe China's success to the state rather than the market? The answer depends on where you go in China…we must avoid crude generalizations about 'state capitalism,' a term that is really not much more valuable today than the Marxist-Leninist term 'state monopoly capitalism' was back when Rudolf Hilferding coined it a century ago."[2]

"State capitalism" theorists try to create a contradiction and contrast between state capitalism and liberal capitalism, defend the capitalist policies and the evil consequences of neoliberalism, and then continue to protect the narrow interests of international monopoly capital and oligopoly (especially financial oligopoly). They assert that as the emerging economies are

---

2 Niall Ferguson, "We are all state-capitalists now," TIMES, February 14, 2012.

becoming stronger and stronger, the United States is becoming more and more restrained, Europe fall apart from inside, G20 replaces G7; and China, the "axis of state capitalism", is getting more and more advantages in the field of ideology, and its economic model which is superior to that of the U.S. will challenge the free market principles and beliefs. They also assert that the rise of state capitalism in the East may encourage some followers in the West, and that worries the companies in the West more and more.

Practice has proven that such strategy of argument is ineffective. At present, neoliberalism promoted by big monopoly capitalists which account for 1% of the capitalists in the West is not only opposed by 99% of the people of their respective countries, but has also harmed the reasonable rights and interests of many developing countries. Even World Economic Forum, which had been praising neoliberalism, had to criticize and reconsider the unjust economic globalization led by the developed countries and discussed about the way out of the current capitalism to echo the international opinion of building a new international economic order, at the new-round annual meeting which will convene at the very beginning of 2012.

As can be seen, behind the fight between the so-called state capitalism and liberal capitalism are Western countries that hold the right to design and formulate international economic and trading rules. They ignore the demands and voices of the vast developing countries and those by far-sighted advanced figures in developed countries, depicted as "necessity to build a new international economic order", instead they simply try to deceive the public and manipulate public opinions.

II. Listing the disadvantages of "state capitalism" so as to deter emerging economies

State capitalism" theorists list the so-called disadvantages of "state capitalism" with the intention to deter people of the emerging economies from making efforts along the development road they have chosen. On the one hand, they assert that the economic momentum of "state capitalism" is great and that the world's most powerful enterprises are practicing "state capitalism"; while on the other, they define "state capitalism" as a system where the state dominates market activities for political interests.

In their eyes, "state capitalism" is mainly made up of solely state-owned companies, state-held companies or companies where the state have shares, sovereign wealth funds and privately-run enterprises supported by the state. Such companies and enterprises actively make merger deals or acquire foreign enterprises around the globe, they struggle for international resources and are keen on independent innovations.

However, "state capitalism" is not good at technological innovation, which will lead to no liberty, corruption and ultimate failure, and will endanger the free market economy and the democratic system. Ian Bremmer, one of the "state capitalism" critic has claimed the following: "The primary purpose of state capitalism is not to produce wealth but to ensure that wealth creation does not threaten the political power of the ruling elite. Those who administer 'state capitalism' fear 'creative destruction'…When old industries die, workers lose jobs and wages, a problem that can drive citizens into the streets to challenge authority." With these words, he intended to persuade the emerging economies (especially China, Russia and Brazil, the "BRIC countries") to abandon international competition that conform to international rules and international practices so as to prevent the positive development momentum of these countries. Looking from the opposite side, it also indicates that some developed countries and their interest groups, due to their fear that emerging economies may take effective measures other than neoliberalism and Keynesianism to achieve rapid development, that they successfully compete internationally and "endanger" their vested interests.

Besides putting the hat of "state capitalism" on some emerging economies, "state capitalism" theorists also try to instigate other countries to discriminate and contain such emerging economies, economically, politically and militarily. Instead of noticing the enormous harms brought about by the capitalist crisis to the world, these people exclaim that "state capitalism" has brought thorny problems to the world economic system. They claim that emerging economies might destroy "the fair and just competition" system of the world. A scholar wrote: "emerging economies try to prove that they are better off, after they have abandoned the market economy, better off with "autocracy" compared to democracy, and they use state-owned enterprises as tools to expand their military strength." Correspondingly, the European Union hinted that it would prevent the state-owned enterprises of China from acquiring European companies on the ground that all state-owned enterprises are in fact a component part of the same economic entity: the huge state trust attached to Chinese government.

Contrarily we see that the so-called countries applying "state capitalism" in their eyes have never mandatorily exported democratic values in recent decades, and the relative expansion of its military strength by China is forced and defense-oriented. The opposite is the case, the real subjects that implement anti-democratic financial control, power politics, unilateralism and new imperialist policy are combinations of international monopoly capital and military interest groups of the Western developed countries which promote neoliberalism around the globe. Their existence posits the biggest challenge against world peace and development.

III. "State capitalism" equaled to and confused by socialism with Chinese characteristics

"State capitalism" theorists view the solely state-owned enterprises, state-held enterprises and enterprises where the state has shares as a part of state capitalism in China instead of a part of socialism with Chinese characteristics. In fact, they confuse the essential distinction between socialist economy and capitalist economy.

Mainstream economic theories both at home and abroad believe that capitalism is a basic economic system where the means of production mainly belong to the capitalists, while socialism is a basic economic system where all or some members of the society should collectively or collaboratively own the means of production. Although components of other ownership forms with different natures exist in both the capitalist society and the socialist society today, it is the predominant ownership that determines and defines the economic nature of any society. If we make a further analysis on the relations between the government and the market, capitalism may be divided into market capitalism (liberal capitalism, as represented by the U.S.) and planned capitalism (state monopoly capitalism, as represented by France), and socialism can be divided into planned socialism ("state socialism", as represented by traditional China and the Soviet Union) and market socialism (socialist market economy, as represented by China since the reform and opening-up and Vietnam), Planned socialism and market socialism have differences regarding the relations between market and planning, market regulation and government regulation, free competition and economic monopoly, resource allocation and economic regulation factors.

Now, the articles in "The Economist", rejecting the rational consensus of mainstream economics both in China and abroad, ingeniously puts forward the new concept of "state capitalism" and confuses the theoretical and practical problems of different forms of ownership and means of economic adjustment around the globe, which can't be justified by any scientific theory. This "state capitalism" is essentially different from both "state capitalism" put forward by Lenin and different from that adopted by China in the 1950s. The latter starts from the perspective that a socialist country led by the Communist Party can utilize the private sector of the economy to develop the national economy, although the private sector of the economy and foreign-capitalist economy can be part of "state capitalism" in nature—. We all know that these sectors are essentially capitalist economic elements that are utilized and controlled by the socialist countries.

The socialist economic system with Chinese characteristics is superior in that it is a socialist economic model where the market plays a fundamental regulating role and the state plays the dominant regulatory role. It is substantially different from the capitalist economic model in the West where monopoly capital controls the national economy and the whole country.

At present, namely in the primary stage of socialism with Chinese characteristics, China adopts a basic economic system which takes the public ownership as the mainstay, the state-owned sector of the economy at the leading position; and allows the co-existence of diverse forms of non-public economic sectors. This basic economic also includes the elements of "state capitalism"[3] like the private sector of the economy and foreign-invested economy. Its way of economic operation and regulation is the double-track system and mechanism where market regulation is the basis and government regulation predominates. It promotes independent and active participation in economic globalization, and follows the international economic rules and practices when implementing the opening-up policies and when competing in the domestic and foreign markets. It is an economic model and development path where systems and mechanisms have global commonalities and national characteristics, and this development path is conformity with the direction of progress of the human society. Its great historical role and competence cannot be simply ignored by any prejudiced label of "state capitalism."

IV. In fact who should be labeled as "state capitalism" more?

Currently, the US economy still remains stagnant; the economic situation in Europe is even worse and the challenges faced by capitalism render all sectors in the West, which urges many people to rethink and evaluate the capitalist system and its mechanisms. Although many advocate state supervision and control of capitalism, lots of Westerners hold a sophisticated attitude towards the rescue of capitalism by the state.

On November 1, 2011, the British magazine "Financial Times" attacked insider capitalism in an editorial entitled "The Big Questions Raised by Anti-capitalist Protests." In the editorial, it pointed out that such insider form of capitalism exploited and indeed created subsidies and tax loopholes on which the insiders prospered, but it also held that capitalism needed the state. "Capitalism should not let the insider form of capitalism managing the economy, but instead it should adjust people's way of managing the economy so that they have to bear the consequences of their acts."

Such contradiction between private monopoly capital and the state often leads to the result that capitalist states, being "ideal total capitalist"—as in Engels' words—, may be able to temporarily ease the tension between private monopoly capital and the capitalist class as a whole, and that between financial monopoly capital and commercial monopoly capital (or industrial monopoly capital) and the social public, through intervention and

---

3   Here we mean state capitalism, subordinate to socialism.

adjustments of interests, but certainly these measures cannot fundamentally eliminate the root causes of those contradictions.

The idea to pin the hope of solving the crisis on Western governments did not prove true this year. As early as on January 22, 2008, "International Herald Tribune" published an article, in which it pointed out that the world's mainstream economic policy was shifting from laissez-faire to government intervention. In practice, the "ideal total capitalists" of the United States and the European nations have chosen to shift the crisis elsewhere, to other countries and over the shoulders of their respective people so as to serve the interests of the monopoly capital groups. If the neoliberal policies prove improper to meet the demands of monopoly capital in the short term, it is in line with the long-term interests of monopoly capital to abandon market fundamentalism which advocates "market decides all" (as underlined by the Nobel laureate Joseph Stiglitz) and turn to support the state capitalism thus forcibly resolve the internal contradictions of the capitalist system.

It has been an inevitable "story" in the Western history of crises that government's regulatory function was used at times of economic crises, and part of the story is that that these governments have timely withdrew from the market after the crises and returned the profit-making space to the "market forces", that is, to private monopoly capital and its owners, and called it by a tricky phrase of "not competing with the people for profits." It was just the case in the crisis of the 1930s, and it has even been the case since the financial and economic crisis in the West in 2008. Helping the monopoly capital groups which are hardly hit by the crisis with generous funds becomes priority, and more profit-making space is returned to monopoly capitalist class after the crises. Although the world economic crisis keeps spreading and further deepens, righteous resistance movements and the international movement of "occupation" by the masses of many countries against the shifting of the burden onto their shoulders are becoming more and more influential, but the governments of the Western countries have begun to seek a government "withdrawal" mechanism, namely giving up their regulatory roles. They seem to ignore the fact that domestic gap between the rich and the poor is unprecedentedly severe and that production and consumption are in serious conflict. Instead they "cleverly" use the rise in government deficits caused by the credit crisis and the collapse of the taxation system as excuses for their "withdrawal". Thus reforming the wealth possession and income distribution system or disturbing the interests of private capital is far beyond their scope, instead they seek to stabilize the capitalist economic system by issuing more currency, reducing laborers' wages, cutting old-pension and other welfare, increasing laborers' tax burden, even putting pressure on other countries, which are simply counterproductive, and help little to eliminate the crisis.

The integration and mutual support of various forms of private monopoly capital and the capitalist states in the West today have given birth to state capitalism, state monopoly capitalism, even international monopoly capitalism, and impose major impacts on the global economic structure. The situation does not exist in socialist countries like China, so "state capitalism" is indeed a mislabeling by the Western critics.

Y. 20

Neoliberalism Worsens Global Labor Relations

Cui Xuedong[1]

Abstract: This paper examines the negative influence of neoliberalism on the labor relations in the US and throughout the world from the four aspects of financialization of economy, privatization of social welfare and security, political party-trade union relations, and the globalization of monopoly capital. Since the current financial crisis has not climbed to the level full fledged crisis of neoliberalism, we do not expect or predict a remarkable deterioration occuring in global labor relations, on the other hand, the financialization pursuit and diminishing of the real economy will continue. Since the dominant position of neoliberal ideology and neoliberal economic policies have not yet been strongly challenged, working class movement and its political forces lack strong motives which can force a progressive change in the labor relations globally. Moreover, globalization process has put the working class at an even weaker bargaining position.

Key words: neoliberalism; financial crisis; globalization; labor relations

---

1 Cui Xuedong, Visiting scholar in the World Socialism Research Center attached to CASS, associate Professor of Nankai University

The US financial and economic crisis since the end of 2007 has become the most grave capitalist economic crisis since 1929. Well, does it mean the end of the US neoliberal model which has been maintained for over 30 years and does it point to a major turning point in labor relations?

Although the financial crisis has erupted in the U.S. due to the declining proportion of labor remuneration, unprecedented inequality of wealth and distribution of incomes, continual diminishing of the manufacturing-centered real economy, economic growth highly dependent to the unsustainable consumer credits, asset price bubbles, all of which do not mean the end of the accumulation and growth model featuring neoliberalism, financialization and globalization. Economic financialization, privatization of social security, inherently deficient political party-trade union relation, and globalization of monopoly capital have all weakened and divided the US working class, making it hard to substantially change the labor relations in the short term.

I. Excessive economic financialization: an accumulation and growth mode where the fruits of labor cannot be shared.

The United States is the most typical country reflecting the financialization of contemporary capitalism. Seen from the mode of capital accumulation, financialization means that non-financial companies are compelled to "make profits via financial channels instead of commerce or commodity production" And if evaluated from the aspect of economic growth model, financialization means "the focus of economic activities shifts from production (including the growing service sector, increasingly) to finance" The finance-dominated accumulation mode is created after a reflection on the Fordist accumulation mode, and substitution of the Fordist accumulation mode after its crisis after WWII.

Under the Fordist accumulation mode, financial capital was highly acclaimed, and bank credits were channeled to productive investments to meet the demand for accumulating industrial capital as the goal of Keynesian fiscal policy and demand of the building of welfare state aiming at full employment in order to provide corresponding social needs for large-scale production.

And in terms of labor relations, —under the Fordist accumulation mode—labor-capital collaboration replaced labor-capital confrontation, trade unions were appreciated and collective bargaining was affirmed, and a benefit-sharing mechanism where wages were adjusted according to productivity was applied; and an international coordination mechanism was implemented to limit the fluctuations and shocks of trade and investments on domestic economy. But since the 1960s, the Fordist accumulation mode has begun to see crises. Neoliberal restructuring, globalization of monopoly capital and financialization as arms of the capital accumulation become three major ways to get rid of the crisis.

Neoliberal restructuring emphasized free competition, which in essence aimed to dis-organize laborers and unions, achieve the goal of shifting the income redistribution from labor to capital, and re-establish the domination of financial capital over industrial capital by halting state intervention and reduction of social security; and strongly emphasizing and pressuring the return to "shareholder's value", which increased the return on capital, on enterprises and through equity restructuring of the capital market. Neoliberal theory argues that the higher the income of capitalist and fewer the wealthy people, the more motivated will they be to expand productive investment and promote employment, thus economic growth will be achieved. And consequently income inequality will be solved through the so-called "trickle-down effect." (Sometimes known as the leakage effect or drip effect) However, neoliberal restructuring and financialization as the arms of new capital accumulation have caused paradoxical results on the US economy in general.

1. Neoliberal restructuring has exacerbated the contradiction of overproduction.

Intense competitions in the product markets has led to the decline of corporate profit rates. Enterprises started labor layoffs, cut down wages and benefits, outsourcing and applying labor-intensive technologies were the main means of competition enterprises adopt in general, and they led to an expanding gap between labor productivity and the rate of increase in labor incomes or wages. In the United States, labor productivity presented an increase of 62.5%, but workers' average pay per hour grew by 12% during 1989 and 2010. Inadequate demand and overcapacity led to long-term stagnation in the real economy. The average growth rate of the US economy was 4% between 1950 and 1979, but in the era of neoliberalism it has dropped to 2.7% between 1980 and 2010. However, mainstream economists in the West have called this stagnation as "great moderation" or "great restructuring."

2. Financialization has become the primary means of recovering, accumulating and increasing the profit margins.

Financialization theory holds that financial liberalization and deepening of financialization can promote productive investments and economic growth. However, the main source of financing for productive investments of the larger US enterprises has always been their reserved profits instead of the gains from financial markets. Since the 1980s, reserved profits that could be used for productive investments by the non-financial companies were transferred to the financial sector in the form of rentier income, but the profits in the financial sector could never pass to the hands of non-financial companies for productive investments. For the pursuit of excessive profits, the non-financial companies in the US have cut productive investment one after another and turned to financial speculation. SP 500 companies' profits from financial businesses accounted for 40% of their total profits. The proportion of profits from financial operations of General Motors and Ford has increased as high as 125% and 157%, respectively. As can be seen, their losses in automotive businesses were offset by their profits by their financial operations.

3. The profits of financial capital come from direct financial exploitation of the working class.

As a result of overproduction and stagnation, the financial sector in the U.S. gained the primary part of profits not from the financing of the industrial and commercial enterprises, but from ever expanding household loans and from commissions received from financial operations including financial investments and consumer loans. Therefore, the finance-dominated accumulation and growth model, which is highly dependent on credit expansion and asset price bubbles, have continually relaxed credit standards and monetary control/regulation and pushed the major part of the population in the game of financial gambling.

Consumer credits only temporarily ease the adverse effects of stagnation in labor wage increases, and allows the working class to maintain a life standard beyond their actual wages, and makes housing a vital necessity of their lives, even an investment tool for the working class. In the long run, both credit booms and asset price bubbles cause a virtual wealth artificially created by financial capital, and it is a way of redistribution to meet the requirements of the current accumulation mode. Along with constant expansion of debts by the working class families, the transfer of wealth from labor to capital has accelerated. The expansion of housing prices means a sharp rise in the minimum cost of living or survival of the working class households and their disposable income keeps depreciating and increasingly need to be reserved for loan repayments, and eventually we arrive at the crisis of inadequate demand and overproduction.

It is hard to reverse the trend of financialization, and transcending the crisis it causes is also complicated due to specific characteristics of its crisis. In the classic crises that occurred under the former industrial accumulation mode, the crises themselves sowed the seeds of recovery; the renewal and updating of fixed capital and the rise in employment became a spontaneous market mechanism for economic recovery. While the recovery of crises in the financial accumulation period includes further increase of the profits by financial institutions and financial corporations, plus worsening the conditions of employment and wages, namely no improvement in "unemployment". Therefore, financialization and financial crises keep dividing and marginalizing the working class, which lead to the heterogeneity in the identity and interests of the working class—first, the number of industrial workers has decreased dramatically; second, marginalized groups in working class has kept growing, third, development of heterogeneity in the identity working class.

II. Privatization of social security: subordination of labor interests to neoliberal reforms

1. On the surface, privatization of social security seems to answer a series of problems like aging of the population, flexible employment and global competition but privatization of social security, as one component of neoliberal reforms, aims to serve the needs of financial capital accumulation

Privatization of social security bears at least three functions: to use the financial capital market instead of corporate and the state to bear the social insurance and security role. Consequently corporate and the state are freed from "the burden" of social security costs, making social security a personal obligation. Secondly; it caters the interests of Wall Street financial capital, by injecting social security capital to the financial market; thirdly it subordinates labor interests and strengthen constraints of capital on labor so that neoliberal reforms would be irreversible.

Privatization of social security started since the Reagan administration. It was mainly about cutting welfare expenditures, raising payroll taxes and the retirement age of workers, in particular reforming the old pension system from defined a benefit plan workers to a one which defined a deposit system.

The former pension system, contained a social compromise and a social solidarity approach and pensioners would receive a pre-fixed amount of old-age pension each month. Under the latter system, the basic old-age insurance premiums, i.e "investment by savings" paid by the individual laborer went entirely to their personal accounts. Their savings are put under the management of institutional investors, like commissioned pension funds, mutual funds and insurance companies, and then becomes a product of the stock and securities markets. Consequently employees' retirement income became uncertain, depending on the amount of retirement savings paid by the workers, and also depends on to the earnings of portfolios of personal accounts in the capital (stock) market.

During the Clinton administration era, the US experienced unprecedented stock market bubbles; and struggle for social security funds (capital) became main objective of business expansion strategy of financial institutions. Wall Street demanded—from the administration—to promote the privatization of social security so that more retirement savings could enter the capital market as a product. Meanwhile, Wall Street demanded relaxation of financial control and regulation. To decentralize and transfer credit risk and overcome inadequate liquidity, it is a must for the bank to make financial derivatives through the non-bank financial institutions directly under its control. A segmented financial system was obviously not conducive to the above objective of financial capital. Under vigorously lobbying by financial institutions, the US Congress passed the Financial Services Modernization Act in 1999 and abolished the Glass–Steagall Act which was issued during Roosevelt's New Deal to restrict financial capital speculation and which had separated investment operations and the business of commercial banks, Instead the Financial Services Modernization Act has removed legal obstacles against the expansion of the business scope of financial capital.

After President Bush took office, the bubble economy had entered into a recession. In order to support and promote the Wall Street-dominated US economy, Bush administration put forward the policy of "ownership society" reform plan to expand the privatization of social security and also the medical services, education and housing was included in the business scope.

Property rights, property inheritance and free choice of property rights became the most seductive sales and promotion slogans in the promotion of privatization of social public needs (medical services, education and housing). It was advocated that an individual's economic freedom and independence depended on his control over his life and wealth instead of relying on social transfers by the state. Individual's such control over his/her private choice (fate) should include housing, enterprises, his/her medical services assets and financial assets. The reform plan aimed to create conditions for recovering the household targeted credit expansion and promote the economic growth driven by asset price bubbles in nature, so it was for the benefit of Wall Street and a handful of the wealthy. However, privatization wave made the costs of education, medical services, retirement benefits and housing needs encountering an increasing rises and the situation of the working class has become even more distressing.

Through the pension funds, the working class indeed became the biggest owner group that have stake in the US companies, but workers failed to take control of the means of production or achieve the "fund socialism" as expected. Pension funds among other financial institutions essentially serve interests of the capital interests. When they apply "shareholder value" to US corporate, the corporate will be forced to layoff laborers, which will cause opposition by laborers. For the working class, losing their jobs will mean losing the ability to control their lives and wealth. "Ownership society" of Bush was actually "a society where individual should rely on oneself"

2. The reform of "ownership society" has the same policy intentions with Margaret Thatcher's "people's capitalism"

According to conservative views, if the working class owns part of marketable assets—such as mortgages, stock investments, private pension fund shares, they will no longer see themselves as workers, but will share common interests with their capitalist bosses. Working class will vote for politicians who promise to improve stock returns instead of those who promise to improve the working conditions.

Class consciousness will become a relic of history. In other words, not only labor-capital confrontation will be eliminated by turning workers into capitalists, but will turn workers to supporters of the free market policies and supporters of the "investor class" conservative party. However, interests bundling is by no means interest sharing, and labor-capital confrontation cannot be eliminated, either. Financial institutions and big corporate are the biggest beneficiaries of social security privatization, which will be financially supported and rescued by the government after a crisis because they are "too big to be allowed going bankrupt"

The working class suffers great losses from their pension savings (funds) in the time of financial crisis. Millions of families have lost their houses (housing investments) in the subprime crisis. Although stock ownership and pension investments by the working class can somewhat bring an investment income to them, it cannot change workers' identities as wage laborers, and will even exacerbated labor-capital confrontation and class polarization. Between 1989 and 2007, the stock assets of the American families 1%, 9%, 10%, 20%, 20% and 40%—from rich to poor—has appreciated by 36.8%, 44.3%, 10.5%, 6.5%, 1.5% and 0.5%, respectively.

If we evaluate net household wealth distribution, in 2007, the wealthiest 1% and 9% among the American families took up 34.6% and 38.5% of all, respectively, and the rest 90% of the American families only held 26.9% of all stock assets. The proportions of the net household financial assets of the above three categories of families were 42.7%, 40.2% and 17.1%, respectively. The ordinary working class received very little earnings from holding and owning of financial assets. Besides, a poll by the Pew Research Center showed that 26% of the respondents in 1988 believed the US to be a society with two major classes, namely the propertied class and the non-propertied. In 2007, the Pew Research Center found that the rate had risen to 48%.

3. Privatization of social security strengthens the subordination of labor to capital

Since social security is highly related to employment, workers have to do their best to keep being employed. No matter how much productivity and productive forces are improved, they must accept low wages, obey high labor intensity and longer working hours so as to accumulate enough retirement savings, for which they even delay their retirement.

4. Privatization of social security strengthens conservative political leanings.

The financial crisis does not shake the dominance of neoliberalism, but triggers the revival of Keynesianism.

III. Formalization of the relationship between the Democratic Party and the trade unions: political dilemma brought by the changes in labor relations

In 2008, as Democratic President Barack Obama became the boss of the White House with a public support rate of 53%, many expected him and the Democrats to wage a reform similarly significant as Roosevelt's "New Deal" in order put an end to the mode of neoliberalism, restore labor-capital collaboration which was prevalent in the period between the end of WWII to the 1970s, and would start a new era for the US working class.

However, the expectation had idealistic colors and was not realistic or feasible. As the core of the capitalist production relations, dialectically labor relations have both sides—confrontation and sharing. Confrontation is the essential nature of labor relations, and that is determined by the nature of the capitalist economic system. Shared labor relations special prerequisites an premises if workers demand to guarantee this won status, thus the temporary status of shared labor relations and cannot be the basis of analyses when examining the capitalist labor relations. Adjustments in labor relations are not randomly or spontaneously achieved, either. Changes in the technologies and new organization of the conditions of laboring, and improvements in labor productivity will only strengthen the actual subordination of labor to capital. Even if a capital accumulation crisis occurs, whether income distribution adjustments are favorable for laborers depends on the contrast between the pressure of capital and workers' resistance.

Party-trade union relations in political system, which were born premature and crippled, have kept weakening the political status of the working class. The US working class is divided into different interest groups with different social identities like race, religion, immigrants and belonging to minorities. Due to the lack of a political party having a solid foundation of laborer support, workers are able to struggle against their employers and against the managers in workshops, against the managers of the neighborhood organizations, even against the city management organ, but they are unable to unite as an independent political force to protect their own interests.

Although trade unions are closer to the Democratic Party, it started since Roosevelt's New Deal reform and was created out of the need of electoral politics. Trade unions provide funds and offer voter support for the Democratic candidate in the presidential elections, and the President of the Democratic Party is expected to keep and realize his political promises made in the campaign after taking office. Therefore, the labor relations in the US—are different from that in Europe where the political programs of the Labor or the Socialist parties contain important stipulations related to "social market model"—thus the labor relations in the US are confined within the framework of Wagner Act. The US Congress enacted the National Labor Relations Act or Wagner ACT in 1935 which said: "protect the rights of employees and employers, to encourage collective bargaining, and to curtail certain private sector labor and management practices, which can harm the general welfare of workers, businesses and the U.S. economy."

It is true that the Act gave workers the right to strike, establish trade unions and practice collective bargaining, but its coverage was very limited; its implementation was not guaranteed; and was checked and restricted by the anti-trade union Labor Relations Act. National Labor Relations Board functions to supervise the election of negotiators assigned by the Unions. It doesn't have the right to force companies to accept collective bargaining, and do not posses any lawful punishment and control rights to restrict improper labor practices like employers' refusal to accept collective bargaining, infringement of collective bargaining agreement and discrimination against labor union members. In 1981, President Reagan ordered firing more than 11,000 air traffic controllers who ignored his order to stop the strike and return to work, and ordered the closure of their union. The event became a watershed in the US history of labor relations, and violated the provisions of the Wagner Act that the striking union workers cannot be discriminated or permanently laid off, making the Act exist only in name.

The current status quo of the US trade unions makes labor law reform extremely urgent. Weakening of the powers of the unions is a strong trend in the developed countries, and it is even worse in the U.S. The proportion of workers organized in the unions in the U.S. was 35% in 1954, but has dropped to 12.3% in 2009. (That rate in the private sector has even dropped to 7.2% in the same year.) Such decline was mainly caused by employers' strong pressure. In 1994, Dunlop Commission of investigation assigned and uthorized by President Clinton confirmed that 57% of the employers threatened their laborers to close their factories down, 47% of them threatened to cut wages and welfare, and 34% of them chose to lay off workers who supported the union organization during 1999 and 2003. Even if unions were set up, 52% of them could not be able to make collective bargaining in one year after their establishment, and 37% two years.

During the 2008 presidential elections, unions proposed The Employee Free Choice Act to amend and reform the Wagner Act hopefully expecting that it could be passed in the US Congress led by a Democratic President and the Democratic Party. The Employee Free Choice Act had three main contents:

First, allowed a union to be certified as the official union to bargain with an employer if union leadership can collect signatures of a majority of workers. The bill removed the former right of the employer to demand an additional, separate ballot when more than half of employees have already given their signature supporting the union.

Second, the Act would have required employers and unions to enter binding arbitration to produce a collective agreement at least 120 days after a union is recognized. Third, the bill would have increased penalties on employers who discriminate against workers for union involvement, which facilitated the establishment of trade unions and the exercise of the right of collective bargaining. As long as over half of the employers agree to establish the trade union, the trade union will be set up automatically and exercise the right of collective bargaining.

Second, concerning employers' behavior of resisting or dragging collective bargaining, the Act provided that after the trade union was recognized by the employer, employers and the Union must produce and reach a collective bargaining agreement, that is, the first bargaining agreement , with the trade union within 90 days. In case no agreement could be reached, it should be submitted for mandatory conciliation. If mandatory conciliation failed, mandatory binding arbitration should be applied.

Third, the Act stipulated increased penalties and more strict regulations on employers who discriminate against workers for union involvement, the interests of employees who joined the trade union should be more vigorously defended. However, like the previous labor law reform attempts, Employee Free Choice Act could not pass the US Senate barrier where the Republicans and conservative faction of Democrats predominated.

If we take an overall look at Europe, we can better understand why no miraculous improvements can be expected related to labor relations in the US, and better understand why the international financial crisis cannot offer any turning point in the improvement of labor relations. Since the mid 1990s, traditional laborers-based middle- left oriented political parties which have been dominating the European political system have suffered large-scale losses in the elections in times of financial crisis, and their public support fell to the lowest level since after the WWII. Conservative middle-right or right wing political parties coming into power have cast a political shadow over the reform of labor relations. It is no surprise the middle-left political parties like the Labor Party and the Social Democratic Party lost their support.

In the 1990s, not only the US Democratic Party but also the European traditional laborer-based middle-left political parties experienced a change in their "political paradigms" "New Social Democratic Alliance" led by Clinton, Blair and Schroeder launched "the third road theory" trying to reconcile neoliberalism with past welfare state so as to deal with negative consequences of globalization. But in essence, they were even more active than the conservative political parties in the promotion of neoliberal reforms. Due to the decline in the number of traditional blue collar industrial workers, these political parties needed to seek cross-class political alliance to reverse the trend of losing in electoral politics or elections, thus they betrayed their traditional laborer voters. Such change of the middle-left political eliminated their certain differences with the right-wing political parties in their political orientation, and dragged them into the situation of losing the laborer voters.

IV. Globalization of monopoly capital causes an irreversible deterioration in labor relations

Globalization enables the monopoly capital to get rid of domestic overproduction restraints and expand its overseas accumulation, but it has caused the disadvantaged status of labor around the globe.

First, outsourcing operations of monopoly capitalism and their direct investment abroad promote the transfer of jobs to overseas countries. The outflow of jobs to overseas countries weakens trade unions in developed countries and their ability of collective bargaining.

Second, labor costs are reduced through global "labor arbitrage" thus jobs move to nations where labor and the cost of doing business (such as environmental regulations) is inexpensive and/or impoverished labor moves to nations with higher paying job. Multinational corporations put the production and processing links—which have the lowest added value, the fiercest competitions and where wages are a competition factor—of the global value chain to the developing countries to effectively control international wage costs, dragging the developing countries under the pressure of severe international competitions and making the labor relations increasingly tense.

Third, it weakens labor protection efforts in numerous countries. Transnational capital threatens to quit from the host country , if they do not reduce corporate and capital income taxes, or reduce labor protection measures, cutting public welfare expenditures, restricting trade unions and collective bargaining and reducing the level of labor minimum wages.

Fourth, global international competition weakens the unity of the working class in many countries of the world.

Well then, can the globalization trend push forward the market economic system, and improve the labor relations models (win-win)?

Mainstream economists in the West hold that those type of labor relations like the promotion of trade union organizations, collective bargaining, workers' participation in the management and employment protection will lead to increase of labor wages, and easily weaken the industries against international competition causing a high rate of unemployment. They argue that the free market economic model in the US and its "flexible" labor relations model are more favorable to timely restructuring in tune with market changes, expansion employment opportunities, reduce cost and favorable for technical innovations, so it is the best model that adapts to global competition.

According to the logic of economic Darwinism (evolutionary economics), global competition will force Europe and Japan to abandon their "rigid labor" relations and follow the U.S model. As regards to industrial hollowing and unemployment caused by globalization in the U.S, they believe that although outsourcing operations and flow of investments abroad, will cause the loss of low-skill jobs, this negative trend will be offset by the expansion of high-skill jobs created by domestic hi-tech and high value-added industrial companies and will result as the net number of increase in job opportunities. Although outsourcing operations will widen the income gap between low-skilled and high-skilled workers, it will improve productivity and reduce commodity prices, that is, it actually improves workers' real wages. All in all, mainstream economists describe globalization as a win-win process for both labor and capital, and purposefully neglect its adverse effects on workers.

However, no evidence shows that globalization has caused a mode of compromise in the labor relations mode of the US, or there appears no evidence that trade unions, collective bargaining and labor protection can impeded a country's technical innovations and international competitiveness, or that globalization is a win-win process for both employers and employees.

The diversification theory of the mainstream economics argues that magnate companies still remain as models which manifest the international competitiveness of developed countries, but the competitiveness of big companies is determined by a series of complementary comparative institutional advantages like local labor relations, company relations, relations within a company and the relations between the company and the finance sector.

Comparative institutional advantages are reflected in different technological innovations and industrial competitiveness. If we take Germany for example, adjustment of the competitiveness of countries applying the market economy is reflected in the traditional automobile- and machinery manufacturing-led high-end manufacturing industry and corresponding incremental technical innovations, as well as the adoption of high-skilled, high-wage, high-quality, high-price and high-profit production strategies. It is closely related to labor relations featuring collaboration and sharing, like stable employment, trainings of industry skills, collective bargaining and the codetermination system. With such complementary labor relations, there would be no competitive advantages. Therefore, they argue that globalization will not lead to a convergent model in labor relations. In fact, although the labor relations in continental Europe and Japan are negatively effected by globalization and neoliberal reforms, they have not completely abandoned their respective reasonable elements. British scholar John Gray used to be a staunch supporter of Thatcherism. He condemned the US-driven globalization of free market economy as "the new Gresham's law", that is, "bad capitalism drives out good" because this kind of globalism impedes the efforts to seek for diversified capitalist development models, and this trend will opposes current trend of neoliberalism.

Unionization, the degree of collective bargaining and international competitiveness are not necessarily related, but if foreign trade surplus is regarded as the competitiveness measure of a country, there is some degree of positive correlation between the both two. Most European countries with a relatively high degree of labor organizations and collective bargaining system are countries with high trade surplus. On the contrary, the United States, the Britain and other countries applying free market economy and with a relatively low degree of unionization and collective bargaining are mostly running foreign trade deficits. In the United States, the decline in the level of unionization was accompanied by a sharp rise in foreign trade deficits, so it is a false proposition that flexible employment can improve a country's industrial competitiveness.

At the core of competitiveness of Nike, Coca-Cola, IBM, General Electric or Ford Motor is in the so-called "intellectual property business or royalty gains" such as controlling and selling franchises, brands, patents, advisements to public sector or to other companies and professional know-how. In their processing and manufacturing, they achieve cost competitiveness mainly through their overseas production sites and outsourcing operations to overseas. They are even like virtual companies that do not engage in manufacturing operations. This mode will surely cause the transfer abroad of the native jobs in the U.S. The jobs transferred are in the manufacturing and service industries, and both low-skilled or hi-tech type jobs are transferred. In 2008, the average proportion of overseas employees in the biggest 18 non-financial multinational companies in the U.S. was 61%, the trend is still growing. The only concern of multinational companies is profits, they do not care about the loss of jobs. Since overseas profits and wealth accumulation are increasingly important for the U.S. companies, the expansion of overseas production and outsourcing of operations has become an irreversible trend. The ratio of overseas profits to their total profits in all U.S. companies rose from 5% in 1950 to 40% in 2008. In the same period, surprisingly and alarmingly the ratio of overseas reserved profits to all reserved profits of the US companies grew from 2% all the way to 93%.

Overseas transfer of jobs does not mean an increase in hi-tech and high-income jobs in the U.S. In 1950, the top ten private employers in the U.S. employed 5% the country's non-agricultural labor force, of which eight were manufacturing enterprises offering high wages, high welfare and stable jobs. In 2008, the top ten private employers, which were all in the service industry, employed 2.8% of the country's non-agricultural labor force, of which seven were in the retail industry. Wal-Mart became the biggest private employer in the U.S. and offered jobs with low wages, low welfare, high flexibility and no development opportunities. The changes in the Dow Jones Industrial Average companies show that an enterprise being big is no longer the symbol of stable employment. In 1987, 16 of the 30 Dow Jones Industrial Average companies had been in this group since the Great Depression of 1929. After 20 years of "shareholder value revolution," only Exxon, General Electric and Chevron Gas has survived. After the current financial crisis, AIG, Citigroup and General Motors withdrew from Dow Jones Industrial Average . The fact is they used to be the biggest among insurance companies, banks and manufacturing companies, respectively, in the U.S. According to the survey of US Census Bureau in 2009, the distribution of educational qualities in the U.S. active labor force has been diminishing in the past decades, and education was not a factor for the layoff or reduction of low-skilled workers and a factor to narrow the income gap among workers. The United States became the country with the most severe wage differentiation/gaps and income inequality among the OECD countries.(Organization for Economic Cooperation and Development).

Mrs. Thatcher once defined neoliberalism, saying that "there is no alternative" to neoliberalism- that free markets, free trade, and capitalist globalization are the best or the only way for modern societies to develop." Of course, that does not make neoliberalism an inevitable and irreplaceable trend. The crisis of neoliberalism is actually one that this mode cannot find the way out to solve its own contradictions. It also shows that contradictions in labor relations, the core of the capitalist relations of production, are fundamental; and that collaboration between labor and capital or improvement of the labor relations need to be guaranteed by specific systems. These special conditions and adjustments are by no means do not appear spontaneously, but are the results of the fights carried out by the working class in hard struggles and social movements.

Y. 21

The Decline of the Western Market Fundamentalism

Yu Zuyao[1]

Abstract: Since the 1970s, neoliberalism has replaced Keynesianism and became the mainstream school of economics that led the ideologies and economic policies and countermeasures in the United States and Europe. Even worse, it gradually became the tool for the U.S. government to pursue world-wide hegemonism externally and to implement "the peaceful evolution strategy" targeting the socialist countries and neo-colonialism targeting the developing countries. Since 2008, the global financial crisis has triggered a new reflection of the world trends and triggered the criticism of neoliberalism and the Washington Consensus. Criticizing financial monopoly capitalism has developed into an irreversible social thought in the Western public. The standard-bearers of neoliberalism in China are still obsessed with market fundamentalism, continue to praise privatization, liberalization and market-oriented "creed," clamor for democratic socialism, and pursue to create a public opinions favoring Washington Consensus.

Key words: neoliberalism; global financial crisis; financial monopoly capitalism

---

[1] Yu Zuyao, visiting researcher of the CASS World Socialism Research Center, honorary member of the CASS, researcher of the CASS Institute of Economics.

Since the 1970s, neoliberalism has replaced Keynesianism and become the mainstream school of economics that leads the ideologies and economic countermeasures in the United States and Europe. Even worse, it has gradually become the tool for the U.S. government to pursue hegemonism externally and to implement peaceful evolution against socialist countries and neo-colonialism against the developing countries. In the modern and contemporary history of economic thoughts, not a single school of economics has played such an enormous role and had such great influences on the world's political and economical life as the neoliberalism did. However, the economic turmoil that started in September 2008 has depreciated its power and tarnished its prestige. The global financial and economic crisis declares the bankruptcy of neoliberalism.

Faced with the crisis which has brought grave disasters to the mankind, the whole world, from scholars and think-tanks to politicians to ordinary people, demand and seek a new way out. It has become a global trend to doubt and review the theories and policies of neoliberalism due to the erupting crisis. However, in China, we observe another trend. The Chinese secondhand dealers who clamor for neoliberalism are opinionated, still stick to their old stands, and continue to praise market fundamentalism. People have the right to question these elite managers who receive high salaries from taxpayers: Where do they really want to drag the 1.3 billion Chinese people? Do you really have social conscience? The two contrary thoughts have appeared in the same issue, and form a sharp contrast, consequently attract people's attention and render them to think deeply.

I. The crisis is both a comprehensive crisis of the capitalist system and an unprecedented severe catastrophe of the mankind caused by Wall Street oligarchs and the U.S. government after WWII

In August 2008, Lehman Brothers declared bankruptcy, and that marked the arrival of the worst economic crisis since the 1930s. The Western world, from politicians to scholars and think-tanks, and to the ordinary people, unanimously agree on the severity of the crisis. "It's hard to overstate how serious the collapse in the economy was," said Mark Zandi, chief economist of Moody's Analytics. "We are in a state of free fall".

The crisis started with the credit crunch by banks, but soon affected the real economy. The United States bore the brunt. In the worst days, the crisis caused 140,000 enterprises to close down, industrial production to drop by 46.2%, and 140 banks to fold up in the United States. Industrial production declined by 37.2% across the Western World. The crisis hit the Western economies, put an end to the bubble economy, and caused the stock market crashes and generally shrinking of capital. The report by the Asian Development Bank on March 9, 2009 showed that, in 2008 alone, global financial assets shrank more than 50 trillion US dollars, that is, global output of a year; that the net wealth of the US households shrank by 36% in the past five years, dropping from 102,900 US dollars to 66,800 US dollars; and that about 23% of all U.S. homes were worth less than the mortgage loan amount[2].

According to the data of the US Federal Reserve, the recession has destroyed the US people's wealth that was saved and accumulated for nearly 20 years, "The median net worth of families plunged by 39 % in just three years, from $126,400 in 2007 to $77,300 in 2010. These developments has reduced the American people's living standards roughly to the level of 1992"[3] There was also a sharp increase in unemployment. According to the report of the International Labor Organization, about 50 million jobs have disappeared since 2008; ILO has forecasted a global unemployment rate of 6.1% in 2012, with total world unemployment rising from 196 million in 2011 to 202 million in 2012. Employment rate will reach the level before the 2008 crisis only by the end of 2016. Unemployment rate even rose to nearly 10% in the U.S. before fluctuating around 8%. The unemployed population in the EU in the first quarter of 2012 reached 24.7 million, that is, 193,000 more than that in the previous quarter and 2.1 million compared with the same period of the last year. In order to control recession, the EU adopts austerity policies, which has further exacerbated the un employment situation in Europe, and a large number of unemployed people have joined the huge proportion of poor people.

The crisis has exacerbated the polarization between the rich and the poor, and the originally affluent society is declining to social impoverishment. Due to the burst of the bubble economy and the sharp shrinking of residents' assets, the middle class is in a very difficult situation. Western media holds that the middle class is disappearing. The middle- and low-income earners are the severest losers. According to the report published in the website of Mexican newspaper El Universal on January 24, 2012, the latest U.S. census statistics show that economic recession has dragged 46 million Americans into poverty, the highest ever in nearly 52 years. "Impoverished" population and the proportion of such population have reached the highest level ever since 1975. Nearly 21 million people have an annual income of only 5,272 US dollars. According to the report of the U.S. Congressional Budget Office (CBO) (issued on October 25, 2011), during 1979-2007, the after-tax income of the 1% richest American families grew by 275 %; but that of the 20% poorest American families grew by 18% only. In 2010, the incidence of poverty in the United States grew to %15.1.

---

2 Available at the website of American newspaper Christian Science Monitor on June 18, 2012.
3 Available at the website of Washington Post on June 12, 2012.

In 2009, people receiving food coupons from the state reached 32.2 million. The crisis hurt not only laborers in the developed countries, but more seriously, it hurt laborers of the developing countries. According to a report issued by United Nations University World Institute for Development Economics Research in December 2006, the 10% richest people around the globe held 85% of world wealth, and half of the world population at the bottom held only 1% of world wealth. Per capita income gap between the richest and the poorest countries in the world was 44:1 in 1973, and 227:1 in 2000, that is, 15.5 times greater. According to the data of the Food and Agriculture Organization (FAO) of the United Nations on June 19, 2009, the people suffering from hunger around the globe was 1.02 billion, and were expected to reach 2 billion in the next decade. After the outbreak of the crisis, the United States and European countries resorted to economic and administrative means to shift the crisis to developing countries and let the latter suffer double disasters.

It has been five years since the crisis has started. When capitalist state intervened and took measures to rescue the market, in haste some people couldn't wait but declared, "the world has entered the post-crisis era" However, the facts give them a heavy blow. No trace of full economic recovery is seen; the unemployment rate still remains high; there are fiscal deficits; the debt crisis is extremely serious; the measures to save the market seek temporary relief regardless of the consequences; and social contradictions have exacerbated. The "Occupy Wall Street" movement foreshadows people's awakening, and the economic crisis fuels political unrest. The future is so dim and hangs in the balance. All In all, the entire Western world is filled with "uncertainties"

II. Reflecting on the economic crisis, criticizing neoliberalism and the "Washington consensus", challenging the U.S. economic hegemony, and attacking financial monopoly capitalism have become an irreversible trend of thought among the masses of the West, and the crisis is a big school that allows people to renew their world view.

On September 17, 2011, in the United States, the heart of the Western world, "Occupy Wall Street" movement was initiated, marking that the majority of the lower classes in big Western countries have become strongly dissatisfied with the capitalist system and with this movement the state ideology—the so-called freedom, democracy and human rights—has turned from pure ideology to organized political action of the masses and such dissatisfaction had developed from pure speeches to a mass organized political action. The society has lived an awakening. In this movement, protesters have declared: "We are the 99% that will no longer tolerate the greed and corruption of the 1%". A distinct and important character of this movement is its highly political nature which targeted directly, the Wall Street financial oligarchs and the neoliberal economic policies adopted by the US government. Secondly, participants were the masses, covering all social classes, who have supported left-wing, middle and right-wing parties, and all kind of mass organizations. Thirdly, the movement has spread to big and medium cities all across the United States, and deeply effected all kinds of schools and enterprises. Fourthly, it effect on the social order was huge, for this reason it was harshly suppressed by the US the police forces, causing grave casualties. The movement has spread to over 700 cities in 71 countries of the world.

Although the "Occupy Wall Street" movement did not have strict organization nor any political program, the movement will never halt at this point and the inherent contradictions of capitalism that has led to this political movement also remain unresolved. The crisis is far from being ended.

—In the West, many scholars, government officials and politicians who had embraced neoliberalism in the past, after facing the crisis and the new reality, started to re-think and profoundly review and criticize neoliberalism.

Iwao Nakatani, a distinguished Japanese professor of economics, wrote a new book entitled *Why Did Capitalism Destruct Itself?* and his book evoked great repercussions in Japan. this was not because he had made a major academic discovery, but because he revolted against neoliberalism. Iwao Nakatani has studied in the United States in his early years, and got a doctor's degree in economics from Harvard University in 1973. Returning to Japan, he taught in a number of universities, and served as a member of the think tank group that served to several Japanese prime ministers. His book Introduction to Macroeconomics is a textbook in many universities. After the outbreak of the global economic crisis, he carefully reflected the mainstream economics he learned, taught and used. But his book, *Why Did Capitalism Destruct Itself?*, seems like a confession or self-criticism of his neoliberal academic course. He said, "I honestly reflect on my ideas so far. I think they are all wrong" "I am so regretful for my wrong ideas" "I just can't keep silent when the world is in such an extremis" According to his own words: "I have too naively believed in the value of capitalist globalization and the supremacy of the market regulation." He has once praised: "If Japan would follow free market economy like in the United States and become a society where the market mechanism functions properly, Japanese people may become as rich and happy as the U.S. people". While serving in the think-thank organization, he strongly advocated the adaptation of the US economic policies and system into Japan. The crisis has disillusioned and caused him to finally say soberly: "it will be wrong to decide Japan government's economic policies with the logic of US economics" He then sharply pointed out: "the American economics is regarded as the universal human truth just because it has been a tool used by capitalism to cover its greedy wants." "Capitalism is an ideology of the greedy profit-seekers aiming for capital proliferation. American society is characterized by insatiable, excessive expansion of individualism and absolute tolerance towards narrow individual interests." "The American-style capitalism has begun to self-destruct" He criticized strongly: "It is indispensable to oppose against following the US-style structural reforms where the disadvantaged groups are further pushed down."

Professor H. Hosokowa from the Waseda University, pointed out: "the outbreak of the crisis has declared the failure of market fundamentalism. Like it or not, the governments must intervene the economy to some extent in the future," "governments must adopt, under the premise of maintaining the market and its functions a revisionist market economy' allowing the government intervention."[4]

Professor Jiro Yamaguchi, from the Hokkaido University, pointed out: "the global financial crisis that erupted on September 2008, told people that the era of neoliberalism which has lasted for 30 years in the past cannot continue anymore. A series neoliberal policies and theories were vigorously praised, but these policies and theories themselves have become the root of gravest problems. Reversing neoliberalism and rewarding social justice should become the main task of the new era.[5]

Alan Greenspan, the former chairman of the US Federal Reserve, is the renown top official serving four different administrations, and was in charge of the finance governance of the US under four governments. He has promoted the neoliberal monetary policies, and was one of the several chief architects behind the crisis. On October 23, 2008 when testifying in the Congress, he revealed that he made a mistake when leading the US Federal Reserve—he neglected supervision and regulation over the financial industry and contributed to financial liberalization; that the modern risk management paradigm had "gone astray". All these comments by him have demonstrated that his faith in the policy of loose supervision on the financial industry had "shaken"

G. Soros, the Hungarian-American business magnate, renown global financial predator G. Soros has also sharply criticized the market fundamentalism. He pointed out: "what is happening right now is incredible, this is the result of market fundamentalism of laissez-faire, expected to automatically regulate the markets—as I call it.." ... "the crisis was not caused

---

4 Japan, Journal of Diplomatic Forum, February 2009.
5 End of Neoliberalism and Regime Choice, Japan, World, Monthly journal, November 2008.

by some external factors or a natural disaster, but by the system itself—a cleavage has occurred within."

—A new trend which shifts from criticizing neoliberalism to criticizing the complete current capitalist system is a remarkable change in the ideological sphere of the West in the recent years. In the 1980's and 90's, global public opinions including the media had favored the capitalist system, and the socialist system was strongly vilified and slandered. However, at the turn of the century, the United States, the boss of the global empire, did not live up its followers expectations, the financial and economic storm tore up the "emperor's new clothes, leaving him naked."

No doubt, the current crisis is grave, but it does not mean that capitalism a social system will soon perish. However, myths about capitalism have been mercilessly exposed by the capitalist crisis. "The American Model" which was adored by the Western elites are blamed and discredited. Spanish website Third Piece of Information published an article "Twelve Myths of Capitalism" which became very popular—analyzed the propagated myths of capitalism like freedom, democracy, equality, common prosperity, universal welfare and irreplaceable principle of democracy one by one. In early 2012, British daily "Financial Times" published a series of articles under the general title "Capitalism in Crisis", the author of the first article was written by Lawrence H. Summers, former director of the National Economic Council for President Barack Obama until November 2011, currently the Charles W. Eliot University Professor at Harvard University. In his article "How Justified Is Disillusionment with Market Capitalism?" he listed those issues such as rising unemployment, unfair distribution, a sharp decline in social mobility, and commented: "unless due attention is paid to such issues, there will never occur a self-correction."

Sharan Burrow, general secretary of the International Trade Union Confederation (ITUC), believed that capitalism "has already become outdated at turn of the 20th century, and no longer conforms to the demands and the circumstances of the 21st century; capitalism neither created secure jobs, nor a fair distribution of wealth.[6]

Klaus Schwab, chairman of the World Economic Forum at Davos, put forward the issue of fighting against "institutional corruption", and commented: "people certainly believe that capitalism in the current form is no longer suitable for the current today.[7]

Kenneth Rogoff, chief economist of the International Monetary Fund, has also listed numerous flaws of contemporary capitalism and pointed out: "in the final analysis the current institutional forms of capitalism are all

---

6 Available at the website of the German daily, The Welt January 25, 2012.
7 German: Financial Times, January 25, 2012.

transitional, the current dominance of the Anglo-American model will certainly be replaced by other models[8].

The economic crisis has also revealed the corruption and hypocrisy of the Western political system. The so-called "democracy" in the West, though praised as "democratic voting" is actually "money politics". The US economist Robert Reich has supported the "Occupy Wall Street" movement, and argued to build a clean democratic system not undermined by "money politics". He argued that when earnings and wealth are concentrated in the hands of so few people, this tiny group of wealthy individuals would have enough money to control and manipulate democracy, which would then inevitably destroy democracy.[9]

—The world economic crisis, this catastrophe was caused by the US financial oligarchs in collusion with politicians and the literati, which fully exposed the false information about the US society, its institutions, systems, model and path fabricated by these three groups. Compared with the true facts, a myth, a superstition or a lie—even if they repeated for thousand times can never persuade people. Some progressive politicians and scholars in the West have made wise suggestions as follows: British journalist David Pilling (editor in chief of Financial Times, Asia) has argued that the of capitalism also poses threats for the prosperity of Asia.[10]

Meghnad Desai, professor of London School of Economics and Political Science, pointed out that Western capitalism has entered its old age times, and energetic capitalism has moved to the East. However, the arrogant sense of accomplishment of the Asian countries ends with this. He believed that the capitalist crisis in the West is also worrisome for the East. According to him, many countries have decided to follow increasingly "capitalist" policies and paths to arrive at prosperity. But it has been disclosed that this path has great dangers, therefore for the vast Asian countries, the capitalist system and path may very possibly be the worst economic system of all.[11]

Former German Chancellor H. Schmidt has been an old friend of the Chinese people. It was him who advocated and designed "social market economy" in Germany, and when Zoellick and those people who shared his ideas put forward the so-called "top Design" reform plan to undermine and finally destroy the socialist state-owned sector of China and achieve overall privatization, H. Schmidt said something quite remarkable: "State-owned enterprises are the lifeblood of the Chinese economy. privatization should be rejected." H. Schmidt has argued: "privatization of state- would

---

8 Is Modern Capitalism Sustainable?, available at the website of Singapore newspaper The Straits Times on December 6, 2011.
9 Available at the website of British newspaper Financial Times, February 1, 2012.
10 Available at the website of British newspaper Financial Times, January 16, 2012.
11 Available at the website of British newspaper Financial Times, January 16, 2012.

not necessarily be conducive to economic efficiency and favorable for the majority of the people, privately-owned enterprises do not care about the overall interests of the society."

—Not only the Western academia gave blows directly targeting neoliberalism, but students of a famous university walked out of the class in solidarity with the "Ocuppy" to protest the lecture of a neoliberalism advocate.

On November 2, 2011, a walkout act happened in the Harvard University that shocked the U.S., even the world academia; students walked out of the class of G. Mankiw, a staunch advocate of neoliberal economics and a "star professor" of Harvard University. G. Mankiw has been the author of Principles of Economics, a book that has been translated into more than 20 languages and issued over one million copies worldwide, and used to be chairman of the Council of Economic Advisers under the administration of President George W. Bush. Students participating in the walkout said that they are part of "the 99%" in the US society, and would no longer tolerate "the greed and corruption of the 1%" They walked out of Mankiw's class to express their "discontent with the biased content of his lecture. They walked out of the campus of Harvard to join the Occupy Boston march organized by the "Occupy the Wall Street" movement. The marchers also entered the Harvard University to support the students, holding a red banner writing "University for the 99%!"

In *An Open Letter to Greg Mankiw*, the striking Harvard students wrote, "Today, we are walking out of your class, Economics 10, in order to express our discontent with the bias inherent in this introductory economics course. We are deeply concerned about the way that this bias affects students, the University, and our greater society. ...Instead, we found a course that espouses a specific—and limited—view of economics that we believe perpetuates problematic and inefficient systems of economic inequality in our society today."

The striking students continued in the letter, "A legitimate academic study of economics must include a critical discussion of both the benefits and flaws of different economic simplifying models. As your class does not include primary sources and rarely features articles from academic journals, we have very little access to alternative approaches to economics. There is no justification for presenting Adam Smith's economic theories as more fundamental or basic than, for example, the Keynesian theory". "If Harvard fails to equip its students with a broad and critical understanding of economics, their actions are likely to harm the global financial system. The last five years of economic turmoil have been proof enough of this". "We are walking out today to join a Boston-wide march protesting the corporatization of higher education as part of the global Occupy movement. Since the biased nature of Economics 10 contributes to and symbolizes the increasing economic inequality in America, we are walking out of your class today both to protest your inadequate discussion of basic economic theory and to lend our support to a movement that is changing American discourse on economic injustice. Professor Mankiw, we ask that you take our concerns and our walk-out seriously". The walkout of Harvard University students has brought forward many questions, and deserves our careful evaluation.

—The outbreak of the world economic crisis has led to the decline of neoliberalism, and triggered an ideological crisis in the Western countries. In this context, Marx's works and Marxist theories, after experiencing a cold spell for a period of time, has been popular and appraised again in the Western world, and even has led to a "Marx fever" that we should not overlook. The decline of neoliberalism in stark contrast with the "Marx fever" constitutes an important characteristic of the current political ecology in the West.

In the Western world, after the disintegration of the Soviet Union, there was a trend of anti-Marxist thoughts. Marxism was vilified, coarsely criticized and treated biased. Back then, the US professor F. Fukuyama asserted that the disintegration of the Soviet Union and Eastern European socialist countries was the end of history, that the mankind had reached its best form and "there is no alternative to capitalism, and that the victory of liberal democracy and capitalism has put an end to history".

However, faced with the naked reality of eruption of such a big crisis, he had to say: "What the crisis did, however, was to underline the instability inherent in capitalist systems—even the ones which are as developed and sophisticated as the United States" "…historians may well point to this financial crisis as the end of US's economic dominance in global affairs" "…The West, and in particular the United States, is no longer seen as the only center for innovative thinking about social policy"[12]

The phenomenon of "Marx fever" that is developing in the West has the following characteristics: First, it has appeared in the background of the global economic crisis which still continues. World countries had taken two different approaches and countermeasures against the great depression during the 1930s. The Soviet Union being a socialist country, in the hope of modernizing its national industries and improving people's material and cultural lives, had focused on expanding domestic demand while making full use of the opportunity created by the Western economic crisis to introduce advanced equipment, technologies and talented experts to develop the Soviet Union. On the other side Western countries applied Keynesianism and implemented expansionary fiscal and monetary policies, and promoted the militarization of their economies to produce weaponry and Roosevelt's New Deal policy was implemented to lead their economies out of the

---
12 Foreign Affairs, monthly, Issue 2011/2.

danger zone. In the 1970s, since the economy was stuck in stagflation and inflation, the leading mainstream status of the Keynesianism was replaced by neoliberalism. But the recovery did not last long and at turn of the new century, a financial storm and turmoil followed by an economic typhoon swept the whole world, and revealed the true face of neoliberalism. It was in such a situation that some people with insight and the general public have turned their attention to Marx, as the "the thinker of the millennium". According to a news report published by the "Guangming Daily" on December 15, 2008, Marx was said to have "infinite charm" in the newspaper Hamburger Abendblatt; that even P. Steinbrück, the German Finance Minister has started reading Marx's *Capital*. P. Steinbrück said, "We have to admit that certain parts of Marx's theory are correct." Another characteristic of the phenomenon of "Marx fever" is that it has spread globally from Europe to the US and to Asia, and from the financial empire to developing countries, and attracted people from all walks, ranging from scholars to politicians, from entrepreneurs to managers, from young students to ordinary laborers, from clergymen to the ordinary people—almost all industries and groups. According to a "Guangming Daily" news report from its Berlin correspondent on November 10, 2008, German monthly journal "Der Spiegel" has published an article online, in which it claimed that "a specter is hovering German universities". Many German universities have organized symposiums to "Revisit Marx" and after the beginning of the new semester 31 German universities have encouraged their students to learn Marx's *Capital* by organizing study groups and holding seminars, over 2,000 students have participated in them. The general manager of the Dietz Verlag publishing company said: Marx's *Capital* is heatedly demanded again because more and more people were encountered by severe problems, so they are trying to seek answers from Marx's works. Along with the phenomenon of "Marx fever" the publication and sales of Marx's books grew rapidly. For example a new version of *Capital* published by the Dietz Verlag saw a sales volume of 3 times greater than that in 2008.

The emergence of "Marx fever" is a spontaneous wave, not organized. After the dissolution of the Soviet Union, in the sphere of ideology Marxism was marginalized in Without the recent world economic crisis occurring or the decline of neoliberalism, "Marx fever" would never develop so fast. But this trend also reflects an inevitable trend of objective development of the world history. However, we have to remain sober and realize that the "Marx fever" does not mean that neoliberalism and its leaders have surrendered and laid down their swords. The struggle will be long-term and tortuous.

Y. 22

A Research on the Policy of Neoliberalism and Its International Influence

Tian Chunsheng[1]

Abstract: The international academic community has different opinions and interpretations on the global financial crisis. Most of the arguments view the global financial crisis from the aspect of financial globalization and the international financial system. This paper, argues that neoliberalism has evolved from an economic theory of the U.S. and the European countries into the economic policy of world's major countries, and consequently formed the neoliberal policy and thoughts, a policy which ran rampant all over the world. "Washington consensus" marked the evolvement of neoliberalism from economic theories into a policy This is the deep source behind the international financial crisis and the global economic turmoil. Neoliberalism as an economic policy in many countries also has also some influence on our country's policies, that means China should have a higher degree of awareness on the issue and give proper responses.

Key words: neoliberalism; international financial crisis; policy; influence

---

1 Tian Chunsheng, visiting researcher of World Socialism Research, Chinese Academy of Social Sciences, professor of China Youth University for Political Sciences.

I. Major opinions on the international financial crisis

Both at home and abroad there are two most representative opinions on the international financial crisis.

The first approach focuses and discusses various problems and manifestations of the financial sector as an international financial system, its institutions and mechanisms. In recent years, —both at home and abroad—most arguments on the international financial crisis are from the aspect of examining the "financial crisis" itself. Accordingly this approach has arrived certain conclusions from the angle of financial globalization and the flaws of the international financial system. In the U.S., both the government and decision-makers have acknowledged several problems and flaws of credit and financial liberalization, the lack of global financial regulation and the unchecked capital flows and broadly agree that it is necessary to strengthen financial supervision and also reform the international currency system. Many economists have also criticized that "the rules of the game" in the current international financial system are mainly dominated by developed countries, others cannot participate in decision making thus non-democratic, thus leading to the lack of fairness, justice and effectiveness in the current international financial system.

Based on the common knowledge that the core issue of the global financial crisis is mainly caused by the flaws of the US financial and currency system, the international community has appealed for all countries to unite and pursue for reforming the international financial system, especially to strengthen supervision of the U.S. finance industry and banks. This is the main consensus reached by world countries after facied by the financial crisis.

The second approach

The second approach clearly points out that the root cause of the financial crisis is neoliberalism. After describing the outbreak of the U.S. financial crisis concretely and explicitly, famous U.S. economist and professor David Kotz said: "neoliberal capitalism is the deep-seated reason behind this financial crisis." In his book The End of Neo-Liberalism? Joseph Stiglitz wrote that "market fundamentalism" held by neoliberalism is the basis of Thatcherism, Reaganomics, and the so-called "Washington Consensus".

Some Western economists, Marxist economists, or non-Marxists, all believe that the international financial crisis and the following economic recession are originated from neoliberal capitalism or related to the emergence and development of neoliberalism, thus neoliberalism is the root cause behind the world economic crisis.The questions are: Why do economic crises take the form of "financial crisis" as the primary form more and why are "financial crises" more frequent since the 1990s? Why are the consequences of the financial crisis so serious that they even lead to global sovereign debt crises? Do the financial crisis and sovereign debt crisis bear the same characteristics? To answer these questions, it is necessary to make an analysis of neoliberal doctrine—which is the ideological basis of financial crisis and sovereign debt crisis—in the 20th century especially its development since the 1980s. Additionally we should analyze neoliberal doctrine's transformation from a ideological doctrine to a policy (neoliberal policy).

II. Neoliberal policy and the international financial crisis

The doctrine, policies and views of neoliberalism became dominant in the U.S. and the world economic systems, consequently the basic contradiction of the capitalist economy was exported to other regions all around the globe along with globalization. From a higher perspective, the international financial crisis originated from the U.S. instead of India, nor from Poland or some welfare states in the Northern Europe. Also the international financial crisis originated from the Western economic theory of neoliberalism promoted by the U.S. and Britain. The outbreak of the financial crisis indicates the failure of neoliberalism and that the theory (neoliberal theory) behind it does not work

1. Core arguments of the neoliberal economic theory

Main arguments of the neoliberal economic theory can be generalized as: neoliberalism tries to prove the necessity, rationality and superiority of market's regulation of the economy, refutes Keynesian state intervention, then criticizes the flaws of the theory and policy of government intervention in the economy.

In the 1980s, neoliberalism has transformed from an economic theory into an economic policy and behavioral norm in the Western world, and was first promoted in the United States, Britain and some Latin American countries.

Since the 21st century, neoliberalism has imperceptibly influenced the economic policies of many countries, and been widely applied in the international economic practice. This wave of neoliberalism has made the US and British governments more liberal on their respective economic policies, and they have used the international organizations like the International Monetary Fund and World Bank to export these economic policies to the other countries.

2. "Washington consensus" marked the evolvement of neoliberalism from a theory into a policy

With the introduction of the "Washington consensus" in the 1990s being, the neoliberal economic theory—as one of the classical economic theories—gradually evolved into an ideology and an economic policy.Before the recent crisis when neoliberal theories and policies were popular, its core aims included "marketization, privatization, liberalization" and "global economic integration"

The landmark event in the process introducing the neoliberal "Washington consensus" was the seminar held in 1990 in Washington, where the International Monetary Fund, the World Bank, the Inter-American Development Bank, researchers of the U.S. Department of the Treasury and representatives of Latin American countries, were the invited by the US-based Institute for International Economics. The seminar aimed to provide solutions and countermeasures for the economic reforms in Latin American countries. At the seminar, the then head of the Institute for International Economics, John Williamson, in agreement with the above other institutions proposed 10 policy measures for the domestic economic reforms of the Latin American countries, known as "Washington consensus"

"Washington consensus" soon—with consensus—became a leading policy of the whole Western countries in their domestic and international economic policies and "Washington consensus" not only played a major role in the economic policies of the Latin American countries, but made significant impacts on the transitional policies of the Russia and Eastern Europe (transition economies) and consequently "shock therapy" policy implemented by the Soviet Union and numerous other countries was the demonstration and result of "Washington consensus" policies. This economic policy not only serves the interests of the international big capitalist class, but also reflects the policies of the International Monetary Fund and the World Bank at the end of the 20th and in the beginning period of the 21st century. The practice of "Washington consensus" policies have proved they have failed, consequently instead of delivering the expected results in Latin American countries or Russia or in some other countries of the Asia region "Washington consensus" was severely criticized and condemned by them. Thus we can say that the current international financial crisis was an inevitable result of the promotion and practicing of the neoliberal theory and neoliberal policies for many years in the past.

3. Policies of the "Washington consensus" and the international financial crisis

If we analyze the neoliberal economic theory and its implementation as policies, they have impacted on the economies of most countries, which has finally led to an economic crisis in the most vulnerable sphere of the global economy—broke out in the international financial sector.

(1) Excessive privatization of large-scale state-owned enterprises, price monopoly.

Privatization policy is an important economic policy of neoliberalism. Since the 1990s, influenced by Coase Theorem and property rights theory of Western economics, privatization was considered to be the only way out for solving the problem of inefficiency of state-owned enterprises. In the developed countries, the UK began to implement the privatization policy since the 1980s. It was first promoted in the public sector industries, and then extended to the social welfare sector of the economy. Throughout the 1980s, a total worth of state-owned assets amounting 60 billion pounds were sold or resold to private investors. Any public activity, from running prisons to the issuance of passports, have become the subjects of privatization. The changes in employment figures reflects the scale of privatization back then in the UK: In 1979 when Margaret Thatcher came to power, 770,000 people were employed by the government for civil services, but only 50,000 had been maintained till the mid 1990s. In developing countries, at the beginning of the 1990s, over 80 developing countries had completed the privatization of 6,800 state-owned enterprises. The Mexican government alone had sold hundreds of solely state-owned companies. According to relevant data published in Mexico, the wealth and assets held by 25 holding trusts had amounted to 47% of the GDP of Mexico. Five among these 25 holding trusts controlled 75% of the banks and credit markets and 66% of the investment assets. Most of them were state monopoly enterprises which engaged in public services (water, electricity, communication services).

(2) Deregulation and high-degree of financialization in the economy

The neoliberal liberalization policies are fully demonstrated in the field of finance. Since Reagan took office in the 1980s, the neoliberal economic theory began to dominate the United States. The U.S. government kept loosening controls over financial operations and vigorously pushed forward financial liberalization policies. Financial Services Modernization Act promulgated in 1999 which mainly aimed mixing financial and non- financial operations—in favor of financialization—has completely substituted and eliminated the restrictions of the US Banking Law that had been implemented in the past, for over 60 years.

Financial liberalization in the international financial markets and relevant changes in the international financial market were promoted. After 2001, the U.S. adopted expansionary fiscal and monetary policies and loosened financial controls, which caused excess liquidity, and excess liquidity flowed to the stock market and to the real estate market which has later caused bubbles in the two markets.

The U.S. financial institutions and banks granted mortgage loans to low-income earners and to those with low repayment capability, which led to vigorously expanding subprime loans.

It was at this time that the U.S. government further increased liquidity, in order to maximize the profits financial institutions and banks, designed asset securitization and structured financial products on the basis of subprime loans, this act shifted the credit risks from the credit market to the capital market through mortgage-backed securities (MBS) and collateralized debt obligations (CDOs). (Securitization of subprime mortgages.)

The securitization of subprime mortgages into mortgage-backed securities (MBS) and collateralized debt obligations (CDOs) was a major contributing factor in the subprime mortgage crisis. Subprime securitization were attractive to investors due to the higher interest rates they offered versus assets backed by prime mortgages.

These new products (MBS and CDOs) developed rapidly, besides the rate of defaults in the subprime mortgage market grew substantially; and a lot of mortgage institutions, especially those in the subprime mortgage market, faced troubles or went bankrupt.

According to available statistics, between November 2006 to mid August 2007, over 80 subprime mortgage institutions were closed or went bankrupt across the U.S., causing a loss of hundreds of billions of US dollars. Over 50 banks and hedge funds in Britain, Germany, France, Switzerland, Netherlands, Japan and Australia were affected, and suffered a total loss of tens of billions of US dollars. The most serious consequence was that wealth growth in the world was contributed greatly by the fictive virtual economy, not from the development of the real economy.

(3) Global flow of international capital and global inflation.

Globalization and liberalization of capital are important manifestations of neoliberal policies in the international economy. In the recent 20 years, international economic institutions continue to demand that developing countries open their capital accounts and allow free capital flows. Seen from the global capital market, imbalanced development of the world economy has led to both capital shortages and surpluses in different countries. Also because of the highly information-based nature of the society today, international capital flows rampantly among different countries, and is known as "floating capital" or "hot money". Short-term capital, which is speculative in nature, seeks profits in the emerging market countries in the form of big capital swallowing the small capital. No matter in the Mexican financial crisis breaking out in 1994 or the Southeastern Asian financial crisis breaking out in 1997, or the international financial crisis which erupted in 2008, this speculative "hot money" played a crisis fueling role. In recent years, with the rise of emerging economies, the excess capital from the center has kept flowing into the emerging economies, leading to frequent financial crises and growing inflation there in the recenti more than a decade.

(4) Increases in residents' incomes are slow, even stagnant

Neoliberal policies imposed demand cutting social welfare expenditure and government subsidies like unemployment insurance so as to eliminate or reduce government regulation of income distribution. Since the 1980s, influenced by neoliberal policies, cutting social welfare has become an economic reform policy taken by the governments of Western countries. Take the U.S. for example, The Omnibus Budget Reconciliation Act passed during the administration of Reagan cut 32.5 billion US dollars in social welfare expenditures in 1982, 44 billion and again 51.4 billion in 1983 and 1984, respectively. After that, the U.S. government's ability to regulate income distribution was weakened. For example, the 1% of the richest Americans have taken 40% of the national wealth, while the proportion of people living under the poverty line has increased to over 15%, the highest ever in the past half a century. More than 40 million people can't feed themselves, and are supported by the state's food stamps. After the crisis, the middle class people were faced with pay cuts, layoffs and bankruptcy, while the blue-collars at the bottom of the society were faced with unemployment. Economic development caused by the economic bubbles would be the starting point of economic recession once the false prosperity consumption boom awakens with the reality, which was one of the reasons for the "Occupy Wall Street" movement in the United States.

As can be seen, in the two or three decades when neoliberalism has dominated the world economy, a whole set of economic policies, including international economic policies, macro and micro economic policies and various specific policies, has been developed and implemented. Some policies have been legalized and carried out in the form of laws and regulations. The core of these policies are liberalization, marketization and privatization, and they essentially protect the interests of capital and harm laborers' interests. Global recession caused by the international financial crisis is an inevitable result of the impacts and promotion of neoliberalism.

III. The Impact of Three New Liberal Policies on China's Economic Policies

On whether the trend of neoliberal policies have impacts on China, and on what such impacts are, opinions vary in China. For some people, China is the only exception in the global promotion of neoliberal policies and "Washington consensus" by Western countries. Some opposite view says: "Neoliberal policies are applied smoothly in the United States, Europe, China and India" and argue that they do not have any negative impacts on China; while others believe that neoliberalism has great impacts on China since the implementation of reform and opening-up strategy. Although there are disputes among the Chinese economists, one thing is certain, that is, neoliberalism has been the mainstream discourse in some aspects of Chinese economic academia so far. It has been proven in practice that China is not an exception related to neoliberal policies and "Washington consensus", and that its impacts manifest themselves gradually.

1. Neoliberal policies and the "Washington consensus" have indeed made impacts on China's economic academia.

More people generally believe that in the 20 or more years since neoliberal economic theories were introduced to China, China has been taking the Western market economy as reference, guided by the Western economic theories, using Western economics as textbooks for its university students; and the leaders of economic reforms have been using language, concepts, definitions and the methods mostly barrowed from the Western economics, so their core concepts have been influenced by the trend of neoliberalism. The introduction of liberalization, privatization and deregulation has made great impacts on some of the economic theories in China, especially the economic reform theories. For example, some have suggested to use (Coase's) neoliberal property rights theory to guide the property rights reforms in China; the trend of liberalization has caused the state to relax control and supervision, especially on education, medical services and social security. In China, there are only a few people who advocate neoliberal policies and hold that neoliberalism's impacts on China are positive, so they credit the success of the socialist reform and opening-up in China to the "Washington consensus."

2. Neoliberalism and the "Washington consensus" has made impacts on China's reform policy.

Neoliberalism is borrowed as the mainstream academic discourse in China, because China must to leave some space for capital and the market, in order to develop the economy, this is the basis borrowing. In ths process of borrowing, people try to emphasize the role of capital and the market extremely, which made impacts on China's policies and imbued China's policies with the marketization theory of neoliberalism. The first result of this was the argument that efficiency is everything; and that capital and profit are the only tools to achieve maximum efficiency, and the two are also the symbols of maximum efficiency. The second characteristic of the impact is that, the power of the Chinese state is used to blaze new trails for opening spaces for private capital, and that capital is combined with power, thus create favorable conditions for the monopoly of international capital. The third characteristic of the impact is that it ignores even sacrifices the rights and interests of the ordinary citizens. The current various contradictions in China like polarization between rich and the poor and other problems in the social sphere are not unrelated with the influence of the neoliberal policies of the early days of the reform and opening up.

3. Neoliberalism and the "Washington consensus" have made impacts on China's socialist market economic system.

Neoliberal economic theories has been able to mislead many countries in their economic practice because its system partially has some reasonable elements. For the initial period of reforms in China, back then neoliberal theories had some reasonable elements that could be borrowed in establishing China's socialist market economy, like utilizing the positive role of diverse forms of ownership, and the need to give full play to the positive role of diverse forms of ownership besides public ownership, since China still needs the market and capital at the primary stage of socialism. Like the other countries which apply neoliberal policies or its economic theories, China also witnesses the emergence of problems such as polarization of wealth, serious social injustices, the resurgence of social conflicts, and the loss of ethics, loss of civil rights because of neoliberalism. In the present conditions of China, the market system is yet to be improved, and also regulating and supervising the markets need to be strengthened, and also the need for a proper legal system is obvious.

We shoul carefully summarize the impacts of neoliberalism on China's economic and social policies from both theoretical and practical policy aspects. Under the conditions of globalized market economy, it is hard to eliminate periodical economic crises, which we have to fully understand and properly deal with.

Y. 23

Problems of The Western Labor Movement as Demonstrated in the "Occupy Wall Street" Movement

Wu Jinping[1]

Abstract: The basic contradiction of the capitalist social formation is mainly reflected in the antithesis, contradiction and conflict between the two big basic classes—the working class and the bourgeoisie, and it is expressed in the movement of working class and other working people against the rule of the capitalist class and movements for their interests and rights. On November 30, 2011, an unprecedented big strike was launched in Britain which attracted over 2 million people. This strike was organised by various unions and the Trade Union Congress evaluated it as the biggest strike in a generation. Nearly two-thirds of England's 21,476 schools were closed, except the 33 schools, Scotland's 2,667 state schools were closed and 7,000 due operations in the hospitals were postponed. Twenty-one arrests were made, as Occupy London activists marched from Piccadilly Circus to Panton House, the headquarters of international mining company Xstrata, which employs the highest paid CEO in the United Kingdom. The activists entered the building with a large banner saying "All power to the 99%" and subsequently entered onto the rooftop and strapped the banner to the front of the building. In this paper, the contemporary problems in Western labor movement reflected by the "Occupy Wall Street" movement in the U.S. and by the social protest movements in many Western countries will be analyzed.

Key words: "Occupy Wall Street" movement; economic and social crisis; labor movement in Western countries

---

[1] Wu Jinping, visiting scholar at the World Socialism Research Center attached to the CASS and Ph.D. candidate of Marxism Studies, in the Graduate School.of CASS.

Facing the current widespread and profound international financial and economic crises, the United States is debt crisis-ridden; and Europe is witnessing a fermenting sovereign debt crisis; and many Western countries have already stuck in the quagmire of sovereign debt crisis, they face high unemployment rates, especially in the youth. Laborers are forced to rise and resist against the austerity policies of the governments that cuts workers' and other the masses' welfare expenditures and against the exploitation and domination of the capitalism. Started and fueled by the "Occupy Wall Street" movement launched by the US people on September 17, 2011, this movement spread world-wide and "occupation" movements have occurred in many Western countries, starting from the "Occupy Wall Street" launched by the US people on September 17, 2011, and on November 30, 2011, an unprecedented big strike was launched in Britain which attracted over 2 million people, This strike was organised by various unions and the Trade Union Congress evaluated it as the biggest strike in a generation. Nearly two-thirds of England's 21,476 schools were closed, except the 33 schools, Scotland's 2,667 state schools were closed and 7,000 due operations in the hospitals were postponed. Twenty-one arrests were made, as Occupy London activists marched from Piccadilly Circus to Panton House, the headquarters of international mining company Xstrata, which employs the highest paid CEO in the United Kingdom. The activists entered the building with a large banner saying "All power to the 99%" and subsequently entered onto the rooftop and strapped the banner to the front of the building. And we have seen other movements fighting against the capital domination, oppression and also shifting of the crisis to other Western countries. It is therefore of great practical significance to examine and analyze the labor movement against the capitalist class rule in the Western countries.

I. Problems of the labor movement in the Western countries as reflected by the "Occupy Wall Street" movement

If we analyze and observe the emergence way and the organizational nature of the "Occupy Wall Street" movement it is obvious that the protesters or participants do not have any leadership organ or structure. Consequently, the "Occupy Wall Street" movement obviously does not have theoretical guidance, let alone a clear specific target. Because of that, participants of the movement cannot have a common ideological understanding or action. With such deficiencies, the movement was doomed to fail from the very beginning.

The one thing the protesters in "Occupy Wall Street" movement have in common was the slogan "We are the 99%, that will no longer tolerate the greed and corruption of the 1%" That is to say, although the movement is rooted from the common demands of the public, to some extent, it is the protesters' spontaneous or instinctive action instead of a self-conscious movement. "Occupy Wall Street" movement, which has not yet ceased, was a protest movement participated by individuals who have voted for different political parties. It opposed the plutocracy formed by the alliance of government, magnate banks, big business enterprises or against the "power of money" regime. Another common target among the demonstrations of the "Occupy Wall Street" was that they were all against government corruption, privileges enjoyed by the big enterprises, and the richest 1% of the Americans holding the decision-making power, dominating the fate of the %99. Demonstrators shouted the slogans such as "The whole system has got to go, capitalism is an organized crime", "Power to the people", "No war but the class war", "Those who make peaceful revolution impossible make violent revolution inevitable", "Revolution generation", "We need jobs. We need revolution", "The revolution has begun" and "Class war further ahead" From these slogans, we can see their consciousness status and spirituality in the struggle.

On the other side, in many Western countries political parties and other organizations of the working class have failed to seize the opportunity and utilize the current full-fledged economic and social crises in the West, although it was an opportune time to educate the angry masses and propagate the program of the working- class party. The opportunity to encourage and mobilize the masses and especially the broad strata of vast working masses, to take effective actions, thus in this way changing the negative and unfavorable situation into an opportunity for progressive reforms, favoring the "99%" was missed. This was the only way to lead the people out of their difficulties, miseries and from the challenges they were faced with. This situation reflects that the political party and other organizations of the working class in Western countries are faced with certain limitations in launching and mobilizing labor movements. It is indeed necessary to make an in-depth examination on this important problem of the Western labor movement.

II. Current factors influencing the occurrence of labor movement in the Western countries

1. The objective reasons behind the low tide status of the labor movements in the Western countries

Mainly, the rapid development of productive forces is the objective reason for the low tide of labor movement in the Western countries; neoliberal policies launched by the Western bourgeois governments to oppress the labor movement is its direct reason; and thirdly the adjustments or certain reforms in the governance policies of the Western states have eased labor conflicts and reduced the frequency of labor movement.² However, external reasons are just conditions for the changes and movement of a thing, and internal reasons are the main basis for changes and movement. External causes become operative only through internal causes.

2. Current internal factors behind the low tide status of the labor movements led by the working class organizations and political parties in the Western countries

Absence of class consciousness or lack of belief among the working class in western countries.

Since the 1970s, traditional working class in developed countries has been declining, in absolute or relative numbers. The working class, which unconditionally supported the progressive labor movement in the past, has shifted its support the political parties advocating economic liberalism. Due to increase and abundance of material social wealth in the society, the working class in the Western countries has lost its past class consciousness and belief, that is, they generally do not believe that only through unity, solidarity and collective class action can bring about a true improvement of livelihood for all.³

Due to absence of class consciousness and loss of belief, they no longer conceive that they should rely on their own independent collective struggles so as to win and defend their own interests, nor do they conceive that it is critical to develop class consciousness and foster the joint action capabilities of their class.

Individualistic thoughts and individualistic values being prevalent in the working class of the Western countries cause difficulties for the political parties and unions of the working class in uniting and organizing the working class and launch effective labor movements. Currently, due to rapid scientific and technological advances and consequently enormous changes in the social, political aspects of the society, employment conditions of the working class have become severer; under these new conditions a lot of working people have lost their jobs or can't even find a job; and numerous flexible forms of employment have increased; consequently labor relations and laboring conditions have become more and more individualized, and people have more chances to choose the social relations—the job, occupation or engagement—they would like to be within, rather than passively accepting them as they had done in the past.

---

2 Wu Jinping, Status Quo and Development Trends of the Labor Movements in Developed Capitalist Countries, Social Sciences Abroad, Issue 2011/1.
3 Eric Hobsbawm, The Century of Labor Movement, trans. by Zhang Shipeng, Contemporary World and Socialism, 2002/6.

Under these conditions the collective and common class identity of the working class which had formed in long years has brought its class consciousness to the brink of disappearance and disintegration.[4]

Workers in the Western countries no longer believe in the class value that the whole working class shares the same class position, status and fundamental interests. The differentiation of and occurrence of different segments in the working class of the developed capitalist countries leads to different interests among the class and lead to internal conflicts, on the other hand, individualistic values make it hard for workers to unite and participate in collective struggles.

Trade unions and the mass organizations of the working class in the Western countries, are split and have become diversified which constitute adverse effects for the occurrence of effective labor movements.[5]

Many trade unions in the United States have become the speakers of certain interest groups other than workers; with the decrease of their members they are reduced to a small group representatives trying hard to negotiate with the employers and this situation hinders the workers' overall solidarity and interests. If we evaluate from the aspect of technical organizational conditions, it is almost impossible to hold nationwide general strikes or other collective actions in the current system. Trade unions divided by industries, domains and interests do not have the ambition or the capacity to organize collective actions or respond to employers' pressures.

The working class and the trade unions are negatively influenced by trade unionism trend of thought or its ideology. Trade unionism trend of thought of the working class first originated in Britain in the mid 19th century. Proponents of trade unionism proposed to organize trade unions and struggle for further economic interests and political rights of the workers with collective efforts, but refusing to "touch" or disturb the existing political and economic institutions.

The conditions of the U.S. were extremely suitable for the growth of trade unionism. Like employers, most of the workers in this country of immigrants, as its long historical tradition firmly believed in liberal capitalism and liberal employment system. Unless a labor conflict develops to the extreme, leaders and members of trade unions would want to create a "win-win" deal with the employers. The reformism of trade unionism advocating "class-peace or class cooperation" denies class struggle, rejects socialism and embraces liberalism and capitalism. To a certain degree, it reflects the political and ideological immaturity of the labor movement. Undoubtedly,

---

4 Ding Jiqian, Reasons for the Decline of the French Labor Union Movements, Foreign Theoretical Trends, Issue 2003/5.
5 Yai Hairong, Disorders in the American Labor Movement, Dushu (Reading), Issue, 2006/11.

the reformism prevalent in the trade unions restricts the development of collective actions by the working class and weakens the labor movement.

The influence of reformism in the working class.

The doctrine of class collaboration between labor and capital as a form of social ideology is the theoretical basis of the reformism trend in the working class. In practice, the working class have ceased fighting against the attacks of capital by forming united joint actions, or fighting for the goal of ultimate elimination of laborers' subordination to reliance on capital and the capitalist system—upon which the social conditions that put laborers at a disadvantage resides.

The working class has lost the clear goals it possessed in the earlier phases of the labor movement, and the life of working class has evolved into a status within which capitalism has offered better social redistribution (welfare state) conditions, which is another important reason for the decrease in the collective struggles of the working class.

The working class in the Western countries abides by and invests trust in the legal system of the ruling state.

After long-term and painstaking struggles of the working class and its trade unions, the bourgeoisie governments had to compromise and introduce a whole set of progressive legal systems and mechanisms to adjust the relationship between labor and capital, working and living conditions, welfare expenditures and social security mechanisms for the working class were improved and some legal democratic rights which favor the laboring masses have formed a relatively stable labor relations.

In the Western countries, in the course of its development, labor movement has changed from a fighting force outside the system, to a constructive component part within the system. The working class in the Western countries prefers legal and peaceful means when fighting for and defending their interests. On the other side, collective bargaining practice, other laws and legal mechanisms and policies developed by the governments to coordinate the labor-capital relationships play a role in dispelling workers' collective actions.

Although collective bargaining right was obtained by the working class after long and arduous struggles, workers seem to have forgotten the history of the labor movement featuring fierce fights between workers and employers. Since collective bargaining provides a platform for solving the conflicts and contradictions between workers and employers and the working class has gained a more effective and relatively peaceful choice, the working class takes collective bargaining as the first option, unless when they are forced to unbearable situations or become desperate, in such an adverse situation they resort sharper collective actions.

Today, trade unions in most of the developed countries have the right of collective bargaining, which in some way and to a certain extent weakens the will and practice of the working class to ultimately solve the contradiction between workers and employers. Here I do not intend to ignore or belittle the practical significance of collective bargaining, reject the importance of the hard-won fruit obtained by the working class after so many struggles, same applies for the maintaining the welfare state benefits or other social institutions hardly won in the developed countries. The working class in the developed countries should not narrowly indulge in the temporary advantages of those institutions such as collective bargaining and welfare state.

Here the author just holds that the working class in developed countries has to think profoundly and see through the true essence behind the phenomena such as the collective bargaining, welfare state. The true essence hidden deep under all these institutions and behind the "peace, justice, benevolence" granted by the ruling class, reside the capitalist class rule and the capitalist exploitation and oppression of the working class, the antagonistic labor-capital contradiction and struggles.

III. The possibility, necessity and the reality of labor movement in Western countries now

1. The possibility of the labor movement

Individualism in the working class of developed countries has affected and will affect their collective actions of the working class negatively, but may not necessarily lead to full disappearance of their collectivism and full disappearance of their inherent ability to take collective actions, so the possibility remains. French sociologist Emile Durkheim held that individualistic way of thinking is bound to grow along with increasingly complex division of labor. However, even if there is diversification and independent labor life, the solidarity and unity among workers will not weaken, because organic solidarity and unity (commonness) thoughts among the workers are built on the basis of collective conscience.[6] Durkheim wrote: the division of labor generated all sorts of interdependencies between people, as well as key elements of organic solidarity, like a weaker collective conscience. Despite the influence of individualism, the working class has a collective conscience which will possibly make a corresponding effect to mobilize collective thinking and action whose natural outcome will be labor movements waged by the working class.

---

6 Ding Jiqian, Reasons for the Decline of the French Labor Union Movements, Foreign Theoretical Trends, Issue 5, 2003.

2. The necessity of the labor movement

Marx had predicted that the majority of the people in the society would live by wages and labor remunerations, and their interests as wage earners would be completely different from the employers'. Consequently the contradiction between the wage earners and employers would require the former take collective actions. Class struggle, regardless of whether is endowed with certain political meaning, will continue to occur.[7] Therefore, the collective actions taken by the working class in the capitalist countries against the rule of capital would occur despite everything.

External factors like state institutions (governments) will also push and facilitate the working class to take collective and coherent actions. Feng Tongqing, wrote: "Now Obama believes that trade unions are not where the problem lies, but they are the subjects to cooperate in order to solve the problem. Therefore trade unions all declared readiness to develop communication and dialogue with him, Obama said: "arrange your unity before talking about communication."[8]

In the United States and some Western countries the tripartite cooperation system—namely 3 cooperative parties as employers, workers and the government— is implemented to solve collective bargaining issues and labor policy issues. This tripartite cooperation system constitutes a prerequisite for solidarity of the workers and their collective thinking and action in order to take part in the tripartite bargaining system. Consequently this institution in these countries, causes the workers and workers' unions to increase unity, solidarity and collective action, to a certain extent.

3. The reality of the labor movement

In the capitalist system, the collisions caused by the fundamental antagonism between the working class and the bourgeoisie due to their different economic, political and social statuses and situations will definitely lead to class struggles and trigger the labor movements. The "Occupy Wall Street" movement held by the American people on September 17, 2011 in New York to protest the rule of financial capital has spread to many US cities, and spread to a number of countries including Canada, Britain and Holland. On November 30, 2011, 30 trade unions in Britain organized a big strike with the participation of over 2 million workers. On December 1, 2011, the trade unions in Greece organized huge strikes. Such demonstrations or strikes held by the working masses either targeted directly capital exploitation and oppression or against the austerity policies taken by

---

7 Eric Hobsbawm, The Century of Labor Movement, trans. by Zhang Shipeng, Contemporary World and Socialism, Issue 6, 2002.

8 Feng Tongqing, Trade Unions in the United States under Financial Crisis: Information and Thinking, Issues of Contemporary Socialism, Issue 4, 2009.

the government which decreases laborers' general social welfare and social security. But fundamentally speaking, this opposition and fight by the working masses are inevitable because the capitalist system—by itself—is unable to get rid of or cure its inherent basic contradiction and chronic illnesses, that is the contradiction –class struggles—between the working class and the capitalist class.

Currently, class struggles in Western countries indicate that the collective actions taken by the working class against the rule of capital is an inevitable regular law and is bound to occur independent of anyone's will, under the capitalist social and political system Although labor movement is in a low tide situation in the Western countries, the workers' and masses' strikes and demonstrations against the reduction and reversal of their rights and interests will continue to occur.

A summary

All in all, it is possible, necessary and a reality that the working class in Western countries would unite, take collective actions and launch labor movements due to their common fundamental interests. Both practice and the reality have proven that they are able to take collective actions, have carried out and are carrying out labor movements.

Collective struggles and solidarity are the powerful means for the working class to achieve its goals the objectives of labor movement and correct path of the liberation of the working class. The working class in the western countries has a deep understanding of the significance of the workers' movement, and with nurturing the spirit and consciousness of acting in unity and collectively actions, the working class in Western countries must have the courage to explore and release the possibility and potentiality of launching collective actions consciously; fight against the united forces of capital by achieving the broadest unity when launching stronger collective actions of the laboring masses; be good at winning victories so as to effectively protect, enhance and ultimately realize the rights, interests and welfare of the working class.

Y. 24

Occupy the System: Confronting Global Capitalism– A Commentary on International Left Forum 2012

Lu Weizhou[1]

Abstract: Left Forum 2012 was held at the Pace University, NYC between March 16-18. The call of the Forum was "Occupy the System: Confronting Global Capitalism. More than 400 panels were organized and participated by more than 4500 attendees, including various type of left progressive organizations scholars, intellectuals, political activists, movement organizers, unionists and those interested from general public. Participants expressed a wide range of critical perspectives on global capitalism. Generally revolving around the "Occupy Wall Street" movement, the participants have discussed and exchanged ideas on the crisis of capitalism, alternatives to current capitalism and the new revival of the left.

Key words: Left forum, occupy, capitalist crisis, global capitalism

---

1 Lu Weizhou, visiting researcher at the World Socialism Research Center attached to the Chinese Academy of Social Sciences and researcher at the Academy of Marxism attached to CASS.

The Global Left Forum 2012, which is known as the largest annual gathering of the Left and cohesion of the Left power was held at Pace University, New York city on March 16-18, 2012. The topic of the forum was "Occupy the System: Confronting Global Capitalism". Organizers set up more than 400 panels, and more than 4,500 people, including left progressive intellectuals, political activists, movement organizers, trade unionists, and the interested public participated. The participants discussed and shared ideas revolving around theoretical and practical issues, including the occupy movement, economic crisis, globalization, social transformation, labor movement, party construction, revival of the Left, regional politics, socialism, communism, environmental issues, feminism, anarchism, colonialism, neo-liberalism as well as conservatism. Since the Forum was held against the social and historical background of unceasingly deepening international financial economic crisis, instantaneous spreading of the European debt crisis as well as the rising of mass movements one after another "occupy movement", the crisis of capitalism, alternatives to current capitalism as well as the revival of the Left movement has become major concerns of the forum.

I. History, status quo, and future of the occupy movement

As one of the most influential events in the US society or even the world throughout 2011, the occupy movement erupted in the New York city on September 17, 2011, dispersed to major cities such as Boston, Los Angeles, San Francisco, Washington, Denver, Philadelphia and Salt Lake City, and others like a hurricane, and further spread to more than 80 countries and thousands of cities throughout the world. The occupy movement was first fueled by The US public's original resentment towards the greed of Wall Street, but currently the world-wide public apparently aim to censure the rich of the whole capitalism. Demonstrators, coming from dozens of different countries, held massive demonstrations to protest against the greed of Wall Street and a handful of people's unfair possession of social wealth, and simultaneously demonstrated anger due to government's concessive bailout policy for infamous financial institutions amidst financial crisis. Under this backdrop, the occupy movement became the focus of the global Left Forum 2012, and participants attached great importance to the history, status quo, and future of the occupy movement.

Among all those 400 panels, about 1/4 of them were directly related to the occupy movement. Participants gave detailed descriptions about the specific conditions of the occupy movement in various countries and regions as well as cities, solemnly discussed and shared ideas concerning the historical origin, development, strategic policies, impact, challenges, future prospects, and development of the entire movement.

1. By combining historical facts with used methods, the Forum conducted an in-depth interpretation and analysis of the history, status quo, and future of the occupy movement from both theoretical and practical aspects.

Numerous left wingers, including the famous The US Marxist economist David Kotz, Marina Sitrin as well as Allen Gupta, who have participated in the occupy movement and helped to launch many journals about the movement, actively participated in those panels such as "The origin, history, and status quo of the occupy movement" by the anarchist scholars and intellectuals, the "Root source and potential impact of the Occupy Wall Street movement" by the journal "Science and Society", and the "History of the Left and occupy movement in 2011, 1999, 1968, and 2012" by "The Platypus Review", the "Occupy Wall Street: its origin and future direction" by the "International Socialist Review" as well as the "History of social movements and future of the occupy movement".

During the discussions, panelists have all agreed that the occupy movement was the product of previous new Left movement and women's liberation movements. Another common view has suggested "global social movements with great diversity" could promote anti-capitalist thoughts and sentiments, simultaneously form a new labor movement. One important problem currently confronting the occupy movement is how to further develop into a more organized power and more directly strike a blow against the US and global capitalism.

Forum carried out in-depth discussions on issues such as strategies, lessons learned as well as development prospect of the occupy movement from a historical and global height. In a set of panels such as "The road to sustainable development: strategies of occupy economy", "Strategic prospect of the occupy movement", "Digital strategies of occupy Wall Street", "Occupy in pursuit of genuine democracy: experience of Egypt, Spain, New York, and Argentina", "The North America's occupy movement from a global perspective", "From occupy to organizing public" as well as "Occupy Nigeria! Social media and its role in promoting democracy and combating corruption" Participants recognized the role of the new tools such as Internet and social media in the occupy movement in various countries and regions. Forum actively discussed and shared ideas on a series of specific issues such as how the occupy movement can affect media, drew on the experiences in history, experiences of various regions as well as how to get more people involved in the occupy movement. Given the fact that the occupy movement was triggered by the "market fundamentalism" the star of mainstream economics and was an inevitable result of international financial-economic crisis spreading to the social-political area, the forum paid more attention to occupying economy. Organizations and institutions such as the journal Reflection on Marxism, the Rosa Luxemburg Foundation from Germany as well as The Platypus Review, launched many symposiums concerning occupying economy, including "Study on occupying economy", "How To Occupy The US economy", "Occupying non-capitalist economy", "Occupying banks: if possible, how should socialists deal with the banking system" as well as "Financial capital and occupation: a Marxist perspective". Richard Wolf, a famous The US left-wing scholar and economics emeritus professor at the University of Massachusetts Amherst Hurst, professor David Schweickart from Loyola University of Chicago as well as Frances Fox Piven, a politics and sociology professor at the City University of New York Graduate Center had all joined in these discussions. They had not only criticized the neo-liberal economic theory and policies but also actively put forward various alternatives for the operation of local and global economy such as worker cooperatives, social market practices, and an equitable and sustainable economy etc.

2. The forum had not only explored the development process and direction of the occupy movement theoretically, but also paid direct attention and provided support to its practice.

Since March 17, 2012 coincided with the half-year anniversary of the "Occupy Wall Street" movement, so numerous participants of the Left Forum, especially active organizers held demonstrations to commemorate the movement. That night, the principal speaker of the Left Forum, Michael Moore, known as the most fearless political critic, a well-known promising film producer, a left activist highlighted causes and the significance of the occupy movement in his speech. He said, "Before the financial crisis, most of our fellow The US people still believed hard work could bring wealth and everyone could realize their goals as long as they worked hard, however, people no longer believe in it due to the financial crisis". Michael Moore also actively called upon participants of the Left Forum to forge ahead towards lower Manhattan Zuccotti Park, he took the lead in the demonstration. Joseph Ramsey, an activist in the Occupy Boston movement, delivered a speech titled "Put Theory Into the Street" in the symposium debating "Establishing A Red And Green Revolutionary Strategic Alliance". During his speech, he expressed his doubt that the occupy movement faces the danger of being submerged due to solely focusing on specific demands. Instead he suggested, people should combine the specific struggle on public transport with the distribution of wealth in society, and he also probed into issues such as protest against the public service cuts and rise in Boston public transportation expense etc.

Generally speaking, the Left Forum gave full affirmation to the significance and future of the occupy movement and also conducted an in-depth discussion on problems and challenges faced by the occupy movement. It is commonly accepted that the "Occupy Wall Street" is characterized by an anti-capitalist tendency and problems such as concentration of wealth, inequality as well as threats imposed on democracy may increasingly become one of the most critical topics of the globally unfolding anti-capitalist occupy movement. The occupy movement sent a clear message; a handful of people, accounting for only 1% of population living in the world's richest countries grab the lion share of wealth, which is used to corrupt politics while the majority of people are plagued by unemployment, loss of housing, debts as well as poverty. Everyone agreed that the occupy type mass movements emerging in those places like Egypt, Greece, Latin America and in the United States, and other countries could provide new opportunities for the development of the Left forces. Therefore, participants placed great expectations towards occupy movement and proposed slogans as "occupying the earth", "occupying the world", "occupying each place" as well as occupying various fields, including economy, politics, culture, society, and ecology etc. on the basis of the current state of occupy movement in the United States, Europe, Asia, Africa, and Australia. Especially in the era characterized by the struggle between capitalism and socialism, the forum, increasingly focused on ideology issues, highlighted the importance of ideology, accordingly symposiums focusing on occupying academy, occupying research, occupying university, occupying ethics, occupying philosophy, occupying consciousness, occupying imagination, occupying cartoon as well as occupying Hollywood were organized. Speakers also conducted in-depth analyses related occupy movement in these ideological fields.

Zuccotti Park, built in the 1960s, was originally called the Plaza Park. In 2006, it was renamed as the Zuccotti Park. The park, located in the Wall Street financial district, between the Broadway Street in Manhattan, the Liberty Street, and the Cedar Street, is quite popular. It was the camping site of Wall Street occupiers since September 2011.

II. The root causes, impacts and trend of the crisis of capitalism

Associated with the occupy movement, the global Left Forum 2012 also conducted an extensive and in-depth analysis on issues such as the root causes of the capitalist crisis, its impacts as well as its development trend and alternatives to capitalist system.

1. Forum made a relative comprehensive interpretation about the causes of crisis, which erupted in the United States, then spread through entire capitalist world, ruining millions of people's life.

In a set of symposiums including "The root cause of economic crisis: financial inflation resulting from the housing bubble and debt", "Causes of the economic crisis: how did the US economic crisis develop into a worldwide economic crisis", "Politics and economy in the global crisis: origins and future prospects" as well as "Crisis and resistance in the Neo-liberal globalization", many left-wing figures participated in the discussion, including Paul Garver, an American democratic socialist and one of the leaders of the International Food Trade Union, and David McNally, a professor of politics at York University in Toronto. Those participants commonly agreed that the 2008 global financial crisis was a consequence of the Neo-liberal economic policies over the past 30 years, especially due to the lack of financial regulatory policies. Financial de-regulation policies allowed broad space for speculative transactions and highly speculative financial instruments which in turn incited speculative greed, its one prevalent result was the real estate bubble. Forum also discussed and elaborated ideas on the manifestations of the crisis in fiscal and monetary spheres, the evolution trend of the crisis during the deflation period as well as the significance of carrying out class struggles and political opposition movements. Moreover, Forum also explored the nature of imperialism and its relation with crisis and wars, all kinds of occupy movements combining and embracing 99% of the population worldwide—from Cairo, Egypt to Nigeria's Kano, from Athens to Oakland and from Wisconsin to Wall Street— should fight against the powerful 1%.

For example, in the session titled "Uniting 99% of the world's population to fight imperialism: Root cause of the crisis and war" launched by "Initiative for Iran's anti-imperialist struggle for democracy" and the International League for People's Struggle, participants pointed out that imperialism is the birthplace of those powerful 1% and also the root cause of the crisis. Many left-wingers indignantly expressed that there exists the danger of a new and more extensive imperialist war, and discussed how to establish a global unified front aimed at overthrowing imperialism, bringing a brighter future for human beings.

2. A hot issue in the Forum was the ecological environment crisis caused by capitalism.

In the session titled "decolonizing the occupy movement: defending the mother earth and confronting the US capitalism", participants pointed out that the earth is increasingly confronted with serious ecological threats and discussed how to combine the global occupy movement with local movements so as to jointly protest U.S's constant looting of mother earth. In the symposium titled "Climate disaster: 99% of all solutions" launched by the journal "New Politics", which discussed the acute ecological problems, socialists, historians, environmentalists, lawyers, and scientists expressed their ideas on problems such as "our distance from the climate tipping point", "the relationship between worldwide social movements and the threat imposed by climate change related disasters", "can the Left provide

99% the population with a future prospect characterized by a positive and ecological utopia?". In the symposium "Rio+20 conference on sustainable development–green crony capitalism" launched by the Rosa Luxemburg Foundation, Germany, participants criticized, "Though increasingly serious climate crisis, the global politics fails to respond to this challenge. Speakers critically analyzed the prospects of emerging "green capitalism", and discussed the damages caused by oil companies and their counter lobby activities, faced by the green struggles of the labor and environmental movements. In the symposium "Capitalism, Imperial Geopolitics and the Climate Crisis: Where Next for the Climate Justice Movement? co-hosted by the Hippocampus Bookshop and the Monthly Review, "A New Green Deal: Interpreting the crisis of work and climate" by the Green Party of New York City and the "Occupy The Environment" by the journal The Platypus Review, participants carried out a relatively in-depth discussion on the ecological and environmental crisis of capitalism and its solutions. Combining environmental crisis analysis with the endless expansionist trend of capitalism, The US author Stephanie Macmillan argued that capitalism and life are in a fundamental contradiction, only a new economy enjoying a sustainable and virtuous relationship with the nature. She also stressed, only joint struggles inspired by socialist and green traditions could be able to transcend capitalism.

3. Based on an overall evaluation of the development prospects of the contemporary capitalism, the Forum deemed that depleted global capitalism has already come to a dead end.

In the session "Is this the final crisis?" launched by the journal Critical, people such as a famous The US Marxist scholar and professor of politics at the University of New York, Bertell Ollman and Hillel Ticktin, a well-known British left-wing scholar, discussed the meaning of "final crisis" and its significance for true class consciousness and revolution. In the symposium "Is the capitalism in a dead end? Socialist revolution during the period of crisis" initiated by the journal Workers of the World International, a left-wing paper, speakers have analyzed the development trend of the crisis of capitalism and commonly agreed that this crisis of capitalism can no longer be solved by relying on the capitalist system. The rapid development of contemporary capitalist science and technology and each new investment propels cutting down the number of jobs, thus pushes more and more people into unemployment. Therefore, capitalism becomes a low wage social system characterized by an increasing amount of unemployment and insufficient employment. At present, the capitalism has come to an eternal crisis and still influences workers in developed imperialist countries. Examples such as unrest in North Africa and Middle East region, massive strikes and occupy movements in the peripheral countries of Europe (Greece, Ireland,

Portugal and Spain) as well as the US occupy movement are all initial responses to this final crisis.

Forum stressed the importance and necessity of an alternative to capitalism, analyzing the issues surfaced during the crisis, strategies adopted by the contemporary capitalism to overcome the crisis and their impacts and feasibility. In the symposium "Global capitalism in crisis: Flash point of oppression and resistance node of changes" launched by the journal Critical Sociology and "Crisis of the capitalism and global struggle against austerity measures" initiated by the International Socialist Review, participants made an in-depth analysis on capitalist governments' policies, actions, their efficiency while handling the crisis. Speakers have commonly argued, since the eruption of the 2008 international financial crisis, the global financial system is trapped in a long-term crisis. Though there emerged widespread skepticism towards 30-year domination of neo-liberal model with the eruption of the crisis, the international ruling class still adopts austerity policies as the only solution, and seeks further cuts in social welfare expenditures, thus favoring monopoly capital class. Consequently, these policies and measures have further widened the gap between the rich and the poor and triggered massive worker strikes, protests, and revolts throughout Europe and The US. Currently, the crisis has already engulfed the entire capitalist world and extended to economic and social fields, which sets the scene for the outbreak of dissatisfaction. Various kinds of occupy and social movements such as the 2011 "Occupy Wall Street" and "Arab Spring" are manifestations of the general public's increasing dissatisfaction towards the so-called "crisis solution" measures implemented by the ruling class.

Based on a comprehensive analysis of different aspects of the current crisis of capitalism and its impacts on various spheres, the Left Forum delivered elaborations on the alternative of the capitalist system and clearly pointed to socialism as its alternative.

An important group in the Left Forum, left wingers have also argued their ideas on the alternatives of the capitalist system. As to their panels, I can mention "The ecological, economic and political alternatives of capitalism" by the journal New Politics, "Occupying Wall Street, Theme Street and White House in both a special and social sense: The design of socialism" by the journal Economy and Society, "For the sake of democracy, putting an end to capitalism or for socialism? Various discussions about strategies and tactics" co-organized by the journal Political Affairs and the US Communist Party (CPUSA) "The next system: Exploring into the economic alternative of capitalism", "An in-depth analysis of the Mondragon cooperative and socialism in the 21st century", "The Return(s) of Socialist Humanism and the Need for an Alternative".

Majority scholars and activists in the above panels have demonstrated agreement that severe economic, social and ecological crisis has already fully revealed the unstable, decadent, unsustainable and parasitic nature of the capitalist system, all of which explicitly indicates the extreme importance of developing and emergence of a positive alternative model.

Mondragon is a small town located in the Basque country, Spain. Next to Spain, it is famous for creating a new cooperative economic model. Currently, Mondragon cooperative enterprise has become a symbol of the Basque country cooperative system. Vitality of this model and its economic impacts in the region is unprecedented. Since its establishment in 1950s, it has enjoyed worldwide reputation. Similar patterns can be found in England, Wales, and the United States.

With regard to the crisis of capitalism and its development trend, some panelists have explicitly pointed out that "it is inevitable for the capitalism to perish and be replaced by socialism, and now it's time to compare, comment, and seek consensus concerning the prospect of the capitalist society" Compared with the capitalist system, which is in jeopardy, socialism has already been a more promising option. So, leftists should abandon the traditional view that people can only make a living under the capitalist system and there is no alternative to capitalism. The forum also illustrated the development prospect and blueprint of socialism from various perspectives such as economy, politics, culture, ecology, and society. For example, some of them explored the economic alternatives of capitalism by proceeding with the destruction of industrial capital resulting from financial crisis. With an eye on the polarization caused by capital greed, some other panelists put some new ideas worker cooperative, as a substitute for capitalism and private property aimed at ending poverty, they also discussed those achievements and challenges faced by worker cooperative movements in U.S and other countries. In their opinion, the rapid growth of cooperative movements has already become an option for workers to form their own workplaces based on equality and democratic management.

III. The current development status and trend of the Left-wing

Just like all those previous global left forums, core themes of the global Left Forum 2012 current were development status, strategies, and prospects of the left wing parties and other organizations. Centering on the theme of "occupy the system: confronting global capitalism", the forum paid high attention to the occupy movement and confronting capitalist system. The forum set up numerous symposiums and conducted positive discussions on a series of extremely realistic and important problems concerning the current development status and trend of the left wing forces, especially on how the left wing should respond to the current occupy movement, achieve rejuvenation with the help of this movement, and adapt to the increasing uncertainties in global politics thus make practical contributions to the cause of combating capitalism.

1. An in-depth analysis of the opportunities and challenges faced by the left wing against the background of the financial crisis

Since the late 1970s, especially after the collapse of the Soviet Union and the dramatic upheaval in Eastern Europe the global left wing movement has lost its strong position both theoretically and practically. In contrast, the Neo-liberalism advocated by the right wing has not only played an extremely significant role in economic policies of western countries but also dominated reality and discourse in politics, media, and academia, which restrained the development of the left wing, substantially. The international financial crisis erupted in latter the half of 2007 disrupted the popularity of Neo-liberalism in the west, on the other side Marxist theories, socialist values including moral values and policies have regained popularity. With the outbreak and wide-spreading of the international financial-economic crisis, left-wing forces sought strategies and proposals to deal with the crisis in and hoped restoring its former glory and achieve a thorough rejuvenation. However, as we observe, the development of the left wing against the backdrop of the international financial crisis is by no means so smooth; instead it has encountered numerous problems and setbacks. In the symposiums "the Arab spring in winter, challenges faced by the left wing in the past one year" and "The third party and the left wing: problems and prospects" initiated by the journal The Platypus Review, participants carried out an in-depth discussion on problems and challenges faced by the left forces. It is commonly recognized that although the coalition of left wing forces has achieved certain developments and sought larger coalition possibilities and breakthrough to benefit from new opportunities, yet inner family conflicts, especially those confrontations and struggles among certain groups and factions still severely weaken its fighting capacity. Consequently, though opportunities exist, the left has failed to formulate a set of practical action plans, thus still cannot play expected roles. The forum also evaluated the Arab Spring in Tunisia and Egypt as a case and discussed current problems faced by the left wing: How should left wing acknowledge the rigorously soaring democratic aspirations in the Arab world and help them turn the potentials into reality? How should left wing adapt to the increasing uncertainties in the global politics and make practical contributions to progressive demands of the people in this region? In addition, Forum also evaluated the case of the US and European left and analyzed their setbacks and problems, a hot issue here was the independent electoral strategies to be adapted by respective parties, including communist and left wing parties including Labor Parties, the Greens, the Socialist (Social-democrats) and even radical-liberal parties.

2. The forum also held a series of panels conducting an extensive discussion on strategies and tactics required by the left wing

In those panels "Left wing and crisis", "How should the left wing theory respond to the new social movements?", "Left wing strategies to be adopted after the occupy movement", "Occupy and independent left wing electoral politics: the green party, socialist party, radicals and occupy movement", "The participation by communists to capitalist electoral process", "Occupy Wall Street and the future of the US's democratic left wing in coming 50 years" as well as "Crisis and opposition during the transformation: basis for a democratic socialist party", left wingers coming from different countries and parties discussed and shared ideas on the role and function of left wing in the occupy movement. It was widely accepted that the current capitalist structural crisis triggered a worldwide occupy movement and mass movement aiming democracy, equality, and sustainable development, and has shifted people's attention from inflation, living costs and employment issues to another related sphere: economic and political inequalities. Of course this change provides a rare opportunity for the development and rejuvenation of left wing parties and organizations. The eruption of financial crisis has opened up a new space for the left wing to confront capitalism. In Europe, although the power of unions and social movements is still relatively weak, the general public has begun to realize the fact that the common currency (Euro) and the European central government in Brussels, Strasbourg enlarged the existing gap between the privileged and the unprivileged, the rich and the poor and capital versus labor, they do their utmost to fight against austerity measures which further frustrates workers and other wage earners. In Asia, the development of capitalism has led to huge inequalities, whereas in Latin America the emerging new social class opposition and democratic participation demand has once again inspired the hope of achieving a worldwide revival of the left wing.

In view of the current situation facing the left wing, participants also probed into those factors, which promote the formation or impede its development. Accordingly, new organization forms, new strategies, newly emerging parties, and social movements were debated.

In a nutshell, the global Left Forum 2012 was held against the historical background of widespread outbreak of capitalist crisis and the vigorous blast of occupy movement in different parts of the world. Evaluating the issues and destiny of capitalism from a systemic perspective, Forum conducted an in-depth and critical thinking on the economic system, development pattern, and democratic political system of capitalism. It directly criticized the capitalist system and called on people to rebel under the slogan "Occupy the system: fight against the global capitalism."

In the morning of September 17, 2012, "Occupy Wall Street" protesters assembled near the New York Stock Exchange to commemorate the first anniversary of the "Occupy Wall Street". Simultaneously in more than 30 cities throughout the world, parades, protests, and demonstrations were held to commemorate this day. Occupiers protested the social injustice caused by greed of the %1, unfair bailouts of major banks and financial institutions by capitalist governments, condemned the US government's incompetent administration over the financial industry, all of which had greatly exploited the overwhelming majority. Scholars and intellectuals also reflected profoundly on gains and losses of the occupy movement and pointed to progressive perspectives for the future.

Y. 25

"Occupy Wall Street Movement" on Its First Anniversary: Gains, Losses and Prospects

Zhang Xinning[1]

Abstract: On the occasion of the first anniversary of "Occupy Wall Street" demonstrators have gathered to protest the social injustice by greed, simultaneously expressed their anger against bailouts of big banks and financial institutions. This paper summarizes views of US scholars on the important movement. Occupy movement, to a degree has made a substantial impact on the US society raising the banner of concepts, social equity and justice, and its future form is yet to be restructured.

Key words: "Occupy Wall Street" movement; anniversary

---

1 Zhang Xinning, guest researcher at the Socialism Research Center of the Chinese Academy of Social Sciences and a doctoral student at the Marxism Institute.

I. The general public: A comeback

James, as one of the hosts of the occupy movement, commented that the first anniversary was a great concern to them, the 99% once more demonstrated their demands and filled the streets. On September 15, more than 300 people assembled in the Zuccotti Park, which is located in the Wall Street financial district, New York to celebrate the anniversary in advance. On September 17, hundreds of occupiers gathered in the financial district of New York, the birthplace of the "Occupy Wall Street" movement, and blocked the street during the morning rush hour. Protesters planned to besiege the New York Stock Exchange, block the path to the New York Stock Exchange, and commemorate the first anniversary of "Occupy Wall Street" by sit-ins, strikes, and demonstrations. On their way to the New York Stock Exchange, protesters cried the famous slogans of the occupy movement—"We are betrayed" and "We will occupy Wall Street all day long or for all week!" etc.

In San Francisco, the main prestige object of the city is the Bank of The US tower located in California street No. 555. Occupiers fastened a big slogan on the iron fence in front of the building's black marble artwork, reading "greedy heart of bankers" Another slogan written with scarlet letters over the white background said: "Occupy San Francisco Bay Area and unite together"

Meanwhile, they declared their movement being non-violent. The police sought to disperse or arrest the protesters, thus they couldn't approach the New York Stock Exchange, though several repeated attempts. As the last effort the mass split up into groups and forged ahead from different directions, thus starting a "cat and mouse game" with the police, combat has lasted for hours.

Since the unfolding of the "Occupy Wall Street" movement, financial tycoons has not taken any responsibility for the financial crisis that caused great suffering for the %99, instead their CEOs still enjoyed generous pays and benefits after being saved by bailout policies. According to the data obtained from the US Budget and Policy Priorities Center, the income share of US's 1% richest population from the national income kept rising since 1980 and reached its peak in 2007, 23.5%.[2] Although the number has slightly declined after the financial crisis, it still remains high -about 20%, which effectively reflects the current state of gap between the rich and the poor.

Meanwhile, the unemployment rate in the United States in August 2012 was still as high as 8.1%. Thus far, unemployment rate in the US has been more than 8% for 43 consecutive months. Some protesters expressed their

---

[2] Miao Qi: The first anniversary of the "Occupy Wall Street", First Financial Daily, September 18, 2012.

dissatisfaction of the current state and confused feelings towards the future. Benson, a protester coming from Puerto Rico, commented: "Almost nothing has changed in the past year, the richest men still exploit the national economy and Wall Street still rules the politics. Another protester Bree said that big business of Wall Street was the common target of their struggle and part of 1%, which have robbed 99%, and their wealth. They tried to commemorate the first anniversary of the "Occupy Wall Street" movement by expressing their opinions.[3]

II. Scholars and intellectuals evaluating the Occupy movement: Mixed reflections

Since the eruption of the occupy movement in September 2011, American scholars kept paying great attention to this issue, opened up research courses, published a large number of papers, and even initiated occupy movements targeting the US's philosophy and social science field. On March 16 to 18, 2012, the theme of the International Left Forum, held at the Pace University located in lower Manhattan, New York, was the "Occupy the system: confronting global capitalism". It was a direct response to the "Occupy Wall Street" from a global and historical perspective. Recently due to anniversary, American scholars have again actively elaborated on the gains and losses of the "Occupy Wall Street" movement.

Some scholars have argued that the occupy movement in itself is a victory. Ganz, a professor at the Kennedy School of Government attached to Harvard University and an organizational behavior theorist, believed that occupiers have found a way to release their desperation as the plutocracy is just like in an iron cage. The most popular slogan in the demonstrations is: "Rescue banks by betraying us!"[4] The occupy movement has helped some people to express their thoughts, that is, pushing capital powers to face a moral crisis. This outstanding and creative movement is an attempt to reconstruct morals in the society.

Professor Todd Gitlin of the Columbia University wrote that the occupy movement changed the political culture of the United States and "deactivated the conservative political forces, this puts banks under great pressure. Some banks have reduced big bonuses, while other banks have canceled the so-called compensations given to high directors. Some local movement organizations successfully prevented or interrupted relocation events enforced by the courts, thus protect those house-owners from being forced out of their house, everybody knows they unable to repay the loans. Ruthless

---
3 Li Dajiu: Supporters of the "Occupy Wall Street" movement held demonstrations to commemorate its first anniversary, Guangzhou Daily, September 19, 2012.
4 Todd Gitlin: The Occupy movement 2.0?, The Deutsche Welle, from a Chinese website, September 17, 2012.

lenders (including some well-known large banks) are to blame for those events.[5] One former professor and an anthropologist at Yale University, David Gray made a resounding slogan for the "Occupy Wall Street"; "We belong to 99% of the population. Since 1% richest Americans dominate the country's wealth and politics, and have all benefits of economic growth in the past 10-15 years, then why not we make a clean break with them?"[6] Just as Dr. Nathanson from the Fordham University in New York City said, occupying itself did not have a broad prospect; instead it was the intense movements triggered by occupying that had such kind of broad prospects.[7]

However, there are still some scholars holding a negative attitude towards the importance of the occupy movement. In their opinion, the "Occupy Wall Street" movement still doesn't have its own policies and programs. "In sharp contrast, the Tea Party movement of the right wing is quite different; they gather strength and foster their favorite candidates for general election of November 2012, eagerly try to strengthen their political power". Steins Cabo, a professor of government and sociology at Harvard University, said, "Politicians will only pay attention to elections and consider those people organizing votes and donating the candidates. That was what the Tea Party has achieved while the Occupy Wall Street has not"… "Therefore, I think this movement has no significance at all."[8]

A columnist from Market Watch, Weidner analyzed the reason why the "Occupy Wall Street" movement failed to become an important social and political power. The reasons are as follows: "firstly, the messages they sent is quite disordered; secondly, their bizarre clothes, different dress styles, or even masks made it impossible for the "Occupy Wall Street" movement to gain support from among center oriented American people; thirdly, their opponents were quite wealthy and powerful; fourthly, they also seemed too aggressive with their masks similar to those worn by the hacker group Anonymous" In addition, Weidner argued that the occupy movement still lacked a clear objective, "although occupiers wished to achieve a series of objectives such as exempting student loans, ending the foreclosures, carrying out bank reforms as well as balancing the distribution of income etc., yet there was no agreement concerning details of those issues.[9]

---

5   Ibid.
6   Nina Easton. Is it still OK to be rich in The US? Fortune, September 24, 2012.
7   Feng Yu: Questioning the Occupy Wall Street movement, the China Press, September 17, 2012.
8   The Sinovision Net: Hundreds of people held demonstrations to commemorate the first anniversary of the "Occupy Wall Street" movement, The Sinovision Net, September 16, 2012.
9   David Weidner, "How the Tea Party beat Occupy Wall Street," Market Watch, August 21, 2012.

III. Profound impacts of the Occupy Wall Street on the US society

The occupy movement has already exerted some impact on the US society in terms of social equality and justice to be further accepted by the general public. The occupy movement itself is a campaign reflecting on the system, and the process of occupying is a kind of democratic practice, which tries to discuss problems, objectives, and strategies in directly democratic ways.

Economically, the United States government began to pay some attention to inequalities when planning its economic policies and also care more for the extreme unhealthy elements/rules in the financial system. According to a Los Angeles Times report, one important achievements of the "Occupy Wall Street" movement was; "before September 17, 2011 Washington's political struggle mainly focused on how to raise the debt ceiling of citizens and avoid credit defaults, but after this movement, following political negotiations, focus shifted to practical problems such as economic inequalities, how Wall Street capital ruined the country's political system and stole peoples' democratic rights.[10]

Politically, another game has started in the US politics. Obama had once proposed to raise the tax rate of those rich Americans with an annual income of one million dollars or more to at least 30%.[11] Although this proposal failed to pass in the United States Congress in 2012, it has still exerted great impact. Currently, the United States presidential election is another good opportunity for the occupy movement to come back to the scene. Since the election is characterized by fierce competition among various political and social forces, it is possible for the occupy movement to benefit from the election as long as it has feasible objectives conforming to the public taste and if it can demonstrate such a leadership good at grasping the overall situation.

The eruption of the "Occupy Wall Street" movement also left deep impacts on communists, and even on extreme right conservatives like Newt Gingerich. He began to attack his opponent Mitt Romney as a predatory capitalist while competing for the Republican Party presidential nomination. As a result, if the occupy movement, which expressed its dissatisfaction towards the current social and economic status quo with actions, could get rid of its biased image as anarchist or vagrant, then it will most likely become an important force in the future of the United States.

---

10   Feng Yu: The anniversary of Occupy Wall Street, perspectives of the grassroots movement, the China Press, September 18, 2012.
11   Li Yang: Ups and downs in the first year of "Occupy Wall Street". International Finance, September 19, 2012.

IV. Future: expectations for reconstruction

One protester said that what happened last year was a ceaseless movement, protesting against social injustice. But what's the prospect of the "Occupy Wall Street" movement? Some scholars and activists believe that occupy movement of the future should be reconstructed or regenerated.

Nelson, a professor at the Fordham University in New York City, said that the "Occupy Wall Street" movement has no future but the movement it inspired is another thing: that aspect is quite promising. Many US protesters held up an occupy banner such as "Occupy the Ministry of Education" and "Occupy Brooks", all of which have assumed an occupying style.

Socialist Cole Deidra Guzman at the City University of New York argued that the occupy movement has already been transformed. Occupiers are no longer obliged to aim camping in a square, instead they can start a new wave of protests by using the social networks, and internet media. In order to achieve this goal, occupiers must welcome more broader public involvement rather than joining the political coterie 100%.[12] The United States also needs anarchists and revolutionists, dedicated to transform the country.

If the revolution will have a next stage, then it should be based on the foundation laid by the occupy movement. On the other hand, the people also needs a movement with solid and clear objectives. Therefore, the regeneration and construction of the occupy movement should be launched by various kinds of networks and vertical organizations, the horizontal organization forms will not mobilize broad opposition.

12　Todd Gitlin, "Occupy Nation: The Roots, The Spirit, and The Promise of Occupy Wall Street," New York: Harper Collins, 2012.

Y. 26

Some Questions to be Heeded in the Research of "International Secretive Groups"

Jing Xianghui[1]

Abstract: Current research about the secretive international groups groups generally covers a wide range of issues such as religious, political, financial, demographic and ethnic ones, and is thus very complicated. Due to their secretiveness, mystery and scant evidence, there exist some misapprehension in related documents and literature, e.g instigating hostility towards the Jews, and an oversimplified stigmatization of secretive groups like the Freemasons. We think such literature can easily mislead the public. At present, it is both important and necesarry for China to spread healthy information and guide public opinion, so as to maintain ideological, financial, political and cultural security.

Key words: secretive international groups; religion; racism

---

[1] Jing Xianghui, guest researcher at the Research Center of World Socialism attached to Chinese Academy of Social Sciences.

In recent years, "conspiracy theory", "Freemasonry" and "secret international groups" gradually become the focus of the Chinese society, especially with the widely visited web blog of He Xin and certain other Internet resources. The issue has aroused great interest among the ordinary people. Looking from the aspect of available literature and historical practice, "conspiracy theory" is not simply a conspiracy but has certain roots in reality, this also applies for the secretive and shadowy international groups acting behind the scenes. In the academy, the secretive international groups are studied under the branch of international strategic studies. This study field involves religion, politics, finance, population, race, culture, food, medicine and other fields, which are comprehensive and complex in content. And, the covert powers behind exists in private and we still lack solid facts, evidence and reference when studying them. Even though the available public literature and Internet materials are abundant, it is hard to trace their activities. Many narrations need to be proved and studied combining history, reality and practice, in order to grasp their true psychology and missions. We think this issue urgently needs a proper ideological guidance and public education, and an urgent task with strategic significance for the ideological security of the nation, and even related to economic and financial security, political security, and cultural security. For example, in the Chinese history some famous Freemasonry organizations have created abundant Chinese literature which can offer us hints to reveal their aims and strategies. Below, we will discuss a part of them with the most impact.

I. Meeting Minutes of Zion Elders

This is the most important historical literature research of Freemasonry which was first published in the newspaper The Standard between August 27, 1905 to September 7, in St. Petersburg, Russia with the title of The Jewish Programme to Conquer the World" It is said the original title of it was The Meeting Minutes of World Alliance of Freemasonry and the Sages of Zion Elders. It was re-published in 1911 and 1917 and then translated into different languages.

The book Meeting Minutes of the Zion Elders reveals the content of the secret meeting by the Freemasonry group which planned to dominate the world. Due to its surprising consistence with certain trends in the contemporary world history, it has attracted was widespread interest and caused a huge impact. This was recorded in details in the book The Holy Blood and the Holy Grail.[2] It is worth mentioning that the public version has been

---

2   He Xin: "Rule the world: The Mysterious Secretive Masonic Secret" China Books Press, March 2011, First edition, p. 145; "The Holy Blood and the Holy Grail", Co-authored by Michael Baigent, Richard Leigh, and Henry Lincoln, World Knowledge Publishing House, 2008, 1ˢᵗ edition, pp 174-178

severely distorted, and contains elements of incitement to discrimination and hostility targeting the Jews. It is quite hard for the general readers to distinguish between true and false. This is also an issue requiring special attention in the research of the Freemasonry.

II. "The World's Finance Is Designed by Rothschild" authored by Yoshiro Abe

This book by the Japanese author reveals certain facts related to the first generation of the Rothschild finance group, Mayer Rothschild held a secret meeting in Frankfurt.[3] This meeting studied the plan of how to monopolize its control over the world intelligence, power and resources, and launched a 25-item-"World Revolution Plan". This book pinpointed the Jewish financial family, the Rothschilds as the main planner of the world wide conspiracy and manipulation behind the closed doors—Rothschild family. But Yoshihiro Abe also admitted, "This document is a very old record, authenticity of which can not be fully proved. But what's more important is the Rothschild family and his allies have been faithful to this plan for generations."

III. The Secret of the FED, Written by Eustace Mullins in the U.S.

The author of the book claims to authority for his work revealing the secret behind control over the issuance and circulation of the world's major currencies, especially the US dollar, the book is also accepted as a major work which reveals the secret of the U.S. FED.[4]

The Currency Wars written by Song Hongbin in China which largely refers to his book, revealing the origin of Rothschild family, the establishment of the FED system. The circulation and impact of Song Hongbin's book was also huge.

IV. Rule the World: Disclosure of the Mysterious Freemasonry—Compilation of the Material by He Xin

The research data of the book were updated on Sina and Sohu, the top blogging websites in China. The pages were viewed by tens of millions and the daily visits to the page reached tens of thousands. The impact was huge. He Xin's book cited the original articles of the above books, which further expanded its ability to influence the Chinese public.

---

3 Yoshihiro Abe: "The World's Finance Is Designed by Rothschild", translated by Yang Jiajing , Chongqing Publishing House, March 2009 First edition.
4 Eustace Mullins: "The Secret of the FED", translated by Li Xiaoyan, Jilin Publishing Group,September 1st, 2011.

V. Series of articles published in the personal blog of Shan Ze

The personal blog run by scholar Shan Ze, published an article in May 2011, which clearly put forward the question "Who is China's Rival?", analyzing this issue in detail.[5] He also wrote a series of articles titled as "The Palace Jew and The Western Capitalism", "Ruling Model of Capital Centralization" and "Why Should We Firmly Oppose Democratic Regime?" targeting Jewish financial capital groups, which has made certain influence in the academy.

VI. "Secrets of the Tomb: Skull and Bones, the Ivy League, and the Hidden Paths of Power", by Alexandra Robbins

The book revealed a secret society with only a handful of elites who gather on High Street in the Yale campus at the tomb. It is said that many presidents, chief judges of the Supreme Court, a number of senators and representatives and members of the cabinet are members of this society. Bush when he served as the ambassador to China, said: "I once spoke to a member of the Skull and Bones who paid me a visit, I said I would like to participate in the presidential elections. The member asked, "Which is the company you act on behalf of?" Bush laughed and answered "The United States of America."[6] His words were very impressive. The sole purpose of Skull and Bones is to get members into positions of power and then to have those members hire other members to prominent positions.

VII. Other Works

The Secret of the Freemasonry by Peter Blakestock; *The Freemasonry of Russia and the Political Transition of Russia* by Zhao Shifeng; *Christianity and the Constitution: The Faith of Our Founding Fathers* by John Eidsmoe, *Invisible Hand* by A. Ralph Parsons, "Shadow People: Inside History's Most Notorious Secret" by John Lawrence Reynolds, *Currency Great Wall* by Jiang Xiaomei, *Financial Assassin—Financial Battles Series, Illustration of World Finance—Popular Finance Readings Series* and so on. Other foreign materials and network resources will not be discussed here.

---

5 Web blog of Shan Ze: "Who is China's Rival?", Http://blog.sina.com.cn/s/blog_52345b4d0100rpw5. Html.
6 Alexandra Robbins: "Secrets of the Tomb: Skull and Bones, the Ivy League, and the Hidden Paths of Power.",translated by Qi Dong , CITIC Publishing House, November 2010, Second edition, pp 176-177.

Looking from the aspect of history and reality, China's huge population base, huge demand for energy resources, its strong ability to govern and its vigorous momentum of development posit huge challenges for the two Western powers. And looking from the aspect of the current complex international and domestic situation, to a certain sense and degree, China has become the focus of attention of the covert international groups. Under the severe and volatile international environment, how to handle the relations between struggle, competition and cooperation while enabling China to maintain its own core interests and reduce the external risks to the minimum worth serious attention and needs deeper study endeavor.

VIII. Several Issues Worth Paying Attention During Contention and Cooperation

1. Importance of the research on the issues of national sovereignty under the new situation

The report presented to the 18th Party Congress of the CPC has repeatedly underlined the importance of safeguarding national sovereignty, "Advance democracy in international relations, respect sovereignty, share security"; "We are firm in our resolve to uphold China's sovereignty, security and development interests and will never yield to any outside pressure."; "We will oppose any foreign attempt to subvert the legitimate government of any other countries...." and "There are signs of increasing hegemonism, power politics and neo-interventionism, and local turmoil keeps cropping up." ... "China opposes hegemonism and power politics in all their forms."

These evaluations have special guiding significance for our studies related to national sovereignty. The changes in the connotation of the traditional sovereignty and ideology in the new era and situation should be correctly grasped, for instance, who founded the U.S.? Which groups affect and even control its domestic and international policies? What's the special relationship between the U.S. and UK? It is known that, the Britain is the major investment target for the U.S. And according to the official BEA statistics, in 2011, the largest stock of direct investment in the United States was from Britain, and amounted 442.2 billion dollars; the largest direct investment stock in the UK is also from the US, amounting to 300 billion pounds.[7] If we review the historical developments since the WWII, the relation between Britain and the United States is like the head and the body, i.e., UK proposes the theory and the U.S. puts it into practice. The British Keynesianism in the post war era not only became the mainstream in the US academy but also had a significant influence on the US government's policy making; "The Third Way" theory was also originated in the UK and

---

7 This data is provided by Luo Zhenxing, from American Studies Center attached to CASS.

was fully accepted and put into practice by the U.S. These issues are worth our attention and thinking seriously. The same consideration applies for the analysis of other countries such as the Japan-US relations and the relationships between Britain and Japan.

2. Significance of the research on the world's major religions and their relationships

The relevant literature reveals that the Vatican and its alliance with the British royal family may be the largest covert power behind many religious issues. These two have been nurturing the politics of hate against socialist countries. Religious organizations have been active in the riots and "Color Revolutions" promoted in different countries around the world. Therefore, great importance should be attached to the religious strategic research in order to fully understand the religious' money making, brain washing, intelligence collection, political command and other functional historical research. Special attention should be given to strengthen to the research on Vatican's role, the Church of England and the Mormons in the U.S.A and other international Christian churches, especially on the role of global religious organizations in the modern Chinese history. Attention should also be given to the research on the complex inheritance relationship between the Judaism, Christianity, Catholicism, Orthodox Church, Buddhism, Manichaeism and other major religions.

3. We should attach greater importance to the research of the British history

The UK has the extremely important status in the history of the modern world and a country imbued with a high degree of aggressiveness. According to the latest research by the British historian Stuart Laycock, Britain invaded almost 90% of the countries in the world in different periods.[8] Based on the analysis related to the history of the 200 countries, only 22 countries were not invaded by Britain, which includes the countries such as Guatemala, Tajikistan and the Marshall Islands which are quite far from the UK, and also includes the Luxembourg which is located near the UK. Special importance should be attached to the research of the British royal family, the Church of England and the British invasions world wide in the modern history.

4. Be vigilant against racist tendencies in the field of ideology

Racism is still deeply rooted in the reality. Globally, there is a deteriorating trend of hatred and intolerance towards Jewish and Muslim religions, which is worth paying keen attention. According to a news report

---

8 Ye Yan: "British Empire—Its Global Footprints," November 10, 2012, http://article.yeeyan.org/view/309313/331198.

published by the Associated Press on the October 27, 2012, the public attitude towards racism has not changed in the four years after the first African-American president, Obama was elected. About 51% of white Americans directly expressed negative attitude against African Americans; and 52% of the non-Hispanic whites expressed negative sentiments against Latinos. Deutsche Welle Radio website released an investigation report made by the Germany Friedrich Ebert Foundation, which revealed that the 9% of the Germans are far-right oriented. The proportion of those people who believed that Nazism did not pose danger was higher in the group of teenagers between 14-16 than in the group of age over-60. Approximately, in today's German population 1 out of 11 tend to be sympathetic with anti-Semitism.[9] What is alarming is that most of the literature we have introduced above, which examine the covert international groups possess the tendency of racism.

5. Freemasonry cannot be simply and superficially regarded merely as an evil force

According to the relevant available literature analysis, there are many branches and genres of Freemasonry, such as the British, the US Freemasonry, and the Jewish Freemasonry which have all kinds of secretive clubs named as "Knights" the Family", Skull and Bones society, clubs, committees and other global public or private organizations, highly active in political, military or financial intelligence fields. Different schools of the Freemasonry have different development history and have played different roles in the development of the modern world history, among which, there are also the Freemasonry schools which has supported the international communist movements, an issue which needs further study. Even within a same Freemasonry organization there are divisions of roles, attitudes and policies, for instance, this is obvious between the U.S. Democrats and Republicans. In addition, the group consciousness is easy to be used by other people having ulterior motives who aim to incite certain factors of instability. Generally speaking, the attempt and manipulation of global structure and arrangement of the world population and resources, determining and manipulation of the world population and resources through biological strategies and transgenic technologies, plus vaccines and by using culture to control minds of world people is one macro-strategy of the Freemasonry and other covert international groups. This is the ultimate mission of the shadowy global government—as a top level designer—staying at the pinnacle of the world pyramid an hierarchy. For example not a word of what is said at Bilderberg meetings can be breathed outside. No reporters are invited in and while confidential minutes of meetings are taken, names are not noted. It can be seen that capitalism externally advocates the universal

---

9   Xinhua, October 29, 2012 and November 21, 2012; "News Archive" Section.

human values and pluralism as its core value system, but internally advocates the theory of racial superiority, based on natural selection and evolution. However, the socialist core value system advocates solidarity, mutual help, humanist-orientation, helping the poor, comity and tolerance. which is one important content of "scientific outlook of development", so our party has devoted itself to fight against the financial magnates and any "ruling elite" which make policy decisions without public scrutiny. by uniting with the workers and peasants. The struggle/competition and cooperation between the two co-existing systems, capitalism and socialism constitute and compose a symphony of contemporary world history, which has become a macro perspective when viewing the complex prospect and panorama of the world history.

Realizing the interests of a hereditary society is the ultimate goal and mission of covert international groups and the implementation of this mission aims to dominate and manipulate the fate of those people making the 99% of the human society. Since this strategic goal serves the interests of minority social groups and targets colored people and their existence, this determines that it embodies obvious racial and discriminative characteristics. We can ask the following critical question, who is the sanctioned judge that will decide the macro or "supra-racial values of humans? Who gave such a Godly leading judgment power to the Anglo-Saxons and some other races?

If we recall history, we can see that the modern mighty countries of the West, that have risen to top position in the "world's food chain in the nature" (in the jungle-like world), do not necessarily owe their success to the efficacy of their system.

On the other hand although China has huge population, it lacks abundant recourses and restrained by several other resource deficits which determines that its development becomes extremely hard, yet it has made remarkable achievements which attracts the global public. Certainly it owes this development achievement to the system of socialism with Chinese characteristics.We should advance with the times, draw on both experience and lessons from the development of China itself and other countries, make a deeper reflection and deepen our understanding of the laws governing the development of human society, and promote the self-improvement and growth of the socialist system, give full play to the advantages of our system in order to maintain China's sovereignty, security, territorial integrity and interests of national development.

The report of the 18th National Congress has pointed out: "We should carry forward the Party's fine traditions and conduct and make its members and officials develop a firm and correct worldview and a firm and correct

attitude toward power and career, take a committed political stand and become better able to tell right from wrong on major issues of principle."
..."Young people should respond to the Party's call, foster a correct worldview, outlook on life and sense of values and always cherish deep love for our great country." It is cardinal for us to correctly observe history, be keenly aware of potential dangers, recognize and distinguish between friend and foe, and remain clear-headed which is very important for establishing correct world outlook, correct values and views on life.

Y. 27

An In-depth Investigation among the Working Class of Beijing: An Experience and Reflection

Lu Gang[1]

Abstract: Marxists hold that the proletariat is the basic driving force of social transformation. For the hundreds of millions of workers, the poor and difficult factory work and life experience and hard living environment compel them to launch strikes again and again as an instinctive resistance to these conditions. Since the "May workers movements and strikes" in 2010, existing labor conflicts hidden in the industrial field have revealed themselves and have become an important factor of social conflict and unrest. Since the May 4th movement in 1919 the working class of China climbed to the stage of history and demonstrated its vigor to change the Chinese society. Chinese proletariat obviously appeared on the stage of history show their will and power to change the Chinese society. The history of international communist movement indicates that labor movement is not born to be the fellow traveler of socialist cause and its vanguard party. For the Communist Party of China, just from the beginning the power of labor movement has been an important driving force to change the society, but it can also deliver unpredictable risks under certain circumstances; consequently how to win and lead this force for the cause of socialism with Chinese Characteristics is an important historical issue. The campaign of "observing and studying our national conditions" initiated by the CASS leadership for the CASS Graduate School students gave an opportunity for Marxists to go among the worker groups and make further investigations.

Key words: build socialism with Chinese characteristics; labor movement; Communist Party of China; Investigating National Conditions

---

[1] Lu Gang. Guest Researcher at World Socialism Research Center attached to Chinese Academy of Social Sciences; Doctoral Student of Marxism Study at the Graduate School of CASS.

During the last year, the Chinese Academy of Social Sciences has initiated the campaign of "Concentrate on the Grass roots, Alter the Style of Work, Change the Style of Writing" which included going into the masses and making investigations among them to better learn the real conditions of the people and country, which has achieved significant fruits. As a grade 2011 doctoral student studying Marxism at the Graduate School of CASS, I came up with the idea of making investigations among the worker groups. Also, being one of the leaders of the Society of Seeking the Truth at the Graduate School, a student organization which focuses on the study of Marxism, I do not only read the classics of Marxism-Leninism, but actively participate in social practices. Consequently, I chose to be a day laborer in the Beijing Economic and Technological Development Area-Yizhuangi for one day, with the intention to explore the practicability of organizing students for day labor and permanent work during the school holidays so that we could develop in-depth understanding of the working class and acquire first-hand materials useful for our investigation. In the history of socialism, carrying out investigations by directly observing the workers' factory life have produced a large number of literature with academic value such as The Condition of the Working Class in England by Engels and The Condition of the Working Class in Russia by L. I. Ostrover and others.

In order to get a day work in a factory, laborers need to apply submit to a professional employment agent company and have to gather in front of the company door at 6 a.m.. Hence, I went to Yizhuang the day before and stayed in a simple and low-budget hotel for 20 yuan a night, and early in the morning through an agent I got a job in a printing factory and worked for a day.

The day's labor made me exposed to the harsh living conditions of the workers – their long working hours, intensive work, poor environment and low income.

I worked from 8 a.m. to 8 p.m., with less than two hours for lunch and supper. There was no overtime wage for day laborers but only several yuan per hour for overtime for the permanent workers. Working in the factory, I realized that workers eat to work and in order to better cooperate with the machines. My job during the day was sorting out the semi-finished products that came out of the folding machine. The work was simple but it was extremely intensive. The daily workload of a folding machine is 48,000 revolves, each revolve with one semi-finished product. That is to say, I sorted out 48,000 semi-finished products a day. Worse still, I had to work standing on my feet, without a slim chance to sit down. As a result, I could not feel my legs in the afternoon. The working environment was like the salt on the wound. The workshop was full with folding machines and overwhelming noise came along when they were on. Despite the warning of "Wear Ear

Protectors" on the wall, most of the workers did not wear protectors and just only a few wore earplugs. You cannot imagine how harmful it is to work under those conditions for a long time.

Then, what is their payment? Through chats with the workers during the meal time, I learned that the monthly salary of a common permanent male worker is 3,000 yuan, with 12 hours a day, meager overtime wage and less than 2 days off per each month. It was worse with day laborers. Their daily wage is 120 yuan, 50 yuan of which is commission fee for the employment agent. Hence, they are actually paid 70 yuan for a day. To me, I had only 50 yuan left because I had to spend 20 yuan on the accommodation for the night before. Many people worked as day laborers in Yizhuang during weekends, but not all of them stay in a hotel like me. Some young people chose to save 10 yuan by staying overnight in a net bar at a cost of 10 yuan.

I met a 22-year-old girl coming from a village in Hebei, who worked in an electronics factory for a monthly salary of 2,000 yuan. After paying 300 yuan for house rent, plus other daily expenses, she almost had no money left. In order to pay her brother's tuition fee, she had to work as day laborer for two days for 140 yuan, but most girl students like us cannot cover the cost of a dress with this money. However, it was a good sum for her family. Moreover, day laborers do not sign official labor contracts with the employers, so if any accidents happen, they have to bear the consequences on their own. In spite that the agents got 50 yuan fee, they take no responsibility for the day laborers.

The day's labor made me exposed to the workers' discontent and even anger towards social injustice.

The workers I met complained to each other about low wages and bad treatment, they seemed somewhat hopeless for themselves and their families, and worked by counting the day. They also complained that the boss of the factory was ruthless and the foreman worker was mean to the workers and even sometimes beat and scolded them. Stories about workers who got injured in the factory but was not compensated was openly talked among them, which intensified their unrest about future and anger against the boss. They are clear that they are in the lowest rung of the social ladder and that most of the people associate them with the rascal yellow-hair hooligans, shameless prostitutes and high crime rate, but they feel they can do nothing about it.

The aforementioned girl envied that I am a student and she proudly told me that she is going to send her brother to university. She said, "Well-educated people like you tend to look down on us poor people, but my brother won't." Those words made me—a so-called well-educated person—ashamed.

In his book Korean Workers, Hagen Koo, a Korean American scholar, described a similar story where a factory female worker who sponsored her brother for education wrote to her mother, "I would also like Siki to receive good education and wear the square academic cap and school badge, on his school uniform. But recently I began to think: maybe college education does not grant the prospect of being a wholesome person. During my eight years away from home, I have seen many cases where the educated look down on the poor and bullied others with the college education they have received." Hagen Koo commented that the story shows that "the girl has seen clearly the ideological fallacy in the mainstream education ideology and felt the social injustice."[2]

The day's labor has improved my understanding on of some the tenets of Marxism in practice

Marx mentioned in Capital that under the conditions of massive industrial production, worker, technology, knowledge and labor will be unceasingly separated.[3]

The only chance for workers to have a rest during the work hours is when the machines break down. Once they break down, the foreman will arrange a repairman, which allows the worker a short break. Short as it is, it is precious for the extremely tired workers. Hence, they often hope that the machines break down and even wish to learn some tricks to make them break down. Such mentality enables me to better understand the Luddite Movement where workers have destroyed the machines in England in the 19th century.

Of course, the introduction of the machines, a modern means of production, represents the progress of human productive forces. However, based on my experience in the factory, I have realized that the more advanced a folding machine can operate more than 48,000 revolves and the chance of it breaking down is slimmer. While it represents the glorious achievement of humans' master of science and technology, it brings longer work hours and more intensive work for the ordinary workers in the printing factory.

The experience has led me to deeper thinking: how Marxists deal with their relations with giant worker groups in modern China.

---

2 Hagen Koo. Korean Workers. trans. by Guangyan Liang & Jing Zhang. Social Sciences Academic Press, 2004.
3 Marx mentioned in Section V entitled "The Strife Between Workman and Machine" of Chapter XIII: "Machinery and Modern Industry" of *Capital* that "the character of independence and estrangement which the capitalist mode of production as a whole gives to the instruments of labor and to the product, as against the workman, is developed –by means of machinery–into a thorough antagonism." (Marx, Karl. *Capital*. People's Publishing House, 1975).

It is noteworthy that recent years have witnessed the increase of workers' movements to safeguard their legal rights, which generally occurred in eastern coastal areas. In May 2010, thirteen people in Foxconn Shenzhen leapt to their deaths, which have triggered the "May Strike Movement". With the strikes started by the workers in Honda Nanhai and 70,000 others in Dalian Development Area, conflict between labor and capital came on to the front stage of public opinions. Some scholars termed the year 2010 as the "labor-capital relationship year". (Guanghuai & Jiangang,[4] Workers' ability to organize, their sense of discipline and struggle tactics they used in the movement were amazing. Since 2010, workers movement to safeguard legal rights began to arouse public attention. Hostility between capital and labor was no longer covert in industrial field, and became one major part of social unrest in the society. By then, Chinese industrial workers' collective movement to safeguard their legal rights has become a force to be reckoned with.

What makes it worse is that liberals at home and abroad and the underground Christian church affected by pro-Western anti-China forces have tried to influence the worker groups through workers' rights protection network, which has become an important threat to national security. As Lenin said, worker groups on the whole possess poor education, so their movement could not give rise to the consciousness of scientific socialism, automatically. Therefore, the development of worker movement harbors unpredictable risks to the building of socialism with Chinese characteristics. During the great upheavals and adverse changes in Eastern Europe, in Poland where the "Solidarity Union" that united most of the Polish workers by the support of the Catholic Church enabled the union leader Walesa to realize peaceful evolution and we should be on alert against such risks.

As Engels mentioned in the preface of The Condition of the Working Class in England, "the conditions of the working class are the real basis and starting point of all social movements, because they are the acutest and most barefaced expression of all social disasters…in order to offer a solid foundation for socialist theories and opinion that socialist theories have the rights to exist and in order to clean up all fantasies and fabrication that are for or against socialist theories, it is necessary to study the conditions of the proletariat."[5] Therefore, to guarantee both national security and the future of our socialist cause, we should be in close contact with workers movement. How to instill the consciousness of scientific socialism into workers movement and correctly guide the working class forces is an important

---

4 Guanghuai, Zheng & Jiangang, Zhu, ed. New Working Class: Relation, Organization and Collective Actions. China Social Sciences Publishing House, 2011.
5 Marx, Karl & Engels Friedrich. The Complete Works of Marx and Engels. Volume II. People's Publishing House, 1957.

historical issue that needs long-term attention all through our path of building socialism with Chinese characteristics. For researchers of Marxism, it is an urgent task to delve deeper into the current conditions of Chinese working class and provide prompt and necessary theoretical support for decision making by the government. For a long time, worker groups have been an object of study and analysis in sociology studies but their historical role has always been ignored by researchers. The Party Committee's campaign of "Concentrate on the Grass roots, Alter the Style of Work, Change the Style of Writing" and "investigate and study our national conditions" practiced by the Graduate School of CASS, provides an important opportunity for Marxists to delve deeper into the worker groups.

As a major in the program of "Basic Tenets of Marxism", I believe that in terms of practice, Marxism requires us to use this opportunity to learn more about the real conditions of the working class observe and study their conditions, demands and confusion. In this way, not only we the intellectuals will have a clearer understanding of the reality but also the workers will better understand both their status and role in the social production process and in historical progress. As Lenin said, (we should) instill Marxist ideology into the workers movement, jointly promote social progress with them and actively rather than passively promote the historical change. In terms of theoretical study, Marxism requires us to analyze the conditions of the Chinese working class, reveal the source of problems about payment conditions, living standards, religion and ethics, and how to develop class awareness, etc. of the working class and at the same time analyze and criticize various non-socialist schools by means of historical materialist views and methods.

Further research, analysis and criticism of these problems above will not only provide a larger space for innovation of the Chinese Marxism, but more importantly, we will be able to grasp the ways to correctly guide the working class forces and ways to raise the socialist consciousness of the working class, and we win this force that may transform China's society under the banner of socialism with Chinese characteristics, and ensure the long-term, stable and healthy development of China.

Selected Titles from Canut Catalogue

English Titles

A New Approach to the Issues of Marxism, Socialism and World Socialist Movement
 Gao Fang

Global Revival of Left and Socialism Versus Capitalism and Globalization and China's Share
 Pu Guoliang, Xiong Guangxing

The Normative and Positive Research of Labor Value: Monistic Living Labor Theory of Value
 Cheng Enfu, Wang Guijin, Zhu Kui

Defense For Marx.
A New Interpretation of Marxist Philosophy
 Yang Geng

Into the Depths of History.
Research on Marx's Historical Materialism
 Chen Xianda

Lenin Revisited.
A Post-textological Reading on Philosophical Notes
 Zhang Yibing

The Subjective Dimension of Marxist Historical Dialectics
Zhang Yibing

Althusser Revisited. A Textological Reading:
Problematic, Symptomatic Reading, ISA and History of Marxism
Zhang Yibing

A Marxist Reading of Young Baudrillard.
Throughout His Ordered Masks
Zhang Yibing

A Deep Plough:
Unscrambling Major Post-Marxist Texts. From Adorno to Zizek
Zhang Yibing

History of Mao Zedong Thought and Truth
of Facts Related to Mao Zedong
Li Shenming, Lie Jie

A Review on Marxist and Left Debates:
Consumer Society, Radical Democracy, Socialism, Ecology,
Feminism, Post-Modernism, New Imperialism
Zheng Zhisheng

The Marxist Theory of Party Building:
Classics, Innovations and the Communist Party of China
Wu Meihua

The New Stage of Capitalism:
A Marxist Update on Its Revolution
Zhang Tongyu, Ding Weimin, Chen Ying

Marx's Practical Materialism:
The Horizon of Post-Subjectivity Philosophy

Wang Nanshi, Xie Yongkang

On Mao's Political Ideology:
Reviewing Chinese and Global Studies 1940-2007

Yang Fengcheng

New Research Into the New Edition of German Ideology

Han Lixin

Between Surging Ideas and Real Changes:
Contemporary Interpretation on Marx's Practice View

Ou Yangkang, Zhang Mingcang

Social Stratification, The White-Collar Group and Its Lifestyle

Xia Jianzhong

Historical Overview, Development Mode of the
International Communist Movement

Du Kangchuan, Li Jingzhi

Lenin's Conception of Socialist Revolution and
Construction after the October Revolution

Liu Peixuan

From Marx to Jameson:
Marxist Thoughts of Literature, Art and Aesthetics.
Its Major Contributors in the Last Two Centuries

Zhou Houzhong

New Research on Stalin's Socialism Thought.
A Historical and Realistic Analysis
  Gu Hailiang

The History of The Kurdish National Movement
  Tang Zhichao

Western Alliance in the Post-war Period
  Zhou Rongyao

Theory & Practice of Western Intervention
  Shi Yinhong, Zhang Yunling

Marxist Theory of Economic Crises and Cycles
  Liu Mingyuan

Sovereignity Issue Over the Diaoyu Island
  Tang Jiaxuan, Sun Dongmin

An Anthology of Japan Studies
  Xia Pengxiang

New Frontiers by Chinese Scholars:
Research Articles on the Crisis of Capitalism, Socialism, Marxist Philosophy, Economics, Chinese Philosophy, Western Marxism
  edited by Deniz Kizilcec

Contemporary Political Trends of Thought in China

German Titles

Zur Verteidigung von Marx:
Eine neue Lektüre von Marxens Philosophie

Yang Geng

Zurück zu Marx.
Die Veränderung des Philosophischen
Diskurses im Ökonomischen Kontext

Zhang Yibing

Ein textuelles Tiefpflügen:
Die textuelle Lektüre der nachmarxschen
Philosophie von Adorno bis Zizek

Zhang Yibing

Zurück zu Lenin:
Eine nachtextuelle Lektüre über die Philosophischen Hefte

Zhang Yibing

60 Jahre Aufbau der Menschenrechte in China

Dong Yunhu

"Ein Gürtel - Eine Straße"

Qin Yucai, Zhou Guping, Luo Weidong

www.ingramcontent.com/pod-product-compliance
Lightning Source LLC
LaVergne TN
LVHW011046100526
838202LV00078B/3328